Sewer of Progress

Urban and Industrial Environments

Series editor: Robert Gottlieb, Henry R. Luce Professor of Urban and Environmental Policy, Occidental College

For a complete list of books published in this series, please see the back of the book.

Sewer of Progress

Corporations, Institutionalized Corruption, and the Struggle for the Santiago River

Cindy McCulligh

The MIT Press
Cambridge, Massachusetts
London, England

© 2023 Massachusetts Institute of Technology

This work is subject to a Creative Commons CC-BY-NC-ND license.
Subject to such license, all rights are reserved.

(cc) BY-NC-ND

The MIT Press would like to thank the anonymous peer reviewers who provided comments on drafts of this book. The generous work of academic experts is essential for establishing the authority and quality of our publications. We acknowledge with gratitude the contributions of these otherwise uncredited readers.

This book was set in Stone by Westchester Publishing Services. Printed and bound in the United States of America.

Library of Congress Cataloging-in-Publication Data is available.

ISBN: 978-0-262-54592-1

10 9 8 7 6 5 4 3 2 1

For Xavier

Contents

Acknowledgments ix

Abbreviations xi

Introduction: From "Mexican Niagara" to River of Death 1

1 Industrialization and Environmental Regulation in Mexico 37

2 Chronicle of a Struggle: The Negation and the Terror 81

3 (Un)regulated Environments and the Santiago River 119

4 The Enemy at Home: Regulatory Capture and Wastewater Discharge 169

5 Corporate Sustainability: Myths and Realities 205

6 Conclusions: The Road Ahead 247

Appendix: Methodological Strategy 263

Notes 275

References 287

Index 321

Acknowledgments

This work was possible thanks to the support of many people. First, I would like to thank the people of El Salto and Juanacatlán, who over many years have helped me to appreciate the history of the Santiago River and the magnitude of its misfortune. In this sense, I am especially grateful to Ezequiel Macías, Enrique Enciso, Sofía Enciso, Graciela González, Alan Carmona, Estela Cervantes, Rodrigo Saldaña, Raúl Muñoz, Manuel Salas, and Francisco Parra. I owe a special thanks to Enrique Enciso, who accompanied me during my fieldwork on many site visits and to interview residents and workers in El Salto, Juanacatlán, Atequiza, and Poncitlán.

I am also very grateful to colleagues and friends who have shared their feedback and perspectives on my research. Darcy Tetreault and Gerardo Bernache Pérez generously provided insightful feedback on different versions of this text. I would also particularly like to thank Cecilia Lezama Escalante, James M. Cypher, Carlos Alba Vega, Luz Emilia Lara y Bretón, Gabriel Torres González, Humberto González, Joshua C. Greene, Timothy Moss, and Susan Street for their comments at different moments. My special thanks also to José Esteban Castro and Karina Kloster from the WATERLAT-GOBACIT network on water research in Latin America.

Perhaps not everyone I interviewed for this research will share my conclusions. This is a controversial issue and touches on important economic interests. Nonetheless, I thank everyone who lent me their time and shared their knowledge, many very generously. The interviews were for me the richest part of this learning process.

My gratitude to Shelley, Marta, and Jack for their ongoing support. My final thanks are for Xavier. Without you, this simply would not have been possible.

Abbreviations

AISAC	Asociación de Industriales de El Salto (Association of Industrialists of El Salto)
AMIA	Asociación Mexicana de la Industria Automotriz (Mexican Automotive Industry Association)
AMLO	Andrés Manuel López Obrador
ANAA	Asamblea Nacional de Afectados Ambientales (National Assembly of Environmentally Affected People)
ANIQ	Asociación Nacional de la Industria Química (National Chemical Industry Association)
BOD	biochemical oxygen demand
BOT	build, operate, and transfer
CCDA	Comité Ciudadano de Defensa Ambiental (Citizen Committee for Environmental Defense)
CCE	Consejo Coordinador Empresarial (Business Coordinating Council)
CEA	Comisión Estatal del Agua (State Water Commission)
CEAS	Comisión Estatal de Agua y Saneamiento (State Water and Sanitation Commission)
CEC	Commission for Environmental Cooperation
CEDHJ	Comisión Estatal de Derechos Humanos Jalisco (Jalisco State Human Rights Commission)
CEMDA	Centro Mexicano de Derecho Ambiental (Mexican Environmental Law Center)
CI	Clean Industry
CNDH	Comisión Nacional de los Derechos Humanos (National Human Rights Commission)

COA	*cédula de operación anual* (annual operating certificate)
COD	chemical oxygen demand
COFEMER	Comisión Federal de Mejora Regulatoria (Federal Regulatory Improvement Commission)
COFEPRIS	Comisión Federal para la Protección contra Riesgos Sanitarios (Federal Commission for Protection against Sanitary Risks)
COMARNAT	Comité Consultivo Nacional de Normalización de Medio Ambiente y Recursos Naturales (National Environment and Natural Resources Standards Advisory Committee)
CONAGUA	Comisión Nacional del Agua (National Water Commission)
CONAMER	Comisión Nacional de Mejora Regulatoria (National Regulatory Improvement Commission)
CONCAMIN	Confederación de Cámaras Industriales de los Estados Unidos Mexicanos (Confederation of Mexican Chambers of Industry)
CSR	corporate social responsibility
DENUE	Directorio Estadístico Nacional de Unidades Económicas (National Statistical Directory of Economic Units)
DOF	*Diario Oficial de la Federación* (*Official Gazette of the Federation*)
EHS	environment, health and safety
EM	ecological modernization
EMP	Empaques Modernos de Guadalajara
EPA	Environmental Protection Agency
FDI	foreign direct investment
GDP	gross domestic product
GMA	Guadalajara Metropolitan Area
GRI	Global Reporting Initiative
IACHR	Inter-American Commission on Human Rights
IDEA	Instituto de Derecho Ambiental (Environmental Law Institute)
IFAI	Instituto Federal de Acceso a la Información y Protección de Datos (Federal Institute for Access to Information and Data Protection)

Abbreviations

ILO	International Labor Organization
IMDEC	Instituto Mexicano para el Desarrollo Comunitario (Mexican Institute for Community Development)
IMTA	Instituto Mexicano de Tecnología del Agua (Mexican Institute of Water Technology)
INEGI	Instituto Nacional de Estadística y Geografía (National Institute of Statistics and Geography)
Instituto VIDA	Instituto de Valores Integrales y Desarrollo Ambiental (Institute of Integrated Values and Environmental Development)
ISI	import substitution industrialization
ITEI	Instituto de Transparencia e Información Pública de Jalisco (Jalisco Institute of Transparency and Public Information)
JTC	Joint Technical Committee
LAN	Ley de Aguas Nacionales (National Waters Law)
LFD	Ley Federal de Derechos (Federal Duties Law)
LFMN	Ley Federal de Metrología y Normalización (Federal Law on Metrology and Standardization)
LSP Basin Agency	Lerma-Santiago-Pacific Basin Agency
MAPDER	Movimiento Mexicano de Afectados por las Presas y en Defensa de los Ríos (Mexican Movement of Dam-Affected People and in Defense of Rivers)
MVA	manufacturing value added
NAFTA	North American Free Trade Agreement
NGO	nongovernmental organization
NOM	Norma Oficial Mexicana (Official Mexican Standard)
NPRI	National Pollutant Release Inventory
NWP	National Water Program
OECD	Organisation for Economic Co-operation and Development
PDC	particular discharge condition
PE	political ecology
PEMEX	Petróleos Mexicanos
PNN	Programa Nacional de Normalización (National Standardization Program)
PPT	Permanent Peoples' Tribunal

PROEPA	Procuraduría Estatal de Protección al Ambiente (State Bureau of Environmental Protection)
PROFEPA	Procuraduría Federal de Protección al Ambiente (Federal Bureau of Environmental Protection)
REF	Region of Environmental Fragility
REPDA	Registro Público de Derechos de Agua (Public Water Rights Registry)
RETC	Registro de Emisiones y Transferencia de Contaminantes (Pollutant Emissions and Transfers Registry)
RIA	regulatory impact assessment
RIS	regulatory impact statement
SEMADES	Secretaría de Medio Ambiente para el Desarrollo Sustentable (Ministry of Environment for Sustainable Development)
SEMADET	Secretaría de Medio Ambiente y Desarrollo Territorial (Ministry of Environment and Territorial Development)
SEMARNAT	Secretaría de Medio Ambiente y Recursos Naturales (Ministry of Environment and Natural Resources)
SRH	Secretaría de Recursos Hidráulicos (Ministry of Hydraulic Resources)
SSJ	Secretaría de Salud Jalisco (Jalisco Ministry of Health)
TBL	triple bottom line
TLA	Tribunal Latinoamericano del Agua (Latin American Water Tribunal)
TNC	transnational corporation
TRI	Toxic Release Inventory
TSS	total suspended solids
UNEP	United Nations Environment Programme
UNESCO	United Nations Educational, Scientific and Cultural Organization
VEC	Voluntary Environmental Compliance
WHO	World Health Organization
WTO	World Trade Organization
WWTP	wastewater treatment plant

Introduction: From "Mexican Niagara" to River of Death

There exists a masterpiece of nature's handiwork, unrivaled in its own peculiar beauties and environments. It is the great waterfall of Juanacatlán. . . . One's ear gradually becomes conscious of a low, distant murmur, which steadily increases to a deep rumble and from that to a mighty roar, and presently the tramcar comes to a standstill at the very brink of a high precipice, from which is viewed through clouds of vaporous mist the sight of thousands of tons of water plunging over a wall of gray granite in a steady unbroken cataract 360 feet in width for a sheer distance of 60 feet into a seething eddying vortex below.

For a time the mind is apt to be held in rapt contemplation of the grand spectacle, then by degrees the senses are awakened to the various characteristics, the effects, and weird vagaries of the foaming, falling waters.

—*Chicago Tribune*, March 10, 1898

I.1 Setting the Scene 1: Arriving at the River

The first thing that hit me was the smell. What I recall from the first times I traveled on the narrow two-lane bridge over the Santiago River, between the communities of El Salto and Juanacatlán, was the urgent need not to breathe. When the bus from Guadalajara neared the bridge, I would take a deep breath and try to hold it until we were on the other side heading up the incline into Juanacatlán and leaving the toxic odors behind.

It was the year 2000, and I was there for a reason unrelated to the river, to collaborate with Ezequiel Macías, an organic campesino farmer from the Exhacienda Zapotlanejo, in the municipality of Juanacatlán. I was on my way to learn about compost and natural sprays made from fermented vegetation, and to write a manual together with Ezequiel. But the smell lingered in my mind. That smell of feces, of acid, of suffocation . . . a vile smell. How could there be a river like this?

Skip ahead to August 2003, when with others I made a first attempt to answer that question. It is a windy afternoon just before sunset, and the sky is gray and clouded. Xavier Romo and I arrive at the bridge in El Salto. We are making a documentary film about the pollution of the Upper Santiago River and Lake Chapala, which is in the middle of its worst crisis since the 1950s. Now you have to walk a kilometer over dusty ground from the pier in the town of Chapala to reach the water's edge (McCulligh and Romo 2003). We head out onto the bridge to film the waterfall from above, capturing the river laid out like a white path, under its thick layer of foam. A strong gust of wind comes and lifts the foam in a whirl of white balls. I turn to run, sidestepping the puffs of toxic foam the size of pillows that float over the bridge. Xavier stays to film the sadly fascinating dance in this landscape of urban-industrial destruction. I run from the bridge because that foam burns, it leaves rashes, it infects.

At that time, we also heard stories from local residents. A grassroots group had recently formed in Juanacatlán, the Institute of Integrated Values and Environmental Development (Instituto VIDA, Instituto de Valores Integrales y Desarrollo Ambiental). The association's president, Rodrigo Saldaña, took us to visit the desiccating mango orchards below the waterfall and other sites along the river. We followed the canal that still carried dark water from the river to irrigate agricultural lands, and spoke with other members of the new group, including Francisco Parra, a physician and native of Juanacatlán.

Seated in his office in El Salto, the doctor recounted the strange story of an event that took place in 1990. He told us about two young contract workers from the Federal Electricity Commission (Comisión Federal de Electricidad), who went to work on the floodgates of the two-meter dam above the waterfall, part of the El Salto hydroelectric dam built in 1893 and which ceased energy generation in 1982 (Patronato de Conservación y Fomento del Lago de Chapala 1997, 24).[1] "They were working in the area of the floodgate from eight in the morning until six in the evening," he retold, "which was when they started to feel ill." Both died later in hospital and, he explained, "the cause of death was acute hydrogen sulfide intoxication, where the lungs were severely destroyed."[2] Hydrogen sulfide is the main gas that can be sensed near the falls, where the waters emanate its characteristic odor of rotten eggs. Standing above the waterfall, to film that video and on many later visits in the company of students, foreign experts, journalists,

Introduction 3

activists, and others, I felt how that smell filled my chest. Many times, I continued to feel it hours later.

Hearing about the degradation of the river, especially from those who enjoyed its clean waters decades before, also meant hearing about the factories that came to the area. In particular, Ciba was often mentioned, in reference to the factory of former Swiss chemical giant Ciba Geigy, which set up shop in the town of Atotonilquillo in 1965. Until it changed hands in 2006, products from this plant ranged from pharmaceuticals and colorants to granulated pesticides (STPS 2006, 23). Stories associated with the factory not only told of the river running red or purple or of the disappearance of fish, turtles, and many other species; there was also talk of a hidden outlet pipe midriver, and of discharges of pollutants late at night and on weekends. It was especially striking to hear the testimony of a former employee who was asked to put on protective gear before pouring a liquid down a drain with an outlet in the river, only for him to be taken by ambulance days later to a private hospital in Guadalajara where he was submitted to numerous tests without ever seeing their results or being informed what he had handled. When we went to shoot images of this factory's effluent in 2003, which that day flowed blue-green, a security guard from the factory came to ask us to leave, although we were on public land.

Learning about the Santiago River in El Salto and Juanacatlán has always meant hearing about what it was; hearing about the "Mexican Niagara" that attracted tourists and was a site for recreation and source of food for those who lived along its banks. "You didn't know what to admire or what to take home to eat, because of all that you could find along the river, from fish to birds," said Ezequiel, speaking to us under a tree in his field. "That was what really caught the eye, the birds, there were so many, and it was incredible how they clouded over the sky as you walked along the lanes. . . . And it was incredible how they vanished, from one day to the next." The explanation of what brought on this destruction was very simple: "What happened was that in those years the industrial corridor started to take shape, Ciba and Cyanamid arrived, and the industrial corridor of El Salto started to grow, grow, grow, and . . . overnight the fish started to float in the river and to die by the ton." "What idiots we were!"[3] exclaimed Ezequiel on one occasion, lamenting how the communities had let this happen to the river where once they had bathed among *chachamol* flowers. "Now we see the river as an enemy because it doesn't give life. It is a latent danger for all of us who live along the river."[4] Residents and doctors told us of that danger: of the cases of cancer, the birth defects, the spontaneous abortions, and the kidney failure and other illnesses they associated with living in this polluted environment.

That sudden change in the river took place in the early 1970s, with 1972 cited by Ezequiel as the last year they could enjoy the waterfall.[5] Some residents blamed others for the death of the river. For the parents of another activist from El Salto, Raúl Muñoz Delgadillo, the culprit, at least in the rumors, was the factory of Japanese chemical company Quimikao: "It set up shop and then everything was wiped out, the fish died, everything died," said his mother. His mother's family are natives of Juanacatlán, and this change had direct consequences for them, as her father and uncles fished in the river. One of her uncles fished daily, and when the water came that killed off the fish, she retells, "he died. He had a heart attack when he saw it all. He started crying and he had a heart attack, because he saw everything that died, the fish died."[6] He died of sadness, she said.

One thing that Sofía Enciso, a young El Salto activist from another grassroots organization, Leap of Life (Un Salto de Vida), points out is that many of those who now live in this area never saw a living river. New residents have been attracted to the area not by the waterfall but by the proximity to the factories. They come to live in one of the irregular settlements or precarious social interest housing developments that have sprouted in the municipality, many located on flood-prone lands and with housing of a deplorable quality (Greene and Morvant-Roux 2020). When they are told about that living river, Sofía says, "it's a story that they can't imagine, that they don't believe."[7] It even seems hard to believe for those who lived it. In that interview for the documentary video in 2003, Ezequiel said,

> Going to the river is going to fish, to select the fish you want to take home, or preparing them right there, taking a swim, spending three or four hours enjoying the water, returning home, and you thought it would always be the same, that you would be able to go back, and that wasn't true. We realized that no, it was a dream, what we lived in the past was a dream.[8]

I.2 Setting the Scene 2: Of Myths and Power

It's April 2008, and there has been a tragedy in El Salto. An eight-year-old boy perished because of the polluted waters. When he fell into the El

Introduction

Ahogado Canal near its confluence with the Santiago River, Miguel Ángel López Rocha swallowed a few mouthfuls of water; he died less than three weeks later. I have been working for several years with the Mexican Institute for Community Development (IMDEC, Instituto Mexicano para el Desarrollo Comunitario), a nongovernmental organization started in the 1960s and with a long history in popular education. Now I find myself in a small meeting room at the Jalisco state Ministry of Environment for Sustainable Development (Secretaría de Medio Ambiente para el Desarrollo Sustentable).[9] It is April 10, and the mega-march for the Santiago River is planned to be held in a few days' time.

The room is crowded with bureaucrats invited by the environment ministry to an interinstitutional meeting on the Santiago River. These interagency meetings on the river started in 2007 but, despite many prior requests, this is the first time that IMDEC and Instituto VIDA have been permitted to attend. After the march in downtown Guadalajara, these meetings will open for a time to other grassroots organizations from El Salto and Juanacatlán. A document outlining the first of these meetings indicated that the state deputy minister of government requested that all agencies contribute to the solution to the problem in the area, "as there is a risk of social movements in the affected communities."[10]

The dynamic of the meeting is that each agency reports to the group what progress it has made or failed to make, based on commitments from previous meetings. The Jalisco State Water Commission (CEA, Comisión Estatal del Agua) is putting together an inventory of the factories in the region; the State Bureau of Environmental Protection (Procuraduría Estatal de Protección al Ambiente) has arranged for drone flights to detect discharges into the Santiago River and the El Ahogado Canal; the Ministry of Rural Development (Secretaría de Desarrollo Rural) is in the process of laying pipes to convey part of the water from this canal. After this tragic death, a small swell of actions has apparently been set in motion.

Once the roll call of agencies is complete, there is a brief presentation by a researcher from the University of Guadalajara. He describes how his laboratory at the university analyzed waters from the Santiago River and one of its tributaries, the El Ahogado Canal, at ten sites near El Salto. This analysis was not restricted to the parameters set out in Mexico's limited environmental legislation, but also contemplated the detection of synthetic organic substances. They found low concentrations of heavy metals in the water, and the researcher particularly highlighted the organic compounds encountered, including organochlorides and other carcinogenic substances. He specifies that these must have come from industrial sources.

After the presentation of this unpublished research, an innocent question is posed: What is the means of contact between people and these synthetic organic compounds? They are volatile and semivolatile, comes the answer, indicating that they are compounds with a high evaporation capacity, and contact is via respiration. In fact, the researcher emphasizes, the characteristic smell of rotten eggs in El Salto, due to hydrogen sulfide, masks the smell of these synthetic chemicals. Meanwhile, the representative of the Association of Industrialists of El Salto (Asociación de Industriales de El Salto) insists that industry is not the only source of river pollution, underscoring the importance of municipal wastewater. Fecal matter comes from cities, states the researcher, who then poses the rhetorical question, Who uses benzene in their home?

A few weeks later, I accompany Rodrigo Saldaña of Instituto VIDA to a meeting in Mexico City. A federal representative for Jalisco, Héctor Padilla Gutiérrez, has invited the mayors of El Salto, Juanacatlán, and two other riverside municipalities to attend a meeting of the Hydraulic Resources Committee (Comisión de Recursos Hidráulicos) of the National Congress. The director of the National Water Commission (CONAGUA, Comisión Nacional del Agua), José Luis Luege Tamargo, is also present, as is Rocío Alatorre, commissioner for evidence and risk management at the Federal Commission for Protection against Sanitary Risks (COFEPRIS, Comisión Federal para la Protección contra Riesgos Sanitarios). During the committee's meeting, Alatorre reports that in 2006 COFEPRIS commenced an initial health assessment for this region of Jalisco. On the one hand, they compared data on mortality due to gastrointestinal ailments in the municipalities of the greater Guadalajara Metropolitan Area (GMA) with national data. El Salto stood out, she said, with rates above the national average and among the highest in the state. On the other hand, they examined mortality data for chronic illnesses for the 2000–2005 period. Juanacatlán and El Salto were above the state-level rates of mortality for several types of cancer. It was simply a preliminary assessment, she emphasized, and had not been published. Speaking after the committee meeting, Alatorre asked Representative Padilla whether it would be necessary to invest in a broader study of the health impacts in this area, or whether they could proceed

Introduction

with what they had. They agreed that a more complete study would not be necessary.

Five years later, it's February 2013 and we have not progressed beyond preliminary evaluations. There is another interinstitutional meeting convened by the renamed Jalisco Ministry of Environment and Territorial Development (SEMADET, Secretaría de Medio Ambiente y Desarrollo Territorial); the main objective is to present a report on the most polluted area of the Upper Santiago River Basin, the El Ahogado Subbasin (CIATEJ 2012). During the presentation, data are scant and there is barely a mention of industrial sources of pollution. Surprised by this fact, a member of IMDEC approaches one of the report authors to inquire about this omission. "Industrial pollution is a myth," responds the researcher.

A caravan called the Toxi-Tour has arrived in El Salto. It is December 2019, and the tour is kicking off here, bringing together representatives of ten countries, convened by the Transnational Institute and the National Assembly of Environmentally Affected People (Asamblea Nacional de Afectados Ambientales). The tour will visit seven highly industrialized regions "characterized by systematic air, water and soil pollution, compounded by unbridled urbanization and the proliferation of landfill sites and dumping grounds for highly toxic waste" (Vargas 2021, 6). Leap of Life, the most active organization in El Salto, has organized the event next to the waterfall and invited local activists and researchers to present a panorama of the devastation. An unanticipated speaker is added to the agenda. Serious and soft-spoken, health researcher Gabriela Domínguez presents the results of a study financed by the CEA and completed in 2011 but never publicly disclosed.

Domínguez works at the Autonomous University of San Luis Potosí, an institution that was hired in the context of the promotion of the Arcediano Dam on the Santiago River, to identify indicators for subsequent epidemiological surveillance in the area that would be affected by the dam. The study evaluated a series of environmental, social, and biological factors in six communities or neighborhoods near the river from Juanacatlán to Guadalajara. Domínguez explained that children in the towns closest to the river, in El Salto, Juanacatlán, La Cofradía, and Puente Grande, presented high levels of blood disorders, skin conditions, learning difficulties, and a higher incidence in their families of neoplasms (tumors), diabetes, and high blood pressure. For the study, they analyzed blood and urine samples from 330 boys and girls between the ages of 6 and 12 to determine their levels of exposure to certain toxins. In the four communities closest to the river, "a high percentage of children exceeded the biological safety limits for the occupationally exposed adult population" for lead, arsenic, and benzene (UASLP and CEA 2011, 268).[11] *The children had higher levels of these toxins in their blood than was acceptable for factory workers.*

These are vignettes of moments in a process that is far from over, and of government (in)action in response to social mobilization calling for the cleanup of the Santiago River. I have selected these moments because, in my view, they help reveal key traits of the power relations that have maintained the Santiago River as a *sewer of progress* that damages the health of people living along its shores. As I will relate in the chapters of this book, government authorities have been adamant in denying the severity of this problem and, even more emphatically, the health impacts and responsibility of industry in this degradation. This negation does not stem, as the vignettes demonstrate, from a dearth of data. It stems, rather, from a configuration of power relations that has endowed the pollution of the Santiago with a certain level of *resilience*.

The term "resilience" has been popularized in recent years, particularly in the context of climate change. The United Nations Office for Disaster Risk Reduction defines "resilience" as the capacity of human communities or ecosystems to "resist, absorb, accommodate to and recover from the effects of a hazard in a timely and efficient manner" (United Nations 2009, 24). Given the risk or hazard of social movements, we can say that the phenomenon of pollution of the Santiago River has been resilient, in the sense it has been able to "resist" the pressures of protest and calls for stricter enforcement of environmental regulations. This resilience, I maintain, is the result of a particular configuration of power relations that normalizes and invisibilizes this pollution, especially that of industrial origin. The entirety of the research presented in this book is aimed at revealing, understanding, and analyzing these power relations.

I.3 Welcome to the Santiago River

"A few words about the Lerma [River] are necessary. It is called the Mississippi of Mexico, as it is the longest river in the country," wrote the American Thomas L. Rogers in 1893. "It originates to the south of us, just east of Toluca, and after a trajectory of four hundred and fifty miles flows into

Introduction

the Pacific Ocean in San Blas. It drains the excess waters of an immense territory" (cited in Peregrina 1994, 45). In fact, the Lerma-Santiago River here described is not Mexico's longest, as both the Grande and Grijalva-Usumacinta Rivers surpass it in length. In the period when Rogers was writing, even though the river changed names from the Lerma to the Grande de Santiago after passing through the "northwestern corner of Lake Chapala," it was recognized as a single river. Today, at least administratively, the Lerma-Santiago is not acknowledged as one river, with the Lerma considered an "inland" river (with no outlet in the ocean) that drains into Lake Chapala, where the Santiago originates (CONAGUA 2014b, 37).

Rogers also visited the waterfall in El Salto and set down his impressions:

> More than evoking, Juanacatlán looks like Niagara Falls. It is really a miniature of the powerful waterfall. . . . The Lerma seems to attempt to pour all the waters of Lake Chapala, and an area of forty thousand square miles, over the waterfall at the same time, as at Niagara the Erie and the upper lakes. (Cited in Peregrina 1994, 46)

The same year these texts were published, the El Salto hydroelectric dam on the Santiago River was inaugurated, the first for the sale of electricity in Mexico (Durán et al. 1999, 102). Later, in 1899, the broad waterfall and its hydroelectric power plant were commemorated on a postage stamp. The image of the waterfall is also found on Juanacatlán's coat of arms, although in the words of the municipal chronicler it is now simply a reminder of the area's history: "as a token of the past, the famous 'El Salto de Juanacatlán' falls, now practically extinct, and thanks to which the region was known both nationally and internationally" (Ayuntamiento de Juancatlán 1997). Hydraulic interventions, population growth, the expansion of irrigated agriculture, and industrial and agroindustrial activities have radically altered the landscape over the past century.

From its emergence in Lake Chapala, Mexico's largest lake, the Santiago flows 562 kilometers to the Pacific Ocean in the state of Nayarit. It is considered the second most important river of the Mexican Pacific in terms of its average annual flow of 7,349 cubic meters per second (CONAGUA 2018, 48). It is part of the country's most populous hydrological-administrative region (región hidrológico-administrativa),[12] as well as the second most significant in terms of its contribution to the gross domestic product (GDP), the Lerma-Santiago-Pacific region, with an estimated population of 24.7 million and contribution to national GDP of 19.8 percent (CONAGUA 2018, 23). Solely in the Santiago River Basin, the population is estimated at

8.7 million, across parts of six states: Jalisco, Nayarit, Zacatecas, Aguascalientes, Guanajuato, and Durango. The majority of this population is concentrated in the GMA, an urban area bordered by the Santiago to the east and north and home to approximately 5.3 million (COCURS 2021). The river, known as one of the country's most polluted, is degraded by untreated sewage from communities along its shores and by agricultural runoff. Furthermore, an industrial corridor stretches from upriver in Ocotlán to the south of the GMA in El Salto and Juanacatlán. It is in El Salto and Juanacatlán where a population of over 260,000 people endure this pollution and local activists denounce the proliferation of health ailments from rashes to respiratory problems and from kidney failure to cancer (INEGI 2020a).

I.3.1 An Industrial Corridor Is Born

Industrial activity in this area dates back to 1866 with the installation, in what is now El Salto, of the Río Blanco textile factory, which later moved to the west of Guadalajara in Zapopan (Durand 1985). Three years after the hydroelectric plant was inaugurated, in 1896, construction of the Río Grande textile factory got underway, together with its industrial housing estate, the precursor of the community of El Salto, located near the waterfall on land purchased from the Jesús María Hacienda (Durand 1986). This factory was the first large textile factory in the state to be located in a rural area, as well as the first major industrial installation in the river basin (Durand 1985; Durán et al. 1999).

Decades later, in Ocotlán, at the other extreme of what would become the industrial corridor, Swiss-owned Nestlé opened a condensed-milk factory in 1935. In the neighboring municipality of Poncitlán, a subsidiary of American chemical company Celanese opened its doors in 1947, producing synthetic fibers (González Corona 1989, 31). This was an era when no industrial development strategy existed in Jalisco, and industrial activity expanded "anarchically" (31). Later, under Governor Juan Gil Preciado (1958–1964), the Guadalajara–La Barca highway was built, linking the city to the communities of Atequiza, Atotonilquillo, Poncitlán, Ocotlán, Jamay, and La Barca, and the so-called Industrial Zone of Western Mexico was promoted, leading to the installation of a further nine factories by 1970. Among them were American chemical manufacturer Cyanamid (now Cytec-Solvay), with a factory in Atequiza that commenced operations in

Introduction

1962, followed in 1965 by Swiss chemical giant Ciba Geigy, with its factory in Atotonilquillo. In 1967, Mexican acrylic fiber producer Crysel (Celulosa y derivados) opened a factory in El Salto. At this time, under Governor Francisco Medina Ascencio (1964–1970), companies came "by invitation" of the government and in the absence of any standards regulating their installation or operation (36).

In this post–World War II period, Mexico sought to spur development by following the model of import substitution industrialization (ISI) (1940–1982), with policies seeking to strengthen the nation's industrial base, restructure the state, and create a new class of domestic industrialists (Cypher 2013). This strategy sparked strong economic growth. "During the decades from 1940 to 1970, the Mexican economy grew at an annual average rate above 6.5%, with a per capita growth rate higher than 3.7%," affirmed Jalisco's development strategy in 1974 (Gobierno del Estado de Jalisco 1974, 36). The same document refers to the industrial decentralization strategy of President Luis Echeverría (1970–1976) and a 1972 decree establishing "new tax mechanisms and other incentives for industries to set up in the less developed regions of the country" (40). Part of this decentralization was the now rebaptized Industrial Corridor of Jalisco (C. Lezama 2004).

The corridor spanned ninety kilometers, from La Barca to El Salto, and included the strip of land between the Santiago River and the Guadalajara–La Barca highway, an area with access to railways, electricity, and surface waters (Durán et al. 1999, 118). An October 1972 report from the Industrial Development Commission of the National Congress conveys the optimism with which Jalisco's corridor was promoted: "This corridor has, in 1970, generated employment for 30% of the state's economically active population [and] has such complete infrastructure that it is promising for the investor, and will undoubtedly become an industrial emporium" (Legislatura XLVIII 1972). Water was seen as key to the development of this future emporium, with the same commission affirming that the "hydraulic resources of the Lerma-Chapala-Santiago Basin, with a volume of 8.2 billion cubic meters, offer water availability for industrial use in practically unlimited quantity." Fifty years later, the idea of "unlimited" water in the overexploited and polluted Lerma-Chapala-Santiago Basin, where conflicts over both water quantity and quality have proliferated for decades, seems incomprehensible.

This industrial corridor was planned following the course of the Santiago River, and the river would be significant for this emporium, not only as a possible source of water. In fact, the vast majority—if not the totality—of companies in the area draw on their own wells to meet their water needs.[13] Rivers fulfill a different function for factories along their banks. As Dan Fagin (2014) narrates for the birthplace of giants in the chemical industry in Basel, Switzerland, factories needed the Rhine River to dispose of the wastes of dye production, after wastes stored in unlined lagoons tainted local wells and made people ill. Fagin affirms that this became standard practice: "Chemical manufacturers all over the world would follow the same strategy for getting rid of their waste. They would dump on their own property first . . . and then if the authorities foreclosed that option, they would then instead discharge their liquid waste into the largest and fastest-flowing body of water available" (chap. 1). Not being a high-flow river, it wouldn't take long for the consequences of using the Santiago as the conveyor of the effluents of the nascent corridor to become apparent.

Thus, the era of industrial decentralization coincided with the arrival of severe problems for the Santiago River. In January 1973, the Guadalajara daily *El Informador* reported "high [levels of] pollution of the Lerma and Santiago Rivers, resulting from the chemical waste emitted by the factories located on their banks," where inspectors from the Department of Fisheries found "many dead fish floating on the waters, mainly of the Santiago River in Ocotlán" (*Informador* 1973). Denouncing a lack of wastewater treatment plants at most factories, the fishermen of Ocotlán voiced their grievances, conveying that the "fish population has practically been eliminated" in a "vast area" where once the fishing had been most productive. The following year, the same paper reported on a study by researchers from the Autonomous University of Guadalajara, who had analyzed samples from the Santiago River and warned that pollution "is eradicating the river's flora and fauna" and that "if this isn't dealt with swiftly and effectively it may soon be irreversible" (*Informador* 1974).

This period saw the arrival of important transnationals, especially to the municipality of El Salto. Spanish tire manufacturer Euzkadi set up its factory in 1971, followed by IBM in 1975, chlorine gas manufacturer Pennwalt del Pacífico (now Mexichem) in 1976, and the El Salto Industrial Park in 1982 (González Corona 1989, 39; Durán et al. 1999, 119).

Introduction

It was at this time, in the early 1980s, that changes in the country's development model commenced that would soon turn Mexico into what James Cypher calls a "neoliberal bastion" (2013, 396). This because the country has been one of the most important laboratories for experimentation with the processes of neoliberalization. As James Greenberg and colleagues (2012, 2) affirm, "Nowhere has neoliberalism been more widely implemented or its impacts been more profound than in Mexico." After almost four decades pursuing a strategy of ISI, Mexico's external debt rose precipitously, ballooning from $6.8 billion in 1972 to $58 billion in 1982. When oil prices dropped, Mexico declared bankruptcy in 1982 (Harvey 2005). This marked the beginning of neoliberal reforms, included as conditions on loans received from the International Monetary Fund, the World Bank, and the US Department of the Treasury. These reforms included cuts to public spending, liberalization of trade, tax reforms, and the privatization of state-owned companies. The government's commitment to privatization and the elimination of subsidies was later bolstered under President Carlos Salinas de Gortari (1988–1994).

The industrial corridor continued to grow through this period. By 1984 there were sixty-one factories in El Salto generating approximately 14,800 jobs, and the figure rose to seventy companies belonging to twelve different industrial sectors by 1989 (Durán et al. 1999, 119). The environmental impacts of the corridor also increased. When Elías González Corona analyzed the situation in El Salto in 1989, he observed that "the Santiago River is now a canal of industrial wastes that have eliminated the fauna and any possibility of using its waters" (1989, 66). He also described the impact at the waterfall: "The air is being polluted and respiratory illness and infection are being spread whose impacts have yet to be adequately gauged" (66). The scenario evident at that time persists today, one of a severely degraded river and of scant scientific evidence to determine the gravity of the resulting health effects for the population.

Urban growth has gone hand in hand with the intensification of industrial development. The population of the GMA grew from just under 0.5 million in 1950 to 2.2 million in 1980 and to 5.3 million in 2020 as it swallowed up surrounding municipalities (SE 1950; INEGI 1984, 1991, 2020a). After 1990, a major area of expansion of the GMA was in municipalities to the south of the city, including in Tlajomulco de Zúñiga and El Salto. These two municipalities also constitute most of the territory of the most polluted subbasin of the Upper Santiago: El Ahogado. Over a thirty-year period (1990–2020), the population of Tlajomulco grew at an annual rate of 32.1 percent (from 68,482 to 727,750) and El Salto at a rate of 16.9 percent (from 38,281 to 232,852).

The severe degradation of the Upper Santiago spurred its inclusion in the campaign platform of the current governor of Jalisco, Enrique Alfaro Ramírez (2018–). A few days after assuming power in December 2018, the governor went to the bridge over the river in Juanacatlán to announce his Comprehensive Strategy for the Recovery of the Santiago River as an emblematic project of his government. From then until mid-2022, however, the aforementioned strategy has not produced clear actions or strategies for the control of industrial pollution.

The area between the source of the river in Ocotlán and the El Ahogado Subbasin in the south of the GMA is home to almost seven hundred manufacturing facilities, including small, medium, and large enterprises, according to information from the National Statistical Directory of Economic Units (Directorio Estadístico Nacional de Unidades Económicas). These companies are not concentrated in one industrial sector. The industrial sectors to which these installations belong include furniture production (20 percent), metal industries (15 percent), food and beverages (12 percent), plastics and rubber (12 percent), and chemical industries (9 percent). Focusing solely on the sixty-three large factories (with at least 251 employees), these are concentrated in the food and beverage sector (19 percent), electronics and electrical industries (16 percent), chemicals (14 percent), metal industries (14 percent), automotive and auto parts (10 percent), and plastics and rubber (10 percent). In this area, seventy-one of the factories belong to foreign-owned corporations.

In chapter 1, I will analyze the existing data on the factories that discharge into the Santiago River or its tributaries, as well as the reports that have monitored the quality of their effluents. Although there have been relatively few studies that have contemplated the monitoring and analysis of industrial wastewater discharged into the river, the results confirm a pattern of noncompliance with Mexican regulations. Moreover, some of these studies went beyond the limited effluent discharge standard (NOM-001-SEMARNAT-1996) and demonstrate that industry is also a source of toxic substances not controlled in existing regulations (CEAS and AyMA Ingeniería y Consultoría 2006; IMTA and CEA Jalisco 2011).

Introduction   15

I.4 How to Create a Sewer of Progress

Before addressing the main arguments of this book, I would like to demonstrate how the Santiago River has been converted into what I am calling a *sewer of progress*—that is, a space for capital accumulation where human and ecosystem health are sacrificed in pursuit of "progress." The term "sacrifice zones" has been used in environmental justice literature to describe urban spaces abandoned to polluting industries and hazardous waste disposal sites that also are home to marginalized communities; in the United States—where this term was coined—they tend to be African American or Latino communities or neighborhoods (Bullard 1993, 25). As Henri Acselrad observes when writing on Latin America, in these sacrifice zones, "there is an overlapping of diverse types of disadvantages and risks for the most dispossessed populations" (2014, 387). In the creation of a sewer of progress, I argue, environmental degradation is normalized to such an extent that it is made invisible. This is the logic behind what I call *institutionalized corruption*.

One of the government employees interviewed for this project, Francisco Javier Silva, then the head of the legal department in Jalisco for the Federal Bureau of Environmental Protection (PROFEPA, Procuraduría Federal de Protección al Ambiente), clearly explained how such degradation is normalized. Silva referred to people from the riverside communities who have asked him, "Why don't you issue sanctions for the damage to the aquatic ecosystem in the basin of the Santiago?" He said that people's point of reference when asking this question is that "twenty years ago or fifty years ago, we swam here or we came here to fish." Given this, he responded, "Yes, but the same authority that administers that resource began to change the classification of that ecosystem to allow that harmful load of pollutants." As the river of old no longer exists, and a lenient classification has been implemented, Silva insisted that "for that reason, *the issue of damage to the aquatic ecosystem of the Santiago doesn't exist.*"[14] Since the pollution has occurred under a regime of regulations and authorized classifications, the problem as such does not exist.

With respect to industry, Silva explained that in the case of the Santiago River, for example, "we find a company . . . that has a discharge with levels higher than the parameters set by the National Water Commission," but the only thing that happens in response to exceeding the limits is that "the company pays the commission for that difference, [and] the commission accepts the payment." In this situation, he asserted,

> this does not become [considered] harm to the aquatic ecosystem because it is within what is permitted by the water system administratively, according to what the commission has determined. Even though the water body is polluted, but according to the commission's criteria, it is a water body that now receives these types of discharges.[15]

That is, it is now a *sewer of progress*. The analysis of why and how the Santiago River has been transformed into that sewer requires examining both the practices that normalize the pollution and their significance in a broader panorama of the capitalist development strategies pursued by Mexico in recent decades, and specifically how environmental regulations have been devised under the general logic of free-market environmentalism.

I.5 Green Mirages: Market Environmentalism for Poor Countries

In the center of this investigation is one of the crucial dilemmas of our era: Can there be development (or economic growth or job creation) without environmental degradation? In the South, is industrial development compatible with a strong system of environmental regulation, or is lax regulation necessary as a "competitive advantage" in a globalized world? Who sets the limits and who monitors how much environmental degradation is to be borne to achieve that development or growth or job creation? On the other hand, from the lands that suffer the degradation, communities demand to know who pays the price for the "externalities" of development. In this case, who pays the price and who is responsible for the severe pollution of the Santiago River from its origins in Ocotlán to the falls in El Salto, at the heart of the main industrial corridor of the state of Jalisco? These questions about the winners and losers of economic activity have been central themes addressed from the perspectives of political ecology and environmental justice.

This dilemma has sparked diverse and polarized responses. For the main promoters of growth and development in government, business, and international organizations such as the United Nations, the World Bank, and the Organisation for Economic Co-operation and Development, the preferred solution centers on the concept of sustainable development and, linked to this, the green economy or, more explicitly, green growth. At the other extreme, activists and academics advocate for degrowth (Latouche 2008;

Introduction

Kallis 2011; Demaria et al. 2013), and there is talk of postdevelopment (Escobar 2005; Gudynas 2013). For many social movements in Latin America, there is a struggle for autonomy, as Raúl Zibechi states, "both from the state as well as from political parties, founded on the growing capacity of the movements to ensure the subsistence of their followers" (2007, 23). This book draws from the field of political ecology with an interest, as Raymond Bryant underscores, in asking how environmental problems are "linked to elite interests and activities that perpetuate the political and economic status quo" (1997, 7). The intention is not to suggest isolated improvements in public policy or standards, to correct the system of government, but rather to point to a systemic logic whereby economic activities are prioritized over environmental protection and human health.

In the context of this dilemma, the question that guides this text is a simple one: After twenty years of citizen demands for river cleanup, why does the Santiago River continue to be polluted by effluents of industrial origin? To this end, the analysis focuses on the practices of three central groups of actors. Primarily, I examine the role of the government authorities responsible for regulating industrial activity, as well as of companies located in the area together with several industry associations. At the same time, I explore the strategies and proposals of the local organizations struggling for river cleanup and protection of the health of the riverside population. To answer this question, therefore, the spotlight is focused mainly on those who generate and those who are meant to regulate this type of pollution.

Based on these analyses, in this book I argue that in Mexico the formulation and enforcement of a regulatory framework for wastewater discharge, under the general logic of free-market environmentalism, has generated a system that permits and normalizes environmental degradation. This is what I call *institutionalized corruption*. At the same time, I argue that there exists a *myth of the multinational*, with reference to a generalized belief or affirmation—which the facts do not support—that large companies, and more specifically transnational corporations, comply with high internal standards that are stricter than Mexican environmental regulations. I seek to demonstrate that this myth plays a key role in justifying a scantly enforced regulatory system that is highly dependent on the self-monitoring of the companies themselves.

At a macro level, I argue that flexible environmental regulations function as a further comparative advantage within Mexico's strategy of insertion into the global economy. Linked to this is the notion that the situation of an individual country, in this case Mexico, cannot be understood in isolation. Rather, a global perspective is necessary to discern how environmental "solutions" in the Global North often represent, more than problems now solved, the displacement of those problems from North to South. At the same time, based on the discourses of development and progress, I argue that a permanent environmental state of exception is generated whereby the state, while taking on the responsibility of bearer of environmental modernity, at the same time justifies the lack of application of regulations, or their laxity, with the argument that at its current stage of development, the country needs to prioritize development and progress.

Based on the notion of institutionalized corruption, therefore, the central argument that I seek to develop in this book is that the Santiago River continues to be polluted by industrial sources due to a capitalist development strategy that promotes foreign direct investment, and more generally the industrial activity of transnational and Mexican corporations, under a system of simulated regulation that responds to the needs of the country as a signatory of trade agreements rather than the commitment to protect the population's health and well-being and the ecosystems that sustain communities. I will demonstrate the existence of a type of regulatory greenwashing that allows authorities to dismiss accusations of environmental dumping, as occurred during the negotiations in the run-up to the North American Free Trade Agreement, while "regulated" dumping may continue in an environment of legal certainty. This type of simulation allows transnational companies to take advantage of double standards in environmental regulation while presenting themselves at the global level as socially responsible, green, environmentally compliant actors. As I will make clear throughout this book, these double standards in the case of the corporations, and the Mexican state's strategy of insertion in the global economy (employing regulatory simulation), devalue human lives and essential ecosystems in Mexico.

This system that puts lives in the South at risk is now dressed in green. Given this, I maintain that the case of the Santiago River is an example of the failure of ideas of sustainable development and, more clearly, of corporate sustainability. Beyond its discursive efficacy, sustainable development does not resolve the aforementioned dilemma, and neither does it impede environmental deterioration or the related negative effects on the health of the most vulnerable populations.

Introduction

The dilemma of environmental protection versus economic growth in a "free market" is not new, as Karl Polanyi captures in his analysis of nineteenth-century economic liberalism:

> To allow the market mechanism to be sole director of the fate of human beings and their natural environment indeed, even of the amount and use of purchasing power, would result in the demolition of society. . . . Nature would be reduced to its elements, neighborhoods and landscapes defiled, rivers polluted, military safety jeopardized, the power to produce food and raw materials destroyed. . . . No society could stand the effects of such a system of crude fictions even for the shortest stretch of time unless its human and natural substance as well as its business organization was protected against the ravages of this satanic mill. (Polanyi [1944] 2001, 76)

Polanyi's observations on the implications of pursuing the "utopia" of the self-regulating market are also important to understanding the logic that sustains what has been called "free market environmentalism" (Anderson and Leal 2001). This free-market environmentalism, in its adaptation for developing countries, is key to understanding the configuration of environmental regulations in Mexico, as well as the relations established between the state and the private sector. The "fictions" referred to by Polanyi, of treating labor, money, and land or nature as commodities produced for sale, were confronted by interventions through which "society protected itself against the perils inherent in a self-regulating market system" (Polanyi [1944] 2001, 80). This is the "double movement" of, on the one hand, the expansion of the global trade of "genuine" commodities and, on the other, the restrictions applied to "check the action of the market relative to labor, land, and money" (79). For the case analyzed here, what is under scrutiny are the power relations governing the interventions applied to mitigate the effects of the "free market" on the environment in Mexico.

Remaining for a moment in the period studied by Polanyi, we can recollect that the devastation of rivers was one of the most notorious symptoms—together with the miserable working conditions—of the new textile factories in England. Coketown was Charles Dickens's fictitious industrial city "shrouded in a haze of its own," where on a "river that was black and thick with dye, some Coketown boys who were at large . . . rowed a crazy boat, which made a spumous track upon the water as it jogged along, while every dip of an oar stirred up vile smells" (1905, 246). Writing in the mid-nineteenth century, Dickens told of the "fragility" of the textile mill owners given any attempt to regulate their production. A factory owner, when "it was proposed to hold him accountable for the consequences of any of his acts—he was sure to come out with the awful menace, that he would 'sooner pitch his property into the Atlantic.'" Such was the threat that had "terrified" the home secretary "within an inch of his life," wrote Dickens (244).

How is this relevant to the matter at hand? Although Polanyi himself believed that the "market mentality" had become "obsolete" following the rise to power of fascism ([1944] 2001, 265), Jamie Peck notes that over four decades after the publication of *The Great Transformation*, "the rise of neoliberal globalism" has drawn attention to the "prescience" of Polanyi's historical analyses, given that new "fables of the self-sustaining market were actively remaking the world in their own image" (2010, 41). The quotations from Dickens also pose the problem that Acselrad calls the "locational blackmail" of corporations, which has increased with globalization and trade openness, whereby "companies . . . may use a lack of employment and public revenue as leverage to impose polluting practices and retract social rights" (2014, 380). This power to exert locational blackmail will clearly be greater or lesser depending on each country or region's strategy of insertion into the global economy, as well as on the relationship between the state and the private interests involved.

Before delving into free-market environmentalism and its deformation for "developing countries," I wish to distinguish between divergent approaches to environmental problems. Acselrad proposes a simple but useful distinction between utilitarian and countercultural logics, where countercultural positions do not reduce the view of nature to one of resources for appropriation but rather acknowledge that there "exist distinct meanings and logics of use linked to distinct societies and cultures" (2014, 378). Struggles for environmental justice and so-called social environmental conflicts, as well as what Joan Martínez-Alier calls the "environmentalism of the poor" (2002), embody these positions that underline the dimensions of power, the unequal exposure of different populations to the risks associated with industrialization and to "environmental and territorial dispossession" (Acselrad 2014, 378). One challenge here, stressed by David Harvey (1996, 401), is to seek out the affinities among local struggles and conflicts by confronting the underlying processes of social and environmental injustice, which would be, in his words, "unrelenting capital accumulation

Introduction

and the extraordinary asymmetrics of money and political power that are embedded in that process."

On the utilitarian side we find, for example, neo-Malthusian texts from the late 1960s and early 1970s such as *The Limits to Growth* of the Club of Rome, with its fear about the "exponential nature of human growth within a closed system" (Meadows et al. 1972, 189), as well as Paul Ehrlich's *The Population Bomb* (1968) and Garrett Hardin's brief but influential text "The Tragedy of the Commons" ([1968] 2009). Evidently, free-market environmentalism fits in the utilitarian field, although unlike the other authors, for those such as Terry Anderson and Donald Leal (2001), their faith in the market and technology allows them to elude scenarios of crisis and the concerns about scarcity on a finite planet put forward by neo-Malthusian authors. From this viewpoint, Malthusian theses "fail to take into account how human ingenuity stimulated by market forces finds ways to cope with natural resource constraints" (3). For "hegemonic utilitarian reasoning," the concern has been "to guarantee the continuity of capital accumulation, fostering the 'most efficient' use of materials and energy" (Acselrad 2014, 377).

Sustainable development and, more recently, green economy and green growth are also key notions of utilitarian reasoning. Certainly, sustainable development and, more clearly, sustainability are contested concepts. Sustainable development in particular has been criticized for being vague, for lending itself to hypocrisy or "fake greenery," and for being in itself an oxymoron (Robinson 2004). Sustainable development attempts to discursively harmonize economic growth with the conservation of natural resources for future generations. This is in consonance with the most widely disseminated definition—or what Subhabrata Bobby Banerjee (2003, 152) refers to as a "slogan"—that of the Brundtland Report, presented to the UN by the World Commission on Environment and Development in 1987. "Poverty itself pollutes the environment," reads the report, decoupling the analysis from global economic relations and blaming the most vulnerable sectors of the population for the degradation of their means of subsistence (WCED 1987, 29). With this lens, part of the required response is further economic growth: "a five- to tenfold increase in manufacturing output will be needed just to raise developing world consumption of manufactured goods" to levels comparable with those of the industrialized world (21). Developing countries thus become the justification for continuing on a path of expanding production and economic growth.

Sustainable development avoids the uncomfortable questions, as Arturo Escobar (1995, 197) asserts:

> The epistemological and political reconciliation of economy and ecology proposed by sustainable development is intended to create the impression that only minor adjustments to the market system are needed to launch an era of environmentally sound development, hiding the fact that the economic framework itself cannot hope to accommodate environmental considerations without substantial reform.

James O'Connor considers the economic framework itself when asking, "Is sustainable capitalism possible?" (1994, 158). In his eco-Marxist critique, O'Connor refers first to Karl Marx to discuss the "first contradiction of capitalism," which highlights the tension between the incentive for individual capitals to increase the exploitation of the workforce (cutting salaries, increasing the productivity of work, etc.) and the undesired effect of reducing demand for consumer commodities as a result of the diminished purchasing power of workers (160). This "internal" contradiction arises from the "demand" side.

O'Connor suggests that a "second contradiction of capitalism" must also be analyzed, this time stemming from the cost side and what Marx called "conditions of production": labor, nature, and space or infrastructure (1994, 162–163). Here the crises would arise on the cost side in two ways. On the one hand, they may result from the actions of individual capitals seeking to "defend or restore profits by strategies that degrade or fail to maintain over time the material conditions of their own production" (162–163). On the other hand, protest movements against these strategies, which demand, for example, better working conditions or greater environmental protection, can also threaten profitability. It is the state, in this formulation, that must ensure access to the conditions of production for capital.

While acknowledging the growing environmental degradation associated with capitalist accumulation, John Bellamy Foster (2002) criticizes O'Connor's focus on the economic crises that are assumed to derive from this second contradiction, as well as his assertion that this has become the dominant contradiction of capitalism. Foster questions the notion that environmental deterioration necessarily leads to economic crises, via a type of "feedback mechanism," as well as the "economism and functionalism" of framing the problem in terms of its capacity to generate such crises (10).

Introduction

In a pessimistic, though no less pertinent, affirmation, Foster maintains that "we should not underestimate capitalism's capacity to accumulate in the midst of the most blatant ecological destruction, to profit from environmental degradation . . . and to continue to destroy the earth to the point of no return" (11). This also has to do with the fact that not all of the nature destroyed is incorporated into accumulation processes, and therefore does not enter into the category of capitalism's conditions of production.

Environmental problems do not derive their significance from the degree to which they can lead to economic crises for capitalism, and Foster points out that "ecological degradation . . . is as basic to capitalism as the pursuit of profits itself (which depend to a large extent upon it)" (2002, 15). For a case such that of the Santiago, the egregious devastation of the river does not seem to have yet, even given the social protest, led to a "cost crisis," so Foster's observations and call to not lose sight of the scale of environmental degradation—beyond what is functional to capitalism—are of consequence for this analysis.

It is instructive to contrast the more structural analyses, such as those of Polanyi, O'Connor, and Foster, with the more optimistic vision of ecological modernization (EM), stemming mainly from environmental sociology. Acselrad categorizes EM theory together with other utilitarian perspectives, as it reaffirms "the market, technical progress and political consensus as the way forward" (2014, 378). EM theory emerged in northwestern Europe in the 1980s and proposes that "advanced modern societies experience changes in industrial structure and production processes, such as via industrial ecology and adoption of renewable energy technologies," which, in turn, lead to reductions in polluting emissions, the consumption of natural resources, and health risks (Perz 2007, 418). EM has been criticized for its Eurocentrism, for paying insufficient attention to questions of social inequality and consumption (not just production), and for its unquestioned technological optimism (Mol et al. 2013). From the Global South, critiques have also emphasized the export of dirty industries to countries of the South as a factor in the reduction of pollution in the North. In this vein, Stephen Perz notes that studies undertaken in the United States, Eastern Europe, Asia, and Latin America have "generally not confirmed EM's theoretical expectations," based on the industrial changes of northwestern Europe (2007, 421).

According to Arthur Mol and colleagues (2013, 22), more recent elaborations of EM have moved away from technological determinism and been more sensitive to social inequality. Nonetheless, from the perspective of this investigation, the understanding of the role of the state, the private sector, and the market in current EM is far from grappling with the power "asymmetrics"—stressed by Harvey (1996)—that influence the favored topic of EM: "the processes and outcomes of environmental reform" (Mol et al. 2013, 15). Based on my empirical work, I concur with some of the common criticisms of EM, in particular the lack of attention to the structural causes of environmental degradation and being excessively "optimistic/naïve" regarding the potential of sustainable development (24). Even more optimistic—though not so naïve—is free-market environmentalism, and the ideas that sustain it are key to understanding hegemonic discourses on environmental regulation and the configuration of the current system in Mexico.

I.5.1 Free-Market Environmentalism as a Neoliberal "Fix"

"Picture a pasture open to all," invites Hardin, and with this bucolic image introduces us to the horrors of the "inherent logic" of the commons, leading "remorselessly" to tragedy; his is a world peopled by "rational beings" always seeking to maximize their own gains (more of their cattle on the pasture), without realizing the limits of the pasture ([1968] 2009, 246). The solution he proposes is private property. The empirical validity of the argument for the unstoppable damage to common-pool resources has been called into question by works such as those of Elinor Ostrom (1990), who explores cases of local cooperative management of common-pool resources in light of arguments biased in favor of centralization or privatization. However, both Hardin and Ostrom acknowledge that situations such as river pollution—cases like that of the Santiago—must be addressed in a different manner.

Given her interest in self-organization, Ostrom focuses on the common-pool resources utilized by groups of a limited number and wherein the members depend to a significant degree on the income derived from those resources. Ostrom explicitly excludes from the analysis of empirical cases situations where "participants can produce major external harm for others," which includes "all asymmetrical pollution problems" (1990, 26). Although Hardin is associated with arguments in favor of privatization, this is not his suggested solution when speaking of polluted rivers. While private property could resolve the issue of the pasture, the "tragedy of the commons as a cesspool must be prevented by different means," since air and water "cannot readily be fenced" ([1968] 2009, 247). These other means would be "coercive laws or taxing devices that make it cheaper for the polluter to treat his pollutants than to discharge them untreated" (247). Thus, a role is conceded for more traditional regulations, although Hardin allows for the possibility that property law may evolve to the point it could address this particular manifestation of the tragedy.

In contrast, Anderson and Leal (2001, 4) reject the option of employing "negative incentives" such as regulations and taxes, while advocating for "positive incentives associated with prices, profits, and entrepreneurship." The basis of their free-market environmentalism is a strong system of private property rights and restriction of the role of government to the definition and enforcement of those rights. Given their dependence on clear property laws and price signals, the authors acknowledge that their solutions are more applicable to certain natural resources. "Pollution concerns challenge the paradigm," they concede, though without abandoning their model (8). They argue that broad regulations have not been effective and have been costly, and that government bureaucracies are inevitably open to co-optation by "special interest groups."

The valid options within this framework include tradeable pollution permits and property rights over the "disposal medium" (Anderson and Leal 2001, 132). Given the difficulty of assigning property rights when the disposal medium is the air or a body of water such as a river, the authors propose a solution based on common law whereby affected parties could defend themselves against the illegal "trespassing" on their property in the form of pollutants. This proposal is based on two clearly questionable assumptions: first, the future evolution of private property rights as regards air and water, and second, the development of novel technologies capable of determining the sources of pollutants once dispersed in the environment. The technologies foreseen by these authors are markers that governments would compel private parties to add to their emissions, allowing for their subsequent detection or, alternately, systems capable of analyzing contaminant dispersal.

Even leaving aside the technological element, affected property owners would be obliged to invest time and money seeking remedy in the courts for harm caused by pollution, providing results of test samples and expert analyses determining the sources of pollutants. In this regard, Peter Menell asserts that "Anderson and Leal provide no explanation for why the world should wait for the development of electronic fencing or tracing technologies before confronting these problems, other than the utter impotence of public institutions" (1992, 502). On the issue of pollution, Anderson and Leal (2001) contend that market-based solutions are losing the battle, except in the case of tradeable discharge permits.

Based on the foregoing, it is clear that there is a drive to employ market logics to address pollution, although given the complexity of applying property rights to such "disposal mediums" as air and water, it is tricky for even the staunchest defenders of the free market to completely eliminate a role for the state in pollution regulation (beyond enforcing property rights). At any rate, it is clear that market-based solutions are the preferred option. In a publication from the World Bank titled *Inclusive Green Growth*, ecological degradation is said to result from a failure to attain the correct "incentives" or "prices," and this is considered "a reality that is harming *economic growth and the environment*" (2012, 45; emphasis added). These imperfections, in turn, may be the result of a series of factors that include "institutional and policy failures; market failures, such as externalities, the public-good nature of many environmental goods; and missing or incomplete property rights" (45). In addressing these failures, the World Bank authors argue that traditional regulations are costly and they affirm that "rules and regulations are generally considered second-best solutions in situations with perfect markets (markets with perfect information and competitive industries)." In the "real world," however, they must grant a role for such regulations as a "useful complement to price-based incentives" (60).

I.5.2 Neoliberal Logics and Environmental Degradation

At this point, I will attempt to link the logic of free-market environmentalism with the broader tendencies of "annihilation" of fictitious commodities such as nature, or the exacerbation of the second contradiction of capitalism (J. O'Connor 1994; Polanyi [1944] 2001, 44). That is, I will seek to explain this logic as a response to the ecological crises engendered by the tendency of capitalist production, particularly in its current neoliberal form, to degrade its conditions of production and nature more generally. One powerful way of understanding how capitalism overcomes this type of contradiction has been accumulation by dispossession (Harvey 2003). This concept has been fruitfully employed to understand the proliferation of socio-environmental conflicts in Mexico (see, for example, Composto and Navarro 2014; Toledo et al. 2015). Focusing on the case of the Santiago River, for example, Mina Lorena Navarro has used the notion of "multiple

Introduction

dispossession" to comprehend diverse "struggles for the commons" in Mexico, including the struggle against pollution in El Salto (Navarro 2015).

Harvey takes up Marx's notion of "original" or "primitive" accumulation, not to conceive of a stage before capitalism but rather to capture with his concept "accumulation based upon predation, fraud, and violence" as an ongoing process (2003, 144). More precisely, Harvey enumerates a series of processes that he sustains Marx identifies with primitive accumulation, to argue that they continue in the "historical geography" of capitalism to the present; these processes include the "commodification and privatization of land and the forceful expulsion of peasant populations; the conversion of various forms of property rights (common, collective, state, etc.) into exclusive private property rights; [and] the suppression of rights to the commons" (145).[16] The role of the state is key in promoting these processes, based on its monopoly on the use of force. Harvey postulates that accumulation by dispossession has become the central characteristic of global capitalism in this period of "neoliberal hegemony" (62). In this way, in addition to expanded reproduction as a means of accumulation, capital "also expands by incorporating resources, peoples, activities, and lands that hitherto were managed, organized and produced under social relations other than capitalist ones" (Swyngedouw 2005, 82). Is this a pertinent way of conceiving the industrial pollution of the Santiago River?

Evidently the river itself is not privatized, but as a commons, the local population has been dispossessed of the river as a site for fishing and recreation, as well as a source of clean water for domestic or agricultural use. More broadly, the communities of El Salto and Juanacatlán have been dispossessed of a healthy living environment given the severe degradation of the river. The Mexican state spearheaded the damming of many rivers as "national" water bodies in the twentieth century—and particularly since the 1950s under the ISI strategy—to increase areas under irrigation and generate hydroelectricity (Aboites 2009; Wester et al. 2009). Based on what has been called the "hydraulic mission," or the idea that "not a single drop of water should reach the sea without being put to work for the benefit of Man" (Molle et al. 2009, 332), in Mexico as in many countries around the world, rivers were dammed in the name of development.

In the case of the Santiago, its damming commenced in 1883 with the construction of both the Corona Dam (for irrigation purposes) and the hydroelectric dam in El Salto, followed in 1906 by the Poncitlán Dam (de

Paula Sandoval 1981). This was during the period known as the Porfiriato (1876–1911), when businessmen and government authorities began to take advantage of new technologies in the construction of hydraulic works for the generation of hydroelectricity, irrigation, and other uses (Aboites et al. 2010). Without naming all the dams on the river, the Federal Electricity Commission has dubbed a series of eight dams the Hydroelectric System of the Santiago River: Puente Grande, Colimilla, Luis M. Rojas (La Intermedia), Valentín Gómez Farías, Santa Rosa, La Yesca, El Cajón, and Aguamilpa (SEMARNAT 2014, 102). In this way, for over a hundred years not only has the river been exploited as a source of water for agriculture and cities—specifically to supply the GMA since 1956—but it has also been fragmented for the sake of electricity generation. Thus, before its flagrant pollution in the 1970s, the Santiago River was exploited as a motor for urban and industrial development over the course of the twentieth century. Its role as an outlet for waste, then, would simply be another facet of the river's use in the same vein.

While the concept of accumulation by dispossession can constitute a useful lens through which to understand the pollution of the Santiago, based on my empirical analysis, I believe other conceptions stemming from studies of the "neoliberalization of nature" are more pertinent to explain the practices that sustain and grant "resilience" to industrial pollution (McCarthy and Prudham 2004; Heynen et al. 2007; Bakker 2009, 2010). To clarify the current logics that sustain the practices in both government and industry in the face of this socio-environmental conflict around river pollution, I draw on the work of Noel Castree (2008, 2010a, 2010b, 2011) and his attempt to understand the neoliberalization of nature in theoretical terms. Castree turns to Polanyi, O'Connor, and other eco-Marxist authors to reflect on the inherent contradictions of continuous accumulation, and from there questions "why it is 'rational' for many different fractions of capital to take a neoliberal approach to nature with the backing of state institutions, pro-business political parties, and advocacy groups" (2008, 146). The answer he arrives at is that neoliberalism, as a particular "shell" of the capitalist mode of production, "offers firms, state bodies, and sympathetic stakeholders a range of 'environmental fixes' to the endemic problem of sustained economic growth" (146).

In addition to a "fix" that basically corresponds to Harvey's accumulation by dispossession, Castree identifies free-market environmentalism as a fix whereby there is a drive to protect or conserve natural resources via their

Introduction 29

privatization or commodification. In countries with preexisting regulations, this tends to entail deregulation and the transfer of responsibilities to the private sector or civil society organizations. For countries without these prior legal frameworks—which would be the case for Mexico—the measures formulated entrust responsibilities to the private sector from the beginning: "Firms and other private interests then step into the vacuum deliberately created" (147). It is important to note that Castree identifies this fix as a way of subjugating conservation to market logics and distinguishes it from a further "fix" that implies the intensification of environmental degradation and the ecological contradictions of accumulation through the real or formal subsumption of previously protected or proscribed aspects of nature. This latter fix is exemplified in the cultivation of transgenic crops and the use of free trade agreements to defend a company's "right" to pollute (McCarthy 2004).

In Mexico, the formulation and application of a regulatory framework for wastewater discharge, under the general logic of free-market environmentalism, without involving privatization or commodification per se, has generated a system that allows for and normalizes environmental degradation. This does not correspond neatly to either of the aforementioned fixes but incorporates aspects of both: the application of market logics to environmental regulation, though not in the name of resource conservation but rather to normalize their deterioration. In the end, as Castree observes (2009, 1792), the typology presented does not purport to be definitive, but rather to draw attention to "distinctively" neoliberal processes. The variability in these processes has to do, as Karen Bakker observes (2009, 1786) in her critique of Castree, with the fact that "different types of socionatures are amenable to very different types of liberal environmentalist strategies, and impose very different types of constraints upon human action." Rivers resist being privatized and, when addressing their pollution, it is tricky to free them from some type of state control. However, it is also essential to interrogate the logic of that state action.

In this regard, Castree's final "fix" deals with the posture assumed by the state in its role as the main entity regulating relations between economic activity and nature. Here, he identifies two positions a state may adopt based on a neoliberal logic. One entails the "hollowing out" of state responsibilities, through their delegation to the private sector or civil society organizations. The other option is the a priori adoption of the position of a "minimal state," an option that tends to prevail "in developing countries with little or no history of state management on the scale Western countries have experienced it" (2008, 149). In Mexico, I would argue that the state has assumed a "minimalist" stance when it comes to enforcing environmental laws and standards, citing budget and staffing limitations while, at the same time, appearing to boast a solid institutional framework on the environment, given the proliferation of laws, standards, and government entities. What we find is an imposing facade, concealing the empty lot behind. This book explores the discourses and practices bolstering that facade, as well as the day-to-day practices that facilitate unfettered environmental degradation and that I argue constitute institutionalized corruption.

I.6 Institutionalized Corruption

Why speak of *institutionalized corruption*? Normally, corruption is understood as an illegal or unethical act for personal benefit and illicit enrichment. In a review of typologies of corruption, Jennifer Bussell (2015) defines the abuse of public office for private gain as the most common characterization of corruption. Distinctions are also often made between "petty" corruption, describing the abusive acts of mid- and low-level public officials in their direct interaction with the public, and "grand" corruption, which refers to the actions of senior government leaders that distort policies or the functioning of the state. Transparency International (n.d.) also recognizes political corruption, which denotes the manipulation of policies, institutions, and rules governing the allocation of resources by decision makers "who abuse their position to sustain their power, status and wealth." The common denominator is the pursuit of individual profit based on state-conferred power.

In the case of environmental regulation of industrial activity, this type of corruption certainly exists among public officials, including inspectors from a diversity of agencies, as well as those charged with approving environmental impact statements or participating in the certification processes for voluntary programs such as PROFEPA's Clean Industry. This may involve accepting bribes in exchange for granting approvals, omitting irregularities from inspection reports, or providing unwarranted prior notice of an upcoming inspection visit, allowing the party to correct any irregularities beforehand. When it comes to environmental enforcement matters, it is common to hear that this occurs, although it is perhaps nearly impossible to accurately determine the prevalence of this type of corruption, precisely because we are dealing with illicit acts. The data generated in my research demonstrate patterns that allow one to infer the existence of this type of corruption, although they are not the central focus of the investigation.

If bias exists in the formulation and application of environmental laws and standards that benefits the private sector at the expense of environmental protection, can this also be considered corruption? It does not directly lead to the enrichment of the public officials involved, nor does it imply that these officials have violated any law or acted unethically: their actions may be both legal and justifiable from their viewpoint. If this is so, would this not be—more than a case of institutionalized corruption— simply an example of business as usual in the comportment of the state? If the compulsion of a capitalist state is to generate the conditions required to attract and maintain private investment, establishing a legal framework to meet this need and enforcing it with such laxity that it might be considered collusion would not be more than doing what is required to achieve the greater good: economic growth.

How can a state that understands its main role as the promoter of economic growth take action that threatens said growth? From there, how can we understand the role of the state in environmental protection? Given a polluting activity, or a large-scale industrial, mining, agro-industrial, energy, or tourism project, the affected communities as well as environmental or human rights organizations tend to appeal to or demand that state actors undertake transparent consultations, enforce environmental laws and standards, and respect the rights of the affected population. At times, state institutions are often the protagonists of such projects or polluting activities, as in the cases of many dams or of the state-owned oil and gas company Petróleos Mexicanos; in other cases, the central actors are private companies alone or operating via state-granted concessions. The responses of government agencies as a rule fail to satisfy citizen demands, and the grievances then allude to the lack of application of legislation and to deficient political will, prevailing impunity, and government inefficiency or corruption. I believe we must understand this lack of action in more structural terms.

But why call it institutionalized corruption? Using this term, I argue, serves to underscore the conspicuous discrepancy between the idea of a democratic state safeguarding the common good and the reality of a neoliberal capitalist state that operates in favor of private profit.

Returning to the conceptualizations of corruption of Transparency International, when describing the political costs of corruption, it maintains that, "in a democratic system, offices and institutions lose their legitimacy when they're misused for private advantage" (Transparency International Kenya, n.d.). Can corruption exist without bribes or illicit enrichment? I would argue that the generation and application of legal frameworks that privilege the profit of private companies over the protection of the environment and public health constitutes a form of corruption that I propose to call institutionalized because it contravenes the hegemonic idea of the democratic state that safeguards the common good. Institutionalized corruption exists where the state apparatus is used to protect the private gain not of individual government employees but rather of the private sector. My focus here is on the industrial pollution of the Santiago River; therefore, I aim to demonstrate institutionalized corruption in this case and as linked to practices and procedures of national relevance.

I.7 Research Strategy

In formulating my research strategy, I adopted elements of institutional ethnography to study the administrative, legal, economic, and discursive practices of private and governmental actors—generators and regulators, respectively, of the industrial pollution of the Santiago River. Institutional ethnography, as an approach to research, was developed and named by sociologist Dorothy Smith in the 1980s and has been applied particularly in the fields of sociology, education, and social work, among others (Devault 2006). The starting point, or "entry point," of institutional ethnography is an everyday situation, frequently a work situation, with the goal of "investigat[ing] policies and social practices in institutional contexts" (Taber 2010, 9). For Smith, as a research method, institutional ethnography is designed to "create an alternative to the objectified subject of knowledge of established social science discourse" (2005, 10). Smith conceives that discourse as part of what she terms "ruling relations," or the "extraordinary yet ordinary complex of relations that are textually mediated, that connect us across space and time and organize our everyday lives—the corporations, government bureaucracies, academic and professional discourses, mass media, and the complex of relations that interconnect them" (10). In this conception, ruling relations do not imply determinism, recognizing

Introduction

the agency of both the actors who apply government regulations or policies and those affected by those instruments, and their ability to both resist and influence those relations (Taber 2010).

From what Smith calls the "people's perspective," an entry point located in the daily lives of people involved in institutional processes, institutional ethnography focuses on how these realities are "embedded in social relations, both those of ruling and those of the economy" (2005, 31). Institutional ethnography begins, then, from concerns or problems that are real for people and that "are situated in their relationships to an institutional order" (32). For my research, the everyday situation is the industrial pollution of the river, and the people who know and experience this situation include residents and activists of El Salto and Juanacatlán, as well as officials and inspectors from CONAGUA, the CEA, municipal workers, and employees of the industries.

Methods commonly used in institutional ethnography include interviews, text analysis, participant observation, and map generation. According to Marjorie Devault, the focus on texts responds to an empirical observation, in the sense that "technologies of social control are increasingly and pervasively textual and discursive" (2006, 294). Institutional ethnography seeks to reveal how texts have an "organizing power" to coordinate "extra-locally" activities taking place in local settings (295). For Kevin Walby, institutional ethnographers "conceive of social relations as organized and enabled by texts" (2007, 1009). For my purposes, I believed that this methodology would allow me to glimpse the relationships that exist between the daily contamination of the river by the factories of the corridor and the discourses and texts of national water policy, environmental regulations, and corporate strategies.

With a starting point in institutional ethnography and the field of political ecology, then, the investigation undertaken comprised, on the one hand, over eighty interviews with government employees, representatives of companies from the industrial corridor or industry associations, members of nongovernmental organizations and local associations, residents, and workers or ex-workers in factories. The majority of the fieldwork took place between 2013 and 2015, with follow-up research between 2018 and 2020. In addition to interviews with representatives of sixteen companies, I toured the installations of ten factories. On the other hand, to test the limits of the information available on industrial activity in this corridor and its environmental impacts, I made approximately two hundred access-to-information requests to state and federal agencies, mainly to the Ministry of Environment and Natural Resources (Secretaría de Medio Ambiente y Recursos Naturales), CONAGUA, and PROFEPA. In addition to digitized information, the responses to these information requests included more than twelve thousand physical copies. This information allowed me to analyze, among other aspects, the discharge permits, annual operating certificates, and environmental licenses for a selection of companies.

Finally, my research also involved participant observation in a diversity of settings. Particularly relevant was the participation in three courses and three congresses on environmental topics of the National Chemical Industry Association (Asociación Nacional de la Industria Química), as well as a business summit and two events organized by the government's now-defunct investment attraction agency ProMéxico. On the governmental side, since 2013 I have participated as a member of the Academic Council on Water of the CEA, and I have taken part in diverse meetings and workshops on the Santiago River organized by SEMADET. With the grassroots organizations in El Salto and Juanacatlán, I regularly took part in a diversity of meetings with members of the different organizations with whom I continue to collaborate (for greater detail on my research strategy, see the appendix).

I.8 Book Structure

To contextualize the case of the industrial pollution of the Santiago River, the book opens with a brief history of the process of industrialization in Mexico and a characterization of the processes of neoliberalization implemented since the 1980s. From there, I outline the development of environmental regulations in Mexico, beginning with the first pollution control laws, with a focus on water pollution control and the agencies charged with oversight and inspections. As part of this, I demonstrate from the Mexican case how market environmentalism is adapted for "poor countries" in ways that empower the private sector in environmental regulations, and the extent to which the regulation of industrial activity in Mexico manifests the general characteristics of neoliberal environmental regulations. Finally, I present an inventory of the companies in the industrial corridor and summarize the data available on industrial effluent discharged into the river.

Introduction

In chapter 2, I trace a brief history of the socio-environmental movement of the Santiago River, relating the main actions of protest and proposal undertaken by local groups and their allies in local and international networks. Although my main objective is not to analyze the conflict or socio-environmental movement, this research is inspired by the actions of local organizations. At the same time, this retelling clarifies how environmental and health authorities have repeatedly sought to deny, obfuscate, or minimize the gravity of the problem.

Next, the focus turns to the functioning of institutionalized corruption, as chapter 3 provides an analysis of the government practices meant to control industrial pollution. First, the actions of CONAGUA are scrutinized to evaluate the effectiveness of enforcement actions through the analysis of inspection reports and administrative rulings for the period from 2000 to 2018. This is complemented with a brief analysis PROFEPA's Clean Industry program. More broadly, I assess the effectiveness of regulatory provisions based on self-reported information and self-regulation, through an examination of a series of documents and environmental permits, including annual operating certificates, effluent discharge reports, and the information companies provide to the national Pollutant Release and Transfer Registry.

In chapter 4, I probe into the web of power relations between government and business elites, analyzing regulatory capture in the process of environmental standard-setting in Mexico. I attempt to demonstrate this regulatory capture through a critical assessment of the National Environment and Natural Resources Standards Advisory Committee (Comité Consultivo Nacional de Normalización de Medio Ambiente y Recursos Naturales), looking specifically at the case of the modification of the national discharge standard (NOM-001-SEMARNAT-1996), which regulates the maximum level of contaminants permitted in discharges to national waters. Linked to this, I consider the cost-benefit logic of the Federal Regulatory Improvement Commission (Comisión Federal de Mejora Regulatoria) and its implications for environmental regulations.

Turning the focus to the business sector, in chapter 5 I explore the myth of the multinational, whereby the good environmental performance of large transnational corporations is assumed a priori, as well as its political consequences. More substantively, I question the veracity of this myth based on data available on the environmental performance of companies in the industrial corridor. This analysis is contextualized in the recent trend of most large corporations, both Mexican and transnational, of adopting environmental management policies, obtaining related certifications, and in many cases generating annual sustainability reports.

What is to be done in the face of the industrial pollution of the Santiago River? The book closes with reflections on evolutionary conceptions of development and on how the category "developing" generates a double standard that allows for the structuring of a system of environmental regulation that facilitates simulation. From there, I review to what extent there exists institutionalized corruption, as evidenced in laws, policies, norms, and enforcement practices, as well as in the institutional arrangements governing the setting of environmental standards. Next, I explain the myth of the multinational as an essential foundation for the current regulatory system. Finally, I draw from my analysis to make a series of proposals for addressing this *resilient* problem and to reflect on how the Santiago River can transform from a sewer of progress into a river of life.

1   Industrialization and Environmental Regulation in Mexico

The surface of the small Las Pintas dam is the bright green of water hyacinths in March 2022 as Graciela González, Sofía Enciso, and several other young activists from Leap of Life begin another Tour of Terror, in this case for a group of university students. The organization has been taking groups of high school and university students, reporters, and sometimes even government officials on this tour of the municipality of El Salto since 2008. The peri-urban landscape it covers, roughly following the trajectory of the El Ahogado Canal from its origin point in this dam to the Santiago River, is a chaotic medley of sprawling factories and industrial parks interspersed between older working-class neighborhoods and new social interest housing developments, many covering barren hillsides in bleak rows of small concrete houses. Trucks lumber down the pot-holed main roads, adding a patina of dust to the garbage-littered sidewalks between metal-recycling depots, junkyards, and small restaurants, shops, and strip clubs. Snaking below the El Verde highway are numerous open canals carrying factory effluents to the El Ahogado dam and canal.

While we pass by the installations of household brands such as IBM, Honda, and Hershey's, we also observe a plethora of faceless industrial warehouses and more modest workshops. Sofía interprets this territory, explaining that "there are these warehouses or industrial facades that don't have a company name or a logo because they work for the large companies and with this the large companies wash their hands and say that they don't pollute. So, it's important to see the entire supply chain that is affecting the population . . . and that there is less regulation in this sense."[1] One of the newer housing developments, Parques del Castillo, offers a lookout point to observe this rapidly changing valley intertwining urban and industrial spaces. New housing developments and industrial parks continue to spring up despite the scarcity of water having led to social protest. Intermittent water services are the norm here (Greene and Morvant-Roux 2020; McCulligh et al. 2020).

"This is a place with a lot of history not only for the municipality but for the country," Sofía tells the group once we have reached the dilapidated parking lot and lookout spot on the Juanacatlán side of the waterfall. From here we have a view of what remains of the installations of the hydroelectric dam built on lands of the Jesús María Hacienda. José María Bermejillo, husband of Dolores Martínez Negrete, who inherited the Jesús María and neighboring El Castillo haciendas, was one of the investors in the hydroelectric dam. In 1896, the state government granted Bermejillo the right to install any hydraulic works necessary on the Santiago River from its origins in Lake Chapala to the new dam to ensure river flow for energy generation (Salas-Mercado 2001). That same year, Francisco Martínez Negrete purchased the land from his sister Dolores to build the Río Grande factory town. In 1907, after it was taken over by a group of French investors, the factory employed 1,650 textile workers. In later decades, the union of the Río Grande textile factory became known for its combativeness and was influenced by currents of anarchist thought. In 1943, then–state governor Marcelino García Barragán repaid the political support of the Río Grande union by making El Salto a municipality in its own right. The union controlled the municipality until 1980, when its power began to wane (Durand 1986).

By that time, the industrial corridor had begun to grow in El Salto, diversifying the allegiance of the population, and modernization processes that started in the 1950s had reduced the workforce at the textile factory. The factory was nationalized in 1973, rebaptized as Nueva Nacional Textil, then later sold to the union, remaining in operation until the mid-1990s. The ninety-meter factory chimney, constructed with bricks imported from England—the birthplace of the model of the rural factory town—is still visible across the river (Durand 1986).

The landscape of not just the waterfall but the whole region changed from one generation to the next, Sofía relates; from her parents' generation to her own, "this paradise was transformed into this chaos or this environmental devastation." This is much of what has sparked the anger and indignation that has moved Leap of Life members to organize and make a change, Sofía says, "because so much has been imposed on us, from a technical education where we are formed to be a cheap labor force, to the death and disease at an early age that are also imposed on us. Our parents' generation is the first generation of parents to bury their own children." How did this happen? This chapter will tell part of that story through a brief retelling of the process of industrialization in Mexico and in this region in particular. How this happened, though, has to do both with the dynamics of capital accumulation and with visions of progress and development.

A dilapidated sign used to welcome travelers driving out of the Guadalajara airport to the "Silicon Valley of Mexico," conveying a bittersweet message of dreams of modernity and a reality that one could indulgently call disappointing. Arriving thus to Mexico's third-largest metropolitan area places one in the terrain of the Tour of Terror, in the polluted El Ahogado Subbasin. Here, noxious odors are often another welcome, provided by the city's wastewater and mixed with industrial effluents that wind their way sluggishly toward the Santiago River along the El Ahogado Canal.

The sign conveys both aspirations and the desire to imitate, following a path of progress fashioned by others to achieve their successes. Ideas associated with the original Silicon Valley center on innovation, being ahead of the curve, and, of course, wealth generation. South of the border, since the mid-1980s the notion of converting Guadalajara into a Mexican Silicon Valley has been touted due to the growing concentration of electronics companies that began to establish themselves in the region in the 1960s (Palacios 1992). This Mexican version of the valley, however, offers up cheap labor (recently even cheaper than in China), while generating minimal innovation or research activities (Gallagher and Zarsky 2007). It also boasts of working conditions repeatedly denounced by local workers' rights organizations (for example, CEREAL 2015). Read from another perspective, it is a region with the comparative advantages of a "competitive labor cost" and a "good relationship with the unions," as promoted by the government of the state of Jalisco in materials produced by the Ministry of Economic Development (Secretaría de Desarrollo Económico).

Kevin Gallagher and Lyuba Zarsky (2007) assert that a "maquila mentality" has predominated in the information technology sector in Guadalajara, which, focused only on attracting foreign direct investment, generates few benefits in terms of knowledge spillovers, while offering low-skilled and low-paying jobs. Neither do these authors find that multinationals transfer their best environmental practices. In their study of this area, they conclude that a "volatile foreign enclave" was generated with "meager" benefits for domestic development (180). This accords, in general terms, with the conclusions of James Cypher and Raúl Delgado Wise, who describe the current socioeconomic system in Mexico as one of "transnational dependent capitalism," based on the exploitation and export of low-cost labor, which serves the interests of the productive system and corporations of the United States while generating some "rentier" benefits for Mexican elites (2010, 11). This system, in addition to exploiting cheap labor, also exploits the environment, a situation that has led to a sharp increase in the country of so-called socio-environmental conflicts (Toledo et al. 2014; Tetreault et al. 2018).

Understanding the conflict surrounding the Santiago River requires an examination of the type of capitalist development that has been experienced in Mexico, and more specifically how the Mexican manufacturing sector is inserted into the global economy and how environmental regulations have developed. In this chapter, I address these topics by first briefly sketching the history of industrialization in Mexico and the transition from an import substitution industrialization (ISI) model to an export-led model under neoliberal policies. In the second section, I outline the evolution of environmental regulations in Mexico, emphasizing the neoliberal "bias" of policies developed in the run-up to the North American Free Trade Agreement (NAFTA) and in the years that followed. From there, I touch on the water pollution crisis that exists in the country, exacerbated in this era of neoliberalization policies. Finally, I describe the current configuration of the Ocotlán–El Salto Industrial Corridor, which has turned the Santiago River into a sewer of progress.

1.1 Industrialization Strategies in Mexico

Industrialization in Mexico dates back to the period of the regime of dictator Porfirio Díaz (1876–1911), known as the Porfiriato. While manufacturing before this time was characterized by small-scale artisan workshops, it came to be dominated by large factories in the period from 1890 to 1910. For the production of cotton textiles, for instance, most of the machinery used toward the end of the 1940s was installed before 1910, since the industrial capacity built during the Porfiriato was not destroyed during

Industrialization and Environmental Regulation in Mexico

the Mexican Revolution (1910–1917) (Haber 1993). Likewise, companies that came to dominate the production of beer, cement, steel, paper, and glass in the 1930s were founded between 1890 and 1910. Some of these companies still exist, such as Vidriera Monterrey, now Grupo Vitro, or the Moctezuma and Cuauhtémoc breweries (merged in the 1980s and bought by Dutch-owned Heineken International in 2010) (657). Industry at this time operated under the protection of government tariffs and subsidies, and Stephen Haber aptly characterizes the mostly foreign owners as "merchants and business-men whose main talent was to make deals so as not to have to operate in a competitive market, and to manipulate the economic apparatus of the state to protect them from foreign and national competitors" (675).

Industrial production in Mexico grew rapidly during the Great Depression, when the Mexican currency experienced two devaluations, thus making imports more expensive and directing demand toward domestically produced goods. Between 1932 and 1940, real industrial production increased at a rate of 10 percent per year. In addition to the devaluations, the agrarian reform implemented during the presidency of Lázaro Cárdenas (1934–1940) and the nationalization of oil and gas production in 1938 led to a transfer of resources from commercial agriculture to industry (Cárdenas 2000, 180). Public investment at this time in roads, dams, energy generation, and other infrastructure works, as well as the creation of development banks, coincided to support industrialization. At the same time, foreign investment in manufacturing increased in the 1930s—for example, in the automotive sector—while national conglomerates continued to develop, with the oligopolistic style inherited from the Porfiriato (181). Enrique Cárdenas (2000, 182) describes what happened in this decade as a process of ISI "stimulated by market forces" given the devaluation in the exchange rate that shifted demand to domestic production. This was a first experience of ISI, but not one driven by government policies.

During World War II, the United States demanded Mexican imports, and this external demand spurred industrial growth. Trade deficits emerged at the end of the war, and it was in 1947 that Mexico began to make large investments in infrastructure and promote heavy industry through the development bank Nacional Financiera (Cypher and Delgado Wise 2010). Throughout the 1950s, measures to promote domestic industry increased, with the idea that any new industry that began to substitute imports would receive protection through the establishment of import quotas. This was applicable for both domestic and foreign companies and led to an important flow of transnational corporations that established plants in the country, sheltered by these protective measures and with the promise of a captive market (Cárdenas 2000). This trend continued until "Mexicanization" laws were introduced in the 1960s, imposing limits on foreign investors (192). In contrast, the Border Industrialization Program began in 1965, leading to the establishment of a first generation of maquiladoras along the northern border, mainly American electronics and clothing companies. Thus, the ISI model was not applied in a "pure" form, as it coexisted with export-oriented maquiladoras (Guillén 2013, 37).

This period also witnessed a transfer of resources from agriculture to industry and the urban sector, through the price system. Progressively, the strategy pursued gave rise to an internationally uncompetitive industrial sector, while strengthening an "oligopolistic industrial structure" (Cárdenas 2000, 193). The 1970s saw growth in the number of parastatal companies, with the government investing both in ventures that were less attractive for the private sector, due to low profitability or because they required long terms to mature, and in areas considered strategic, such as electricity, steel, fertilizers, and petrochemicals. These ventures were largely financed with external debt. At the same time, imports of manufactured goods increased, particularly of capital and intermediate goods, and the trade deficit grew (Cárdenas 2000; Guillén 2013, 35).

The administration of President Luis Echeverría (1970–1976) spearheaded a strategy of "shared development," seeking to stimulate economic growth and improve income distribution (Cárdenas 2000, 196). This was based on incurring public debt to grant subsidies and invest in infrastructure and parastatals. A first financial crisis took place in August 1976, but it coincided a few months later with the discovery of large proven oil reserves. With this oil as guarantee, Mexico took on debt with credits from international banks involved in aggressive "loan pushing" during the oil boom period (Cypher and Delgado Wise 2010, 31). While the government continued to invest, loan repayment required high oil prices, and with the fall in oil prices in 1982 and interest rates rising globally, Mexico entered into a debt crisis.

Later that year, Miguel de la Madrid became president (1982–1988), and a struggle ensued within the political elite between those who continued to advocate state intervention to promote economic development and those who supported the adoption of a neoliberal model. Actors outside the government were among those lobbying for the adoption of a new economic model, especially representatives of the International Monetary Fund, the World Bank, the US government, and, in Mexico, a new high-level business organization, the Business Coordinating Council (Consejo Coordinador Empresarial), founded in 1975 (Schneider 2002; Cypher and Delgado Wise 2010, 32).

Various authors maintain that by this time the ISI model had been "exhausted" and no longer had the capacity to generate economic growth or development in a broader sense (for example, Cárdenas 2000; Guillén 2013). From a critical perspective, Cypher and Delgado Wise argue that the ISI model had hardly been tested in Mexico, since a "light or shallow" version had been implemented, with policies focused on credit subsidies, tax exemptions, and tariffs. This would be in contrast with ISI models applied in Asia that contemplated long-term investment in science and technology and relied less on foreign direct investment, among other policies (Gallagher and Zarsky 2007; Cypher and Delgado Wise 2010). At this point, it should be noted that the Mexican economy grew at an average annual rate of 6.2 percent between 1940 and 1970 and at a rate of 6.8 percent between 1970 and 1981 (Moreno-Brid and Ros 2009, 261). At the same time, the manufacturing sector became the "engine" of the economy, with a growth rate of 8.0 percent annually between 1940 and 1982 (Cypher and Delgado Wise 2010, 28).

In favor of abandoning the ISI model, René Villareal wrote in 1976 that what existed in Mexico was a "prolonged" ISI model that could generate *"growth but without development"* (7; emphasis in original). Here Villareal defines development as achieving not only growth but also "employment, income redistribution and independence from abroad" (21). In order to achieve growth with development and reduce the "imbalance" resulting from external dependence on imports, investment, and loans, the route was to adopt an export substitution model (7). This is presented by Villareal as a necessary step in the evolution of countries toward modernity:

> The historical evidence on the evolution of the "backward" capitalist countries towards industrialization and "modern" growth makes it possible to distinguish precisely the transition stages in which the mode of organization and operation of the economic system acquires defined characteristics, such that we can speak of them as economic models of transition towards modern growth. (21)

At that point, Mexico had to take the step to the export-led "stage."

By 1985 it was clear that the proponents of the new economic model would prevail, with the defeat of the "development coalition" and the country's application to join the General Agreement on Tariffs and Trade, consolidated in 1986 (Cypher and Delgado Wise 2010, 19). With the ensuing "unilateral opening process," Mexico rapidly lowered customs tariffs and eliminated quantitative restrictions and import licenses (Guillén 2013, 39). Neoliberal policies were brought in, and to date Mexico has been recognized as one of the countries with the most faithful application of these free-market ideas.

In itself, the term "neoliberal" is a slippery concept, described by Neil Brenner and colleagues as "promiscuously pervasive, yet inconsistently defined, empirically imprecise and frequently contested" (2010, 184). In particular in the academic literature, Jamie Peck highlights how—despite its widespread use—it continues to be employed in a "confusing and inconsistent" way (2010, 13). The ideas of neoliberalism are mainly associated with authors such as Friedrich Hayek and Milton Friedman. The Austrian Hayek, in his famous work *The Road to Serfdom*, expounds on the peril of socialism and planning inevitably leading to fascism and authoritarianism, and argues for a state limited to creating the conditions for competition and defending private property (1944, 38–39). For his part, Friedman espouses his faith in the market—for example, in *Capitalism and Freedom* (1982)—or his "probusiness/antistate manual" (Cypher and Delgado Wise, 2010, 30). Peck (2010) and Brenner and colleagues (2010), among other authors, prefer to refer to the processes of "neoliberalization" rather than employing the static term "neoliberalism."

In abstract terms, Peck maintains that "neoliberalization refers to a contradictory process of market-like rule, principally negotiated at the boundaries of the state, and occupying the ideological space defined by a (broadly) sympathetic critique of nineteenth-century laissez-faire and deep antipathies to collectivist, planned, and socialized modes of government, especially those associated with Keynesianism and developmentalism" (2010, 20). A key part of the "deeply contradictory" nature of neoliberalism is that, despite its characteristic anti-state rhetoric, "neoliberalism, in its various guises, has always been about the capture and reuse of the state, in the interests of shaping a pro-corporate, freer-trading 'market order'" (4, 9). This point is key to the argument I develop throughout this book, and I will return to it at the close of the chapter.

Underlying the use of the term "neoliberalization" is a critique of the notion of neoliberalism as a "unidirectional logic" in which global institutions "impose disciplinary constraints 'downwards' on national states" (N. Brenner et al. 2010, 195). This leaves little room to inquire about the "conflictual, volatile and contested *interaction* of (transnational) neoliberal regulatory experiments with inherited (national and subnational) institutional landscapes" (195; emphasis in original). Neoliberalization processes, then, are inherently incomplete, and the generated crises and moments of regulatory failure have been used "paradoxically" to deepen regulatory reorganization following the same market logic (218). The unequal character of neoliberalism in different countries is also addressed by David Harvey when speaking of the "competition between territories" and concluding that "the general progress of neoliberalization has ... been increasingly impelled *through* mechanisms of uneven geographical developments" (2005, 87; emphasis in original). Highlighting the uneven geography of these processes calls attention to the fact that they do not lead to a global convergence or homogeneity of regulatory systems but to the "*systemic* production of geoinstitutional differentiation" (N. Brenner et al. 2010, 184; emphasis in original).

In the Mexican case, new loans in 1985 and 1987 were conditional on structural adjustments, in particular on trade liberalization, fiscal reforms, and the privatization of state-owned companies. While in 1982 there were 1,115 state-owned companies, by 1992 only 15 percent remained, the largest being the oil and gas parastatal Petróleos Mexicanos (Greenberg et al. 2012). The process of privatization of parastatal companies is also notorious for having benefited people close to President Carlos Salinas de Gortari (1988–1994) and for creating large private fortunes—for example, with the sale of the telecommunications company Telmex to Carlos Slim, who was the fifth-richest man in the world in 2019 (*Forbes* 2019). Trade liberalization was not the only key change in this process of restructuring and "redeployment" of the state, as the relationship between the state and the private sector also began to shift. The country's economic policy makers began to lose autonomy as part of a "complex change ... wherein the CCE [Business Coordinating Council] and other peak organizations became crucial participants in what had been heretofore a largely closed policy-making process," where the business sector even went so far as to "set the parameters" of the process (Cypher and Delgado Wise 2010, 43; see also Schneider 2002).

In the economic sphere, it is worth reviewing the results of the new economic strategy, particularly for the manufacturing sector. First, we can recall that the arguments behind the reforms of the mid-1980s were that "the elimination of trade protectionism, coupled with the acute reduction of state intervention in the economy would significantly encourage private investment and set the economy onto a path of high and sustained export-led expansion with macroeconomic stability" (Moreno-Brid 2013, 216). Although nonoil exports have grown, economic growth has not met expectations, nor has it been associated with improvements in wages for workers. Remuneration levels in the manufacturing industry (adjusted for inflation) fell 38 percent between 1982 and 1988 (Cypher and Delgado Wise 2010, 45), and they have continued to decline. Between 1988 and 1998, in real terms, manufacturing wages fell by 45.9 percent. From their peak in 1976, in real terms wages had fallen 75 percent by 2002 (de la Garza Toledo 2004, 108). More recently, the International Labor Organization (ILO) reported for Mexico that real wages decreased 1.7 percent between 2008 and 2017 (ILO 2018).

It is not surprising, therefore, that the *Financial Times* published an article in January 2016 entitled "Want Cheap Labour? Head to Mexico, Not China" (Kwan Yuk 2016). With data from Bank of America Merrill Lynch, the National Institute of Statistics and Geography (INEGI, Instituto Nacional de Estadística y Geografía), and the ILO, the piece affirms that from an hourly wage level in the manufacturing sector that was 183 percent higher in Mexico than in China in 2003, since 2010 wages have been lower in Mexico. Due to both the increases in wages in China and the devaluation of the peso against the dollar since 2013, by the beginning of 2016 the hourly wage in Mexico was 40 percent below the cost in China. Further, Mexico was the only one of the so-called emerging countries of the G20 where real wages fell between 2008 and 2017 (ILO 2018).

The wage situation in Mexico does not reflect improvements in productivity in the manufacturing sector either. Enrique Dussel Peters and Samuel Ortiz, for example, report that between 2007 and 2013 the gap between productivity and wages increased in twelve manufacturing subsectors, a phenomenon they consider significant, given that "a wide gap points to a worsening in the distribution of the income generated by manufacturing" (2015, 36).

In terms of exports from Mexico, the new economic strategy saw resounding growth after the signing of NAFTA in 1994. This slowed down between 2000 and 2013, as growth in exports fell to only a third of the rate between

Industrialization and Environmental Regulation in Mexico

1994 and 2000 (Dussel Peters and Ortiz 2015, 24). It is also important to note several factors related to exports. First, as shown in figure 1.1, imports of goods have kept pace with the ups and downs in exports; in fact, exports of goods have only exceeded imports in three years since 1994 (1995, 2012, and 2019).

The data also reveal the strong dependence of Mexican manufacturing exports on the US economy. With information from the first quarter of 2016, the Ministry of Economy reported that 83.1 percent of Mexican nonoil exports were to the United States, a level slightly below the percentage in the same period in 1994 (85.2 percent). The origin of imports has diversified; 70.7 percent of nonoil imports came from the United States in 1994, while in 2016 (first quarter) it was the origin of 44.1 percent. Here the factor of note is the rise in nonoil imports from China, which amounted to 18.7 percent of the total at the beginning of 2016 (SE 2016).

The trade deficits experienced, Héctor Guillén clarifies, are due to the fact that exported manufactures are highly dependent on imported inputs.

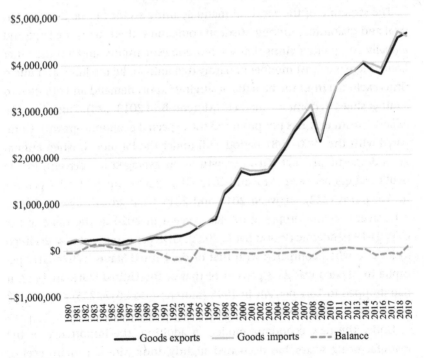

Figure 1.1
Exports and imports of goods in Mexico, 1980–2019 (current US$).
Source: Author's elaboration based on World Bank (2022).

In the case of the maquiladoras, he notes, "they do not use more than 5% of local intermediate products." (2013, 43). However, the phenomenon is not limited to maquiladoras, since nonmaquiladora manufacturing export companies are also dependent on imports. In general terms, "[it] is estimated that around 70% of Mexican manufacturing exports are produced by assembling imported inputs that arrive in the country protected by preferential regimes" (43). Cypher and Delgado Wise refer to the maquiladora sector to encompass both maquiladoras and "disguised" maquiladoras (2010, 107), which are also mainly based on the export of manufactured products, and they highlight that in 2008 these companies generated 76 percent of manufacturing exports, 90 percent of which were destined for the United States. In part because of this, they describe NAFTA not as a trade agreement but as "an investment/production restructuring agreement . . . that enabled US firms to shift production to Mexico" (169). The transfer of part of US industrial production to Mexico has obviously applied pressure on manufacturing wages in that country.

The structure of the Mexican manufacturing sector can be described as dual and disjointed. Among Mexican companies, there are some large and globally competitive firms that use few domestic inputs, and, on the other hand, there is a "vast number of hardly dynamic small, medium, and micro firms excluded from the benefits of surging export demand and oriented to a rather sluggish domestic market" (Moreno-Brid 2013, 224). This when the export-led strategy has not produced the expected economic growth. Compared with the 1960–1981 period, still under the ISI model, when annual gross domestic product (GDP) growth levels averaged 6.7 percent, in the neoliberal era between 1987 and 2012 GDP grew annually by 2.7 percent in real terms (222). Between 2013 and 2019 GDP growth averaged only 2.1 percent, before dropping to –8.3 percent in 2020 in the wake of the COVID-19 pandemic (World Bank, 2022). GDP per capita has also declined in Mexico when compared with that of the United States. While GDP per capita in Mexico was 23.3 percent of that of the United States in 1982, it had dropped to 16.1 percent in 1995 (Moreno-Brid 2013, 225) and to 15.2 percent in 2019, according to data from the World Bank (2022).

Under the new economic model, in addition, the importance of the manufacturing sector has decreased slightly, indicating a certain level of deindustrialization. From representing 20.2 percent of GDP in 1998, in 2019 the manufacturing industries generated only 17.3 percent of GDP

(INEGI 2021b). Currently, Mexican manufacturing exports are strongly dominated by two subsectors: the manufacture of transportation equipment (which includes the production of cars and trucks, auto parts, and aerospace equipment) and electronics, electronic equipment, components, and accessories. The manufacture of transportation equipment accounted for 45.9 percent of manufacturing exports in 2019, while the electronics and electrical equipment sectors represented 25.3 percent (INEGI 2021a). The dominant companies in these sectors are foreign owned.

In 2016, *CNN Expansión*'s ranking of the five hundred most important companies in Mexico listed thirty-eight companies in the automotive and auto parts sector, of which only five were Mexican. Of the ten companies in the electronics industry on *CNN Expansión*'s list, only one was Mexican, the home appliance manufacturer Mabe. Three of these ten corporations in the electronics industry have their main activities in Mexico in the state of Jalisco: Flextronics Manufacturing, Jabil Circuit, and Sanmina-SCI Systems (*CNN Expansión* 2016).

It is given the elements just outlined that Ilán Bizberg qualifies the strategy pursued in Mexico as one of "disjointed or externally-linked *international subcontracting capitalism*" (2015, 83; emphasis in original). These external linkages are with the US economy, and as we have seen, the economic model "requires low wages, since it is based on attracting foreign investment to productive areas with high labor requirements" (83). In this age of free trade and globalized manufacturing, "flexible" environmental regulations can serve as a further investment pull factor. In the next section, I explore the evolution of environmental regulations in Mexico, particularly as relates to water pollution.

1.2 Environmental Regulation in Mexico

In May 1991, the US Environmental Protection Agency (EPA) presented a preliminary report on environmental laws, regulations, and standards in Mexico. This was during the NAFTA negotiations when diverse American organizations expressed their concerns about the possible migration of industry from the United States to Mexico, taking advantage of less stringent environmental regulations and motivating a "race to the bottom" (Behre 2003; Liverman and Vilas 2006; Greenberg et al. 2012). In this context, the EPA report reached flattering conclusions for the promoters of NAFTA. EPA officials claimed that their investigation with their Mexican counterparts had demonstrated that "Mexico has a strong commitment to protecting its environment which is reflected in: budgetary and staff increases, particularly in the areas of inspection and enforcement; [and] efforts to ensure that new sources meet pollution standards comparable to U.S. environmental standards" (EPA 1991, 2). This, in addition to factory closures recently undertaken, was proffered as evidence of a commitment to achieving "strict" compliance with environmental laws in Mexico.

As regards water pollution control specifically, the document also painted a positive picture when comparing regulatory systems, despite some nuances. In general terms, the report authors concluded that the legislation for water pollution in Mexico "contemplates a regulatory system that if fully implemented would control point sources of pollution as broadly as the U.S. CWA [Clean Water Act]" (EPA 1991, 14). The nuances emerge from the fact that the system in Mexico is not as "comprehensive" as in the United States, due to the low levels of coverage of discharge permits at that time, as well as the fact that enforcement "appears to cover only discharges of conventional pollutants rather than toxic metals or organics" (16). Those nuances, thus, are not minor. Even so, the overall message of the document remained that "Mexico's environmental laws, regulations, and standards are in many respects similar to those in the United States" (2). In other words, NAFTA would not provoke environmental dumping on the part of companies that take advantage of regulatory disparities to transfer polluting activities to Mexico, given the roughly equivalent systems. To put these statements in context, we can review how environmental regulations in Mexico have evolved since the 1970s, and in the years before and after the signing of NAFTA.

1.2.1 Evolution of Environmental and Water Regulations

In the nineteenth century, the functions of the state in terms of environmental management were limited to matters such as water supply, sewerage systems, and food inspection (Gandy 1999). That changed radically in the twentieth century, with the development of institutional structures, both within and between nations, to address everything from biodiversity conservation to climate change. Using the example of the United States, Matthew Gandy describes a process of expansion of environmental policies and regulations in the 1960s and early 1970s, followed by a retreat that began in the 1970s and deepened in a neoliberal context that diminished the possibility for state intervention. By the early 1990s, the anti-regulatory lobby had captured legislative agendas and proceeded to implement setbacks from previous achievements in environmental regulation. This neoliberal deregulation can also be understood as an intensification of a preexisting situation. As Gandy asserts, "environmental regulation has always existed in a state of dynamic tension with prevailing centers of economic and political power" more than academic studies have contemplated (1999, 62). At the same time, this deregulation has paradoxically coincided with increased environmental risks and related public anxiety.

The trajectory of environmental regulation in Mexico has followed a different chronology. During much of the ISI period of rapid industrialization, there were no environmental laws or regulations governing polluting emissions (Mumme 1992; Simonian 1999). The first law to regulate pollution in Mexico was the Federal Law to Prevent and Control Environmental Pollution of March 1971, which covered air, water, and soil pollution. The ministries charged with its application were the Ministry of Health and Assistance (Secretaría de Salubridad y Asistencia), in coordination with the Ministry of Hydraulic Resources (SRH, Secretaría de Recursos Hidráulicos) as related to water pollution and the Ministry of Industry and Commerce (Secretaría de Industria y Comercio) in relation to industrial activities. This legal instrument contemplated a broad definition of pollution and forbade the dumping of polluting wastewater into sewage networks or water bodies (Article 14). Despite this "prohibition," the law charged the SRH, together with the Ministry of Health and Assistance, with dictating the conditions for effluent discharge. The supervision of "works, facilities and uses that could cause water contamination" was left to the SRH, as up to now the inspection of discharges into national waters has been largely under the jurisdiction of the National Water Commission (CONAGUA, Comisión Nacional del Agua). In the SRH, however, pollution was a low priority and the agency attempted to address the issue while dedicating "the least possible resources," according to a 1976 SRH report (cited in Aboites 2009, 43).

In 1973, the Regulation for the Prevention and Control of Water Pollution was issued, which included fiscal incentives for industrial decentralization, as well as for the acquisition of pollution control equipment. This regulation required the registration of discharges with the SRH and set fairly lax limits for five parameters, which would apply to discharges that were not to sewage systems starting three years after registration. The SRH was empowered to monitor water treatment, as well as to set specific discharge conditions according to a classification of water bodies. José Urciaga and colleagues point out the fragmented nature of Mexican environmental policy at this time, which entrusted pollution issues to the health authorities, "while those related to the conservation of natural resources continued to be approached with a productivist vision," assigning responsibility to the authorities of each sector (2008, 85).

Also in 1973, the SRH implemented a first pollution prevention and control program that covered both municipal and industrial wastewater discharges. The program charged the SRH with preparing "classification studies for the country's water bodies and establishing quality criteria based on which the authorities should set the particular discharge conditions" (Jiménez 2001, 309). However, when the Ministry of Agriculture and Hydraulic Resources (Secretaría de Agricultura y Recursos Hidráulicos) inherited this program in 1976, on absorbing the SRH, it later abandoned the program "given its inability to handle the large number of applications" (309).

In 1982, the Federal Environmental Protection Law replaced the law of 1971. The new law did not institute significant changes with respect to water, but it included a chapter on inspection and surveillance and another on criminal penalties for polluting activities, specifying prison terms as well as fines. It was not until 1988 that a law with broader regulatory capacity was approved, the General Law of Ecological Balance and Environmental Protection (Ley General del Equilibrio Ecológico y Protección al Ambiente), which also laid the foundations for the decentralization of environmental management to states and municipalities (Tetreault et al. 2010). In terms of water pollution control, also in 1988 the Ministry of Urban Development and Ecology (Secretaría de Desarrollo Urbano y Ecología) established the first twenty-five technical standards for effluent discharge, to which two were added in 1990 and six in 1991, for a total of thirty-three standards that set the conditions for effluent discharge of a series of categories of industry and for services such as restaurants and hospitals (Jiménez 2001). One year later, in 1989, CONAGUA was created as the sole water authority.

The environmental institutional framework was strengthened in Mexico in 1992 with the establishment of the National Institute of Ecology (Instituto Nacional de Ecología), the National Commission for the Knowledge and Use of Biodiversity (Comisión Nacional para el Conocimiento y Uso de la Biodiversidad) and the Federal Bureau of Environmental Protection (PROFEPA, Procuraduría Federal de Protección al Ambiente). That same year, Article 27 of the Constitution was amended, opening communal lands to privatization, and the National Waters Law (LAN, Ley de Aguas Nacionales) was approved. The LAN granted broad powers to CONAGUA, despite contemplating steps toward decentralization in water management. This decentralization began with the changes to Article 115 of the Constitution in 1983, which shifted the responsibility for the provision of water and sewerage services from the federal government to municipalities (Torregrosa et al. 2010). More recently, state water commissions have been created and CONAGUA has formed basin councils and transferred control of irrigation districts to users. Despite this, Philippus Wester and colleagues note how under the 1992 law, CONAGUA "was made the country's sole water authority, charged with managing water resources both qualitatively and quantitatively. [Thus], the hydrocracy achieved its objective of re-establishing bureaucratic autonomy to a large degree" (2009, 407).[2] The LAN also laid the groundwork for the privatization of hydraulic infrastructure and the growing participation of the private sector in the provision of municipal water services.

Regarding discharges to national waters, in 1995 the National Institute of Ecology issued a further eleven technical standards, increasing to forty-four the regulations for industrial sectors and municipal wastewater. These regulations established specific parameters for each sector and suggested a list of particular discharge conditions that could be included in discharge permits. However, they were repealed shortly thereafter, with the argument, according to researcher Cecilia Tortajada, that they were "unrealistic: they did not anticipate gradual compliance by users, in accordance with existing technical and economic capacity" (2002, 240). What came in their stead was referred to as a "simplification" of effluent regulations (Jiménez 2001, 312). Between 1997 and 1998 three standards were published in the *Official Gazette of the Federation* (*Diario Oficial de la Federación*), and they remain the only ones in force to date: NOM-001-SEMARNAT-1996, which sets limits for pollutants discharged into national water bodies; NOM-002-SEMARNAT-1996, which establishes the limits for discharges to municipal sewerage systems; and NOM-003-SEMARNAT-1997, which regulates water quality for reuse in public services, such as irrigation of parks and gardens. Due to the focus on discharges to the Santiago River, my interest here is mainly in the NOM-001-SEMARNAT-1996 standard (hereafter NOM-001), which leaves a wide range of substances uncontrolled, in particular those of industrial origin.

The NOM-001 standard was in effect unchanged from 1997 until March 2022, and it only regulated twenty parameters: eight basic parameters, eight heavy metals, cyanide, pH, fecal coliforms, and parasites. For this reason, the standard has failed to control industrial pollution, and even wastewater complying with the standard has been a source of emissions of toxic pollutants. In this vein, a study by researchers from the Mexican Institute of Water Technology (IMTA, Instituto Mexicano de Tecnología del Agua) affirmed that while industrial effluent from different sectors may comply with the NOM-001, the standard does not take into account the specific pollutants generated by diverse industries, thus "causing the incorporation of toxic substances that deteriorate the aquatic environment and provoke the loss of flora and fauna, as well as limit the uses of the recipient body" (IMTA 2006, 4). To address this deficiency, the study proposed the inclusion of acute toxicity tests "that can identify those effluents that introduce toxic substances and that are not detected by conventional analyses" (4).

In the United States, the EPA has effluent guidelines for almost sixty industrial categories, regulating the specific contaminants they generate according to their production processes. In the case, for example, of facilities that produce organic chemicals and synthetic fibers, sixty-two compounds are regulated, of which only six (metals and cyanide) are included in the Mexican standard (EPA 2022). The NOM-001 has allowed other substances, such as benzene, toluene, and phthalates, to be dumped with impunity in this country, even though their health effects are recognized. Several industries from this sector have facilities in the Ocotlán–El Salto corridor.

Continuing with the evolution of environmental institutions, at the end of 1994, during the presidency of Ernesto Zedillo (1994–2000), the Ministry of the Environment, Natural Resources and Fisheries was created, with CONAGUA, PROFEPA, the National Institute of Ecology, the National Commission for the Knowledge and Use of Biodiversity, and IMTA under its purview. In 2000, responsibility for fisheries was transferred to the Ministry of Agriculture, to remain since then as the Ministry of Environment and Natural Resources.

Thus, the 1990s did not witness a process of environmental deregulation, as Gandy states was the case in the United States, but were a period of opening to privatization of communal lands, services, and infrastructure. Despite the legal aperture to the privatization of hydraulic infrastructure and the implementation of novel economic instruments, James Greenberg and colleagues assert that Mexico "has some of the strongest [environmental] laws and created the first agency in the world devoted to balancing conservation and development" (2012, 20). However, they also acknowledge that the laws are contradictory, enforcement is "arbitrary," and regulatory efforts have not curbed environmental degradation (12).

Many of the environmental laws, regulations, and institutions in the country were forged at the time of NAFTA negotiations, with the neoliberal economic model already fully assumed, and reflect this bias. In their analysis of "neoliberal nature," James McCarthy and Scott Prudham (2004, 276) define four main ways in which, bolstered by discourses of competitiveness, the role of the state in environmental regulation is restructured and diminished: privatizations; profound fiscal and administrative cuts; changes to the scale of governance, with the devolution of responsibilities to local governments (without the transfer of resources or capacity), as well as the transfer of regulatory powers "upwards" to international institutions that lack transparency; and the shift from obligatory standards to voluntary regulatory frameworks, self-regulation, and public-private agreements. A further mechanism of institutionalization of neoliberal policies, noted by Nik Heynen and colleagues, is the "restructuring of state regulatory apparatuses in ways that tend to enhance private and corporate authority over economic, environmental, and social action" (2007, 6). This last point is important to take into account for the analysis that I undertake in chapter 4 on the power of private actors in the formulation and modification of environmental regulations.

Environmental regulations are generally divided into two broad categories: command and control measures, which constitute direct or traditional regulation, and so-called indirect regulation, associated with the liberalization of environmental governance or with "market environmentalism," and which include everything from taxes and voluntary regulations to subsidies and other incentives (Menell 1992; Jenkins and Mercado 2008; Bakker 2014). The use of command and control regulations is criticized by economists, such as Rhys Jenkins and Alfonso Mercado García in their analysis of industry and the environment in Mexico, for its "inefficiency" (2008, 25). They argue that this inefficiency arises, on the one hand, from the fact that any pollution source has to comply with the same standard "regardless of the marginal costs of compliance"; and, on the other hand, from the lack of incentive to go beyond minimum compliance with standards (25). To understand this logic of inefficiency, ecological economists Joan Martínez-Alier and Jordi Roca Jusmet explain that economists usually define the efficiency of an environmental policy as "achieving the objective [of the instrument] at the *lowest cost*" (2000, 150; emphasis in original). What this approach does not address, however, is the cost of not complying with regulations. The starting point, then, is a perspective from which the right to pollute precedes control, and that control has to be justified in economic terms.

This type of direct regulation also requires that authorities have the information and technical capacity to identify the causes of pollution, set what are considered safe pollutant emission levels, and monitor and regulate polluters. As Dara O'Rourke points out, however, pollution is a complex phenomenon, and "state agencies have had difficulty gathering and processing the information they need to effectively enforce pollution laws" (2004a, 9). From their investigation of the ecological norms applicable to industry in Mexico, Mercado García and María Lourdes Blanco highlight another weakness, specifically how inspections often focus on "verifying compliance with administrative requirements," rather than providing a true picture of the environmental impacts of a factory or other installation (2005, 232). Maintaining in order the administrative matters of logs, signage, and other records may be sufficient to pass an inspection, even if this does not guarantee that a company's operations are environmentally benign.

An example of indirect regulation is the duties charged for discharges to water bodies, under the "polluter pays" principle, as stipulated in the Federal Duties Law (LFD, Ley Federal de Derechos), Article 278, with questionable results that I explore in chapter 3. This principle was introduced for water in the LFD in 1991, establishing duties per cubic meter of water discharged and per kilogram of chemical oxygen demand (COD) and total suspended solids (TSS). Over the years, the parameters contemplated in the calculation of the fees to be paid have been changed, but the duties collected have remained low. In itself, the "polluter pays" principle assumes that the damage caused by pollution can be compensated for or reversed through the application of technology with the funds collected. This premise is erroneous, given that irreversible harm may be caused by certain toxins whose removal through treatment systems is difficult. In the Mexican case, this principle is not accompanied by incentives that promote pollution prevention or water reuse and recycling, nor by penalties that represent an economic incentive not to pollute.

Voluntary standards range from private certifications, such as ISO 14000, which certifies environmental management systems, to governmental ones, such as PROFEPA's Clean Industry program, which I analyze in chapter 3. The United Nations Environment Programme (UNEP) classifies voluntary standards into four main types: contractual agreements between industry and government; government initiatives; voluntary programs driven by industry, without government involvement; and third-party programs, which are verified and audited by an independent organization, such as International Organization for Standardization certifications (Jenkins and Mercado García 2008, 29). Verónica Medina-Ross (2005, 2008) identifies several weaknesses of voluntary initiatives, particularly for their application in so-called developing countries. The main deficiencies include the nonexistence in many systems of monitoring and surveillance, as well as the absence or weakness of the penalizations contemplated.

The key debility of such voluntary certifications, in my opinion, is the impossibility of verifying whether the adoption of this type of initiative has resulted in improvements in the environmental performance of the companies. In the absence of external oversight, Medina-Ross states bluntly, "there is no way to ensure that codes of practice are not just general statements of business principles, but actual regulations that apply to company operations" (2008, 244). Even with this lack of transparency and independent supervision, voluntary standards do not simply represent declarations of principles but also constitute "a justification for dismantling the regulatory capacity of the state" (Medina-Ross 2005, 100). In Mexico, this regulatory capacity is already diminished.

In general terms, a neoliberal bias marks many of the environmental and water policies in Mexico. For example, the main source of information on effluents discharged to national waters is self-monitoring in the form of the quarterly or semiannual reports that permit holders must undertake and submit to CONAGUA. In chapter 3, I will detail how several of the regulatory mechanisms implemented to control industrial activity depend on self-reported information that, in practice, is not reviewed or considered reliable by government authorities.

Another clear example of this neoliberal bias can be observed in the trends to privatization in water management in Mexico. This is not only the context of the problem studied here, but water pollution can also be understood as one of the facets of these privatization processes. Water privatization processes have four main facets or "faces": the privatization of municipal water services, the sale of bottled water, private control of hydraulic infrastructure, and water pollution (S. Ribeiro 2005; McCulligh 2011).

Thus, a facet of privatization that is not new is the use of water bodies as "free" repositories for pollutants generated by productive activities. In economic terms, these are considered externalities or market failures, where "the market does not work properly and prices do not reflect all the benefits or all the costs" (Aguilar Ibarra et al. 2010b, 221). Water pollution represents a private benefit in terms of the savings of treatment costs, while these costs are transferred to others in loss of water uses (for drinking water; in irrigation, fishing, or other productive activities; and for recreational or cultural activities) and in loss of health and quality of life more broadly. This pollution deprives others of access to clean water and effectively turns rivers and lakes that are part of the commons of humanity into private sewers.

Here the use of the term "privatization" is not literal, as it does not involve assigning property rights to the polluted waters, but precisely their status as a commons is used to accumulate private profit. Seen as a broader process, however, it shares roots with the processes of privatization of water services, hydraulic infrastructure, and the commodification of water associated with the logics of the neoliberalization of nature (McCarthy and Prudham 2004; Castree 2008; Bakker 2010). Within these broader processes, there are proposals to control water contamination from a market rationale. This is part of what Karen Bakker calls the "liberalization of governance," under the umbrella of "market environmentalism" (2014, 471). In the introduction, I discussed this free-market environmentalism as part of the logic undergirding the system of environmental regulation in Mexico. In that regard, in the next section I will demonstrate how this logic is adapted for "developing countries" through an analysis of two texts on environmental management from the Organisation for Economic Co-operation and Development (OECD).

1.2.2 The Logics of a System

The first document from which I will extract elements that help make explicit the logic of the system of environmental regulation analyzed in this book is an OECD policy brief, dated 1992, on environmental management in developing countries (D. O'Connor and Turnham 1992). It starts from the conventional assumptions that environmental degradation stems from either market or policy failures and that developing countries lack resources and tend to suffer from "problems of weak political commitment and governance" (3). The policy brief sets the scene of fragile systems of property rights and resource constraints that limit the ability of governments to implement traditional command and control regulations. From there, the report authors promote the "broad-based use of economic instruments, with a sparing use of regulation," this despite conceding that developed countries have not abandoned traditional regulations because "regulation is often required to ensure that minimum acceptable standards of environmental performance are met" (6, 19). At the same time, they encourage greater participation of the private sector and communities in environmental management. This participation, particularly that of the private sector, is based on several striking assumptions.

The policy brief distinguishes between the large corporations of developed countries and local companies from developing countries, where the latter have little incentive to halt polluting activities. Many of the former, O'Connor and Turnham maintain, are ever more sensitive to critique related to their environmental performance and find that the adoption of strict internal environmental management standards "can to a large degree 'pay for itself' through efficiency gains and reduced waste" (1992, 9). In a succinct enunciation of what I term the myth of the multinational, the document affirms that "a growing number of multinationals are adopting common environmental standards worldwide (normally based on those in their home countries) as a matter of policy" (10). From there, governments are urged to "co-opt" the technical knowledge of these corporations, particularly experts from multinationals, to train local personnel.

Another way in which governments are encouraged to take advantage of the capacities of corporations is through an aspect I consider essential to understanding Mexico's regulatory system: self-monitoring. O'Connor and Turnham put forward self-monitoring as a way to compensate for the weak oversight capacity of governments, and they declare that it will be successful if combined with periodic "spot checks" and effective penalties in case of inaccurate reports. "By involving firms themselves in the monitoring process," the brief affirms, "governments can avail of the former's in-house technical expertise" (1992, 21). Governments are urged to involve industry associations in self-regulation, in order for more responsible companies to motivate the compliance of laggards.

To minimize the risk of strict regulations on paper that governments cannot enforce in practice, the OECD brief advises a "consultative approach," wherein regulated parties should be consulted during the formulation of regulations. O'Connor and Turnham adduce three justifications for this approach. First, they invoke the generalization that the cultural traditions of many developing countries "emphasize consensus building and compromise over confrontation" (1992, 20). Second, they note the technical knowledge to be found in the private sector, which governments may not have access to. Third, they indicate that consultation may furnish a route to voluntary compliance, given the generally limited capacity of governments. The goal is consensus, and they acknowledge as only a last resort that a government can establish the regulations it deems necessary, if agreement is not reached.

Despite this promotion of regulations set via consensus and negotiation, the document does not mention the risk of regulatory capture. While not a binary condition, regulatory capture is associated with the collusion of regulatory authorities with the companies to be regulated, at the expense of the public interest (Zinn 2002; Etzioni 2009; Carpenter and Moss 2014). Close negotiations and the dependence of the authorities on the technical information of regulated parties should at a minimum be identified as factors increasing the risk of capture. The only mention of regulatory capture in the document, however, is with regard to the involvement of communities and nongovernmental organizations in monitoring polluting activities—citing their reliance on jobs in the polluting companies as a possible conflict of interest. With respect to the relationship between regulator and regulated parties, the possibility of capture is not even hinted at.

From these general recommendations for developing countries, I turn to an example of the application of this logic to the system in Mexico, in this case the OECD's 1998 *Environmental Performance Review of Mexico*. The OECD has undertaken subsequent evaluations (OECD 2003, 2013); however, for my purposes this document contributes more to elucidate the logic of how the system has been fashioned. The evaluation praises the promotion in Mexico of self-regulation and voluntary compliance programs, as well as the fact that "co-operation between government and industry has . . . improved lately" (OECD 1998, 22). Despite acknowledging that the inspection and monitoring of discharges is weak, that duties collected from the application of the "polluter pays" principle are low, and that Mexico has some of the most degraded water resources of the OECD countries, the overall tone of the evaluation is positive. Even in relation to water, it concludes that "Mexican authorities have clearly diagnosed the problems to be solved and have adopted a set of water laws and policies that is in line with, and sometimes ahead of, those of the other OECD Member countries" (70). In fact, the evaluation argues that Mexico is a success story in achieving a win-win configuration in environmental regulation: "Mexican experience has shown that *environmental protection is not incompatible with competitiveness and employment.* . . . Mexican authorities and industry representatives maintain that competitiveness, in the new context of globalization, trade agreements and opening of markets, requires new rules in which environmental policy and regulation work in synergy with industrial development" (129; emphasis in original). In this brave new world, apparently, no sacrifice is required in the robustness of environmental regulation to achieve economic goals.

When this logic is translated to a specific example in the evaluation, however, the reality is different. The example refers to the forty-four discharge standards that, as I mentioned earlier, were replaced by the NOM-001, a fact here celebrated as a case of simplification. I will again cite the evaluation at length, as it calls into question the win-win logic that supposedly reigns in the country:

> The withdrawal of elaborate, technology-based and industry-specific effluent limits in favour of a simple system based on receiving water standards . . . *could be interpreted as leniency towards polluters.* However, . . . the mix of measures now being implemented can also be seen as *recognizing economic realities* while giving Mexican industry the signals and the time to install cleaner technology as it renews its production capacity. (72–73; first emphasis added)

It is difficult to imagine that this is what it means to be "ahead of" other OECD countries, especially if we take into account that, for example,

Germany has fifty-seven different industry-specific effluent standards, while the United States has guidelines for about sixty categories of industry. It is rather the "economic realities," one must presume, that lead to this apparently lenient norm—that is, offering up flexible environmental regulations as a further comparative advantage of the country.

To close this section, I would only emphasize that the myth of the multinational becomes evident throughout the evaluation, which asserts that many of the large corporations in the industrial sector "meet most national and international environmental standards and many are increasingly aware of their environmental responsibilities" (OECD 1998, 30). In contrast, the authors state that 70 percent of small and medium-sized enterprises do not comply and, therefore, must be the target of government programs. In addition, associations between small and large companies are recommended for technology transfer and dissemination of environmental responsibility.

While I undertake a more empirical analysis of this myth in chapter 5, in light of information available for several transnational companies in the Ocotlán–El Salto Industrial Corridor, here I would stress the flimsy arguments deployed to support the idea that these companies have adopted global environmental standards. If, as the proponents of free-market environmentalism Terry Anderson and Donald Leal maintain, "everyone accepts that managers in the private sector would dump production wastes into a nearby stream if they did not have to pay for the cost of their actions" (2001, 11), why would one assume that large corporations everywhere comply with the standards of the countries where they are headquartered? While I do not share the assumptions of Anderson and Leal, in their vision of "man as self-interested" (5), it would be equally erroneous to base a system on the view of economic actors as universally responsible and vigilant of the common good. This can be contrasted, in addition, with Milton Friedman's take on corporate social responsibility. For this ideologue of neoliberalism, in a free economy, "there is one and only one social responsibility of business—to use its resources and engage in activities designed to increase its profits so long as it stays within the rules of the game" (1982, 133). Based on this precept, then, it would be irresponsible for a company to apply the strictest environmental standards (of its home country, for example), unless this generated profitability or was an obligation or "rule of the game." The only reasoning presented here in favor of the myth is that these companies will have found savings in clean production.

1.3 A Crisis of Contamination

> Access to safe water is a human right. However, the right to pollute and discharge contaminated water back into the environment, polluting the water of downstream users, is not.
>
> —From the report *Sick Water? The Central Role of Wastewater Management in Sustainable Development* (Corcoran et al. 2010, 16)

> We all have the right to pollute and to impact, the point is knowing how, when, and up to what point, that is the key to how to pollute.
>
> —Aciel Gaitán, during the 2013 Environmental Legal Actualization Seminar of the National Chemical Industry Association[3]

Does there exist a right to pollute a river, lake, aquifer, or other body of water? In that it is an activity regulated through permits or other regulatory instruments by many governments, in practice it does exist. Given the state of urban infrastructure in many parts of the world, as individuals we may also contribute to the deterioration of a body of water through our domestic sewage. When it comes to private actors, however, whose profit increases via these "environmental externalities" in the form of polluted effluents, do they have that right to pollute? If we accept that productive activities are not likely to cease generating wastewater flows, to what extent do they have this right, and how should it be regulated? Why is it important to think about water pollution on this thirsty blue planet in the first place?

It has become common in recent years to speak of water crises, and even of current and future water wars (see, for example, Shiva 2003; UNESCO 2003; Barlow 2007). In Mexico, there are multiple disputes related to water supply to urban centers, such as the fight against the El Zapotillo Dam in the Highlands region of Jalisco and previously against the Arcediano Dam in Guadalajara; that of the Yaqui community against the construction and operation of the Independencia Aqueduct to supply water to Hermosillo; and the protests of the Mazahua Front against the impacts of the Cutzamala System that provides water to Mexico City. In the so-called water and energy nexus, since 2003 the Council of Ejidos and Communities Opposed to the La Parota Dam (Consejo de Ejidos y Comunidades Opositores a la Presa La Parota) has led a successful struggle against this dam in the southern state of Guerrero, while other communities organize against hydroelectric projects such as Las Cruces in Nayarit, Paso de la Reina in Oaxaca, and El Naranjal in Veracruz. Socio-environmental conflicts around water also occur as a result of toxic pollution, where water bodies become a source of disease for local populations, as in the case of the Atoyac River in Puebla and Tlaxcala, the Coatzacoalcos in Veracruz, the Lerma River from the State of Mexico, and Lake Chapala in Jalisco. Although it would be wrong to liken these to water wars, this very partial list shows how communities are opposing the projects and practices of both governments and private companies when it comes to water management and use.

This is part of a broader surge in socio-environmental conflicts in Mexico, especially in the last two decades (Tetreault et al. 2012; Paz 2014; Toledo et al. 2014; Navarro 2015; Tetreault et al. 2018). These conflicts have been triggered by dam, road, and wind farm projects; by the impacts of mining activities, energy infrastructure, garbage dumps, and tourist developments; by chaotic urbanization; and by the impacts of industrial pollution of water, land, and air. In this broader panorama, water pollution and overexploitation were identified in a one study as the cause of the highest proportion of socio-environmental conflicts in the country. María Fernanda Paz (2012) analyzed a total of ninety-five socio-environmental conflicts, registered between 2009 and 2011 in twenty-one states, and found that water was the resource affected in 39 percent of the cases. Furthermore, they were not conflicts related to water scarcity; rather, in 70 percent of the conflicts over water, pollution was at the center of the dispute.

In the "official" interpretation of the rise in water conflicts, as expressed in CONAGUA documents, they are presented in economistic terms as the result of competition between users: "The social, economic and political stability of Mexico has been compromised by various conflicts that have arisen in some basins in the country due to the growing demand and competition for water among the different users" (2014a, 28). At the same time, in keeping with the focus on water as an input for economic development, more attention is paid to its availability and ensuring its use in productive activities than to its role as receptor and purifier of the waste generated by these activities.

The explanation of the water problems in the country seems to be found, from the perspective of CONAGUA, in a simple logic of demographic growth and a mismatch between population and rainfall distribution. "In Mexico," states a CONAGUA evaluation of the country's aquifers, "the adequate

Industrialization and Environmental Regulation in Mexico

preservation of the resource represents an extraordinary challenge derived largely from population growth" (2015, 5). From 25.8 million people in 1950, the Mexican population grew to 126 million in 2020 (INEGI 2020a). That population also urbanized. While 57 percent of the population lived in rural communities in 1950, by 2020 only 21 percent remained in rural areas. At the same time, two-thirds of the Mexican territory is considered arid or semiarid (with less than five hundred millimeters of precipitation per year), contrasted with the southeast, where rainfall exceeds two thousand millimeters per year (CONAGUA 2014a, 13). Thus, CONAGUA documents often emphasize that 77 percent of the Mexican population lives in the center and north of the country, where there is only 33 percent of the country's renewable water; conversely, 23 percent of the population lives in the south-southeast with access to 67 percent of renewable water resources (CONAGUA 2017, 24).

Population growth has resulted in a decrease in the renewable water available per capita, which CONAGUA reports "has fallen drastically in recent years," from 18,000 cubic meters (m^3) per person per year in 1950 to 3,663 m^3 in 2020 (2014b, 28; CONAGUA 2022a). The Lerma-Santiago-Pacific region, which includes the Santiago River Basin, is the fifth most restricted, with an availability of 1,374 m^3 per person per year, one of the levels that CONAGUA qualifies as "worryingly low" (CONAGUA 2014a, 28; CONAGUA 2022a). Groundwater sources are also under pressure, with 157 of 653 aquifers in Mexico classified as overexploited. These overexploited aquifers are the source of 80 percent of the total volume of extracted groundwater in the country (Moreno Vázquez et al. 2010, 80). Globally, the United Nations Educational, Scientific and Cultural Organization (UNESCO) estimates that by 2025, 1.8 billion people will live in countries or regions with absolute water scarcity and two-thirds of the global population will suffer from water stress.[4]

There is no reason, therefore, to dismiss concerns about the growing overexploitation of freshwater sources. However, dominant representations of scarcity often obscure the causes of unequal access to water. As Basil Mahayni warns, in many discourses on water governance, "there is too often a linear path from scarcity to impending crisis to market-based reforms, and consideration of alternative means of confronting water-society dilemmas is sidelined" (2013, 39). What tends to prevail in academic and governmental analyses, Lyla Mehta notes, is a focus on "volumetric and physical measurements, especially with respect to both a growing population and competing demands for water" (2007, 654). In addition to market-based solutions, faced with these numerical and biophysical assessments, science and technology are often "evoked as the panaceas" (655), frequently in the form of large hydraulic works to provide new sources of water supply. What these representations of scarcity leave out, moreover, are the historical context and power relations that determine inequalities in access to water (Mahayni 2013, 41). When the biophysical analysis is put at the center, scarcity is not conceived as "the result of powerful actors getting away with resource appropriation and thus enhancing degradation" (Mehta 2007, 655). Industrial pollution is a form of this appropriation with impunity.

Scarcity and pollution are also intimately linked. Pedro Arrojo, currently the UN special rapporteur on the human rights to safe drinking water and sanitation, has argued that the water crisis "does not lie so much in problems of scarcity itself, but in the quality of the available waters," affirming that behind the tragedy of 1.2 billion people worldwide who lack access to drinking water is the "lack of sanitation and the direct discharge of urban and industrial wastewater to the natural environment" (2009, 35). Recent UNESCO and World Bank reports conclude that the issue of water quality has received less investment, scientific support, and public attention compared with issues of water quantity (UNESCO 2012; Damania et al. 2019). This despite the fact that an estimated 80 percent of the water used globally is not collected or treated, and toxic contamination from industrial sources and hazardous waste sites is considered "a major threat and expense to the provision of safe water in the developing world" (UNESCO 2012, 96).

According to estimates by UNEP, industry globally dumps between 300 million and 400 million tons of heavy metals, solvents, toxic sludge, and other waste into water bodies each year (Palaniappan et al. 2010, 17). Even if they receive treatment, furthermore, many substances of industrial origin are not susceptible to treatment in conventional systems. There is an additional trend relevant to this case: the transfer of polluting industries to countries of the South. Thus, while there are improvements in industrial waste treatment levels in developed countries, the UNEP report underscores that, given the disparities in the stringency of regulations, "many industries are moving from high-income countries to emerging market economies, leading to severe environmental and human health concerns and often hindering future economic development" (60). It is clear, then, that pollution is a cause of water scarcity and the deterioration of ecological systems and human health, and that it is not merely a question of technological solutions but of justice and power.

1.3.1 Green Growth in the Blue Sector

In Mexico, reliable water quality data are scarce, as are clear strategies and concrete actions to clean up polluted surface waters. Until 2003, CONAGUA measured water quality through a water quality index, calculated based on nineteen parameters. In that year, only 6 percent of surface waters were considered unpolluted, while 73 percent were classified as polluted and 20 percent as acceptable. In the Lerma-Santiago-Pacific region, 96 percent of water bodies were categorized as polluted (slightly polluted, polluted, or highly polluted) (CONAGUA 2003, 34). As of 2004, the official manner of reporting surface water quality changed, with results reported separately for only three parameters: biochemical oxygen demand (BOD),[5] COD,[6] and TSS.[7] This implied, as Blanca Jiménez (2007, 46) points out, that "the interval to classify water as highly polluted was reduced," among other changes that impeded any clear determination of whether water quality was improving or deteriorating (Aboites et al. 2008).

The number of sites included in the National Monitoring Network (Red nacional de monitoreo), the source of surface water quality data, rose from 209 in 2003 to 4,655 in 2019. While greater coverage of this monitoring network is positive, it also represents another challenge when seeking to compare data over time. UN-Water, which coordinates UN efforts on water and sanitation issues, asserts that in Mexico "more than 70 percent of the water bodies have some degree of contamination: lakes, rivers, mangroves and coasts are polluted, affecting humans, animals and plants that inhabit these ecosystems" (UN-Water 2013). For the state of Jalisco, based on samples for 2012 to 2020, CONAGUA classified 41.2 percent of water bodies in the state with a red water quality "stoplight"; 34.2 percent received a yellow light and only 25.3 percent a green light. The red light indicates levels were exceeded for COD, BOD, acute toxicity, or fecal enterococci, while the yellow light indicates limits were not met for fecal coliforms, *Escherichia coli*, TSS, or dissolved oxygen. This is evidence of serious problems in much of the state.

Untreated sewage is a persistent problem despite official statistics citing rising levels of municipal wastewater treatment, and to a lesser extent of industrial effluents. Between 2004 and 2019, the level of treatment of municipal sewage in Mexico rose from 25 percent to 56.4 percent and of industrial wastewater from 15.3 percent to 40.7 percent, according to official data (CONAGUA 2022a). Even so, the same official data indicate that the pollutant load discharged (untreated) into water bodies has risen, as measured in terms of organic matter (BOD). CONAGUA reports the BOD load generated and removed in treatment systems for both municipal and industrial wastewater. Between 2004 and 2019 the BOD load not removed rose 35 percent, a phenomenon exclusively due to industrial effluents, since in the period analyzed, the BOD load from municipal sources fell by 29 percent, while *that of industrial origin rose by 54 percent.*

Mexico's 2020–2024 National Water Program (NWP) highlights the impact of industrial wastewater, stating that in terms of the BOD load generated, "industries contributed the most organic pollutants and up to 340% more pollution than that generated by municipalities" (CONAGUA 2020, 15). Previously CONAGUA estimated that industries in Mexico "produce a pollution equivalent to that generated by 300 million inhabitants," or about 2.5 times the country's population (2014a, 42). At the same time, certain industrial sectors also represent "the highest risk of release of heavy metals, toxic compounds, [and] persistent and bioaccumulative substances" (CONAGUA 2020, 15). At present, however, the diverse toxic pollutants released by industry in Mexico go unmonitored (Jiménez 2007, 51). Industrial effluents, explain René Schwarzenbach and colleagues, are "not only a source of BOD but also a point source of chemical pollution of heavy metals and synthetic organic compounds" (2010, 124). With more than one hundred thousand synthetic compounds registered globally, many of which exert toxic effects at extremely low concentrations, significant efforts are required to prevent these pollutants from reaching aquatic ecosystems (111). In Mexico, these efforts do not exist.

While successive planning documents have set goals aiming to improve surface water quality and wastewater treatment, they have been both ambivalent and ineffective (CONAGUA 2011a, 2014a, 2020). The ambivalence is clear, for example, in the 2013–2018 NWP. Despite diverse strategies to improve water quality in river basins and aquifers, on analyzing the document in its totality, the lack of real commitment becomes evident. This can be affirmed based on a glaring omission: *CONAGUA did not propose to achieve any improvement in the quality of the country's waters.* The NWP specifies as

Industrialization and Environmental Regulation in Mexico

indicators for water quality the percentage of water bodies classified as excellent and good quality according to the ranges established by CONAGUA for three parameters: BOD_5, COD, and TSS. What is strange is that no improvements were proposed for these indicators. Thus, while the percentage of monitoring sites with a good or excellent classification for the base year of 2012 is 66.8 percent for BOD_5, 47.3 percent for COD, and 86.8 percent for TSS, the goals for 2018 are identical (CONAGUA 2014b, 134). Even with that low bar, they failed for two of the three indicators. For 2018, CONAGUA reported that only 62.7 percent had excellent or good quality for BOD_5, and for COD the figure was just 35.4 percent of sites (CONAGUA 2022a).

The 2020–2024 NWP continues the pattern of vague objectives with respect to reducing and controlling pollution to curtail the degradation of water bodies and ensuing health impacts (objective 4.2). Thus, the document sets a similar goal regarding the proportion of surface water monitoring sites with excellent, good, or acceptable quality; indicates the baseline figures; and then sets no goal to be reached by 2024 (CONAGUA 2020).

It is interesting to note that the seeming disdain from CONAGUA for actions to curb water pollution is aligned with the recommendations of one of the most important promoters of so-called green growth, the World Bank. A 2012 World Bank publication, *Inclusive Green Growth*, recommends that developing countries prioritize green growth strategies that generate synergies such as immediate benefits that will be perceptible to the local population, as well those considered more urgent, and understood as necessary to avoid irreversible actions or "lock-in." The priorities, according to these principles, are urban planning and mobility policies, together with "family planning" and the construction of large-scale multipurpose dams (161). On the other side of the scale, among the issues considered to have few local and immediate benefits and to be of low urgency for developing countries are actions such as the implementation of stricter wastewater regulations. Thus, it seems that the scant action taken in Mexico to protect and restore water quality does not contradict the goal of green growth: "green" does not imply stricter environmental regulations, at least for the waters of so-called developing countries.

To explain the context of this research and the problem of industrial pollution here, I close this chapter with a brief description of the Ocotlán–El Salto Industrial Corridor, to assess the magnitude of the environmental problem associated with industrial effluent in this region.

1.4 The Ocotlán–El Salto Industrial Corridor

In the introduction, I touched on the contours of the Ocotlán–El Salto Industrial Corridor and its growth during the ISI period, as well as the first testimonies of severe river pollution and mass fish kills in the early 1970s. Writing in the mid-1980s, when the country's market-led strategy was just beginning, Patricia Arias emphasized that, although foreign capital had arrived in the Guadalajara Metropolitan Area, what continued to predominate in the city was the production of basic goods with an important contingent of small workshops, which, the author believed, "would continue to be the distinguishing characteristics of the industrial activity of Guadalajara" (1985, 117). This would not be the case, however, as the policies of the neoliberal period favored the export manufacturing sector, in particular the electronics, beer, tequila, plastics, and steel industries (C. Lezama 2004, 75). Arias wrote of the "big city of small industry," but the entry of products from Asia hit producers from various traditional sectors, including shoe and clothing workshops, printers and publishers, and the basic metals industry (Barba and Pozos 2001, 199).

After the right-of-center National Action Party won the governorship in Jalisco with Alberto Cárdenas Jiménez in 1994, his administration made efforts to attract investment, particularly foreign investment, in the electronics, communications, and automotive sectors (Barba and Pozos 2001). When crisis struck the electronics industry between 2001 and 2002, with an economic recession in the United States and the bursting of the stock bubble in its technology sector, and with the entry of China to the World Trade Organization (WTO) in 2001, the consequences were felt in the electronics sector in Mexico and particularly the so-called Silicon Valley of Guadalajara (Dabat Latrubesse 2004; Ordóñez 2006). Jobs were lost and a number of electronics companies withdrew from Guadalajara, moving to China (Gallagher and Zarsky 2007). China was already attractive due to its low wages, its productive capacity, and the size of its domestic market, but Kevin Gallagher and Lyuba Zarsky (2007) highlight its accession to the WTO as a key global change, with the concomitant reduction in tariffs and obstacles for foreign direct investment (FDI).

The departure of companies to China, according to Alejandro Dabat Latrubesse (2004, 35), was "not the result of their low labor costs, as is unjustifiably believed." According to this author, it stemmed from the important role of the government and universities in promoting the electronics industry in China, with the creation of a large number of national companies as well as partnerships with some of the most important transnationals of the sector. This is similar to the analysis by Gallagher and Zarsky (2007, 9), who critique the idea prevalent in Mexico that economic liberalization is sufficient to attract FDI and thus ensure job creation and industry expansion. One of the lessons that these authors indicate can be drawn from the Guadalajara case is that FDI is not a magic pill: "Supportive public policies are needed to nurture domestic industries and capture the benefits from FDI" (10).

Currently, the electronics industry in Guadalajara continues to be an important source of jobs, representing 22 percent of the personnel employed in the manufacturing industry in 2016 (INEGI 2017). The electronics sector is highly concentrated; in 2014 only fourteen large facilities provided 96 percent of employment in the sector and generated the same percentage of gross census value added (IIEG 2016). In the manufacturing sector in general, in 2014 there were 33,609 economic units in Jalisco, of which 89 percent were microenterprises and only 1 percent were large companies. The large firms, however, provided 43 percent of employment in the sector and generated 66 percent of gross census value added (IIEG 2016).

Jalisco is one of the states with the greatest concentration of manufacturing activities, generating 9.1 percent of Mexico's manufacturing GDP in 2018 (IIEG 2019). Table 1.1 presents some of the most important states in the country for manufacturing activities, ordered by total employment in the manufacturing sector, based on data for 2018. Jalisco was ranked third in terms of manufacturing employment and was the fifth most important state in terms of the total gross production and the number of manufacturing units (INEGI 2019).

The municipality of El Salto, as well as other municipalities of the Ocotlán–El Salto Industrial Corridor, is among the main manufacturing municipalities in the state, particularly as measured in terms of total gross production and the number of people employed in manufacturing (table 1.2). While much manufacturing activity continues to be concentrated in the city's central municipalities of Guadalajara and Zapopan, this also has impacts for riverside communities like El Salto, which receives the runoff from the El Ahogado Subbasin, a formation that encompasses parts of the municipalities of Zapopan, Tlajomulco de Zúñiga, and Tlaquepaque. The relevance of El Salto as an industrial municipality can be appreciated

Table 1.1

Principal manufacturing states, in terms of employment, total gross production, and number of economic units (2018)

State	Total employment—manufacturing		Total gross production—manufacturing (millions of pesos)		Economic units	
	Ranking	Number	Ranking	Amount	Ranking	Number
National total	—	6,493,020	—	$10,800,994	—	579,828
State of Mexico	1	626,924	2	$1,182,643	1	61,840
Nuevo León	2	548,255	1	$1,326,684	13	14,001
Jalisco	**3**	**507,266**	**5**	**$744,999**	**5**	**35,702**
Chihuahua	4	502,532	16	$297,851	21	8,671
Guanajuato	5	499,649	3	$1,050,831	8	31,508
Baja California	6	422,816	12	$365,099	22	8,114
Coahuila	7	405,912	4	$996,438	19	9,436
Mexico City	8	352,501	7	$474,297	7	32,384
Tamaulipas	9	323,720	11	$369,691	20	8,844
Puebla	10	300,009	6	$546,191	3	50,091

Source: Author's elaboration based on the 2019 Economic Census (INEGI 2019).

by noting that the total gross production in manufacturing activities is estimated at MX$567,802 per inhabitant per year, with population data from 2020, versus an estimate of five times less for the municipality of Guadalajara at MX$111,172 per capita (INEGI 2019, 2020a).

In 2018, the most important industries in Jalisco in terms of employment were the food and beverage sector (112,622 people), the electronics industry (65,343), the manufacturing of metal products (43,927), automotive and auto parts (39,658), plastic and rubber manufacturing (39,063), and chemical industries (34,362) (INEGI 2019). As at the national level, in Jalisco manufacturing exports are dominated by the electronics and automotive sectors. In 2018, 59.7 percent of exports from Jalisco came from the electronics industry and 12 percent from the automotive and auto parts industry. These sectors are followed by plastics and rubber manufacturing (9.9 percent), the beverage industry (7.4 percent), and the chemical industry (3.4 percent) (IIEG 2019). Since 2004, between 75 percent and 80 percent of exports from Jalisco have come from just three sectors: electronics, automotive and auto parts, and food and beverages. These exports, particularly those of the electronics and automotive industry, contribute little to the

Table 1.2

Main manufacturing municipalities of Jalisco, by total gross production, employment, and number of manufacturing units (2018)

Municipality	Total gross production (millions of pesos)		Total employment		Economic units	
	Ranking	Amount	Ranking	Number	Ranking	Number
Guadalajara	1	$154,044	2	113,477	1	8,007
Zapopan	2	$137,565	1	121,731	2	4,395
El Salto	3	$132,214	4	44,696	7	896
Tlajomulco de Zúñiga	4	$89,248	3	51,833	5	1,136
Tlaquepaque	5	$68,942	5	41,699	4	2,556
Lagos de Moreno	6	$37,358	6	17,497	8	840
Ocotlán	7	$11,484	9	7,985	9	836
Tepatitlán	8	$11,153	8	9,165	10	669
Atotonilco El Alto	9	$9,234	18	2,719	30	229
Tequila	10	$9,137	22	2,136	16	297

Source: Author's elaboration based on the 2019 Economic Census (INEGI 2019).

state's economic growth due to the scant local value added, as well as the "weakness in the local productive chains" (R. Cervantes and Villaseñor 2014, 197). The industrial corridor studied includes companies in all the main export sectors, as well as a large number of mostly smaller companies catering to the domestic market.

To provide a more accurate picture of manufacturing activity in my study region, I compiled a database of the industrial facilities located here.[8] This included manufacturing companies in the municipalities of the Ocotlán–El Salto corridor, including the entire El Ahogado Subbasin, as well as in the three main municipalities of the Zula River Basin: Arandas, Atotonilco El Alto, and Tototlán. I included companies classified by INEGI as large (251 or more people employed), medium (51 to 250 people), and small (11 to 50 people).[9] This leaves out microenterprises while capturing the vast majority of the manufacturing output. At the national level, INEGI reports that although manufacturing microenterprises (up to 10 people employed) represent 93.7 percent of economic units, they generate 19.4 percent of employment and only 2.3 percent of total gross production (INEGI 2020b, 26).

In the Ocotlán–El Salto corridor, I identified a total of 675 manufacturing companies, of which 63 are classified as large, 176 as medium, and 436 as small enterprises. Of these, 71 are foreign-owned companies, which represents 11 percent of the total.[10] Twenty-seven of the foreign-owned companies are headquartered in the United States, 23 in European countries, 7 in Japan, and another 15 in different parts of the world. It is also worth noting that 80 percent of foreign-owned factories are from five industrial sectors: electronics and electrical equipment (23.9 percent), chemical industries (16.9 percent), automotive and auto parts (15.5 percent), food and beverages (12.7 percent), and plastics and rubber (11.3 percent) (table 1.3).

In general, no single manufacturing sector predominates in the corridor. Including both Mexican and foreign companies, the sectors with the

Table 1.3

Number and percentage of companies by industrial sector and origin of capital, Ocotlán–El Salto corridor

Sector	Total		Mexican		Foreign owned	
	Number	Percent	Number	Percent	Number	Percent
Food and beverage	84	12.4	75	12.4	9	12.7
Automotive and auto parts	25	3.7	14	2.3	11	15.5
Electronics and electrical	25	3.7	8	1.3	17	23.9
Metal industries	101	15.0	95	15.7	6	8.5
Machinery and equipment	24	3.6	23	3.8	1	1.4
Nonmetallic minerals	45	6.7	44	7.3	1	1.4
Furniture	136	20.1	136	22.5	0	0.0
Paper, wood, and printing	50	7.4	45	7.5	5	7.0
Plastics and rubber	84	12.4	76	12.6	8	11.3
Chemical and petrochemical	60	8.9	49	7.9	12	16.9
Clothing, textiles, and footwear	28	4.1	27	4.5	1	1.4
Others	13	1.9	13	2.2	0	0.0
Total	675	100.0	605	100.0	71	100.0

Source: Author's elaboration based on the National Statistical Directory of Economic Units (Directorio Estadístico Nacional de Unidades Económicas).

Industrialization and Environmental Regulation in Mexico

largest numbers of installations are furniture manufacturing (20.1 percent), metal industries (15 percent), plastic and rubber production (12.4 percent), food and beverages (12.4 percent), and chemical industries (8.9 percent). In terms of the sizes of the facilities by number of employees, it is worth noting that 69 percent of Mexican factories are small, 24 percent are medium, and 6 percent are large. On the other hand, only 25 percent of foreign-owned factories are classified as small, 38 percent as medium, and 37 percent as large enterprises. Figure 1.2 presents a map indicating the distribution of industrial units by size and by origin of capital.

As a tributary of the Santiago, the Zula River Basin is relevant to understand the problems of the Upper Santiago. The Zula unites with the Santiago at Ocotlán. Due to hydraulic interventions, however, the waters of the Zula do not flow year-round into the Santiago River. During the rainy season, the gates of a dam on the Santiago River in Poncitlán are closed to channel the waters of the Zula into Lake Chapala. Thus, for several months a year the runoff of the Zula and the first stretch of the Santiago flows "backward" toward the lake. The justification for this hydraulic management is to safeguard lake levels, given recent crises in the volume of water stored in Lake Chapala, which often receives a low flow from its main tributary, the Lerma River.[11] In the Zula Basin, I identified sixty-three companies: thirty-nine small, twenty-four medium, and three large factories. Of these companies, seventeen are dedicated to the production of tequila, including five foreign-owned distilleries.

If we add the manufacturing facilities of the municipalities of the Zula Basin, there are a total of 741 manufacturing facilities in this region (66 large, 200 medium, and 475 small). Some of these facilities, located in urban areas, discharge their effluents to municipal sewer systems, where they may or may not receive treatment, depending on the municipality, its collector sewers, and the status of treatment plants, where they exist. The remaining factories, particularly the larger ones, emit their liquid waste directly to the river or to streams or canals that flow into the Santiago. In the following section, I outline the characteristics of those direct emissions.

1.4.1 Sketches of the Enigma Effluent

Although the information is partial and not regularly updated, several studies have given an indication of the magnitude of the impact of discharges from the portion of companies that discharge directly into the river or

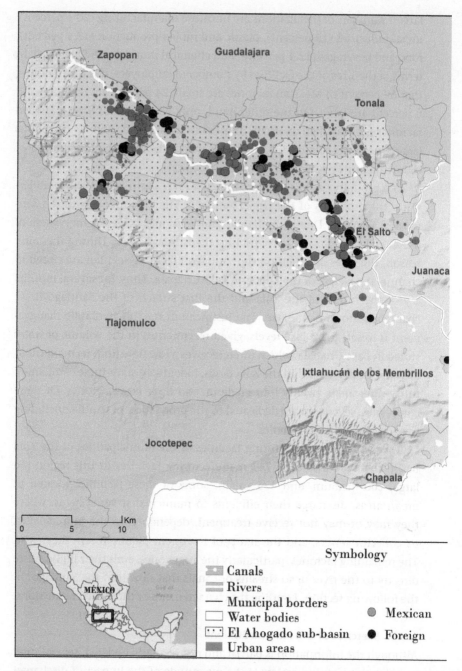

Figure 1.2
Industrial installations in municipalities of the Ocotlán–El Salto corridor, by size and capital of origin.

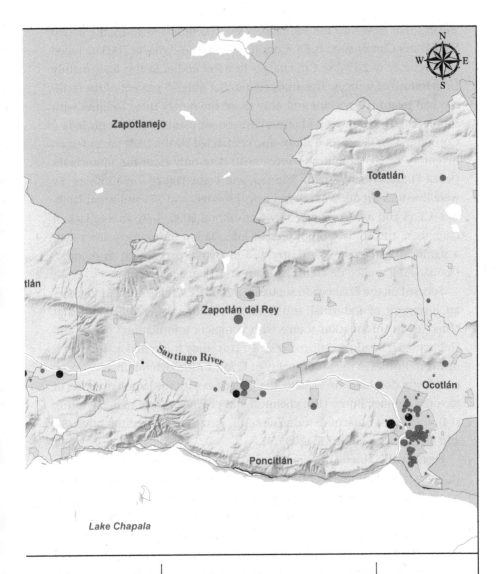

- • 11–30 employees
- • 31–50 employees
- • 51–100 employees
- • 101–250 employees
- • 251+ employees

Projection: UTM Zone 13N
Datum WGS84
Source: Authors' elaboration based on
DENUE and INEGI vectors
Authors: Cindy McCulligh
and Jorge Alberto Cruz Barbosa

streams that flow into the Santiago. A study commissioned by the Jalisco State Water Commission (CEA, Comisión Estatal del Agua) in 2003 included an inventory of 265 direct discharges to water bodies in this area, mainly from industrial sources. This study found that only 35 percent of the facilities had treatment systems and only six of the ninety-three facilities with some form of treatment had tertiary treatment plants (AyMA Ingeniería y Consultoría 2003). A 2006 study, also contracted by the CEA, presented an inventory of 305 pollution sources, with data only from the municipalities of El Salto, Juanacatlán, Tototlán, and Poncitlán; of these sources, 14 were livestock production, 20 municipal sewage, and 271 industrial facilities (CEAS and AyMA Ingeniería y Consultoría 2006, 1–9). Due to lack of data, then, this study did not present information for municipalities with a significant presence of industry and industrial parks, such as Arandas, Ocotlán, Tlajomulco de Zúñiga, Tonalá, and Tlaquepaque.

Focused on the El Ahogado Subbasin, a 2005 CEA study brought together an inventory of industrial and livestock facilities, after indicating that "there is no information source with complete information" (CEAS and Gobierno del Estado de Jalisco 2005, 4). This study integrated an inventory of 151 industries in the municipality of El Salto. Although no single category of industry dominates in El Salto, the categories with the largest numbers of factories are metallurgy (15), chemical and pharmaceutical manufacturing (14), metals and machine industries (10), electronics (9), automotive (9), and food and beverages (8) (2005, 6).

Even in the absence of continuous analyses of industrial effluents in this area, several studies confirm them as an important source of contaminants. The most comprehensive study that included an analysis of industrial effluent was undertaken by IMTA for the CEA. This study analyzed twenty-six industrial discharges over three monitoring campaigns between March 2009 and May 2010. These discharges include several from large transnational corporations with factories in the area and with wastewater treatment plants, such as the companies that will be looked at in greater detail in chapter 5: Nestlé, Celanese, Huntsman, and Quimikao.

Even given the lax discharge standard, the levels of noncompliance found in the IMTA study are high. In fact, the study concludes that "industrial discharges were more polluting than municipal discharges, as between 87 and 94% of industries did not comply with at least one of the parameters of standard NOM-001-SEMARNAT-1996" (IMTA and CEA 2011, XI-2). In addition, this study sought to detect the presence of synthetic compounds both in effluent and directly in the river and its tributaries. In the analysis of volatile and semivolatile organic compounds, a total of *1,090 substances* were detected either in effluent or in the waters of the river and its tributaries (XI-3). Substances or classes of substances that were encountered frequently include phthalates (used to make plastics flexible), toluene, chloroform, benzene, phenol, and hormonal compounds. Several of these substances are also known to be harmful to human health. Certain phthalates cause reproductive and hepatic damage; toluene and phenol affect the nervous system; benzene is carcinogenic; and chloroform can damage the liver and kidneys with prolonged exposure.[12] The significance of this IMTA study is that it is one of the few sources of reliable information on effluent quality, and it directly contradicts the insistent claims—from government and industry—of high levels of compliance by the industrial sector.

Further monitoring has confirmed the contribution of industry to the degradation of the Santiago River. Based on an analysis of monitoring carried out along the Upper Santiago by the CEA between 2009 and 2015, researchers from the National Autonomous University of Mexico determined that "due to its biological and chemical water quality, the Santiago River is in a critical state" (Bollo Manent et al. 2017, 114). The researchers classified the river's chemical quality as "always very low," highlighting that there is "pollution along a large stretch of the river caused by industrial production and the lack or inadequate treatment of domestic waste" (112). This study drew attention to the levels detected of total phosphorus, aluminum, ammonia nitrogen, sulfides, fecal coliforms, methylene blue active substances (surfactants), COD, dissolved oxygen, mercury, barium, and total suspended solids, which exceeded the permissible limits in more than 400 of the 832 samples analyzed in this period. In general terms, they emphasized that the majority of the chemical contamination encountered "is associated with industrial activities" (112).

*   *   *

In this chapter, I have briefly reviewed the history of industrialization in Mexico and the current configuration of manufacturing in the country. I have described an economic strategy that, guided by policies of neoliberalization, is centered on attracting FDI through low wages and other "competitive" advantages, and which has not led to the desired levels of economic growth. The manufacturing sector in Mexico is highly dependent on the US economy, with exports concentrated in the electronics and automotive sectors.

The second part of the chapter focused on the history of environmental regulation in Mexico, with an emphasis on water pollution control. Here, I underscored how most of the existing environmental institutions, laws, and regulations were created after the adoption of neoliberalization policies in Mexico and, consequently, favor the opening of previously public-sector activities to privatization, while also empowering the private sector through a reliance on self-monitoring and self-regulation. This has to do with the "capture and reuse" of the state, in favor of private interests, which Peck refers to as the hallmark of neoliberalization processes, despite the accompanying "antistatist rhetoric" (2010, 4, 9). From the regulatory system, I moved the focus to the context of multiplying socio-environmental conflicts in the country, where pollution is one of the main causes of water-related conflicts.

From the general situation in Mexico, I turned to look at manufacturing in the Ocotlán–El Salto Industrial Corridor, and the type and origin of the companies with factories here. I outlined the available information on industrial effluents discharged directly into the Santiago River or one of its tributaries. Garnering public access to this evidence of industrial pollution was an achievement of community actors and their allies in the movement for the cleanup of the Santiago River. That movement and the strategies and discourses of state and private actors to evade responsibility and obfuscate the causes of river degradation are the subject of chapter 2.

2 Chronicle of a Struggle: The Negation and the Terror

The school overlooked the waterfall and was housed in a building that had once formed part of the Jesús María Hacienda. It opened as a school in 1926, when El Salto was still a factory town for the Río Grande textile factory, and a local newspaper reported that eighty generations of students had completed primary school there before it was closed in 2015 (Lomelí 2015). Named for striking textile workers killed in 1907 across the country in Veracruz, the Martyrs of the Blanco River school was where Josué Daniel studied in the late 1990s. His classroom had a balcony with a view to the waterfall. When the floodgates were opened above the falls in the rainy season, the river filled with foam, sometimes as high as the falls themselves. Flying balls of foam fell over the school and, "with the innocence of children," Josué Daniel says, "we went out to see the falls and the foam. Because we thought it was strange . . . but it was pure chemicals and we played with those chemicals."[1] Kids smeared the balls of foam over their faces, he recalls.

At 32 years of age, Josué Daniel now has three children of his own and struggles with chronic kidney disease that led to a kidney transplant. The US Renal Data System presents data on the incidence of treated end-stage renal disease for fifty-six countries or regions. In 2019, Jalisco was the country or region with highest incidence, above Taiwan and the United States (US Renal Data System 2021). In Jalisco, El Salto is one of the hot spots for renal disease (CEDHJ 2022). Shortly after his transplant, when Josué Daniel began to recover and was able to return to work in the main plaza in El Salto, the floodgates were opened on the river. It was the dry season, and when water began to flow over the falls, noxious gases were dispersed into the air. "It started to smell so bad that I lasted more than a week intoxicated. . . . As soon as I got up to leave, I was already dizzy from the smell! . . . I got really intoxicated . . . for more than a week, with nausea, vomiting, dizzy all day. I don't know what I absorbed, but whatever I absorbed hurt me."[2]

The smell of the river often permeated the classrooms at the Martyrs of the Blanco River school in the mornings. Now, Josué Daniel's children will also comment, "It smells of river." "They say it smells of river because it smells bad, but the truth is that a river does not have to smell bad," he reflects. "Many will imagine a river [and think of] nature, fish, and here smells like a river [means] like egg . . . like poop, everything you can imagine. So, it's not normal, what we are experiencing here in El Salto is not normal."[3]

Juan Carlos also grew up in El Salto and, now in his early thirties, received his kidney transplant when he was 25. A change in the medicine provided by public health services recently put him at risk of rejecting the transplanted organ. His doctor advised him to buy another medicine himself if he didn't want to become his twentieth patient to lose his kidney. Living with kidney disease involves coping with medical bills and inadequate public health services, traveling to clinics in Guadalajara, and returning home to the polluted environment that many view as the cause of their disease.

As a kid, Juan Carlos used to ride his bike with friends on the bridge over the river between El Salto and Juanacatlán. "We didn't know anything, catching the foam, but the foam fell on our skin and left marks." Now he knows six other young people with kidney disease within a three-block radius of his home in downtown El Salto, where two other patients have already died. "There are really a lot of us, in a range of two or three blocks and we are six sick and two dead, that is not something normal."[4]

One of the objectives that Leap of Life (Un Salto de Vida) seeks in their community and advocacy work, and which they share with participants in their Tours of Terror, is breaking with the "dictatorship of normalcy." For them, that means breaking with a "notion of progress and development where those of us who are surplus must be sacrificed, where they turn us— along with our territory—into inputs, into labor or into a resource" (Agencia Subversiones 2017). The grassroots questioning of what is normal in El Salto and Juanacatlán started several decades ago. That questioning was what led to the closure of the Martyrs school and what sparked an important social environmental conflict in Jalisco. Not surprisingly, the first questions also arose in a school.

It was the absences of children from school that sparked some of the first actions calling for river cleanup, according to Rodrigo Saldaña. Saldaña was

Chronicle of a Struggle

president of the parents' association at a primary school in Juanacatlán, and the school principal informed him that the absences were due to "headaches, dizziness, vomiting, flu, stomach infections, hives, rashes, [and] eye infections."[5] This was in 2001, and it prompted Saldaña and other concerned people to begin discussing the issue at various community meetings: "'Hey, why are the children missing school so often?' Or, 'Why is there this smell?' Or, 'Why is the river so foul smelling?' And that's how we started to decide that we should do something." That something, as a first step, was to sign a letter in July 2002, together with the president of another parents' association, addressed to the then-president Vicente Fox (2000–2006). The letter called attention to the "social emergency" that existed due to "industrial pollution of the Lerma Santiago River," stressing that "the most dramatic aspect of this situation is the observed diseases." In this regard, they cited both gastrointestinal and respiratory tract infections, an increase in cancer in young people, and the high incidence of kidney failure, spontaneous abortions, and birth defects.[6]

The letter was sent by the Office of the Presidency to the Federal Bureau of Environmental Protection (PROFEPA, Procuraduría Federal de Protección al Ambiente), which accepted the case as a citizen complaint (*denuncia popular*). Thus began the litany of insufficient and dismissive government responses and attempts to manage citizen demands around the Santiago River. This government handling is a key contextual element of this research, as these responses have not emanated from recognition of the seriousness of the problem but rather represent an effort to refute the concerns of residents regarding both the health effects of living in a contaminated environment and the severity of the pollution itself. As I will narrate in this chapter, the tenor of the response has shifted over time from outright denial of the problem to minimization of its gravity, with the constant delineation of jurisdictions and powers by different ministries and agencies seeking to offload responsibility. In this sense, environmental authorities characterize the situation as a health issue, while public health authorities define it as an environmental problem; meanwhile, the environmental health conditions along the river continue to worsen. Authorities have been particularly insistent in downplaying the issue of industrial pollution and proclaiming the good environmental performance of the factories operating here. In more recent years, it has not been possible to deny the problem entirely—although the health authorities have insisted on doing just that—nonetheless, elected officials and bureaucrats maintain that the problem is under control and will be resolved through proposed government programs and infrastructure investment.

This chapter explores the public face of the conflict, including the discursive strategies of authorities and industry, and several instances of "manufacturing uncertainty" to undercut evidence of toxic pollution and related health impacts (Michaels and Monforton 2005; Conde 2014). While David Michaels and Celeste Monforton (2005) coined the term "manufacturing uncertainty" to describe the actions of diverse industries to generate uncertainty regarding scientific evidence supporting stricter environmental or public health regulations, the instances I will highlight involve government agencies either questioning the validity of studies that demonstrate significant levels of toxic pollution or developing studies ad hoc to subvert evidence of the health effects of pollution. In other cases, state agencies attempted to prevent studies from coming to light.

Such action by state actors also highlights the question of the role of the state in social environmental conflicts. Addressing conflicts related to water quality in Mexico, Alejandro Von Bertrab and Javier Matus Pacheco (2010) discuss conflict resolution and present what I consider a naïve understanding of how divergent interests can be reconciled. "Within a democratic regime," they affirm, "the authority (executive, legislative and judicial) must assume its role as the supreme conciliator of the needs and interests of the social groups it governs," while avoiding becoming a "party" to those conflicts (275). Without considering that not infrequently the authority *is* party to the conflict, as promoter of the projects that give rise to conflicts, they argue that the negotiation "depends on the will of the authority to assume a truly neutral position with respect to the parties involved" (277). The weakness of this interpretation lies, in my opinion, in its erroneous conception of the role of states in what are denominated "democratic" regimes.

This vision shares similarities with that of the National Water Commission (CONAGUA, Comisión Nacional del Agua) articulated in the 2014–2018 National Water Program, which states that conflicts are due to the increase in demand and competition between "users" (2014a, 28). This competition, which would surely be subject to negotiation, is part of the depoliticized vision presented by CONAGUA, in which conflicts are naturalized by linking them to population growth. A contrasting vision of socio-environmental conflicts is held by María Fernanda Paz, who has

Chronicle of a Struggle

made significant efforts to understand the causes and logics of this type of conflict in Mexico (2012, 2014).

Paz registered 133 conflicts in 2014, which appeared in the national press or were presented before the National Assembly of Environmentally Affected People. When environmental impact or deterioration is the cause of the conflicts, Paz maintains, "there is no negotiation possible," since what is at stake is the existence as such of the affected groups (2014, 17). This vision directly contradicts both the focus on reconciliation and the official version from CONAGUA that represents conflicts as disputes over a contested resource. In the words of Paz, "These are not conflicts of interest or [cases of] competition for access to a good or resource. What is in dispute in socio-environmental conflicts of this nature are the material (ecological), social and cultural conditions that make life possible outside the hegemonic project" (17). The most dramatic of these conflicts, according to Paz, are those triggered by the pollution of surface and underground waters, given the damage to health that they entail (19). What unites these cases, among them the struggle for the Santiago, is the presence of industry, as well as a state that acts as an "accomplice of the abuses" and is reluctant to accept the allegations of contamination (23). In general, this type of conflict coincides with what Joan Martínez-Alier calls the "environmentalism of the poor," which refers to movements "related to survival" (2008, 14).

With conflicts over pollution, Martínez-Alier highlights that they should be seen as protests of a "structural" nature and not NIMBY (not in my backyard)–type phenomena. This structural nature is related to the fact that, from the point of view of social metabolism, it is clear that the generation of "externalities," rather than instances of market or government failures, is of an "inevitable systemic nature," due to the increasing flows of materials and energy through the economy, which necessarily generate waste (2008, 19, 12). They are also protests or movements that are part of the international movements for environmental justice (Schlosberg 2007; Carruthers 2008).

In the studies of socio-environmental conflicts, then, there tends to be a rejection of the conception of the state as a neutral mediator of conflicts and rather an identification of it either as a protagonist of conflicts (when the projects are promoted directly by the state) or as an adjunct to the private interests that spearhead the projects or processes of environmental deterioration. As Victor Toledo and colleagues summarize well, "Each environmental conflict is a battle between private or business interests and the wellbeing of citizens . . . and in these battles the state almost always takes the side of the former in the name of 'progress,' 'modernization,' and 'development'" (2015, 144–145).

Along the shores of the Santiago River, in the face of the denials and inaction of state actors, grassroots organizations have deployed a diversity of creative strategies and developed an array of alliances with researchers and nongovernmental organizations (NGOs) both nationally and internationally. Those strategies have also evolved over time, with some of the first organizations formed, such as the Institute of Integrated Values and Environmental Development (Instituto VIDA, Instituto de Valores Integrales y Desarrollo Ambiental) and the Citizen's Environmental Defense Committee, becoming less active, while Leap of Life has become the key local voice in denouncing threats to the community, from the neighboring garbage dump to uncontrolled urbanization and, at the heart of the problem, the failures to protect and restore the Santiago River. This chapter will bring to light some of those strategies, while particularly highlighting the role of government agencies and industry actors in downplaying industrial pollution and the severity of the environmental crisis in El Salto and Juanacatlán.

2.1 The Negation Begins

That first complaint by Juanacatlán residents was combined with another from 2001, presented by an environmentalist from Guadalajara, Jaime Eloy Ruiz. This complaint denounced the deterioration of the river as well as of Lake Chapala—at that point in the midst of one of its most serious crises in the last century due to the decreased volume in Mexico's largest natural lake, which had ebbed to just 15 percent of its capacity at the time of the complaint (CEC 2012, 95). PROFEPA's resolution of these complaints is worth noting. PROFEPA requested reports from the Lerma-Santiago-Pacific Regional Office[7] of CONAGUA. In two letters, Raúl Antonio Iglesias Benítez,[8] who headed the regional office for more than ten years, summarized the situation of the Santiago River and the actions of CONAGUA.

The first letter described the water quality monitoring undertaken by CONAGUA, through its National Monitoring Network, and indicated in relation to the degradation of Chapala and the Lerma and Santiago Rivers that "it is mainly due to the pollution generated by companies, towns and cities, farmlands, and livestock production." In the case of these bodies of water, Iglesias also explained that the anaerobic degradation of organic matter "generates a gas that is very irritating and can become highly toxic, that is, hydrogen sulfide," which has the characteristic odor of rotten eggs.[9]

The second letter from CONAGUA indicated that according to the "rigorous" water quality index applied to the Santiago River in the vicinity of El Salto, the "results demonstrate that it is *Highly Contaminated,*' and that it is only suitable for restricted industrial and agricultural uses."[10] At the same time, Iglesias declared that the government of Jalisco was implementing a sanitation program for the El Ahogado Subbasin, which would improve water quality in the river. Following these reports, which in themselves did not deny the problem, the director of the complaints area at PROFEPA informed Saldaña that the complaint had been deemed closed given "the non-existence of infringements of environmental regulations."[11] "A neophyte," Saldaña responded to PROFEPA, could "visually verify" the pollution of the river. In a letter full of astonishment and indignation, Saldaña affirmed, "I repeat, it is not credible that any regulations are complied with when daily we see a dead river and waterfall, which emit unbearable odors."[12] Not only was it not credible, but it was also not even in line with the information provided by CONAGUA. Nevertheless, when PROFEPA was confronted with these first citizen complaints, denial of the problem was evidently seen as an option.

Also in 2003, Saldaña and other Juanacatlán residents took the issue of the Santiago River to the international arena, joining the Guadalajara-based Environmental Law Institute (IDEA, Instituto de Derecho Ambiental) and other NGOs and activists in signing a citizen petition presented to the Commission for Environmental Cooperation of North America (CEC). The CEC was created as a result of the environmental agreement signed in parallel to the North American Free Trade Agreement (NAFTA), the North American Agreement on Environmental Cooperation. Articles 14 and 15 of the environmental agreement established procedures for the presentation of citizen petitions denouncing the nonapplication of the environmental legislation in any of the three countries of North America. In this case, IDEA and eight other organizations alleged a lack of effective application of Mexican environmental laws in the Lerma-Chapala-Santiago-Pacific Basin, focusing the petition on the deterioration of Lake Chapala, the Santiago River in Juanacatlán, and the proposed Arcediano Dam, the construction of which was planned on the same polluted Santiago River downstream of El Salto in the

Oblatos-Huentitán Canyon, north of the Guadalajara Metropolitan Area (GMA). I will return to this petition later, as it took ten years to reach the culmination of this process, with the publication of a so-called factual record.

In light of what has happened in the years since these first complaints, this strategy of presenting the situation to the authorities in hope of immediate action may seem naïve. When Martínez-Alier writes of the "environmentalism of the poor," he describes how "these struggles ... most often begin by addressing letters and petitions to persons of authority, in the state administration ... as if the mere knowledge of injustice would, by itself, bring remedy to it" (2002, 205–206). When this hope is not realized in practice, the struggles tend to move toward other forms of protest or "direct forms of confrontation," as well as appeals to "a wider national and international audience." NGOs also often play a key role in translating petitions into a language of "environmental, human and territorial rights," which facilitates linkages with international networks and organizations (205–206). In the case of the Santiago River, as we have seen, shortly after the first local denouncements, the petition was also taken to an international body. Even so, this hope of achieving improvements by presenting the case to the authorities has persisted, although as new local organizations have emerged, there have been those critical of the state whose strategies center on more autonomous forms of community work and organization.

Still in 2003, Instituto VIDA took its demands to the state governor, Francisco Ramírez Acuña (2001–2007), requesting a study of the pollution in Juanacatlán, and that the Ministry of Health carry out "an epidemiological study in the region so that we are made aware of the reason for the incidence of diseases such as cancer," birth defects, spontaneous abortions, and other ailments. Unfortunately, when this request was turned over to the Jalisco Ministry of Health (SSJ, Secretaría de Salud Jalisco), they responded by merely setting out possible actions to control mosquitos near the river, making no mention of the requested study. Certainly, the chemical control of mosquitoes is much simpler than an epidemiological study of the effects of multiple sources of pollution on health. This trend, of seeking simple solutions and evading complexities, was also seen in the first intervention of the Jalisco State Human Rights Commission (CEDHJ, Comisión Estatal de Derechos Humanos Jalisco).

"Lethal, the Waters of the Santiago River" was the headline of an article in the Guadalajara newspaper *El Occidental* in March 2003, calling attention to

Chronicle of a Struggle

the rising rate of mortality from cancer in El Salto and Juanacatlán. This and other press reports led the CEDHJ to commence an ex officio investigation. Strangely, the CEDHJ focused its investigation on the wastewater treatment plants (WWTPs) in the towns of El Salto and Juanacatlán—quite minor points among the plethora of pollution sources upstream. When its investigators' site visits found the treatment plants in operation, this convinced them that "they are not the cause of environmental pollution in the area." In addition, after sending petitions for information to diverse government agencies, they concluded that "the commitment and willingness of the authorities to provide a solution to the problem caused by the contamination of the waters of the Santiago and Zula rivers is clear."[13] As the CEDHJ only has powers to scrutinize the acts and omissions of state and municipal authorities, they conveniently pointed out that the agency responsible for national waters was CONAGUA—whose actions the CEDHJ is not empowered to examine.

While the CEDHJ closed its investigation, the press coverage that gave voice to the concerns of riverside residents continued to multiply. This was also the period when members of the affected communities and their allies began to generate studies to confront the official negation of the problem. Instituto VIDA members had river water tested by a certified laboratory in Guadalajara and provided support for two studies on the health impacts of exposure to hydrogen sulfide—the source of the intense odor of rotten egg that invades the towns. One of these studies was undertaken by an Instituto VIDA member and medical doctor, originally from Juanacatlán, who focused on exposure symptoms in children (Parra 2006), and the other by a geographer from the Jalisco Center for Research and Assistance in Technology and Design (Centro de Investigación y Asistencia en Tecnología y Diseño del Estado de Jalisco) who looked at the presence of hydrogen sulfide near the waterfall (Gallardo 2005).

At the same time, Instituto VIDA began to connect with the movement against the Arcediano Dam, which had become part of the Mexican Movement of Dam-Affected People and in Defense of Rivers (MAPDER, Movimiento Mexicano de Afectados por las Presas y en Defensa de los Ríos). Instituto VIDA members participated in the Second Encounter of MAPDER, held in the Santiago River Canyon, at the site of the displaced community of Puente de Arcediano, where only the temple and the house of Guadalupe Lara, the sole inhabitant who resisted dam construction, remained (Lara and McCulligh 2014). The so-called Arcediano Declaration called for the "intervention of the [World Health Organization] to investigate the cases of leukemia caused by contamination of the El Ahogado basin in the communities of Juanacatlán, El Salto and Cajititlán" (MAPDER 2005). In this period, the Mexican Institute for Community Development (IMDEC, Instituto Mexicano para el Desarrollo Comunitario) promised to collaborate with Instituto VIDA in shooting a documentary video and preparing a report to document the violations of the rights to health and a healthy environment (McCulligh et al. 2007).

Two new grassroots organizations concerned with river cleanup were founded in El Salto in 2006, Leap of Life and the Citizen Committee for Environmental Defense (CCDA, Comité Ciudadano de Defensa Ambiental). These organizations have been more critical of the authorities and reluctant to participate in government-convened spaces for dialogue, and they have spearheaded protest actions more frequently than Instituto VIDA.

Debates on water raged in Mexico in 2006, when Mexico City hosted the fourth World Water Forum. Criticized as a forum for the promotion of water privatization policies, a series of alternative events were convened by various national and international networks. One of those events was a hearing of the Latin American Water Tribunal (TLA, Tribunal Latinoamericano del Agua), an ethical tribunal that seeks to contribute to the solution of water conflicts. IDEA, IMDEC, Instituto VIDA, and other organizations presented the case of the Lerma-Chapala-Santiago Basin before the TLA, focusing on the degradation of Lake Chapala, the risks of the Arcediano Dam, and the river pollution in El Salto and Juanacatlán. The verdict, issued by a jury of water and justice experts, was more forceful regarding the case of the Arcediano Dam. On the contamination of the Santiago, the recommendations were generic, calling for the enforcement of environmental regulations and compensation for affected people and communities (TLA 2006). Even so, the situation in Juanacatlán made an impact on TLA president Javier Bogantes, who visited the community a few weeks before the hearing in 2006. This was largely the motivation for holding a further TLA hearing in Guadalajara in October 2007.

The report produced through the collaboration between Instituto VIDA and IMDEC, *Martyrs of the Santiago River: Report on Violations of the Right to Health and a Healthy Environment in Juanacatlán and El Salto, Jalisco, Mexico*, was presented in April 2007 in the public square in Juanacatlán (McCulligh et al. 2007). As one of the authors, I addressed the five hundred people

Chronicle of a Struggle

gathered on that occasion and felt how cold and even irrelevant the data on types and qualities of effluents discharged into the river sounded in light of the heartbreaking testimonies of men, women, and children who shared their experiences living in a poisoned environment. The report was disseminated quite widely to municipal, state, and federal authorities, to NGOs, and to UN offices in Mexico (UNICEF, the Pan American Health Organization, and the Office of the High Commissioner for Human Rights). The *Martyrs* report was also presented as the basis of a complaint before the CEDHJ that would result, almost two years later, in the so-called macrorecommendation of the Santiago River (CEDHJ 2009). In parallel, in late April 2007, two thousand people rallied in Juanacatlán petitioning for the declaration of a public health emergency (*Informador* 2007).

Shortly after the complaint process was initiated with the CEDHJ, members of Leap of Life filed a complaint with the National Human Rights Commission (CNDH, Comisión Nacional de los Derechos Humanos). This was significant because the CNDH could evaluate the actions of the federal authorities, in particular CONAGUA. In a setback, in November 2008 that complaint was closed without leading to a recommendation, after having been deemed "without substance." CNDH officials reached this implausible conclusion since, according to one official, "the construction of the macro-wastewater treatment plant El Ahogado is about to take place," and this, according to "the National Water Commission and the State Water Commission, will provide a complete solution for the pollution problem" (Torres 2008). This confidence in the impact of a single treatment plant that would treat only municipal wastewater, although it reflects a skewed view of reality, was expressed on numerous occasions.

The TLA jury did not find the case "without substance" when it analyzed the situation in El Salto and Juanacatlán in October 2007 at the public hearing in Guadalajara. Despite the local venue, it was not surprising when environmental and water authorities ignored the invitation to appear. Only representatives of the SSJ and the federal Commission for Protection against Sanitary Risks (COFEPRIS, Comisión Federal para la Protección contra Riesgos Sanitarios) attended the hearings. In her testimony, the commissioner for evidence and risk management at COFEPRIS, Rocío Alatorre, stated that they had carried out an initial review of mortality data for this area without being able to reach definitive conclusions. Alatorre indicated that a further phase of study was required and that "the [federal] Ministry of Health is aware of and concerned with the case and, if [a cause-effect relationship] is demonstrated, [the ministry] has sufficient legal powers to take action" (Pérez 2007).

In the end, the TLA (2007, 3) verdict called for the declaration of a health emergency in the area and recommended that authorities undertake an "interdisciplinary, independent and participatory epidemiological study, to determine and analyze the specific damage to the health of the inhabitants of El Salto and Juanacatlán" attributable to the pollution of the Santiago. Moreover, the TLA called for "constant monitoring in the main industrial corridors" in the basin, and for results of this monitoring to be made public (4). The latter has not happened, nor has a serious epidemiological study been carried out. Shortly after the TLA verdict, the state minister of health, Alfonso Gutiérrez, ruled out undertaking such a study: "We have not felt the need to do it [the study] because in the last five years there has not been a significant variation in terms of deaths from cancer," he asserted (Atilano and Hernández 2007). This was not the same conclusion reached by COFE-PRIS officials, as will be seen later.

2.2 A Tragedy That Sparks Protest

Even a neophyte could perceive the pollution of the river, Rodrigo Saldaña told PROFEPA in 2003. The TLA jurors also considered it "evident" when they visited the waterfall before judging the case (Palomero 2007). In the words of Enrique Enciso of Leap of Life, "Even a five-year-old child knows the quality of depredation or devastation of our territory . . . even a six-year-old child knows that this river is dead" (cited in McCulligh et al. 2012, 170). This reality of pollution evidently harms the health of people who are daily exposed. However, there are many difficulties in establishing a cause-effect relationship between the presence of certain pollutants and the manifestation of specific diseases in the population (Auyero and Swistun 2009; Lora-Wainwright 2021). In El Salto and Juanacatlán, the sources of contamination are also diverse: untreated municipal wastewater flows in canals and the river; factories of a variety of industrial sectors emit pollutants into the air, water, and soil; and the Los Laureles landfill generates leachates and gases. Studies have also found groundwater contamination, which may affect water supplied to the population (McCulligh et al. 2020). A 2016 World Health Organization (WHO) study estimates that 23 percent of deaths globally and 22 percent of the disease burden are attributable to environmental risk factors, including pollution (Prüss-Üstün et al. 2016). At the same time, a previous WHO report acknowledged that "in many cases, the causal pathway between environmental hazard and disease outcome is complex" (Prüss-Üstün and Corvalán 2006, 9). Not being able to establish the causal pathway, however, does not imply that there is no impact on health.

The difficulty of substantiating the health impacts of environmental pollutants is addressed in a revealing study by historians Gerald Markowitz and David Rosner (2013). Their book narrating the toxic consequences of lead emissions and the production of polyvinyl chloride in the United States presents a detailed history of industry actors concealing and misrepresenting information related to the toxicity of these substances. Markowitz and Rosner question traditional ways of evaluating both the impacts of toxic substances and their effects on human health. In this regard, they question the ability of epidemiology to account for the diverse impacts on human health of industrial pollution after its dispersion in a complex and dynamic environment. They demonstrate the limitations of epidemiology with cases in the state of Louisiana, where the studies requested by the communities affected by the chemical industry in the end weakened their demands when it was not possible to statistically verify the relationship between pollution and the diseases encountered.

Acknowledging the limits of traditional tools to assess these hazards, Markowitz and Rosner conclude that "science is often unable to give us the knowledge we need," and call for transparency and access to information about industrial activities (2013, 305). By tracing the history of epidemiology and analyzing it in light of the case of cancer deaths linked to chemical contamination in the town of Toms River, New Jersey, Dan Fagin reaches a similar conclusion: "For all its advances in mathematical technique, the rise of statistical epidemiology had the unintended effect of making it harder than ever to investigate patterns of cancer cases in places like Toms River" (2014, chap. 4). This is because the methods require large numbers of cases to demonstrate the "normal" distribution and hence be able to identify an abnormal cluster.

In El Salto in late January 2008, a tragic death crystallized and evidenced the impact of pollution as no study has done to date. Eight-year-old Miguel Ángel López Rocha fell into the waters of the El Ahogado Canal near its confluence with the Santiago, just two blocks from his home in the social interest housing development La Azucena. When he became seriously ill, his mother took him to the hospital, where he fell into a coma and died nineteen days later, on February 13. I recall sitting in a meeting in El Salto, with members of various local organizations and personnel from the municipality's Ecology Department, when a person came to inform us that a child had fallen into the river, accidentally swallowing some water, and was in the hospital in Guadalajara.

I was also among the curious to show up in La Azucena at the home of Miguel Ángel to speak with his mother and understand what had happened. His mother, María del Carmen Rocha, told me that they had been unaware of the neighborhood's proximity to the river when they purchased their house. "If they had told us, we wouldn't have come here," she said.[14] *Where what you love most lives,* read the advertisements posted at that time along the streets of La Azucena, which also touted an "Atmosphere of Tranquility." This was the publicity for a deplorably constructed social interest housing development located in a flood zone. It is one of the many new developments built far from consolidated urban areas and without basic services, which Luis Felipe Cabrales (2010, 82) has called "macro-developments of mini-houses" or "residential underdevelopment," promoted since 2004, during the presidency of Vicente Fox, and generating a real estate boom around many Mexican cities, including the GMA. "Money is what matters to them, they don't care who dies," said María del Carmen days after the death of her son. "Unfortunately, until this happened, people didn't realize that we are all in danger," she also observed.

While Miguel Ángel was still in a coma at the Hospital General de Occidente, the results of testing for arsenic levels in urine were released, showing a concentration of 51 micrograms per liter, when the normal range is between 5 and 12 micrograms per liter, according to toxicologist Luz María Cueto (Robles 2008). Before this became known, Alfonso Gutiérrez, minister of health in Jalisco, had tried to claim that the boy was in a coma as a result of a physical blow, while a hospital official hinted that it was due to opium consumption. After his death, rumors arose of domestic violence or that the child had been poisoned by his own mother. The cause of death was the subject of such rumors and debate for one simple reason: it pointed the finger of blame at the industrial sector. For that reason, this was one of the few occasions when industry representatives spoke out to defend their sector.

That defense was memorable but unfortunate. First, there were statements from the vice president of the Association of Industrialists of El Salto (AISAC, Asociación de Industriales de El Salto), Rubén Reséndiz, also the manager at the Honda plant. Reséndiz did not deny that there were companies that did not comply with environmental regulations or that even lacked treatment plants. In fact, he said that only half of the 150 companies settled in El Salto had a WWTP. However, he shifted any blame firmly to the government authorities. In response to data presented to him of AISAC companies whose effluents failed to comply with regulations, Reséndiz declared, "They have to be investigated, they have to be checked, I repeat, the authorities have the information, if the companies are not complying, it is their responsibility." On the other hand, in the absence of actions against the companies, he asserted, "if there have been no punitive actions by the authorities against the companies, it means that things are being done well" (cited in Estrada 2008). The authority thus served to take the blame for any noncompliance, while government inaction was proffered as evidence of the "innocence" of industry actors.

At the same time, Reséndiz complained about the demonization of companies and laid the blame for pollution on clandestine workshops and effluents discharged into the Lerma River from its upper reaches in the State of Mexico (Estrada 2008). On behalf of CONAGUA, the director of the basin agency, Iglesias Benítez, emphasized that municipal wastewater was the most significant source of pollution and assured that the industries did not seriously breach regulations. "Currently they comply with what is indicated for a type A water body, according to our monitoring," he said, referring to the least stringent classification for discharges in the relevant standard, the NOM-001-SEMARNAT-1996 (NOM-001). At most, they had "minimal" violations, being 10 percent above the stipulated limits, Iglesias affirmed (cited in del Castillo 2008). This version of events is at odds with the results of several government-funded studies, as I will detail later.

The truly unfortunate statement from industry came from the coordinator of the Council of Industrial Chambers of Jalisco (Consejo de Cámaras Industriales de Jalisco), Javier Gutiérrez Treviño. "No one gets poisoned there," he told the media. "If I swallow a mouthful of water, nothing will happen. I would do it, and what will happen, whenever you want, I'll go and nothing will happen. This [situation] has existed for 40 years" (cited in Romero 2008). The invitations to accompany this industry leader to take his mouthful of water from the Santiago River did not take long to arrive. The fiercest response to his statements came from the respected forensic doctor Mario Rivas Souza, who had performed the autopsy on the child. His reaction was published in the press: "Bullshit . . . total bullshit. I've never heard such bullshit as this, what does this bastard know about it?" Miguel Ángel's death was due to the water he ingested from the canal: "Very polluted water entered his lungs, stomach and that was the cause of death," Rivas made clear (cited in Ferrer 2008).

The original toxicological diagnosis was confirmed in March 2010 in a recommendation on this case from the CNDH. Therein, they concluded that Miguel Ángel "presented acute arsenic poisoning derived from the serious state of contamination of the Santiago River" (CNDH 2010, 17). Even at the time, despite the controversy surrounding this death, the outrage over the condition of the river among the population and the media increased pressure on environmental and health authorities to respond, open up to citizen participation, and develop feasible action plans to begin a recovery process for the Santiago River.

2.3 Early Studies of Industrial Effluents

Given the debates during the period just described, it is worth reviewing the data that then existed on industrial effluents released into the Santiago River. Information on the quality of industrial discharges in the country is scarce, and the situation in the case of the Santiago Basin is not different. However, while community groups in El Salto and Juanacatlán clamored for river cleanup, downstream plans were proceeding to build the Arcediano Dam on the same river. Promoters sought dam construction from 2001 until the state government canceled plans in 2009. Parallel to the protests in El Salto, then, organizations in Guadalajara grouped in the Jalisco chapter of MAPDER insisted on the nonviability of Arcediano, given the poor quality of the water that it would capture to supply around 4 million people in the GMA. In support of the dam project, the State Water and Sanitation Commission (CEAS, Comisión Estatal de Agua y Saneamiento)[15] contracted various studies on the quality of the water in the Santiago River and its tributary, the Verde River. Some of these studies included analyses of discharges to the river.

The first of these studies, carried out in 2003, includes an Inventory of Discharges in Jalisco, recording 280 point source discharges from the industrial and service sectors, of which 265 were direct discharges to the Santiago River. In quantitative terms, the study estimated a flow of 227 liters per second of industrial effluents, of which 36.5 percent originated from chemical-pharmaceutical factories, 15 percent from food and beverage industries, 12.3 percent from the textile industry, 7.4 percent from paper industries, and 2.1 percent from tequila distilleries (AyMA Ingeniería y Consultoría 2003, 4-19). The same study also contemplated analyses of effluents from a hog farm and four factories: Celanese/Industrias Ocotlán, Nestlé, Cydsa Crysel, and Ciba, none of which complied with the parameters of the national discharge standard (NOM-001) (4-40). In fact, the authors calculated the pollutant load measured in terms of biodegradable organic matter (five-day biochemical oxygen demand) of these facilities, except Ciba, and concluded that, "excluding the [GMA], their load exceeds that of any other community in the study area"— and this was only for three factories and one hog farm (4-40).

In 2004, CEAS commissioned a second study from researchers at the University of Guadalajara. The study generated a stir when it was made public in 2005 after officials at CEAS initially refused to release it in response to a request for information. In what I consider an instance of "manufacturing uncertainty," the version finally made public was preceded by an opinion from CEAS questioning the reliability of the results. Although CEAS had commissioned the study, the institution was apparently not pleased with the outcome. Authorities from the University of Guadalajara defended their investigation and "categorically" rejected the disparagements of the commission (Ferrer 2005). The goal of this study was to determine the presence of heavy metals and organic compounds in sediments and waters of the Verde and Santiago Rivers. The results were not propitious for dam promoters, as they found "high levels" of chromium, lead, cobalt, and arsenic in the sediments at almost all the sites sampled along the Santiago River (CEAS and Universidad de Guadalajara–CUCEI 2004, 2-10). The points near the discharges of the Celanese and Ciba factories, as well as the waterfall in El Salto, stood out for their high levels of pollution. The report authors also alerted that diverse samples contained more than one hundred different organic compounds, and they called attention to the presence in the river of compounds that are "very hazardous to health," such as benzene, toluene, and xylene (2-50).

That same year, CEAS contracted out a report on the El Ahogado Subbasin that included an inventory of industries in El Salto. The report recommended the construction of a treatment plant specifically for industrial wastewater, concluding that, "due to the complexity of this basin, it is recommended that special surveillance be carried out of industrial discharges and, if possible, a sewer main be constructed for industrial wastewater, to receive treatment and then be pumped to the intake of the El Ahogado treatment plant in order to prevent industrial discharges from reaching the Santiago River" (CEAS and Gobierno del Estado de Jalisco 2005, 7). Construction had not yet begun on the El Ahogado WWTP, which was inaugurated in 2012, and which still only receives municipal wastewater—not industrial wastewater as here proposed.

Based on a survey of 145 industries in El Salto, the study reported that "only 31% (41) of the companies have a wastewater treatment plant (including the treatment plant at the El Salto Industrial Park)" (CEAS and Gobierno del Estado de Jalisco 2005, 51). Likewise, the report presented results from the analysis of twenty-six samples of industrial effluent. Nineteen of the samples exceeded limits for at least one parameter of the NOM-001. The effluents that did not comply include those from Hershey's, Empaques Modernos de Guadalajara, Mexichem, Quimikao, Industrias Gosa, Envases Universales, Crown Envases, and the Guadalajara Industrial Park.

In many cases, these effluents exceeded the stipulated limits multiple times, not by the 10 or 15 percentage points that CONAGUA claimed to encounter in their monitoring. In addition, some discharges that met the standard had high levels of chemical oxygen demand (COD), a nonregulated parameter that measures the presence of both biodegradable and non-biodegradable organic matter. For example, of the effluents in compliance with the NOM-001, Urrea Valves (2,819 mg/L) and ZF Sach's (800 mg/L) had relatively high COD values, in addition to Mexichem (2,133 mg/L), which also violated a parameter of the standard. As a reference, from 2008 to 2013 the Federal Duties Law (LFD, Ley Federal de Derechos), which sets the limits of pollutants in discharges for fiscal purposes, established a COD limit of 320 mg/L for type A water bodies and 100 mg/L for type C waters. Above these concentrations, the corresponding duties had to be paid (Article 278-B), ostensibly in accordance with the "polluter pays" principle.

A final Santiago River study, carried out by the consulting firm AyMA Ingeniería y Consultoría, included the analysis of effluents from seven tequila companies and ten factories from diverse industrial sectors, as well as leachate from the Los Laureles landfill, the largest in the GMA (CEAS and AyMA

Ingeniería y Consultoría 2006, 3-1). Even with the small number of samples taken, the study provided clear evidence of violations of the discharge standard. Six of the ten samples from manufacturing facilities did not comply with at least one parameter of the NOM-001: AGyDSA, Nestlé, Quimikao, Ciba-Huntsman (the plant was acquired by Huntsman in 2006), Celanese, and Santorini (PepsiCo). These noncompliant discharges include at least four from factories with treatment plants: Nestlé, Quimikao, Ciba-Huntsman, and Celanese (CEAS and AyMA Ingeniería y Consultoría 2006, 4-3). The two leachate samples from the Los Laureles landfill also exceeded pollution limits by a wide margin, as did the vinasse from five of the seven tequila companies.

The same study determined the acute toxicity of effluents using the organism *Vibrio fischeri* (Microtox). Measuring acute toxicity involves determining the percentage dilution of the original sample in which half of the population of organisms dies, and from there the toxicity units of the sample are calculated. A hog farm, GENPro, had high acute toxicity, while seven effluent samples, including those from Ciba-Huntsman and Quimikao, were found to have significant acute toxicity, and the Santorini, Sach's Boge (ZF), and AgyDSA discharges had moderate acute toxicity levels (CEAS and AyMA Ingeniería y Consultoría 2006, 4-21). In addition, the water sample from the El Ahogado Canal was reported to have significant acute toxicity. Thus, the studies that existed at this time presented a consistent pattern of noncompliance, at the same time as they provided clear evidence of nonregulated and toxic compounds in industrial effluents discharged into the river.

2.4 The Megamarch and Other Protest Actions

In the wake of the death of Miguel Ángel, local organizations spearheaded protest actions. Raúl Muñoz of the CCDA presented to the media a register of 477 people with illnesses linked to pollution, including kidney disease, residing in three communities near the El Ahogado Dam (Martín 2008). At that time, the CEDHJ (2008) also released a special report on the Santiago River, as an initial result of its response to the citizen complaint filed in 2007. This report was revealing, spelling out how the different government agencies attempted to evade responsibility, arguing their noncompetence in the matter or presenting the projected WWTPs as the ready solution, while failing to address the problem in its complexity (see also Tetreault et al. 2010).

Thus, in response to written petitions from the CEDHJ, the state Ministry of Environment for Sustainable Development of Jalisco (SEMADES, Secretaría de Medio Ambiente para el Desarrollo Sustentable) and PROFEPA argued they lacked the power to intervene; the Ministry of Environment and Natural Resources (SEMARNAT, Secretaría de Medio Ambiente y Recursos Naturales) simply reported the number of hazardous waste–generating companies in the area, while the State Water Commission (CEA, Comisión Estatal del Agua) and CONAGUA cited the future WWTPs of the GMA. In a further evasion of responsibility, the SSJ asserted that it had not studied the problem because "in its epidemiological and statistical information there was no evidence of impact on health due to environmental contamination," while the federal agency, COFEPRIS, indicated that it had requested resources from the SSJ to be able to carry out an epidemiological and environmental evaluation, but that the SSJ had not provided such funds. Furthermore, the SSJ stated that "environmental pollution" was not its jurisdiction (CEDHJ 2009, 3).

The most important action by civil society during this period when debate raged in the communities and in the media was a united effort of organizations including Leap of Life, the CCDA, and Instituto VIDA. In mid-April 2008, more than 2,500 people from El Salto and Juanacatlán closed the main avenues in downtown Guadalajara for several hours, while another contingent from downstream in Puente Grande closed the highway from Guadalajara to Zapotlanejo. The protesters' demands were summarized in a petition that was delivered to a representative of the state administration. Therein, community residents demanded the declaration of a state of environmental and health emergency,[16] advances in wastewater treatment, an inventory of industries with characterization of their discharges, and a public dialogue. On the topic of the Los Laureles landfill, protesters called for the concession holder's request to extend the operational life of the landfill to be refused.

Up to that point, the government response in the wake of Miguel Ángel's death had focused on reiterating that the WWTPs would provide a solution and on constructing a pipe to divert part of the flow of the El Ahogado Canal to enter the river downstream of the waterfall in El Salto. In fact, when first reported in the media, it was said that several kilometers of the Santiago River itself would be channeled, a clearly infeasible feat. It was later specified that the new infrastructure would divert part of the wastewater that flowed through the El Ahogado Canal in a 1.22-m-diameter tube—incapable of diverting even the minimum of wastewater generated in this subbasin in the dry season. The justification was that this would reduce the gases generated at the waterfall, particularly hydrogen sulfide, although it obviously did not represent a solution to the problem.

When government agencies responded to the communities' petitions, they again argued a lack of competence or presented very partial action plans. In this vein, where the demand was for the declaration of a state of environmental emergency, the strategy from SEMADES was to seek to decree a Region of Environmental Fragility (REF). This would be accomplished finally in 2010, and the REF has had meager tangible results to date. When it came to the Los Laureles landfill, SEMADES simply failed to heed community concerns.[17] One response worth highlighting is that of SEMARNAT's delegate in Jalisco, José de Jesús Álvarez, given its lack of basic logic. Álvarez maintained that "with the studies that currently exist, it cannot be assured that the integrity of one or several ecosystems may be or is at risk. Since the problem of municipal [and] industrial discharges most affects the health of people, not of ecosystems [sic]" (SEMARNAT, Delegación Jalisco 2008). According to this assessment, then, toxins released into the environment do not affect ecosystems, an extraordinary finding to say the least.

In turn, the CEA defended its "Comprehensive Sanitation Program," centered on two macrotreatment plants, and acceded to the request for dialogue on alternative solutions only under specific conditions. "We will only participate in a roundtable discussion with individuals who have technical arguments duly supported with sufficient and adequate information," stipulated Ricardo Robles on behalf of the CEA (CEA 2008). Thus, the CEA sought to impose technical criteria while invalidating public concerns that may have lacked a basis in laboratory or engineering studies. It is not surprising either that CONAGUA did not commit to take any action, referring only to its routine inspections program and the data available on discharge permits in its Public Water Rights Registry (Registro Público de Derechos de Agua).

Following the protest in Guadalajara, for a few months an institutional space was opened to the organizations of El Salto and Juanacatlán, inviting them to participate in a series of interinstitutional meetings. These meetings achieved very little, consisting of a roll call of the various agencies—those already mentioned, as well as the Office of Civil Protection, PROFEPA, the SSJ, the GMA's water service provider the Intermunicipal System of

Water and Sewerage Services (Sistema Intermunicipal de los Servicios de Agua Potable y Alcantarillado), the State Bureau of Environmental Protection (Procuraduría Estatal de Protección al Ambiente), and municipal authorities—reporting their progress (or lack thereof) on actions they had committed to undertake. It was not a forum for debate on strategies for river restoration, and the participation of organizations and residents was limited to commenting on the reports or criticizing the process. While these meetings proceeded, protest actions also continued.

Leap of Life was creative in drawing attention to the river, setting up toilets outside the governor's house, Casa Jalisco, in May 2008. This was also when they began distributing a series of decals that read, "Your shit pisses me off"; "In El Salto the pollution is killing us, do you prefer to die or fight?"; and "Government + industries + indifference = death in El Salto and Juanacatlán." Leap of Life also led the calls for closure of the Los Laureles landfill. After filing a complaint with SEMADES, they held a protest at the entrance to the garbage dump in July 2008. This garbage dump, located only kilometers from the municipal seat of El Salto, is run by private concession holder Caabsa Eagle and received 2,500 metric tons of solid waste per day from four municipalities of the GMA (Bernache 2012). The garbage dump generates highly polluting leachates that flow into the Santiago River and filter into the ground surrounding the dump. Gases and noxious odors also emanate from Los Laureles, often reaching El Salto. More than eleven years later, in late 2019, Leap of Life finally obtained the commitment from the current governor, Enrique Alfaro Ramírez (2018–), to commence the closure of Los Laureles (*Informador* 2019).

During this period, broader alliances with national and international networks were also strengthened. Leap of Life, for instance, began to collaborate with members of the Popular Analysis, Information and Training Center (Centro de Análisis Social, Información y Formación Popular), which supported them in 2008 to publish an educational map that explained the environmental and health problems in El Salto. Due to this alliance, Leap of Life was among the organizations that helped found the National Assembly of Environmentally Affected People (ANAA, Asamblea Nacional de Afectados Ambientales) in Mexico City at the end of August 2008. One of the first actions of the ANAA was a march of about two thousand members to the offices of CONAGUA and SEMARNAT to denounce the country's "environmental collapse" and demand attention to the struggles of

Chronicle of a Struggle

the communities participating in the assembly. In May 2009, Leap of Life coordinated the fourth assembly of the ANAA, held on the banks of the Santiago in El Salto, which brought together around two hundred assembly delegates from twelve states (Enciso and Torres 2008).

2.5 River Reclassification and Treatment Plants

Within the limited legal framework for the control of discharges to national water bodies, a positive change occurred in 2008. In November, the National Congress approved the reclassification of the Santiago River up to the site of the proposed Arcediano Dam from types A and B to type C—the classification in the NOM-001 with the most stringent parameters.[18] Despite the fact that the reclassification came into effect on January 1, 2009, a CEA official reported that companies would be granted a grace period to modify their treatment processes (Citlalli de Dios 2009). To understand the implications of this reclassification, it must be recalled that the NOM-001 contemplates three possible classifications for rivers, conceptualized as wastewater "receiving bodies": type A, with the laxest limits, is for rivers classified as for use in irrigation; type B is for urban public use; and type C is for the protection of aquatic life. For the twenty parameters regulated by this standard, the change in classification implies lower permitted levels of contaminants.

Despite the limited nature of this reclassification, it generated expectations of a significant improvement in river water quality, especially in the media. The daily *La Jornada Jalisco*, for example, described it as the application of a "severe regulation that would imply a drastic reduction in residual discharges from municipalities and companies that today dump them untreated" (Nuño 2008). From a more critical perspective, the reclassification was patently insufficient to generate real control of industrial effluents. This is due to the limitations of the standard, the lack of enforcement, and the absence of a regime of sanctions and incentives to motivate a reduction in pollutant releases and reorient production processes toward cleaner technologies. I will explore this topic in greater depth in chapter 3.

Eric Gutiérrez, an official for many years in the Water Quality Department at CONAGUA's central offices, indicated that the reclassification of this section of the Santiago River did not follow the normal administrative process. Gutiérrez explained that in order for a river to be reclassified in the LFD, the Ministry of Finance and Public Credit (Secretaría de Hacienda y

Crédito Público) requires that CONAGUA present a "declaration of classification" of the water body. Declarations of classification are contemplated in the National Waters Law (Article 87) and specify the water body's dilution and assimilation capacity, as well as the maximum pollutant limits in order to establish particular discharge conditions beyond national regulations. These declarations seek to address the problems of nonregulated pollutants or water bodies with limited assimilation capacity.

Gutiérrez reported that he approached the Ministry of Finance regarding the change in the Santiago's classification, but his request on behalf of CONAGUA was not successful:

> I went to the Ministry of Finance and presented them with the problem and everything and they said, "Where is the declaration?" . . . The issue is that the Ministry of Finance says, "There is also regulation. You have to present a declaration, which in turn has to have a cost-benefit analysis and you have to unequivocally demonstrate that the costs are less than the benefits," and that is sometimes very difficult to corroborate.[19]

There are few approved classification declarations in the country. The first was issued in 1996 for the Lerma River, followed by the Coatzacoalcos River in 2008; the San Juan del Río, Nado, and Aculco Rivers in 2009; and most recently the Atoyac and Xochiac Rivers in 2011. A preliminary draft of a classification declaration for the Santiago River was included as part of a 2011 Mexican Institute of Water Technology (IMTA, Instituto Mexicano de Tecnología del Agua) study, although it was never approved. In any case, in 2008 no declaration existed for the Santiago.

Then–general director of CONAGUA, José Luis Luege Tamargo, had promised the authorities in Jalisco to help obtain the river reclassification, according to Gutiérrez. In Jalisco, the CEA had another interest in achieving reclassification: it was a step toward the construction of the Arcediano Dam. For this reason, before the IMTA study, in 2007 the CEA contracted a report to the consulting company AyMA Ingeniería y Consultoría, with the aim of "updating the current classification as receiving bodies of the Santiago and Verde rivers, whose runoff will fill the Arcediano Dam" (CEAS and AyMA Ingeniería y Consultoría 2007, 1). However, as there was no officially published declaration, the Ministry of Finance denied CONAGUA's request. Normally, said Gutiérrez, the Ministry of Finance presents changes to the LFD for vote in a plenary session of Congress. In this case, however, the change was achieved only because a congressman from Jalisco, Joel Arellano, then president of the

Special Commission of the Lerma-Chapala-Santiago-Pacific Basin, pushed for its approval in Congress. Gutiérrez felt, when analyzing this process, that citizen pressure was a crucial factor in achieving the change.

Also in 2008, the tender process began that would lead to the construction of the El Ahogado WWTP, inaugurated in 2012. This was after a long history of delays in sanitation works in the GMA. Since 2003, there had been decrees from the State Congress authorizing the executive branch to contract a loan of up to MX$6.7 billion for the design and construction of treatment plants and water supply infrastructure for the GMA.[20] Later, in 2005, the state government contracted a MX$1.75 billion loan for sanitation works with Banobras and with resources from the Inter-American Development Bank.

The tender for the El Ahogado plant was awarded to Atlatec in association with Trident Water Services in November 2008. This plant would treat 2,250 liters per second of domestic wastewater generated in the southern part of the GMA, which is home to more than a million people (CEA 2012). The other 80 percent of the GMA's sewage was to be treated at the Agua Prieta WWTP, inaugurated in July 2014 by President Enrique Peña Nieto. However, because sewer mains were not completed, this plant does not capture the sewage from the basins to the east of the city, and in 2019 it treated only 3.9 cubic meters per second instead of the 8.5 cubic meters per second for which it was designed.[21] Both plants are managed under privatization schemes for water and sanitation services through twenty-year build, operate, and transfer contracts with subsidiaries of the Japanese group Mitsui (Atlatec and Servicios de Agua Trident) and, in the case of Agua Prieta, with the participation of the Mexican company ICA (Mitsui 2014).

2.6 From the Macrorecommendation to the REF

The long-awaited CEDHJ recommendation on the Santiago River was issued in January 2009. In it the CEDHJ affirmed that violations had taken place of the right to "a healthy and ecologically balanced environment, [the rights to] water, health, food, heritage, legality, social security, work and decent housing, and the rights of girls and boys" (2009, 132). It was called a "macrorecommendation" because it included no fewer than 148 recommendations and twenty-nine exhortations. Most of the recommendations were addressed to the state governor, as well as to the CEA, the Intermunicipal

System of Water and Sewerage Services, and fourteen municipalities of the Upper Santiago River Basin.

From the outset, the government of Jalisco rejected most of the recommendations that involved industry. Among the rebuffed recommendations were those addressing the control of polluting industrial discharges, urging the evaluation of their risk to the environment and human health, and calling for the closure of or imposition of sanctions on industries that do not adequately treat their waste, as well as the proposal that the state government "request the coordinated intervention of federal or municipal authorities" in case of the concurrence of powers (recommendations 7–10, 35, and 45) (239). On behalf of the state administration, Fernando Guzmán Pérez Peláez communicated to the CEDHJ the refusal to accept these points, alluding to the federal jurisdiction—specifically that of CONAGUA—over wastewater discharge, together with municipalities (SGG 2009, 2).

Nor did they accept recommendation 27, which urged state authorities to enter into interinstitutional agreements "in order to assume inspection powers" and thus garner a greater number of "environmental inspectors" (CEDHJ 2009, 242). This recommendation was not accepted because it was asserted that "the competent authorities carry out inspections according to their remit and budget" (SGG 2009, 5). Unfortunately, there is no evidence that a minimally adequate number of inspections are undertaken, as will be demonstrated in chapter 3. Until recently, the various state agencies have reported on their progress in complying with the CEDHJ recommendations, normally on the "anniversary" of the macrorecommendation, and have provided the percentage compliance they purported to have achieved. Thus, on the sixth anniversary in February 2015, the minister of the renamed Ministry of Environment and Territorial Development (SEMADET, Secretaría de Medio Ambiente y Desarrollo Territorial), Magdalena Ruíz, estimated that 32 percent of the accepted recommendations had been complied with, despite acknowledging that this had not improved the conditions of the river or the surrounding communities. As per the accustomed discourse, the responsibility also lay elsewhere: "It is the federal government that has the strongest impact in terms of [achieving] compliance to restore this river to health" (cited in Ríos 2015).

The state government accepted the recommendation to request that the federal Ministry of the Interior declare a state of emergency in the municipalities of El Salto and Juanacatlán. Nonetheless, the government of Jalisco, through SEMADES, instead promoted the creation of an REF in the El Ahogado Subbasin.[22] The agreement for the creation of the REF, published in September 2010, aimed to establish "environmental criteria" applicable to this region, including various criteria related to the control of industrial activities and the monitoring of water and air pollution.

More than a decade after its creation, the results of the REF are not encouraging. It has spurred the preparation of a basic assessment (CIATEJ 2012) and a handful of questionable projects, such as the creation of an "ecological park," which in reality consists of nothing more than a parking lot and lookout point to better appreciate the polluted waterfall in El Salto, inadvertently facilitating the Tours of Terror led by Leap of Life. A strange promotional video by SEMADES captured a fanciful vision of the projected park (SEMADES 2013). To operate the REF, SEMADES established a Joint Technical Committee (JTC), with representatives of municipalities, state agencies, and PROFEPA and CONAGUA. Six JTC meetings were held between March 2011 and February 2013, convened and chaired by SEMADES. The achievements were so few that by the last meeting of the JTC, agreements had been signed with only three of the ten municipalities with territory in the REF.

The reports of the SSJ are illustrative of the dynamic of these JTC meetings. On three occasions, the SSJ presented its actions, which consisted of monitoring the efficiency of drinking water chlorination in the municipalities of the REF. In July 2012, the SSJ also indicated that it had issued letters to mayors in the REF regarding the risks of contact with the treated wastewater from the recently inaugurated El Ahogado WWTP (SEMADES 2012). If the treated wastewater posed a risk, why were they not also concerned with the risks of contact with the waters of the El Ahogado Canal and Santiago River, which receive countless *untreated* discharges?

The SSJ has been insistent in denying any relationship between river pollution and health. A clear example of this and of attempts to manufacture uncertainty was a report produced by the SSJ in 2010 entitled *Perception of Morbidity and Mortality among the Inhabitants of El Salto and Juanacatlán Compared to That in Tonalá, Jalisco*. The empirical basis for the study report was a survey of 150 residents in El Salto and Juanacatlán, and of an equal number in the neighboring municipality of Tonalá. In two short paragraphs, the study concludes there are no differences in the mortality patterns among those surveyed and that "the perception of the population regarding the diseases they present is the same for the two locations studied" (SSJ 2010, 22). On this basis, Minister Alfonso Petersen Farah announced in February 2010, "We did not find any association between inhaling the vapors from the [Santiago] river and health risks for people living in the environment of the river" (Saavedra Ponce 2010). Criticism of this "perception study" and the conclusions derived therefrom was quickly forthcoming, particularly from the University Committee on Emerging and Reemerging Diseases of the University of Guadalajara, whose technical secretary, Víctor Manuel Ramírez Anguiano, declared that "this type of study cannot and should not be used as evidence, or even as a reference to define the damage to health caused by exposure to the river of the inhabitants of El Salto and Juanacatlán" (*Informador* 2010). The SSJ, nonetheless, sought to present its perception survey as a serious study of health effects.

Héctor Castañeda, director of watersheds and sustainability (2008–2013), represented the CEA on the JTC. From his point of view, "because of how the REF was created, it had a much more citizen flavor . . . and later it shifted more towards the government side and I think that was a bad decision."[23] Castañeda compares the REF process with a related interinstitutional collaboration to mitigate flood risks in the El Ahogado Subbasin. In that case, in contrast to the REF, the objectives were achieved. "What I conclude is," Castañeda stated, "if there exists the will to get things done, sometimes the will works better than having decrees." In the case of the REF, we have a decree but not the political will.

With the change of state administration in March 2013, when Aristóteles Sandoval of the Institutional Revolutionary Party became governor, the renamed SEMADET convened two strategic planning workshops for the REF, bringing together officials from municipalities and state and federal agencies, as well as members of IMDEC, Instituto VIDA, and Leap of Life and representatives of AISAC. While the workshops produced an action plan covering about seventy points, the subsequent follow-up or implementation was basically nonexistent. More than ten years after the creation of the REF, my conclusion is that it was a strategy seeking to tamp down social protest more than to actually address the environmental and health problems in the El Ahogado Subbasin: an elaborate but ultimately empty institutional simulation.

2.7 Toxic Rivers and Environmental Devastation

Leaving aside the institutional strategies, local actors gained a new ally in 2012. Greenpeace Mexico made a splash with its campaign denouncing the issue of toxic pollution of Mexican rivers and the Santiago River in particular. On World Water Day, March 22, 2012, Greenpeace Mexico launched its Toxic Rivers campaign in El Salto. Early in the morning, swathed in protective suits and wearing gas masks, volunteers went out on the river in inflatable kayaks to pose among the mounds of foam at the base of the waterfall. The images of that action were memorable (figure 2.1). The message was also clear: "Industrial discharges destroy the country's fresh water," read the information sheet Greenpeace distributed, emphasizing that water legislation in Mexico was permissive and not enforced (Greenpeace Mexico 2012b).

Figure 2.1
Launch of the Greenpeace Mexico Toxic Rivers campaign on the Santiago River, March 2012.
Source: © Greenpeace / Iván Castaneira.

This action took place just days after the inauguration of the El Ahogado WWTP in mid-March 2012. The hyperbole surrounding the potential impact of this WWTP was memorable. For example, the director of CONAGUA, Luege Tamargo, indicated that this plant would "guarantee zero polluting discharges to the Santiago River" and thus would also "satisfy a long-time demand of the inhabitants of this region: comprehensive cleanup of the Atemajac and El Ahogado basins." Raúl Antonio Iglesias, director of the Lerma-Santiago-Pacific Basin Agency, avowed that due to the WWTP, in the Santiago River "there will be no odors or presence of harmful fauna, the appearance will change overnight" (Ferrer 2012). Needless to say, one WWTP could not be—and has not been—capable of bringing about the restoration of this river.

In the summer of 2012, Greenpeace, Leap of Life, and IMDEC held a press conference to make public the study carried out by IMTA in 2011, which remains the most comprehensive study undertaken of the conditions in the Upper Santiago River Basin. Obtaining the study was not easy. After an initial refusal from IMTA, Greenpeace activists filed an appeal with the Federal Institute for Access to Information and Data Protection (IFAI, Instituto Federal de Acceso a la Información y Protección de Datos). IMTA had argued that the study was the property of the CEA, as the agency that paid for the study. In its response, IMTA also maintained that the information should be reserved as an "industrial secret," alleging that if that information were provided to

> one or more of the private entities that are located in the geographical region of the aforementioned river in Jalisco this would in itself constitute a competitive advantage over third parties, by virtue of the fact that they would be in a position to know both their own polluting compounds, as well as those of the rest of their competitors, and on the other hand, this information would allow them to report other parties and at the same time correct or modify the pollutants that other parties were releasing. (IFAI 2012, 16)

This fallacious argument was not only rejected by the IFAI, but the IFAI argued in its resolution of the appeal that if the pollution of the river were made known, "the private entities of the region could correct or modify the pollutants they were releasing, which would lead to benefits for the community as well as a healthy environment" (IFAI 2012, 53). At the press conference in Guadalajara, Gustavo Ampugnani, campaign director at Greenpeace Mexico, highlighted the overwhelming evidence of pollution

Chronicle of a Struggle

from industrial sources in this study and the need for transparency on the issue of the toxic pollution of the country's rivers.

Also in 2012, Greenpeace Mexico, together with Leap of Life and the Union of Scientists Committed with Society (Unión de Científicos Comprometidos con la Sociedad), completed an evaluation of environmental health risks for the population living in the vicinity of the Santiago River and its main tributaries. The report authors, members of the union, sought answers to some of the unresolved questions in this case: "Is there a risk from exposure to chemical substances in the area? What is known about this risk? And who are the most vulnerable people? . . . What chemical substances are present in the river as a consequence of industrial discharges?" (Arellano-Aguilar et al. 2012, 3). To answer these questions, they analyzed several years of water quality and mortality data for the municipalities bordering the river from Ocotlán to El Salto. For the period from 2007 to 2010, they found increases in mortality rates in Juanacatlán and El Salto due to various causes, including kidney failure and hypertensive kidney disease. They also identified rates above the state average for malignant digestive system tumors, mortality from malformations, and slight deviations for lymphoid leukemia and breast cancer. The report concludes that it is "plausible that the incidence of lethal diseases such as those we identified in this study is due to the presence of pollutants in the river" (18). Noting that the contamination of a river by volatile organic compounds, heavy metals, and other pollutants can affect a population that lives within five kilometers of the body of water, and that there is greater risk within the first kilometer, they calculated that between Ocotlán and El Salto 211,331 people live in the high-risk range (one kilometer) and 469,840 live in the region of moderate risk (up to five kilometers).

At this time, harassment of activists flared, affecting the founders of Leap of Life, the Enciso González family. Activist Sofía Enciso recounts how "the aggression against people here in the area worsened as soon as the IMTA [study] was uncovered."[24] In addition to being watched in her home, Sofía says, "we started to receive photographs of our nieces and nephews and other people." In 2012 members of her family, including her parents, Enrique Enciso and Graciela González, were forced to leave El Salto for a period and seek the assistance of human rights organizations. They were not able to return to El Salto until the end of 2013. In addition to being a highly polluted area, El Salto is also a municipality where drug trafficking and violence abound.

In 2013, almost ten years after the citizen petition was presented to the CEC, the CEC published the factual record on the case of the environmental deterioration of Lake Chapala, the pollution of the Santiago, and the risks posed by the Arcediano Dam. This was the culmination of the process, and its publication required the approval of the CEC Council, as not all factual records are made public. When reviewing the record, one can observe, on the one hand, that part of the response presented by the Mexican government to the petition is excluded "due to its confidential nature" (CEC 2012, 37). On the other hand, the usefulness of the factual record and of the entire procedure comes into question given that the authors refrain from evaluating the effectiveness of Mexican policies and, furthermore, that the "factual record does not present conclusions regarding the alleged lack of effective application of Mexico's environmental legislation," reiterating frequently that it only presents "factual information" (185). Thus, as an incomplete factual record (due to confidentiality) that reaches no conclusions, it is of little relevance. Regarding the trajectory of the citizen petition process, Diana Liverman and Silvina Vilas find that there is "little evidence that the resultant investigations have had a significant impact on environmental practices in North America" (2006, 336). Even more bluntly, James McCarthy considers this type of new environmental institution to be "undemocratic [and to] heavily favor market actors over civil society concerns" (2004, 330). A review of this factual record reinforces these critical assessments.

Given the inaction of government authorities, local groups have continued to seek the intervention of external actors, whether by petitioning international organizations such as the CEC or seeking the voice of ethical bodies. In this vein, the ANAA invited its members to participate in hearings of the Permanent Peoples' Tribunal (PPT). The PPT is an ethical tribunal founded in Bologna, Italy, in 1979 by Italian lawyer and senator Lelio Basso. The Mexican chapter of the PPT held seven thematic hearings starting in 2011, including one on "environmental devastation and peoples' rights." For this hearing, Leap of Life presented the case of the Santiago River in three of the prehearings. The communities and organizations that came together in the ANAA accused the Mexican state of committing an "intentional ecocide," focusing mainly on the consequences of neoliberal policies and the role of NAFTA in spurring environmental degradation.

The weakening of the state and the reduction of its regulatory functions, in parallel with the increase in corporate power, changed the role of the

Chronicle of a Struggle

state, the PPT judgment asserted, as it no longer plays the role of balancing interests or protecting vulnerable populations. Rather, the state is forced to function in a "more and more authoritarian" manner to create the conditions to attract foreign investment and to "work with corporations . . . in the development of laws and public policies" (PPT 2013, 11). The members of the jury found that water was at the center of most of the cases presented before the PPT and considered it "in a marked process of deterioration due to pollution and monopolization [of water rights] for industrial and, increasingly, for commercial purposes" (16). The judgment emphasized the evidence presented on the criminalization of environmental activists. Ultimately, it found that the Mexican state was legally responsible for the environmental devastation, based on its role as "guarantor of environmental impunity." Transnational companies were found accountable for transferring their environmental costs to communities in Mexico, and foreign states, in particular the United States and Canada, were called to account for allowing human rights violations by companies operating under their jurisdiction (22).

The second half of 2016 brought the Santiago River back into local headlines with worrisome news and implausible responses. In early September, members of the United Nations Working Group on Business and Human Rights heard the testimonies of activists and residents near the Salto de Juanacatlán waterfall. At the end of their ten-day visit to Mexico, they highlighted the case of the Santiago River in their statement, noting the "strong impact" that resulted from "the view of the river covered by foam and the smell of the strong gases and odours that dispersed as the water flowed over the El Salto waterfall" (OHCHR 2016). Faced with the "obvious exposure to hazardous industrial contamination," they emphasized not only the lack of corrective actions but also the fact that, "the burden of proof is on victims who are suffering health impacts" (OHCHR 2016). A few days after this visit, new evidence of these impacts came to light.

Researchers from the University of Guadalajara spoke to reporters about the results of their research on the genotoxic and cytotoxic effects (damage to DNA and cells) they attributed to exposure to heavy metals in four communities on the banks of Santiago (del Castillo 2016; Gómez-Meda et al. 2017). The study, led by Juan Armendáriz, found "nuclear abnormalities" in residents of El Salto and Juanacatlán, as well as downstream in Paso de Guadalupe. "We are finding the cause of what may be happening with exposure to heavy metals, genotoxic and cytotoxic damage, which can evolve to cancer, kidney failure, liver cancer," said Armendáriz (cited in del Castillo 2016). For the populations of El Salto and Juanacatlán, high levels were found for three of the seven nuclear abnormalities analyzed, with results described by Armendáriz as "conclusive."

This news elicited a response from AISAC and other industry representatives, who shifted the blame outside the state of Jalisco. The president of AISAC, Raúl Güitrón, complained that "we are pointed at directly, the industries of El Salto, but we are the last in the chain, the river is actually polluted from the State of Mexico, Guanajuato and Michoacán, the whole Lerma Santiago Basin" (Velasco 2016). Blaming upstream industries and agribusiness in the Lerma River Basin reflects a lack of knowledge or a misrepresentation of the hydraulic interventions that have fragmented the Lerma and Santiago Rivers. The Lerma River flows into Lake Chapala. Although the Santiago is the natural outlet of Chapala, there are a series of dams and pumping stations that control the water flows from Chapala to the Santiago. Thus, according to CONAGUA personnel, in the rainy season the Poncitlán Dam on the Santiago is closed so that the waters of the Zula River and the first section of the Santiago flow "back" toward Lake Chapala. In the dry season, water is pumped from Chapala to the Santiago, but that pumping is limited to the provision of water for an irrigation district and for water supply to the GMA.[25] The assertion that the problem emanates from the Lerma basin, then, can be interpreted as an attempt to divert attention from the preponderant role of discharges in the Santiago River Basin. In addition to blaming the states of the Lerma basin, Güitrón—who is a manager at the Quimikao factory in El Salto—stressed that within AISAC, "we are working in an environmental committee where we promote good practices and try to ensure that all our members comply with the current regulations" (Velasco 2016).

Then, at the end of November, Greenpeace Mexico returned to the Santiago River to present analyses carried out of water and sediments in the area of the El Ahogado WWTP. Its subsequent report found that the treatment plant does not eliminate toxic substances, as evidenced by the presence of 101 semivolatile organic compounds in the samples it analyzed of the plant's treated wastewater. Of these, it was able to identify 56 substances, including several that are "highly toxic" and classified as "carcinogenic, capable of causing hormonal disruptions, damage and malformations in fetuses and in the female and male reproductive systems" (2016, 21). Although these

Chronicle of a Struggle

115

substances are not regulated in the NOM-001, in the European Union "they are subject to strong regulations and monitoring programs" (10). Greenpeace concluded that the WWTPs built so far are insufficient and advocated for incorporating the principle of zero discharge into water legislation, as well as updating technical regulations.

In response to the Greenpeace report, the PROFEPA delegate in Jalisco, Xóchitl Yin Hernández, ruled out the possibility that large companies were responsible for the pollution, pointing rather to small companies and workshops: "The biggest problem is where we do not know what is there, clandestine [facilities]," she stated. On inspecting larger companies, Yin asserted that PROFEPA only found minor irregularities and that, "as regards the discharges that we review based on the official Mexican standards, I'm not saying that they are the best [standards] but they are what we have and what we apply, they do comply" (cited in Meléndez 2016). In this way, given the evidence of both industrial pollution and worrisome health impacts, industry and government actors have focused on diverting the blame to other states or the specter of clandestine workshops, while defending the performance of the largest companies. If compliance is insufficient, due to the laxity of standards, well, "they are what we have." Cynicism and inaction have persisted in the face of the growing body of evidence of damage to the environment and human health.

* * *

Although the organizations of El Salto and Juanacatlán have never ceased their denouncements and actions of protest, not until 2018 did an apparent shift take place in the institutional approach. In his first public act, in December 2018 Jalisco governor Enrique Alfaro Ramírez announced the Comprehensive Strategy for the Recovery of the Santiago River, known now as Revive the Santiago River. Adopting a top-down approach, the strategy was presented without consultations with communities or experts and lacked concrete actions to combat industrial pollution, with the bulk of investment channeled to the construction and rehabilitation of municipal WWTPs (McCulligh 2022). One year later, in December 2019, the ToxiTour Caravan arrived in El Salto, kicking off a series of visits to six severely contaminated sites in Mexico by a group of legislators and members of social organizations from the United States, Europe, and several South American countries. As mentioned in the introduction, this is also when an important health study conducted in 2010 that demonstrated the accumulation of toxins in children living on the banks of the river finally came to light (UASLP and CEA 2011). I return to these events in the conclusion to present a preliminary balance of the strategy of the state government and the absence of federal authorities despite growing international attention to the problem.

This international attention came in the form of precautionary measures issued in February 2020 by the Inter-American Commission on Human Rights (IACHR) in order to "preserve the life, personal integrity and health" of residents living within five kilometers of the Santiago River in El Salto and Juanacatlán, as well as in several communities on the shores of Lake Chapala in the municipality of Poncitlán (IACHR 2020, 1). In its resolution, the IACHR states that the government response to its request for information centered on the construction of municipal treatment plants. The IACHR found that such plants "are not suitable measures for pollution produced as a result of industrial waste" (8). In addition to calling for actions to mitigate environmental pollution, the precautionary measures call for the state to "offer a specialized medical diagnosis for the beneficiaries [in the affected communities], taking into account the alleged contamination and providing adequate medical attention" (9). More than two years after these precautionary measures were issued, the federal government has presented no clear plan to mitigate pollution.

In this chapter, I have narrated some of the most important events of this conflict and highlighted the roles of the organizations that, from their various perspectives, have sought to protect their communities from pollution. My emphasis has also been on critically examining the responses from the various government institutions that have been called to account or that have adopted strategies to contain social protest. The tale told is one of outright denial of the pollution—in particular from industrial sources—and of a discourse centered on WWTPs as the ultimate solution to this problem. As regards the environmental health crisis, the denial of any cause-effect relationship between the river pollution and health effects has been a constant from the state authorities, who have employed strategies of "manufacturing uncertainty" (Michaels and Monforton 2005), disseminating the conclusions of flawed studies while withholding the results of more serious health research, and thus contributing to what Javier Auyero and Débora Alejandra Swistun (2009, 144–145) have called a "labor of confusion" about the nature and effects of toxic pollution.

Chronicle of a Struggle

At the same time, I reviewed the response from the industrial sector, particularly after the death of Miguel Ángel López. This was one of the few occasions when media and social pressure put this sector in the spotlight. Also, I underscored the information then available on industrial discharges in this area. Thus far I have focused on the actions of a movement that, despite some internal fractures, has persistently called for the cleanup of the Santiago. From here, I will turn in chapter 3 to examine the logic and realities of the practices surrounding the regulation of industrial activities, as well as their legal framework.

3   (Un)regulated Environments and the Santiago River

Institutional practices and logics are at the heart of this research. What institutional logics predominate in water and pollution management? I encountered an interesting example of the divergence between official discourse and the logic of water managers at the 2014 Water, Energy and Climate Conference convened in Mexico City by the International Water Association and the National Water Commission (CONAGUA, Comisión Nacional del Agua). In a workshop on water governance, Víctor Javier Bourguett, then-director of the Mexican Institute of Water Technology (IMTA, Instituto Mexicano de Tecnología del Agua), a federal public institution dedicated to water research and technological development, spoke of a controversial new General Water Law (Ley General de Aguas). In 2012, Article 4 of the Mexican Constitution was reformed to incorporate the human right to water and sanitation, and the reform included the stipulation that a General Water Law be approved within 360 days. The new law, not yet approved in 2022, would replace the National Waters Law (LAN, Ley de Aguas Nacionales) of 1992.

It was to the future implementation of a General Water Law that Bourguett was referring when he shared his vision:

> We have three types of country. In the north, since you don't have much water, society is much more *mature*, our law is going to work in a certain way, I think quite positive. But we have the southeast, where I suspect that with the law and with our best intentions, it will not work well because we are still much more *culturally backward* . . . we have cultural traditions, a certain relationship with the water of our ancestors that simply prevent things from being done as the modern world requires. Maybe it is very nice to respect traditions, the culture of the people, but the sad reality is, *the world economy works differently.*[1]

Here what is "traditional" (code for indigenous) is associated with immaturity and backwardness. On the second "type of country," the center, which would include the Santiago River Basin, Bourguett only commented that in this region water is "very overexploited" and will have to be managed differently. He also made it clear that environmental preoccupations are a further obstacle to progress. After recalling the great legacy of Mexico's civil engineers in dam and infrastructure construction, he regretted that, "unfortunately, fate has caught up with us, and now the environment matters a lot, and what's worse for us . . . we have to take social participation into account. Which implies in a country as immature as ours, that things reach a standstill."[2] In this view, social and environmental concerns are irrational impediments.

Bourguett's comments are also testimony to the persistence of evolutionary and teleological ideas. One of the assumptions of the social sciences, since its structuring in the mid-nineteenth century, which Immanuel Wallerstein insists must be questioned, is that "human history is progressive, and inevitably so" (2000, 146). Linked to this is the assumption that "capitalism (or its surrogate, individual liberty) had in some sense to 'triumph' at some point within particular states" (145). In this teleological version of history, of course, there are those who lead the way in a linear evolution toward higher levels of industrialization, technological development, and consumption. Thus, as Eric Wolf (2010, 5) asserts, the history of the "entity" known as the West is usually taught as an evolutionary scheme, turning "history into a moral success story . . . a tale about the furtherance of virtue, about how the virtuous win out over the bad guys." Who are the good guys and who are the bad guys in this story? That has never been in doubt.

Edward B. Tylor, a nineteenth-century evolutionist considered the founder of cultural anthropology, put it this way: "The main tendency of culture from primaeval up to modern times has been from savagery towards civilization" (1920, 21). And it was clear who could judge what it was to be civilized: "The educated world of Europe and America practically settles a standard by simply placing its own nations at one end of the social series and savage tribes at the other, arranging the rest of mankind between these limits according as they correspond more closely to savage or to cultured life" (26). Here the Eurocentrism is so evident that it does not require comment. However, the interesting point is to observe how these evolutionary ideas continue to manifest themselves and inform our readings of reality, often even those that purport to be critical and progressive.

Within anthropology, there was a revival of evolutionary theories in the mid-twentieth century. In this neoevolutionist vein, Leslie White proposed a "basic law of cultural evolution," asserting cultural evolution is analogous to the amount of energy used per capita, "the efficiency of the techno-logical means with which it is put to work," and the "amount of human need-serving goods and services produced per capita" (1949, 368). There are interesting parallels with the Truman Doctrine, as expressed in Harry S. Truman's inaugural address of 1949, the same year that White published his book *The Science of Culture*. After describing the misery, disease, "primitive" economic life, and poverty that plague "more than half the people of the world," beginning his second term as president of the United States, Truman called on "peace-loving peoples" to share "our store of technological knowledge." "The key to prosperity and peace," declared the president, is greater production, and "the key to greater production is a wider and more vigorous application of modern scientific and technical knowledge." The United States possessed "constantly growing and inexhaustible" stores of precisely this technical knowledge (Truman 1949).

The evolutionary theories of the mid-twentieth century emanated not only from anthropologists but also from economists such as W. W. Rostow. Rostow (1960), in what he characterized as an alternative to Karl Marx's modern history, postulated the existence of five stages denominated "traditional society, the preconditions for take-off, the take-off, the drive to maturity, and the age of high mass consumption" (4). Traditional society, according to Rostow, is characterized by its "hierarchical social structure," a value system dominated by "long-run fatalism," and limited productivity due to "the inaccessibility of modern science, its applications, and its frame of mind" (5). Transitioning from a traditional society to one in take-off, according to this scheme, is associated in most cases with an "external intrusion by more advanced societies," which spurs the collapse of the traditional structure and creates the possibility of economic progress (6). Thus, having overcome the "obstacles" of the static and traditional, "growth becomes its normal condition" (7). This version of "history" seems an apologia for foreign intervention, and a defense of faith in unlimited economic growth and consumption as the pinnacle of human "progress."

Rostow's ideas have an interesting parallel in a 1951 document from the United Nations' Department of Social and Economic Affairs: "Ancient philosophies have to be scrapped; old social institutions have to disintegrate; bonds of caste, creed and race have to burst; and large numbers of persons who cannot keep up with progress have to have their expectations of a comfortable life frustrated" (cited in Escobar 1995, 4). This quote clearly expresses the discourses that Arturo Escobar characterizes as the hegemonic will to transform two-thirds of the world in pursuit of "economic progress." When the idea of development began to emerge after World War II, the belief that "Third World" countries must achieve economic growth in order to overcome their condition of "underdevelopment" was based on the assumption that there were stages of economic growth of a progressive and orderly nature, and development was the process of transition toward replicating the conditions of mature capitalist countries (38). This route to modernization, industrialization, and urbanization was considered inevitable. The financing and technological capacity of rich countries would be what would ensure this global progress.

In critical reflections on development, understood as "economic expansion worshiping itself," Brazilian anthropologist Gustavo Lins Ribeiro observes how since the nineteenth century, and with greater intensity after World War II, "the accelerated pace of integration of the world system demanded ideologies and utopias that could give meaning to unequal positions within the system, that could provide explanations through which peoples placed at lower levels could believe that there would be a solution for their 'backward' situation" (2007, 175, 183). Here, I would point to the way in which pollution and weak regulations in the countries of the Global South tend to be naturalized, as an illustration of the evolutionary qualities of current development discourses.

Returning to Bourguett, cultural traditions, the environment, and social participation appear as irrational phenomena because they fail to recognize that "the world economy works differently." As regards pollution, that logic of the world economy was clearly expressed in an oft-cited 1992 memorandum from the World Bank's chief economist at the time, Lawrence Summers. In the memorandum, Summers asked, "Just between you and me, shouldn't the World Bank be encouraging MORE migration of the dirty industries to the LDCs [least developed countries]?" Asserting that the cost of the health impact of pollution can be measured by the income lost due to increased morbidity and mortality, he stated that from this perspective, "a given amount of health impairing pollution should be done in the country with the lowest cost. . . . I think the economic logic behind dumping a load of toxic waste in the lowest wage country is impeccable" (*Economist* 1992, 66). How to understand this "impeccable" economic logic?

The concept of coloniality can help to decipher a rationale in which the value of the lives and health of different populations can be quantified, with income as the unassailable yardstick. In Eduardo Restrepo's definition, coloniality is understood as a contemporary "pattern of power" and as a "much more complex historical phenomenon than colonialism" (2007, 292). In itself, Restrepo argues, coloniality "operates through the naturalization of racial hierarchies that enable the re-production of territorial and epistemic relations of domination" (292). Is it possible to understand the "logic" of Summers or Bourguett without these naturalized hierarchies?

In one of the most critical moments of social protest around the contamination of the Santiago River, community demands were answered from the same impeccable logic. This was in the voice of the then-minister of the Ministry of Environment and Natural Resources (SEMARNAT, Secretaría de Medio Ambiente y Recursos Naturales), Juan Rafael Elvira Quezada, in response to demands from organizations in El Salto and Juanacatlán and their allies that federal authorities declare an environmental emergency. In March 2009, Elvira rejected the possibility, pronouncing that "the declaration of an environmental emergency entails the paralysis of a very important number of investments in this region" (Alonso Torres et al. 2009). Here was perhaps the clearest statement that industrial interests eclipse concerns over the health of communities.

If this economic logic is as impeccable as it is implacable, why is the environment now intruding into its domain? The logic of modernization has had to confront the "environment," as the environmental costs of industrialization, technological development, and the increasing social metabolism of the global economy have become more apparent. As a measure of the rise in this social metabolism, for example, while the global population quadrupled between 1900 and 2000, "the consumption of materials and energy increased on average up to ten times. . . . That of energy 12 times, of metals 19 times and that of construction materials, especially cement, about 34 times" (Delgado 2012, 17; Martínez-Alier et al. 2014). Furthermore, the rate of extraction and disposal of materials accelerated between 2002 and 2015 (Krausmann et al. 2018). The hegemonic responses, however, do not unsettle the goal of infinite economic growth or the unrestricted confidence in the ability to generate technological solutions to environmental problems.

3.1 The Logics of Environmental Regulation in Mexico

In this chapter, the objective is to delve beyond the official discourse to examine the logics undergirding environmental regulation in Mexico as regards the control of industrial water pollution. I begin with the most direct control action, the inspections undertaken by authorities at CONAGUA. From there, I go on to examine aspects of regulation that are based on self-reported information as well as on self-regulation programs. Finally, I briefly outline the role of state and municipal governments in regulating industrial activity. This and the next two chapters present the key empirical evidence to support my argument of institutionalized corruption. While this chapter centers on the enforcement of regulations, chapter 4 focuses on the processes and actors involved in the generation of environmental regulations, and chapter 5 on the performance and environmental discourses of a series of corporations with factories in the Ocotlán–El Salto Industrial Corridor. The aim is to demonstrate a systemic logic of environmental nonregulation, in contrast to the "reformist" or "progressive" approaches that argue that what is lacking from efforts to achieve the desired level of environmental protection are minor adjustments and greater (financial and human) resources.

Other authors have noted the deployment of a systemic logic of nonapplication of environmental regulations in Mexico. Thus, despite citing an impressive set of environmental laws, policies, and institutions, José Urciaga and colleagues (2008) affirm that there are "alarming" structural problems, including the "inefficient implementation [and] inadequate application" of laws, and the fact that many environmental institutions "suffer from the traditional problems of a 'captured state agency'" (91–92). Captured agencies are those that, owing to their close relations with the regulated sectors, "interpret their function not as strong defenders of the public good, but as partners and facilitators of private extraction or production" (92). This weakness of the state vis-à-vis private interests has also been noted in the water sector.

In his book *The Decadence of the Nation's Water*, historian Luis Aboites illustrates the weak capacity of the state to control water exploitation, whether for locally managed irrigation systems or for the consumption of large farmers and industries. In the case of the latter, referred to as oligarchies, Aboites emphasizes that there exists an "inability, or the frank complicity of the state, to subject these groups to any non-business logic or rationality" (2009, 46). Since the state adopted what Aboites terms a "commercial-environmental model" in water management in the 1980s, he finds that "not only does the state no longer spend on public works but it also fails to exercise its regulatory functions, it does not protect the resource or even collect duties [for its use]. So, what does it do? There is now a certain *notion of deception* in government conduct that would be worth exploring in much greater detail" (2009, 121; emphasis added). This pattern of action of federal authorities is in contrast to "the certainties, wisdoms and the firm march of the oligarchies" (121). What I explore in this chapter is that "notion of deception" in government behavior.

Before probing the specifics of wastewater oversight, I would first clarify the hypothetical function of environmental regulations. According to Rhys Jenkins and Alfonso Mercado García (2008, 25), "Public authorities establish certain limits for the quantity and quality of emissions and discharges, and incorporate them into the legal system; then they monitor compliance with these limits and apply penalties to those who violate them." The contrast with this ideal should become clear in this chapter, which also provides insight into prevailing power relations between industry and the state. If, as Peter Menell and Richard Stewart affirm, "no program of environmental regulation is better than its enforcement system" (1994, cited in Zinn, 2002, 82), we begin with a key point to assess the effectiveness of environmental regulation in Mexico: inspections of discharges to national waters.

3.2 Environmental Enforcement: Negligence or Omission?

In the partitioning of regulatory and governmental competencies, a distinction is made between the wastewater discharged to national waters (directly into permanent water bodies) and that released into municipal sewer systems. In the case of direct discharges, the jurisdiction is federal and CONAGUA is charged with ensuring compliance; since 2012, the Federal Bureau of Environmental Protection (PROFEPA, Procuraduría Federal de Protección al Ambiente) has also assumed these powers. In fact, the LAN provides that both CONAGUA and PROFEPA personnel can carry out inspections of these discharges (Article 88 BIS, Section XI). Legal confusion begins when reviewing the discharge standard, NOM-001-SEMARNAT-1996 (NOM-001), which stipulates that compliance monitoring falls under SEMARNAT's jurisdiction, through CONAGUA, and under the navy's for discharges into coastal waters (paragraph 9.1). The powers of PROFEPA were clarified, nonetheless, in 2012, through changes to SEMARNAT's Internal Regulations specifying its authority in this regard.[3]

These changes led PROFEPA to commence with effluent inspections in 2013, when it undertook about seventy inspections.[4] Between 2015 and

2018, PROFEPA inspected an average of 217 discharges per year in the country, finding "minor" irregularities (a term that is not defined) in 63 percent and carrying out total or partial closures in 4 percent (PROFEPA 2016, 2017, 2018, 2019, 2020, 2021a). Despite its new powers, then, PROFEPA has carried out very few inspections of wastewater discharge to date.

It is interesting, in this sense, to look at the period before the current water regulations were published, a few years after the creation of PROFEPA. The head of PROFEPA at that time was Antonio Azuela de la Cueva.[5] Azuela recalls that, in the midst of intense changes at PROFEPA in late 1994 and early 1995, the minister of the environment, natural resources and fisheries, Julia Carabias, told him, "It seems that people at the National Water Commission don't want to let go of the water inspections." This despite the fact that the idea was for PROFEPA to take over that responsibility. Later, Azuela was invited to lunch by the director of CONAGUA, Guillermo Guerrero Villalobos, and he recounts his words regarding those inspections: "He told me, 'You know what, Antonio, if that function goes to PROFEPA, the profession will be divided.' What we see here," Azuela explained, "is a type of professional unity [among the] hydraulic engineers." The comment, Azuela stated, merits an "ethnographic exploration."[6] This is related to the history of hydraulic engineers in Mexico, or what some have called the "hydrocracy" (Wester et al. 2009). According to Azuela, PROFEPA lacked the capacity to handle wastewater inspections, struggling at that time to carry out its assigned functions, especially when its responsibilities had been tripled with the expansion to natural resources (forestry, wildlife, and fisheries), while its budget had not grown. Whatever the history, to date CONAGUA is the institution with the principal responsibility for inspections of discharges to national waters.

For discharges to sewerage systems in urban areas, there is also some ambiguity regarding oversight. The standard that sets limits for these discharges is the NOM-002-SEMARNAT-1996, where the competent authority is defined as the "governments of the states, . . . and the municipalities, directly or through their public water management agencies" (paragraph 3.5). Here too, although it seems that there could be a concurrence of functions between municipalities and state administrations, in practice, at least in Jalisco, it is interpreted that only municipalities or water utilities can carry out these inspections (Ugalde 2014). For the research that I have undertaken, my focus has been on the inspections of discharges to national waters, because most of the factories in the industrial corridor discharge

(Un)regulated Environments and the Santiago River

directly to the Santiago River or one of its tributaries, such as the El Ahogado Canal; therefore, the focus is on the actions of CONAGUA.

3.2.1 What Inspections There Are

In order to assess the enforcement of regulations for discharges to national waters, I analyzed the number and type of inspections carried out, the number of inspectors, the results of those inspections in terms of the penalties generated, and some of the procedural aspects that mar the effectiveness of the inspections. CONAGUA does not only inspect discharges but also monitors the extraction of surface and groundwaters, as well as the extraction of materials from river and lake beds and construction in or along water bodies. With information up to December 2021, 527,189 permits and concessions are registered in the Public Water Rights Registry (REPDA, Registro Público de Derechos de Agua). The vast majority (75 percent) are surface and groundwater extraction concessions, followed in number by concessions to occupy "federal zones" along waterways (21 percent), with a smaller percentage (3 percent) for discharge permits and the extraction of petrous materials (1 percent), as detailed in table 3.1. In terms of discharge permits, those for industrial uses represent 16 percent of permits, while constituting 42 percent of the authorized discharge volume. In the state of Jalisco, industrial uses represent 36 percent of the discharge permits and 55 percent of the authorized volume.

Table 3.1

Number and proportion of concessions registered in the REPDA by type

Type of concession	National		Jalisco	
	Number	Percent	Number	Percent
Surface water extraction	124,497	22	6,695	16
Groundwater extraction	299,944	53	25,827	61
Wastewater discharge	19,031	3	749	2
Federal zones	117,128	21	9,089	21
Materials extraction	4,321	1	155	0
Total concessions	**527,189**	**100**	**42,268**	**100**

Source: Author's elaboration based on CONAGUA (2022b).
Note: CONAGUA indicates that the sum of the titles for each type of concession is greater than the total number of concession titles because an individual title may contain more than one type of concession.

The information in the REPDA provides an indication of the universe of users that CONAGUA inspection personnel have to monitor, although obviously it does not take into account clandestine extractions or discharges carried out without a valid permit. The number of inspectors to monitor compliance with these concessions has varied over the years. In the period between 2007 and 2014, there were an average of 220 inspectors in the country, although this may include personnel who acted as notifiers but without authorization to carry out inspections. In the same period, the number of inspectors assigned to the Lerma-Santiago-Pacific (LSP) Basin Agency, who carried out surveillance actions in the state of Jalisco, varied between four and five.[7] Under the government of Andrés Manuel López Obrador (AMLO) (2018–), CONAGUA personnel indicated in early 2021 that the number of inspectors nationally had dropped to only eighty.[8]

The number of total inspections carried out by CONAGUA rose slightly after 2010. From an average of 4,258 inspections of any type carried out per year in the period from 2000 to 2009, they increased to 7,694 annually for 2010 to 2018. For inspections of wastewater discharges, the average in the nineteen-year period (2000–2018) has been 1,010 per year (figure 3.1). It should be noted that although discharge permits represent a small proportion of titles, the possible impact of discharges to bodies of water is

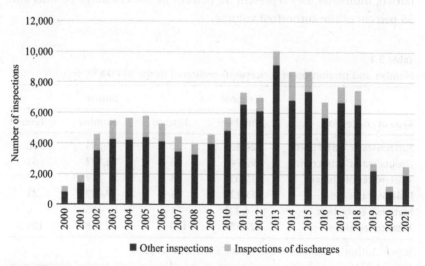

Figure 3.1
Inspections by CONAGUA nationally, 2000–2021.
Source: Author's elaboration based on information from CONAGUA (2022c).

significant and may affect other users as well as the water sources and environments of large populations. A worrying trend can also be observed for the first years of the AMLO administration: between 2019 and 2021 CONAGUA undertook only 2,148 inspections per year, a reduction of 72 percent compared with the 2010–2018 period.

According to then–manager of inspections and evaluation at CONAGUA's central offices, José Antonio Rodríguez, the priorities that determine the type of inspections to be carried out have changed over the years. "Originally the visits were very oriented towards tax collection," Rodríguez stated. Up until 2001, he affirmed, "they were very oriented to verifying that the users who extracted water from the aquifers, or from watercourses, paid for that." In his opinion, the 2001–2006 National Hydraulic Program sparked a shift and "the focus became more towards the preservation of basins and aquifers." Although basin agencies and state offices can prioritize based on local problems, which in certain areas include pollution and therefore discharges, Rodríguez maintained that even to date, "what happens is that the priority has been more towards extraction."[9] Regardless of the priorities, the overall level of inspections is low.

If we take as a reference the average number of inspections between 2010 and 2018 (7,694) and the number of concessions registered in the REPDA of 527,189, and assuming that each inspection is carried out on a different user, *CONAGUA would require sixty-eight years to inspect all users.* The inspections manager in 2015 stated that his goal was to increase the number of inspectors: "We could visit each extraction point, discharge, federal zone or extraction of materials every twenty years, let's say, if we reach 705 [inspectors]."[10] While even in 2015 the number of inspectors was trending down, in part due to voluntary retirement programs, the recent decline is more drastic. Even before this decrease, the deputy manager of inspections at CONAGUA, Luis Miguel Rivera, commented that "the coverage of the inspections is very, very, very low."[11]

For the state of Jalisco, with data from the years 2000 to 2017, an average of 45.2 discharges were inspected per year. Of these, 5.6 were registered to tequila companies, 13.8 to other types of industries, 10.4 to municipal treatment plants or in subdivisions, 9.6 to individuals, 5.0 to agribusiness facilities, and 0.8 to other types of users. Strengthening inspections has long been a demand of citizen groups in El Salto and Juanacatlán, as part of proposed river cleanup actions. In 2012, the director of water administration at the LSP Basin Agency, Óscar Herrera Camacho, after estimating that 20 percent of companies did not comply with discharge regulations, observed that CONAGUA does not have "an army of inspectors to be specifically looking at where each and every discharge is located" (Velazco 2012). For the state of Jalisco, there are now two inspectors assigned to the LSP Basin Agency.

When announcing the results of its first monitoring campaign on the Santiago River in 2009, inaugurating a nominally monthly monitoring program, the State Water Commission (CEA, Comisión Estatal del Agua) stressed the importance of strengthening inspections: "The issue of surveillance and inspection of discharges that are released into the Santiago River is fundamental. CEA . . . will continue to request a collaboration agreement with CONAGUA so that compliance with the water quality of these discharges can be jointly reviewed" (CEA 2009, 5). The CEA's request to CONAGUA was unsuccessful. In 2019, as part of the Alfaro government's river strategy, the Jalisco Ministry of Environment and Territorial Development (SEMADET, Secretaría de Medio Ambiente y Desarrollo Territorial) renewed the petition to CONAGUA to coordinate discharge inspections, though it has yet to achieve a positive response. At the same time, there is further evidence of the deficiency of the inspections undertaken by CONAGUA.

In order to measure the impact of the inspections, I requested a list of the offenders that violated the discharge standard (NOM-001) from 2000 to the end of 2014. For the state of Jalisco, the CONAGUA Basin Agency responded that it encountered no information on users that violated the standard for the years 2000–2009; in 2010, a procedure was initiated against Empaques Modernos de Guadalajara (EMG), a paper and cardboard producer and part of the Mexican company Grupo Gondi, although ultimately no penalties were imposed. Later, twelve fines were assessed based on inspections carried out in 2011 and 2012, four of which were contested by users. From what was reported then, between 2000 and 2014, eight fines were imposed for noncompliance with discharge regulations in the entire state, only one of which corresponds to a company in the industrial corridor. Curiously, the fine was applied to the facilities of Ragasa Industrias in El Salto, which at that time operated only as a warehouse with eleven employees, and the discharge that resulted in the fine came from the restrooms.[12] If this had taken place in the absence of any other evidence, it would perhaps lead one to believe that compliance with regulations is high. Although the available data are not abundant, they do reveal a very different picture.[13]

In addition to the evidence of noncompliance in the IMTA study (IMTA and CEA Jalisco 2011) referenced earlier, a further example of why the fact that CONAGUA detected so few instances of noncompliance is remarkable comes from the response of the General Secretariat of the Government (Secretaría General de Gobierno) to the recommendation of the Jalisco State Human Rights Commission (Comisión Estatal de Derechos Humanos Jalisco). Therein, it mentions that when the State Bureau of Environmental Protection (PROEPA, Procuraduría Estatal de Protección al Ambiente) audited factories in El Salto in 2008, it subsequently turned over to CONAGUA "the information of eight companies that exceeded the maximum permissible limits established in the current environmental regulations to initiate the corresponding administrative procedures" (SGG 2009, 2). This is only to illustrate that other authorities have detected offenders, even though wastewater is not within their remit.

Interviewed in this regard, Héctor Castañeda Nañez, who served as director of watersheds and sustainability at CEA Jalisco from 2007 to March 2013, as well as personnel manager at CONAGUA from 2001 to 2006, questioned the value of CONAGUA inspections based on his experience visiting locations in the industrial zone of El Salto: "I assure you that practically any time you make a discharge-related visit, you will find something that can be improved or, in other words, you will find something irregular." Castañeda explained the lack of enforcement of the discharge standard with one word: "corruption." However, he broadened the scope of this corruption, considering that "inspection and oversight part is a small part of a whole process." He pointed out that it encompasses everything from the selection of the parameters included in the standard to the particular discharge conditions stipulated in individual permits:

> What happens if when the standard that regulates you regulates certain parameters that, for example, you do not have in your process? Well then that is very simple, it's as if your left knee is hurting and you go to the doctor and tell him that it's the right one. Or, if in the particular discharge conditions what they establish for you are some things that are not what you generate, but not because they are mistaken but because there is an intention. . . . Then, in the procedural

> part, I am referring to the records of the inspection visits, if it turns out that at the time you draw up the report, you "make a mistake" about something . . . and then you notify the user that you made an error, then you give [the user] every opportunity to appeal and you don't do anything to them.[14]

Castañeda did not view discharge regulations with optimism: "Either it evolves and is strengthened or eliminate it, because frankly the worst thing you can have in life is a legal weapon to do something and then do nothing."

In some cases, a company's assertion was sufficient to dismiss the imposition of sanctions. For instance, effluent samples taken during a 2010 inspection of EMG revealed a violation in the level of fecal coliforms (a most probable number greater than 24,000, versus a limit in its discharge permit of 2,000). Subsequently, EMG argued that the allegation of noncompliance was "totally false" for various reasons. First, it claimed to have sent a duplicate of the sample taken during the inspection to a certified laboratory that determined a lower number of coliforms (1,500). It also asserted that CONAGUA did not provide further information on the analysis carried out by the commission, nor was there a copy of said analysis in the file; therefore, EMG maintained that CONAGUA had not proved the breach or preserved the company's legal rights. Through another information request, I obtained a copy of the missing laboratory analysis, carried out by Análisis de Agua for CONAGUA.[15] In any case, CONAGUA resolved that "the results presented by [EMG] are sufficient evidence to disprove the facts that it was accused of." Thus, although the laboratory analysis demonstrating the violations of the standard did exist, CONAGUA failed to present the lab report and the company's assertions prevailed.

In the case of an inspection at Hilasal Mexicana, the company's contentions were also accepted, again in the absence of official evidence. When the inspection of this producer of towels and bathrobes was carried out in November 2012, the inspection report indicated that, in addition to the two discharges covered by the permit, there was a third discharge directed through an open channel to the El Ahogado Dam, which the company claimed was rainwater.[16] In CONAGUA's resolution, the deficiencies of the original inspection are evident. Therein, it is recorded that during the inspection no samples were taken from the unauthorized discharge, nor was its provenance determined (neither were samples taken from the two authorized discharges). Hilasal, on the other hand, ordered its own evaluation by an external laboratory of this third discharge, and samples were taken months later, on January 31, 2013. Citing the low levels of chemical oxygen demand encountered, it argued this was sufficient evidence that it was in fact rainwater. This was accepted by CONAGUA, and it resolved that no penalties be imposed on Hilasal. I would note not only that both the inspection and the subsequent sampling were carried out in times with little or no rainfall but also that it was the deficiency in the original inspection that led the company to provide its own evidence, which was not contradicted by the authorities.

Although effluent samples were taken in the majority of the more than 150 wastewater inspection records reviewed for this investigation, the lack of sampling in the industrial zone of El Salto at some specific times is noteworthy. A week after the death of Miguel Ángel López, between February 21 and 26, 2008, CONAGUA carried out ten inspections of industries in El Salto. These inspections had one thing in common: no effluent samples were taken in any of them. As a result of these inspections, which lasted an average of two and a half hours, a penalty was imposed on Distribuidora Chocomex for discharging without a valid permit. In that year, there was only one more wastewater inspection in El Salto, so almost all the visits to discharges in this municipality did not take into account their analysis. Here, the public defense of the industries that was simultaneously undertaken by Raúl Iglesias, then director of the LSP Basin Agency, is interesting.

Iglesias was quoted in the press on February 28 stating that, in general terms, the industries had "minimal" violations of the standard, about 10 percent above permissible contaminant levels. He further stated that

> in the case of the El Salto industrial corridor there is a whole system of sewer collectors to carry the water to the industrial waste treatment plant managed by the State Water Commission. There are also companies that have their individual [treatment] plants, there are other companies that have joined together for this general treatment plant, and there *should not be more than five that discharge directly to the water body*, registered with us. (Del Castillo 2008; emphasis added)

This statement is false on several points. In contrast to this estimate of five direct discharges, a 2003 inventory provided by CONAGUA records 265 discharges to the Santiago River from industrial companies and service activities, all located in the Ocotlán–El Salto corridor (AyMA Ingeniería y Consultoría 2003, appendixes 4-2 and 4-5). The gap between 265 and five direct effluent discharges suggests that Iglesias, on behalf of CONAGUA, represented the situation with neither honesty nor goodwill. Neither can the realization of ten wastewater inspections without collecting samples be considered carrying out an official function in good faith.

Something similar happened in 2010, when CONAGUA inspected twelve factories in the industrial corridor on a single date, April 29. This was a month after CONAGUA refused to accept the recommendation of the National Human Rights Commission (Comisión Nacional de los Derechos Humanos) addressing the pollution that caused the death of Miguel Ángel López. All twelve visits were to verify compliance related both to groundwater withdrawals and to wastewater discharge. Once again, no effluent samples were collected at any of these factories. Not only that, eight of the twelve companies were located in the El Salto Industrial Park and are precisely the companies that directed their wastewater to the treatment plant referred to by Iglesias and managed by the CEA. Thus, these companies were not directly responsible for their own discharges. At the same time, CONAGUA did not inspect the CEA-managed treatment plant. The El Salto Industrial Park treatment plant had the capacity to treat 2.5 liters per second, and it received the discharges from the approximately thirty-five companies installed in the industrial park, not the entirety of industries in El Salto as Iglesias asserted (*Informador* 2012).

I visited this wastewater treatment plant run by the CEA in May 2014. The operator explained that the plant only treated the discharges from the restrooms and general services of the factories of the industrial park. When process effluents were channeled to the plant, they were diverted without treatment to the El Ahogado Dam. He reported that sometimes "very filthy" waters reached the plant, laced with oils or black, green, brown, or white in color. The operator stated that there was a shift toward requesting that companies not send this type of discharge to the plant, where in the past they sometimes went through full shifts without being able to introduce water into the treatment process because they only received heavily polluted effluents. If they incorporated this type of discharge into the plant, it could "spoil" the biological treatment system.[17] If CONAGUA knew, as is evident in the quote from Iglesias, that the companies located in this industrial park sent their wastewater to a common plant, why invest the limited resources for inspections in these visits? In addition, why not address the evidently inadequate management of the CEA plant, which I was able to detect in a simple field visit by speaking with the plant operator? After my visit, this plant was shut down and the wastewater from the industrial park directed to the El Ahogado wastewater treatment plant.

Regarding the now-defunct plant at the El Salto Industrial Park, it is evident that the CEA regularly diverted untreated process effluent from factories in the industrial park to the El Ahogado Dam, from where they would reach the Santiago River. But this was not the only way effluents from the park reached the dam. Shortly before the change of state administration from the National Action Party to the Institutional Revolutionary Party in December 2012, the CEA announced that it was going to present criminal charges against three companies from the El Salto Industrial Park for clandestine connections to the park's storm drains. In addition to damaging the hydraulic infrastructure, Héctor Castañeda declared that "their industrial and sanitary wastewaters are flowing directly into the El Ahogado Canal, contributing to its contamination." The companies targeted were Philippine-based electronics corporation IMI-Electronics, the German steel pipe producer Salzgitter Mannesmann, and Mexican animal nutrition company Vimifos. The CEA reported that the problem was not new and that "practically 365 days a year there is continuous discharge" to the storm drains (*Informador* 2012). If this was the case, why make the report so shortly before the change of administration? It is also unclear whether the CEA proceeded with this legal complaint. In any case, the CEA's ambivalence is evident.

More recently, during the 2015–2018 period, CONAGUA reported fifty-six inspections of industrial discharges in Jalisco; irregularities were found in fifteen, although only three led to the imposition of fines. During many of these inspections, no effluent samples were taken. Of the fifty-six inspections, during forty no samples were taken for analysis, and in April 2019 another six were still awaiting laboratory results *for inspections carried out in 2015 and 2016*.[18]

To understand why inspections find no infractions or why penalties are issued almost exclusively for administrative faults, there are other elements that must be taken into account. Until recent years, CONAGUA notified parties in advance of inspections. The deputy manager of inspections at the national level explained, "Before 2008, 2009, we did indeed leave a summons twenty-four hours before the visit . . . later we realized that notification is not needed for a visit."[19] Having this notice, obviously, provides users the opportunity to modify the conditions of their discharge in advance of the inspection. In recent years, then, CONAGUA's policy has been not to notify that an inspection will take place. However, I heard multiple testimonies to the effect that unofficial advance notice persists. For example, a worker at a Mexican paper factory in El Salto reported, "One day before, they tell us that they are coming to check. . . . We have that privilege, [and] I think it's not just us, any company." As he dealt with the inspectors, this worker received the notice and was aware of this "privilege," which is not part of the lawful procedure.[20]

Even assuming there is no prior notification, the deputy manager of water quality at CONAGUA, Eric Gutiérrez, expressed his misgivings about the effluent samples collected during inspection visits. He explained why they may not be representative of the effluent regularly released to the environment:

> Even when it is no longer necessary to notify, one arrives there, "Yes, of course, come in." This and that, "But let the plant technician come and let me do this . . ." and they spend two, three hours there and then . . . they close and open pipes and water of different types flows since one doesn't know the inner workings.[21]

To bolster enforcement, Gutiérrez proposed the installation of automatic sensors at the outlets of high-volume discharges, which would remain in situ for a period of time to take samples. Pilot tests were undertaken of this type of continuous monitoring system, Gutiérrez commented. "We put automatic meters on discharges that are very, very voluminous and very polluting, and information is transmitted in real time. There they can do absolutely nothing." When they first installed this type of sensor at a textile factory, the company stopped all wastewater discharge for fifteen days and later the automatic device was vandalized on several occasions: "It's interesting that they go to the pipe and, bam! They bust it so we can't take water. So . . . maybe it is the company [doing it]."[22] This type of real-time system would allow continuous monitoring to shore up weak enforcement.

There is another factor that can also constitute an indirect notification to users of a possible inspection. As the inspections manager at CONAGUA, José Antonio Rodríguez, indicated, "I think the problem is that when we start working in the field, people realize it. . . . And they immediately communicate [among themselves]."[23] Here it is necessary to understand how inspections are scheduled. CONAGUA does not receive the budget to sample and analyze discharges from the beginning of the year, nor does it directly take the effluent samples, rather signing contracts with the private laboratories that win annual tenders for this service. In the words of Rodríguez,

> Financial resources are not granted in January but are granted later and you have to complete disbursements in November. So, that already limits your time. Then, since it is by tender, you need to do the bidding. . . . So, it is not convenient for the companies [that win the tender] to have their brigades dispersed and then in another month to continue thus dispersed all the time. . . . If they are moving around and monitor in one municipality and then return two months later, their staff have to move again, and it's very expensive.[24]

This explains the fact that these types of inspections are usually carried out at the same time in a certain area and usually not at the beginning of the year. However, this also constitutes a persistent form of notification, despite the policy change of not providing formal notice. What was the main problem with providing that notification? According to Rodríguez, the argument for not notifying is that, otherwise, "the user prepares and everything is perfect."[25]

This process of awaiting budget approval and carrying out annual tenders explains why the head of inspections at the LSP Basin Agency, Apolinar González, stated in mid-May 2014 that he had not yet received resources and that "sometimes" there were years in which funds were not authorized.[26] The use of private laboratories to carry out sampling and analysis of discharges as part of CONAGUA's inspections can also generate conflicts of interest. This is because, at least in some cases, the companies inspected are also clients of the same laboratories. This is exemplified in the case of the Quimikao chemical factory in El Salto. The laboratory Apoyo Técnico Industrial was employed by Quimikao in 2011 for its regular discharge analyses, and in 2012 it took samples for CONAGUA during an inspection.[27] Although this in itself is not evidence of any act of corruption, it implies that laboratories may be, at one point, service providers for the companies and, at another, an arm of the authority to monitor their legal compliance.

To close the discussion, it is instructive to illustrate how inspections are perceived by industry actors. These opinions are by no means surprising, but rather confirm the picture drawn thus far. In this sense, the manager of the Cytec-Solvay chemical plant in the town of Atequiza, speaking in a personal capacity, linked the country's current environmental regulations to the North American Free Trade Agreement (NAFTA) negotiations. "One of the requirements that the countries negotiated at that time," he stated, "was that Mexico improve its ecological standards, in which we were very, very far behind." However, the creation of such legislation has not implied real control in practice. The manager explained that "overnight,

138

new environmental laws appeared that we had never had before, and the government has never had, neither then nor now, the possibility of verifying that the laws are complied with by industries."[28]

Reflecting on the capacity and will of the country's environmental authorities, the same manager observed, "I see them short of resources, I see them short of muscle, of teeth. As a Mexican, I can tell you that not all companies are treated in the same way . . . because we know that they allow some companies that are not complying to continue working."[29] The teeth referred to would be the authority's ability to punish those who break the law. I have already presented some data on the limited number of fines imposed in the state of Jalisco, but we can briefly analyze the information available for the national level. In response to a request for information on the sanctions applied for violations of the discharge regulations, CONAGUA informed that between 2009 and 2013 an average of 231 economic penalties were imposed per year, with fines averaging MX$180,976, in addition to an average of 113 noneconomic penalties (such as a suspension of activities). If we consider that, on average, in the same period 831 discharge inspections were carried out per year in the country, it means 20 percent of those inspected received economic penalties while 14 percent received noneconomic penalties.

An indicator to evaluate the adequacy or impact of these penalties would be accurate data on the level of noncompliance of users, which do not exist. Nonetheless, we can consider what CONAGUA reports as the levels of wastewater treatment, which went from 42 percent in 2009 to 50.2 percent in 2013 for municipal wastewater and from 19.3 percent in 2009 to 28.9 percent in 2013 for nonmunicipal or industrial wastewater (CONAGUA 2011b, 2014b). This implies that around half of municipal sewage and at least 70 percent of industrial effluent lacked treatment. This helps put the number of penalties into perspective.

Several heads of environment, health and safety (EHS) departments at factories I visited expressed the perception that CONAGUA was more interested in collecting fees than controlling pollution. For instance, at the Japanese Quimikao chemical plant, an EHS engineer related his experience of receiving inspection visits:

> They show up and well, not just the PROFEPA shows up and could take some samples, "Hey, you know what? Well, we need these parameters." "Hey, you know what? You're not complying." So, sometimes you have to pay an extra cost when

(Un)regulated Environments and the Santiago River

you exceed parameters. And then, that's how you work with them in some way. You have to negotiate, finally, what is best for me? Should I pay or it is better to invest.[30]

This company, as will be detailed in chapter 5, regularly exceeds contaminant limits, even in its self-reported analyses, which would indicate that it has not yet decided to invest in improved wastewater treatment. What is also clear is that CONAGUA's inspections do not in fact protect Mexican waters.

3.2.2 Discharge Permits: Minimal Control

Any user who discharges into national waters, including marine waters, or who infiltrates water into the subsoil, with the consequent risk of groundwater contamination, must have a valid discharge permit issued by CONAGUA (Article 88, LAN). Discharge permits indicate the location of the discharge, the annual and daily volume permitted, the receiving water body, and the origin of the discharge, from an industrial process, equipment washing, cafeterias, or another use. These permits specify "particular discharge conditions" (PDCs), or the contaminant limits within which the permit holder must operate, and which may differ from the national standard (NOM-001). The LAN indicates that users must comply with both official Mexican standards and the PDCs set in their permit. However, from the point of view of the deputy manager for inspections at CONAGUA, Luis Miguel Rivera, the obligation of users is to comply with the PDCs established in their permit, rather than with the official Mexican standards:

> The NOM-001-SEMARNAT-1996 standard, which defines the maximum permissible discharge limits to receiving waters, is a reference, but we actually review the particular discharge conditions that are in the discharge permits. Each discharge permit has particular discharge conditions that consider both the activity that generates the discharge and the receiving water body to which that discharge flows.[31]

Thus, at the time of an inspection, the basis are the PDCs registered in the discharge permit.

In theory, this could be positive in terms of pollution prevention, since the LAN defines PDCs as the set of parameters that are established for a user or for a body of water "in order to conserve and control water quality" (Article 3, Section XIV). In this sense, PDCs can establish limits and include parameters beyond what is contemplated in national regulations, if there exists a classification declaration for the body of water or if the authority finds that there are "considerations of public interest or general health" (LAN

Regulation, Article 140). As regards the permit holders, the LAN obliges them to inform the authority if there are "pollutants present in the wastewater that they generate due to the industrial process or the service they are operating, and that were not considered in the established particular discharge conditions" (Article 88 BIS, Section V). So PDCs could compensate for some of the shortcomings of the NOM-001. As Aguilar Ibarra and colleagues point out, in relation to the classification declarations, "Because the NOM 001 is a 'base' standard, the National Waters Law establishes the power to define particular discharge conditions, by means of which protection is achieved against specific problems in a given region" (2010a, 289). Of course, for that to work, PDCs would have to be used to control pollution beyond the general "base" standard.

In the case of the Ocotlán–El Salto Industrial Corridor, I tried to grasp how these PDCs have been employed by examining a series of discharge permits. I obtained fifty-two permits that had been issued for forty factories in the corridor (in some cases I obtained permits from different years for the same company). Analyzing these permits makes it possible to differentiate three periods in the setting of PDCs in this region. To understand these periods, a key moment was November 2008, when the classification of the Santiago River in the Federal Duties Law (LFD, Ley Federal de Derechos) was changed for the stretch from Ocotlán to the (displaced) community of Arcediano, from the lax type A classification to the stricter type C.

The first distinguishable period covers the permits issued between 1994 and 1998. It should be recalled that until the NOM-001 was published on January 6, 1997, forty-four wastewater standards were in force or in the process of approval, and they specified parameters according to the industrial sectors, suggesting possible PDCs for each sector. Of the eighteen permits analyzed from this period, eight established more than thirty parameters, and the permit for the Celanese chemical factory required that it comply with thirty-eight parameters. It can be concluded, then, that at this time PDCs were used to tailor discharge permits according to the origin of the effluent and the specifics of each industrial process.

The next stage covers the permits issued between 2000 and 2008. We can call it the era of least possible regulation. Of the thirteen permits reviewed from these years, twelve established as PDCs only the parameters contemplated in the laxest classification of the NOM-001, for type A rivers, categorized as for use in agricultural irrigation. In only one case, for the Mexican manufacturer of tools and bolts Urrea Professional Tools, the discharge permit includes four parameters not contemplated in the NOM-001: aluminum, barium, iron, and silver. In this period, therefore, it seems that PDCs were not used to control specific pollutants based on the industrial sector or process at each facility, simply maintaining the lowest level contemplated by the regulations: the "base" level.

The last stage covers the permits issued, extended, or modified after the change in river classification on January 1, 2009, when it became type C, the classification for the protection of aquatic life. From this period, I examined twenty discharge permits and, in general, encountered a persistent attempt to maintain the least stringent control, even in contravention of the new classification, or by using novel ways to avoid the somewhat stricter limits. The strategy that I consider novel involves dividing the discharge points between discharges to the Santiago River or one of its tributary streams, for which the type C limits are applied, and an additional discharge point set for irrigation of green areas or soil infiltration, where the lax type A limits remain.

The most worrisome are the six permits that were issued or modified after January 1, 2009, and that included discharges to the river or its tributaries with PDCs in accordance with NOM-001 type A and not type C, as was then required. These include permits for the chemical companies Cytec (Belgium), Zoltek (Japan), and Oxiteno (Brazil); for the voluminous discharge of the EMG paper factory (Mexico); for Emerson Power Transmissions (United States); and for the ZF shock absorber plant (Germany). Legally, this should not have been the case. Thus, Jesús Amezcua, head of water quality at the LSP Basin Agency, explained, "Here they send us the files of all those who request a discharge permit and here the determination is made based on the standard [NOM-001] and based on the classification of the water body in the Federal Duties Law." As of the change to type C for the Santiago, Amezcua stated that "all new discharges and all those who are renewing their discharge [permits] are given the C limits. The C classification means you have to have very efficient secondary treatment so that you can achieve it, which many do not want to do."[32] It seems, then, that CONAGUA officials have used their discretion in the issuance of permits, not consistently respecting the legal classification assigned.

Of the fourteen remaining permits post-2009, seven are permits that maintain lax type A PDCs, but where the receiving body is only specified as soil infiltration or irrigation, implying no wastewater released to surface waters. Two of those permits are for the other Urrea company, a producer of pipes, valves, and taps, for its factory in El Salto, Grivatec. On its website, as part of its promotion as a sustainable company, Urrea indicates that it has a new treatment plant ensuring "zero discharges to the drainage network" (Urrea 2016). Despite the claim to have "zero discharge," when I visited this factory in March 2014, the head of EHS indicated that all the treated water from restrooms and cafeterias is used for irrigation but not all the water from the physical-chemical plant that treats the effluent from the electroplating area, with the baths for chrome plating, nickel plating, and so on. Although the effluent is treated to comply with type C parameters, he affirmed, they had not been able to use 100 percent of that water for irrigation because it killed the grass on the property. For this reason, part of it was released into the El Ahogado Canal. In this way, the visit to the plant revealed an inconsistency with the company's advertising and a breach of its permits, which do not authorize discharge to the canal (Permit 08JAL1380038/12IMOC10).

Three of the remaining post-2009 permits combine a surface discharge point with type C limits and another discharge point for infiltration or irrigation with type A limits. These are the cases of the chemical company Celanese, Plásticos Rex (part of the Mexichem group), and the Dutch company DSM. Some questions arise in this regard. How will an inspection be performed when these different parameters exist? Thinking about what the deputy manager of water quality said on the possibility of opening and closing valves at the time of an inspection, it would surely be at least possible for the water discharged to the river or the canal to be presented at the time of an inspection as water for irrigation, and therefore with the obligation of a less efficient treatment. At the same time, at the factory level, will each factory have multiple treatment plants to achieve the strictest parameters in one and the least stringent in another? Based on this examination, it is clear that CONAGUA is not strictly assigning type C parameters, which is the legal obligation. There are reasons to suspect that the setting of discharge points for infiltration, with less demanding parameters, is being employed as a strategy to mitigate the impact of the change in river classification and allow companies to continue operating without improving their treatment systems.

Leaving aside the issue of the reclassification of the river in the LFD, in recent decades CONAGUA has made scarce use of the option to apply PDCs

(Un)regulated Environments and the Santiago River

to control specific pollutants in accordance with the industrial sector or production process. According to CONAGUA and IMTA officials, there are legal impediments to setting PDCs more frequently. Eric Gutiérrez of CONAGUA stated that only the parameters of the NOM-001 are set as PDCs: "Unless the user informs what [their effluent] has—because [the law] says that they have to declare other types of pollutants and all that—then, they include some additional parameter in [the discharge permit]."[33] The problem here, then, is that the companies themselves have the obligation to self-declare specific pollutants that they discharge. Since this rarely occurs, the PDCs are restricted to the parameters of the standard. In the opinion of Yolanda Pica, a hydraulics specialist with more than twenty years' experience at IMTA, the legal requirements based on self-declaration constrain the authority:

> At CONAGUA . . . they aren't fools, they know very well that a company pollutes, but they don't have evidence because to date everything is under the control in some way of the company itself. . . . The system is somehow rigged or maybe it's made for another type of country, where people don't go around doing this kind of thing and they show themselves openly.[34]

As long as companies do not report the nonregulated pollutants found in their effluents to the authorities, there is only one route for CONAGUA to establish PDCs beyond those in the standard: to demonstrate the harm caused by a particular discharge.

Garnering the evidence required to corroborate this damage is not easy. Gutiérrez explained that "there is a part of the law that says that CONAGUA can establish particular discharge conditions when it reliably demonstrates that there is damage to the ecosystem and third parties and there must be a study." However, in his experience, "we sometimes have a bit of a problem because asserting directly that there are effects on third parties and on the ecosystem is very complicated."[35] In this way, unless companies volunteer the information, PDCs are unlikely to compensate for the limitations of the standard. This problem is closely linked to the next topic I address to understand the operation of environmental regulations in practice: self-reported information from companies on their environmental performance.

3.3 Self-Reporting: Fiction or Faithful Measure?

As environmental regulations are designed in Mexico, even many of the mechanisms of direct regulation depend on the regulated parties themselves self-reporting their performance. As Allen Blackman and Nicholas Sisto note for discharges to sewage systems, "Although presumably factories are periodically inspected by environmental authorities, surveillance depends mainly on self-monitoring" (2005, 10). The same applies to discharges to bodies of water. Self-monitoring occurs in two key points: first, in the discharge quality monitoring reports that must be submitted to CONAGUA by holders of a discharge permit, quarterly, bimonthly, or annually, with the results of their effluent analyses (NOM-001, subsection 4.8; LAN, Article 88 BIS, paragraph XII); and second, for tax purposes, in the declarations of payment for discharges to receiving bodies in accordance with the LFD (Articles 277-B and 278-B).

For the United States, and given the popularity of voluntary programs and their touted "win-win" approach, Jodi Short and Michael Toffel (2008) empirically analyze the relationship between enforcement through inspection and surveillance programs and the disposition of companies to self-report environmental violations. After examining data for 17,464 manufacturing facilities for the period from 1997 to 2003, they find that companies "are more likely to self-report violations when they are subject to frequent inspections and targeted by focused compliance initiatives" (62). In this way, the effectiveness of self-regulation depends on the proper functioning of the regime of oversight and sanctions implemented by the state. The authors indicate that their research "counsels caution in the face of arguments that coercive regulatory strategies are ineffective or obsolete and that government should cede to corporations the unfettered authority to regulate themselves" (66). As we have seen in the previous section, government oversight for wastewater discharges is far from effective and could not be expected to motivate companies to self-report true and reliable information.

In fact, water authorities also express their reservations about the quality of self-reported data, despite working within a regulatory framework that depends on this information. Regarding the policy that users self-report the quality of their effluents, the deputy manager of inspections at CONAGUA stated,

> We have not had good results in general. Users try, obviously, because it involves an expense, to falsify the information on their discharges. I mean, it's normal, it's not reliable, because the users themselves report . . . usually they try to declare the least. It's like when we take the car for an emissions inspection, if it were up

(Un)regulated Environments and the Santiago River

to me to define whether my car complies or not, then it would always comply. I mean, I'm hardly going to say, "No, I'm not complying, I'm going to have to change the exhaust or the catalytic converter." Nope.[36]

Based on his experience at CONAGUA and CEA Jalisco, Héctor Castañeda shared similar reservations about the value of self-reported data:

So, as you leave it up to them, do you think they're going to send an analysis of the worst discharge they have? No, of course not. So, there you are not going to catch anyone. So, it seems to me that the policy that the users themselves are the ones to confess, and then say everything they do or don't do, has not had the results in terms of improvement in the quality of the water in rivers and streams in this country. If that is no longer working, then we should already be implementing the other [policy], which is the stick.[37]

Until now, however, no effective use has been made of the "stick," as I have detailed.

Some of the officials interviewed also drew attention to the role of the private laboratories that carry out the effluent sampling and analysis on behalf of companies in generating information of doubtful reliability. Thus, Yolanda Pica of IMTA questioned the fact that laboratories report first to companies:

At the same time that you issue the report to the company, you should report to CONAGUA. In fact, they do but not until the client agrees. In other words, the laboratory can report to CONAGUA if the client decides, but not until they agree. So, they tell you: "I'm sending you the sample." "Did it go well?" "No." "Don't report it. Let's see, I'll send it to you again and, did it go well?" "No." "Ah, wait a little while, let me adjust here and there and right now." And so on until it complies and then they report. They always report in compliance.[38]

A similar concern was expressed by the deputy manager of inspections, who highlighted the fact that the sampling carried out by the laboratories is done at the time and place set by the company: "The user can even tell them, 'Well, look, sample here. Now that I have fixed my whole process, once everything is fixed, it is beautiful, bottled water comes out, well then, come and take the sample.'"[39]

This information has so little value for the authorities that it is not analyzed and, in the case of a series of discharges from the El Salto industrial corridor, it apparently does not even exist. At the national level, from the department at CONAGUA that receives the reports on effluent quality, Eric Gutiérrez stated that "right now the reports are coming and there is no capacity to analyze them." In addition, for it to be a functional system, Gutiérrez concurs with the study cited earlier that adequate oversight is also required:

> The law says, "Ok, the law is self-declarable, but if I catch you in violation and you are cheating, then yes, I will go after you with everything." So, we have to have that capacity. . . . [We] have to have a much greater surveillance capacity and for that we have to invest in infrastructure, equipment and qualified personnel.[40]

Gutiérrez also echoed the concern expressed by Pica about the role of the laboratories that perform the analyses, noting that in addition to directly monitoring users, CONAGUA would have to "verify the laboratories that perform these analyses and penalize them."[41] More recently, CONAGUA has strengthened precisely this aspect through an online system known as SIRALAB (System for the Reception of Laboratory Analyses), which requires laboratories to report directly to CONAGUA. Nonetheless, companies continue to choose the time and place for monitoring.

To obtain more data on thirty-one companies in the industrial corridor between Ocotlán and El Salto, I requested the results of discharge self-monitoring from CONAGUA for the period from 2000 to 2013.[42] Although the response confirmed that most of the companies named had discharge permits, CONAGUA reported that "it was not possible to locate the chronological analyses and water quality indicators" and declared the information "non-existent." What is particularly remarkable in this case is that for seventeen of these companies, I was able to verify that this information did in fact exist. For those seventeen, I had inspection records from CONAGUA that affirm that the companies had sent reports of their discharges to the commission, and in appendixes to ten of the inspection reports, copies of several laboratory analyses were included. So, rather than a failure to comply with this obligation on the part of the companies, which would be the case if the information were actually nonexistent, it seems rather that the problem is that CONAGUA refuses to make these reports public.

The analyses that the companies entrust to certified laboratories are also the basis for the payment of duties for wastewater discharge, in accordance with the LFD. In Mexico, the legal framework that regulates transparency and access to public information classifies tax information as confidential or reserved.[43] Therefore, when I requested information on the amount of duties paid quarterly by the representatives of the same thirty-one companies, in accordance with Article 278-C of the LFD, for the period from 2000 to 2013,

CONAGUA responded that the information was classified as reserved. However, the Lerma-Santiago-Pacific Basin Agency reported that, in that fourteen-year period, a total amount of MX$1,718,100 was collected from those companies, or an average of MX$122,721 per year. The agency also provided a table indicating the years when it had a record of payment of duties.[44]

Analyzing the information from CONAGUA and excluding companies without a discharge permit and that do not have the obligation to pay, it appears that companies only reported 8.5 percent of the time. Again, there is uncertainty as to whether this is the result of inaccurate information provided by the authority or a breach on the part of the companies, or a mixture of both factors. In fact, several of the inspection records referred to above also have, among their appendixes, documentation of payment for wastewater discharges not accounted for in CONAGUA's information. Does this derive from improper handling of databases and files or a strategy to deny transparency in this regard? Either explanation is troubling.

At the national level, duties collected from discharges to bodies of water are a minimal proportion of the total fees and duties collected by CONAGUA, as shown in table 3.2, gradually increasing to 11.4 percent in 2020. The "polluter pays" principle was adopted by the Organisation for Economic Co-operation and Development in recommendations published in 1972 and 1974. According to the first recommendation, "The principle means that the polluter should bear the expenses of carrying out the [pollution prevention and control measures] decided by public authorities to ensure that the environment is in an acceptable state" (OECD 1992, 13). Principle 16 of the Rio Declaration of 1992 also urged national governments to "promote the internalization of environmental costs and the use of economic instruments, taking into account the approach that the polluter should, in principle, bear the cost of pollution, with due regard to the public interest and without distorting international trade and investment" (United Nations 1992). In Mexico, the provisions of the LFD constitute the application of this principle, but given both the scant monitoring of the self-reported information that is the basis of payments and the low levels of duties collected, it does not achieve such internalization of environmental costs or the maintenance of the environment in an "acceptable" state.

After noting that 94 percent of water bodies in Mexico show some degree of contamination, a 2007 World Bank publication asserts that to reduce pollution, in addition to expanding municipal wastewater treatment,

Table 3.2

CONAGUA duties collected, 2011–2020 (millions of pesos at constant 2020 prices)

	2011	2012	2013	2014	2015	2016	2017	2018	2019	2020
Discharge to water bodies	$379	$407	$511	$818	$1,414	$1,632	$1,754	$1,839	$2,031	$2,454
Total collected	$17,897	$19,264	$19,279	$19,973	$20,173	$21,885	$21,739	$21,521	$22,349	$21,435
Percent of total collected	2.1	2.1	2.7	4.1	7.0	7.5	8.1	8.5	9.1	11.4

Source: Author's elaboration based on CONAGUA (2022a).

"the Mexican government would need to put much greater emphasis on enforcement of the water pollution discharge fee and increasing the rate, as well as providing clear incentives for promoting treatment of industrial effluents" (Olsen and Saltiel 2007, 296). The authors estimate the costs of water pollution at US$6 billion annually (294).

The interviews with officials from the water sector confirm the debility of self-regulation of effluent quality, with self-monitoring reports either not being analyzed or considered of minimal reliability. It is also clear that there are gaps in the information CONAGUA chooses to make public in this regard. CONAGUA denied the existence of information that, as a result of other requests for information, was delivered to me together with inspection records from the same commission. This indicates a clear lack of transparency.

3.3.1 Self-Reporting of Chemical Substances

In Mexico, the creation of the Pollutant Emissions and Transfers Registry (RETC, Registro de Emisiones y Transferencia de Contaminantes) was a commitment that the country acquired from the signing of NAFTA. Its counterparts in the other NAFTA countries are the Toxic Release Inventory (TRI), implemented in the United States since 1986, and the National Pollutant Release Inventory (NPRI), established in Canada in 1992. The purpose of this type of pollutant and emissions registry is to respond to communities' "right to know" about chemical risks. It was the 1984 tragedy in Bhopal, India, that led to the creation of the TRI. That industrial disaster took the lives of thousands of people as a result of the release of a highly toxic pesticide from a Union Carbide factory. At the same time, in 1985 the Environmental Protection Agency reported that in the previous five years there were 6,900 incidents related to the release of toxic substances in the United States, which led to 135 deaths and left 1,500 injured (S. Wolf 1996).

Thus, in response to a strong grassroots movement, in 1986 the US Congress issued the Emergency Planning and Community Right-to-Know Act. The act's right-to-know stipulations around toxic substances created the TRI and, according to Sidney Wolf, required "unprecedented disclosure by industry, as well as citizen access, concerning the presence and release of hazardous and toxic chemicals at industrial locations" (220). What I will succinctly analyze here is the quality of the information provided in the RETC in Mexico, in particular for emissions to water bodies, and whether communities' right to know in fact exists.

The implementation of the RETC has evolved from a voluntary paper report starting in 1997 to an electronic version in 2005, and from a voluntary norm in 2001 establishing a list of 104 substances to a mandatory standard in 2014 broadening the list of substances to 200 (NOM-165-SEMARNAT-2013) (Martínez and Gavilán 2015). The information that makes up the RETC is drawn from annual operating certificates (COAs, *cédulas de operación anual*) presented to SEMARNAT. These are mandatory for industries classified as fixed sources of federal jurisdiction in terms of air emissions, as well as for companies that discharge into national waters and those defined as large generators of hazardous waste. Fixed sources of federal jurisdiction for air emissions are those from the following sectors: oil and petrochemical, chemical, paint and ink, metallurgical, automotive, cellulose and paper, the cement and lime industry, asbestos, glass, electricity generation, and the treatment of hazardous waste (Article 111 BIS of the General Law of Ecological Balance and Environmental Protection).

According to the RETC standard, the substances included are given priority, as they "have the potential to cause environmental harm," measured in terms of "their characteristics of toxicity, environmental persistence and bioaccumulation" (*Diario Oficial de la Federación*, January 24, 2014). In addition to emissions of pollutants to surface waters, the RETC requires reporting on emissions to air and soil, as well as transfers of waste, from reuse and recycling to coprocessing, incineration, or final disposal.

Due to the link to NAFTA, the respective pollution release and transfer systems of the three countries have been a focus of the tripartite Commission for Environmental Cooperation (CEC). The CEC maintains a database called Taking Stock Online (CEC, n.d.) with information from the three registries and generates periodic publications on the results and progress of these registries. An analysis of the three registries repeatedly highlights the differences that impede direct comparisons, since the sectors required to report, the number of substances considered, and the emissions thresholds for reporting vary. Thus, while in Canada the NPRI covers approximately 325 substances, the US TRI covers 750 and the Mexican RETC increased from 104 to 200 substances (CEC 2014, 12). The disparities are particularly striking when looking at the data for emissions to water, where the discharges reported by companies in Mexico tend to amount to less than 1 percent of the total emissions for the three countries, with a maximum of 2 percent of emissions in 2017 (figure 3.2).

(Un)regulated Environments and the Santiago River

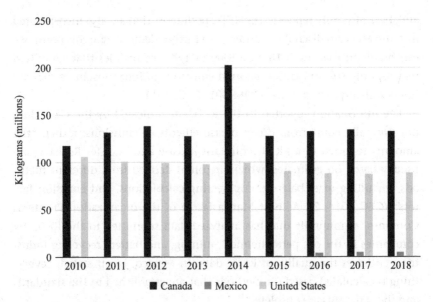

Figure 3.2
Emissions to surface waters reported in Canada (NPRI), Mexico (RETC), and the United States (TRI), 2010–2018.
Source: Author's elaboration based on data from the CEC.

Part of the reason for this huge discrepancy is that, of the twenty main pollutants discharged to surface waters in the region, only six are mandatory for reporting to the Mexican RETC (CEC 2014, 32).[45] Even of those six, only larger quantities of nickel and arsenic are reported as emitted to water in Mexico, while in recent years zero or negligible emissions have been reported for formaldehyde, acetaldehyde, phenol, and benzene from all companies in the country. In fact, reported emissions to Mexican waters are almost exclusively of six heavy metals (arsenic, cadmium, chromium, mercury, nickel, and lead) and cyanide, all parameters of the NOM-001. Between 2010 and 2018, the amounts of these seven pollutants constituted 98.4 percent of the total for substances reported as emissions to water. The remaining 1.6 percent consisted of small amounts of eighteen other substances. This is from a total of 102 pollutants reported to the Mexican RETC in these same years. Thus, despite the increase in the number of substances slated for mandatory reporting to the RETC, the data for water indicate that companies are not reporting emissions of toxic synthetic substances and, basically, only report to the RETC pollutants that are also incorporated into the Mexican discharge standard. To further demonstrate this point, we can highlight that, in 2018, of a total of 1,997 companies that submitted reports, only six companies reported emissions of four substances that are not also incorporated in the NOM-001 (CEC, n.d.).

The information reported to the RETC, as indicated by the CEC, does not normally come from direct measurements of emissions; rather, "the amounts reported to a PRTR [Pollutant Release and Transfer Registry] are usually based on estimates, which are often derived from different methods, including mass balance, engineering calculations, and emission factors" (CEC 2014, 2). Activist Marisa Jacott of the organization Fronteras Comunes, a nonprofit that has analyzed data submitted to the RETC by companies in the oil, petrochemical, mining, and battery recycling industries, criticizes the quality of RETC data. In Mexico, Jacott stated, "everything is calculated based on methods that are established in the standards and the standards are obsolete."[46]

In the case of discharges to water, the then-director of industrial regulation and the RETC at SEMARNAT, Maricruz Rodríguez, believed that the volumes of pollutants released into water normally come from the sampling and testing for the regulated parameters that are almost the only ones reported: "Since those water [parameters] have to be [measured] for regulatory control, that makes it easier for you to use that direct data" versus a calculation such as an emission factor.[47] Furthermore, the explanation for the scant reporting of other substances would be the fact that, as they are not part of the regular monitoring required by CONAGUA, they are not measured. Rodríguez inferred, "Maybe the majority have been heavy metals because that is what is regulated in the standard . . . because it is what they are forced to report and they are only having those analyses carried out." However, in many cases it is evident that the water data also come from estimated calculations. This is exemplified by the data in table 3.3, which presents the discharges to water reported to the RETC for 2018 from five companies in Jalisco, and where it is evident that they do not come from direct measurements of the pollutants in their discharges. In many cases, the same values are reported for various substances or they are simply multiplied. Furthermore, other companies report the same values year after year.

Table 3.3
Emissions of pollutants to water reported to the RETC for 2018

Pollutant (kg/year)	Crown Envases	Cytec	Urrea Herramientas Profesionales	ZF Suspension Technology	Zoltek
Arsenic	1.5505	0	0	3.4	3.1768
Cadmium	1.5505	1.6239	0	1.4	1.5884
Chromium	1.5505	3.2154	1.4717	7.4	0
Nickel	1.5505	9.5789	0.7359	7.4	7.9419
Lead	1.5505	3.2154	1.4717	7.6	7.9419

Source: Author's elaboration based on data from RETC/SEMARNAT.

There are some other general problems with reports to the RETC, and one is that many companies do not report every year. To illustrate this, figure 3.3 indicates whether a series of companies in the corridor in Jalisco submitted a RETC report between 2010 and 2020, as well as whether the report included the discharge of pollutants into surface waters. For these twenty-nine companies, only six reported each year during this period.

Jacott of Fronteras Comunes identified similar problems in her assessment of the RETC: "We see how they report what they want, the amounts they want. . . . We see companies that continue to have the same process year after year and sometimes they report ten kilos of lead and sometimes they report a thousand. . . . Or there's a year that they skip and do not report, other years yes."[48] In terms of imprecise data, there are noteworthy cases from the industrial corridor in Jalisco, such as those of the Sanmina-SCI Systems and Zoltek. Sanmina is an electronics company based in San José, California, serving as a contract manufacturer for some of the original equipment manufacturers. In its factory in the municipality of Tlajomulco de Zúñiga, Sanmina has capacities for the assembly of printed circuit boards and the manufacture of backplanes and enclosures (Sanmina, n.d.).

For the years from 2010 to 2012, Sanmina did not report emissions to the RETC, and in 2013 it reported very high amounts of heavy metals discharged to water: 23,700 kilograms of chromium, 9,562.8 kilograms of nickel, 956 kilograms of arsenic, and 956 kilograms of mercury. In subsequent years, with the exception of 2016, when it did not submit a report, Sanmina sent information to the RETC but reported zero emissions of pollutants to water. Although the 2013 data are most likely the result of erroneous calculations,

Figure 3.3

Reports to the RETC of companies of the Ocotlán–El Salto Industrial Corridor (2010–2020)

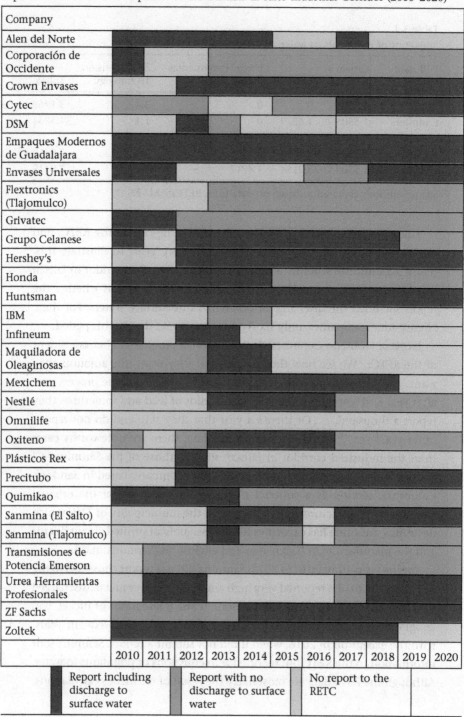

Source: Author's elaboration based on data from RETC/SEMARNAT.

they were not identified as "inconsistent" by SEMARNAT (2013). Inconsistencies are detected, explained Maricruz Rodríguez, based on "two hundred and fifty criteria for the review and validation of the information" provided in the COAs. These "criteria" are incorporated into the software, to detect errors in the information provided.[49]

Another strange data set that was not cataloged as "inconsistent" is that of carbon fiber producer Zoltek, acquired by the Japanese Toray Group in 2014. For 2013, Zoltek reported the discharge of 4,666 kilograms each of chromium, nickel, and lead, in addition to 933 kg of cadmium, 803 kg of cyanide, and 655 kg of arsenic. These releases were far higher than those listed in its 2012 report. In the absence of other information, it is difficult to imagine a technical reason that could explain the increase from 14 kg of chromium as well as lead in 2012 to 4,666 kg of each substance in 2013, or from 2.8 kg of cadmium in 2012 to 933 kg in 2013. For subsequent years, discharges to water were normally reported as below 10 kg.

There are doubts, then, about the veracity of the data reported to the RETC, despite the validation criteria that SEMARNAT claims to apply. Jacott highlighted the fact that it is "approximate" information but maintained that it is useful for nongovernmental organizations, especially since "we don't have many sources of information" on industrial activity. In Jacott's opinion, the successive ministers of SEMARNAT have given no priority to the RETC or to ensuring data reliability.[50] In early 2020, the new head of the RETC at SEMARNAT, José Ernesto Navarro, reported they had two staff members to review the information from over 13,500 COAs received annually—which is an indicator of the lack of priority assigned to the RETC.[51] A further indicator comes from a 2011 report by Occupational Knowledge International and Fronteras Comunes, which noted that "there is no record of penalties ever being imposed for a company failing to report" to the RETC (16).

The limited control over the data is evident both in apparently erroneous data that are not detected as inconsistent and in the fact that many companies do not report to the registry every year. Another critical observer of the RETC since its creation has been Maite Cortés, from the Jalisco Ecologist Collective. Although Cortés appreciates that the RETC exists in Mexico, she maintains that "it does not work . . . as it was intended, for the right to information, that you go in and see who is releasing [toxins] five blocks from your house."[52] Its lack of functioning is quite clear as regards water pollution, as the vast majority of companies do not report substances other than the few regulated by the NOM-001.

3.4 Clean Industry and Self-Regulation

Although space does not permit me to carry out a thorough evaluation, I cannot omit a mention of PROFEPA's Clean Industry (CI) program. The CI voluntary certification, part of the National Environmental Auditing Program, was established in the same year as PROFEPA, 1992, as one of the pillars of its enforcement strategy, along with inspections and citizen complaints (Blackman et al. 2010, 183). Since 1997, the CI certification has been issued to companies that comply with the procedure. Nonetheless, there is no clear evidence that the program has represented an attractive option for industry, as measured in terms of levels of participation. Thus, while participation grew from 78 industrial facilities in 1992 to 7,616 in 2008 (Blackman et al. 2010, 184), in August 2021 only 792 companies held valid CI certifications (PROFEPA 2021b).

In their econometric analysis of CI, Blackman and colleagues (2010) underscore that there have been few studies on voluntary regulation programs in developing countries. Unlike in industrialized countries, where the focus of such programs is on incentivizing environmental performance so that companies go beyond basic legal compliance, they assert, "developing countries generally use [them] to stem rampant noncompliance due to, among other factors, weak environmental management institutions and limited political will for strict enforcement" (182). The authors assess CI based on data on companies participating between 1992 and 2004, as well as the records of all fines applied to companies by PROFEPA from January 1992 to December 2009. In the absence of reliable environmental performance data, fines by PROFEPA are employed as a proxy indicator. From there, they conclude that fined companies are more likely to participate in CI and that, following a period of "amnesty" from inspections during the certification process, there is no significant difference in the rate of fines for companies that had participated in CI versus companies that had not taken part. They affirm that the likely explanation is that the impact on environmental performance was "temporary, not permanent," and that CI "did not have a large, lasting impact on average environmental performance" (191). More such empirical analyses of the program would be important.

The Regulations to the General Law of Ecological Balance and Environmental Protection in the matter of Environmental Self-Regulation and Auditing stipulates that the certification will go to "those who voluntarily and through the Environmental Auditing assume and comply with commitments additional to the legal and regulatory environmental requirements to which they are bound" (Article 3). However, it is not clear to what extent certification can oblige companies to go beyond Mexican laws and regulations. Initially, PROFEPA staff carried out the audits directly, but later this function was delegated to private environmental auditors. Environmental auditors require the approval both of PROFEPA and of the Mexican Accreditation Entity (entidad mexicana de acreditación). This change, according to Armando Montoya, director of audit promotion and conciliation at PROFEPA, happened around 2003 and with the intention of increasing the transparency of the program.[53] Currently, companies seeking certification may hire one of seventy approved environmental auditors (PROFEPA 2022b).

The review carried out for the certification is comprehensive, covering areas including air and noise pollution, water, waste, energy use, natural resources, forest resources, environmental risk, environmental management, and environmental emergencies. On the issue of wastewater discharges, the audit ensures that companies hold a valid discharge permit, have paid duties, carried out effluent analyses with a certified laboratory, and are in compliance with the respective standard.

Although the process is carried out by the auditor together with the company, it can be verified at any time by PROFEPA officials. The respective regulation specifies that PROFEPA, by awarding the certification, is recognizing that, "at the time of its granting, the company operates in full compliance with environmental regulations" (Article 23). In the process, Montoya explained, areas of opportunity are also identified for companies that can result in savings both in process inputs and in economic costs.[54] In this sense, PROFEPA touts the program's environmental benefits by estimating the savings in water and energy consumption, as well as the reduction in the generation of waste and greenhouse gas emissions by participating companies (PROFEPA 2021b).

For companies, the use of the CI seal is one of the benefits of the process. In addition, according to the instructor of a course on CI offered by the National Chemical Industry Association (Asociación Nacional de la

Industria Química) that I attended in 2013, there are other benefits of working with the authorities. The instructor, an environmental manager at a Mexican business group, identified among the benefits of the program the fact that, although PROFEPA would not conceal polluting acts, "the communities already know by the simple fact of having the seal that PROFEPA is on our side. . . . That means that from the outset they are going to agree with us." She expanded on what this close relation entails: "Under this program the industrialist and the government become part of the same team. That is very important. PROFEPA views us favorably . . . and therefore opportunities for dialogue are common and the need for inspections is minimized. That is also a fact that saves PROFEPA resources."[55] This addresses one other important aspect of the program: its links to inspections.

Initially, PROFEPA granted certified companies an amnesty period that exempted them from inspections, but that policy changed. José Domingo Morales, director of program evaluation and monitoring in the industrial inspection unit at PROFEPA, stated that "in the past, companies entered the auditing program so that [the industrial inspection area] would not visit them. That provision was removed. We can visit them whenever we want." Now certified companies are inspected either in the event of a citizen complaint or "if there is a perception that the company is falsifying the documentation it presents." Morales indicated that there may exist a certain "conflict of interest" for the environmental auditor, who works for the company. Although it is not frequent, they have encountered cases of certified companies where "we do find irregularities, which supposedly should not exist. Why? Because the audit was supposed to have detected all those inconsistencies."[56] On the other hand, although Montoya from the environmental auditing department agreed that there is no policy to exempt certified companies from inspections, in order to "optimize" resources, he stated that inspections of certified facilities would not be a priority: "Maybe the inspector is going to say, 'Hey, this company has massive control systems, it has five certifications, let's not make it a priority, let's rather go to this one.'"[57]

A few words are warranted about the inspections carried out by PROFEPA. As with CONAGUA, PROFEPA suffers from a lack of personnel. In early 2014, Morales reported that the industrial inspection unit had 250 inspectors. The universe of companies to be monitored was approximately 194,791 installations, the majority being hazardous waste generators (169,836), with the rest being installations that generate atmospheric emissions (24,955). Capacity and inspections have dropped 60 percent, from an average of 6,651 inspections per year related to industry compliance and natural resource use between 2010 and 2018 to just 2,681 per year in 2019 and 2020 (SEMARNAT 2021b). PROFEPA's budget as a percentage of SEMARNAT's total budget for the environmental sector has also fallen, from an average of 4 percent of the budget between 2001 and 2004 to 2 percent between 2013 and 2020. The total budget of the environmental sector has also undergone a dramatic drop in recent years, shrinking 46 percent between 2016 and 2020, from more than MX$55 billion to less than MX$30 billion (SEMARNAT 2021a).

From the PROFEPA delegation in Jalisco, the head of the legal department, Francisco Javier Silva, reported in 2013 that they had five inspectors for industry. To strengthen their inspection area, they signed an agreement with the State Bureau of Environmental Protection (PROEPA) so that the state entity could carry out inspections in matters of federal jurisdiction, thus increasing to a total of between fifteen and eighteen inspectors. However, he believed that "the agreement is not enough, but more or less we're doing what we can."[58]

On the subject of PROFEPA's inspections, Marisa Jacott of Fronteras Comunes expressed the concern that parties "are generally notified . . . and it may be that although they are not notified, generally the industrialists are aware, in some way there are leaks and communication between the authorities and industry." Morales from PROFEPA affirmed that "most are surprise" visits, which is essential to observe the normal operating conditions of the companies. Nonetheless, he acknowledged that there are situations where inspectors are asked to wait on arriving at an industry because the legal representative is not present: "So, they ask you to come back the next day, then they are told or an agreement is reached on the place or date and time when we will return."[59]

Returning to the CI program, the fact that audits lack the "surprise factor" was highlighted by Jacott to question their effectiveness: "The way these certifications are done with prior appointments, that is, there is an entire preliminary administrative procedure and preparation to be able to obtain the certification." Ongoing oversight is also insufficient, in her opinion. "In Mexico, a Clean Industry certificate implies that I've already dealt with them," said Jacott. "I'm an example, nobody bothers me again, and it's like a protection . . . but they don't do any follow-up."[60]

In Jalisco, several of the largest companies in the corridor currently hold CI certifications, among them Alen del Norte, Continental Automotive Guadalajara, Effem Mexico (Mars), EMG, Flextronics, Honda, Oxiteno, and Quimikao (PROFEPA 2022a). In the interviews carried out, I encountered varying perspectives on the program. For some of the transnationals, although they voiced positive views of the program, it is not considered of high value. Two EHS managers that I interviewed at an American food company with a factory in the corridor explained that they have not seen anything "that pushes us to become certified" in CI. Although the company has its own environmental management system, they observed that "Clean Industry makes you invest in that you have to hire an adviser to come and do the assessments . . . and in the end you aren't released from the inspection program" of the government. One of the managers explained that, as a company, "we always seek a win-win relationship," and therefore the mere fact of "having the piece of paper that says that you are Clean Industry" is not reason enough to seek certification.[61]

The manager of the Nestlé factory in Ocotlán, in the same vein, indicated that they let their CI certificate expire, although he considered the program "valuable," in that "it represents the respect of a series of standards." In his opinion, however, there are companies that make inappropriate use of the certification: "sometimes this type of emblem is misused and, for example, there are companies that seek it out just to sell" the image.[62] For one of the American electronics companies in the corridor, although it held the CI certification between 2000 and 2010, it subsequently determined the expense was not a priority. In this sense, the head of EHS explained that their clients are almost exclusively outside Mexico and that "they come asking [for] ISO 14000, that is, a client has never asked us [for] Clean Industry."[63] There may be other reasons as well for dropping the CI certification.

From the German auto parts manufacturer ZF, the environmental protection coordinator reported that, although it is a "magnificent" program, they have not been recertified since 2011 due to factory expansion, as they first hoped to "stabilize" their new production processes before attempting to renew their certification. The coordinator related that "an auditor came and did a pre-audit and told us what the areas are that we have to improve. Because as we have changed [processes], he told us, 'Wait for that to expand and we'll make sure that the water you generate there doesn't affect the treatment plant.'"[64] Thus, they let their certification expire and to date they do not have a valid certificate. Similarly, from another US electronics company in the corridor, the environmental manager clarified that they have not sought CI certification due to the "exponential" growth of their plant: "Really we have started many processes, new buildings, etc., and the truth is that right now it is complicated."[65] Hence it seems that while some companies are not interested in the program, others leave it when they cannot guarantee full compliance with regulations.

For certified companies, interviewees highlight several benefits of the CI program. From the Mexican company Urrea, the EHS coordinator emphasized the tax incentives linked to CI, incentives that were later no longer included in the 2014 Income Tax Law (PROFEPA 2014). In addition, he spoke of improvements in community relations and in the work environment that led to a decrease in staff turnover, improved customer recognition, and the fact that "it helps you to springboard and achieve ISO 14001."[66] For the Japanese chemical company Quimikao, the safety supervisor pointed out that "the fact of being certified gives us an image that we are doing things well and that we are validated," since CI provides their clients with "the confidence that we are complying." It also has an impact on relations with environmental authorities, even when it does not exempt them from PROFEPA inspections. In this sense, the safety supervisor stated, "We have a little leeway in this regard, because they know our weak points"; they are given certain "consideration" because "we obviously open up our information, and there is that trust."[67] In this way, they earn the trust of both customers and authorities.

I have underscored how, despite the proclaimed target of certified companies going beyond the requirements of legal standards, the CI process focuses only on ensuring legal compliance and, when a company cannot guarantee that compliance, it simply has the option of letting the certification expire. This is the conclusion reached by Blackman and colleagues (2010) about the CI certification, which in general did not lead to long-term environmental improvements for the participating companies and focused on addressing regulatory breaches rather than encouraging companies to exceed legal standards. The lack of regular oversight by PROFEPA implies that whether compliance is maintained is often not verified after certification is achieved.

3.5 State- and Municipal-Level Regulation

In this last section, I will touch on the regulation of industrial activity by state and municipal authorities, who have limited powers in matters of discharges to national waters. Enforcement of environmental regulations is fragmented, with oversight for different sectors and types of emissions assigned to federal, state, or municipal authorities. In relation to wastewater discharge, the then-director of legal and environmental compliance at PROEPA, Edgar Olaéz, explained that when conducting inspections, they only verify the existence of a treatment system: "Of the industries that we visit that are within our competence . . . we are going to check from the door inwards, that prior to making a discharge they have a treatment system." However, PROEPA does not verify whether this treatment system is adequate: "The quality of this system depends on whether it is supervised by CONAGUA or the municipality. I can't go in to ask them to comply with the standard, nor can I ask them to treat it properly, which is a bit of a paradox."[68] Focusing only on wastewater discharge, then, the constrained scope of action of the state government is evident.

State governor Enrique Alfaro (2018–), as part of his Revive the Santiago River strategy, announced that PROEPA's inspection capacity would be strengthened; however, the initiative was short lived. The strategy involved increasing PROEPA's budget, which rose from MX$16.7 million in 2018 (under Governor Aristóteles Sandoval of the Institutional Revolutionary Party) to MX$66.9 in 2019. Unfortunately, this financial bolstering has eroded. The head of PROEPA explained in 2021 that the increased resources in 2019 allowed them to hire ten to twelve new inspectors and pay for a study of discharges in the Upper Santiago River Basin, but with the advent of the COVID-19 pandemic there was a "setback,"[69] and the PROEPA budget dropped to MX$52 million in 2020 and only MX$25.9 million in 2021 (Gobierno del Estado de Jalisco 2022).

In another area of action, since 2012 SEMADET has promoted a CI-style program, known as Voluntary Environmental Compliance (VEC). Similar to CI, the VEC program analyzes compliance with federal, state, and municipal regulations, although it contemplates the option of only reviewing state standards. In the event that a company chooses only an assessment of compliance with state regulations, however, they are not allowed to make use of the Environmental Commitment seal. In mid-2014, it seemed that the program had not provoked great interest from the industrial sector, since the then-director of the Sustainability of the Productive Sector Department at SEMADET, Luz Marcela Fernández, affirmed that only sixty-five companies were enrolled in the program and twelve had been certified. Of the sixty-five registered, "there were approximately forty from the manufacturing sector or with some type of industrial process, and the rest are from commerce and services."[70] In 2016, twenty-three companies were certified from a universe of potential establishments estimated at 53,736 companies (Gobierno del Estado de Jalisco 2017). At the same time, fifteen of the manufacturing plants certified in the state program were also certified in CI.[71] Not only are few companies certified, then, but it seems that the program is also far from capturing companies that the CI program does not attract, as Fernández stated was their goal: "we want to focus or have focused more on sectors of medium and small companies or even micro" enterprises.

With that goal, the VEC program is more flexible than its federal counterpart. To lessen the companies' fear of exposing existing infractions, for instance, Fernández specified that "there is an agreement that states that [PROEPA] will not inspect them until after the process is finished, unless there is an environmental emergency or an environmental complaint."[72] A final incentive, compared with the CI program, is the option of using the seal directly on product packaging. Such use is not permitted with the CI seal. Regardless, participation in the program remains low.

The same department at SEMADET is also responsible for regulating certain aspects of industrial activity in the state. In this regard, Fernández lamented that of the "seventy-five thousand companies in Jalisco . . . less than 10 percent—between 7 and 10 percent—have completed some type of [regulatory commitment] with the ministry." One of the procedures that is obligatory for a portion of these companies is the filing of a state COA. Although it has been required since 2007, Fernández reported that there has been little progress in compelling companies to file their certificates: "Last year [2013], only for atmospheric emissions, we received approximately 550 [COAs]. It's almost funny, because the [environmental] licenses we have granted are 2,000, or 2,200, or 2,300, out of 8,000 more or less fixed sources that exist in the state. So, it's not at all representative." Attempting to access these state COAs for a number of companies led to another case where the transparency of government information came into question. In September 2014, I submitted a request to SEMADET for the state COAs of thirty-four companies in the corridor for the period from 2007 to 2013.[73] SEMADET denied having this information. Subsequently, I filed an appeal for review with the Jalisco Institute of Transparency and Public Information (ITEI, Instituto de Transparencia e Información Pública de Jalisco), providing evidence from SEMADET's website that confirmed the existence of the requested information.

The ITEI judged the appeal valid and ordered SEMADET to issue a new response to the request for information. Likewise, it warned the director of environmental protection at SEMADET of "possible breaches" of the state transparency law, advising that "if such omissions are incurred again, it will be reason to order the opening of the corresponding Administrative Responsibility Procedure."[74] Following the ITEI resolution, SEMADET responded that the COA reports consisted of 22,510 pages of information, in addition to thirty-one maps and sixty-seven compact discs; accessing that information, therefore, would have a cost of MX$35,071.50.[75] Given this cost, I sought direct access to review the files in person. After multiple requests, SEMADET staff alleged that the information was not available and that they did not have the time to prepare a public version of the documents for my review. So, despite the successful appeal, it was not possible to consult the information and a lack of transparency prevailed.

Finally, a few brief remarks on authorities at the municipal level who are responsible for overseeing discharge to sewer systems and for granting municipal permits. Here I encountered a scarcity of human resources, a lack of technical capacity, and testimonies indicative of corruption. The director, Víctor Castellanos, remarked that of the fifteen or sixteen people assigned to the Ecology Department in the town of Ocotlán, population 106,050 (INEGI 2020a), "the bulk of the staff are gardeners."[76] Therefore, as director, he had to perform many of the regulatory functions himself: "I really need to have operational personnel, because being honest the truth is, I have to divide myself into a thousand at times." Although at the time of the interview he indicated that they were about to hire five new people for the department, due to the low salary levels offered, he was not hopeful they would be able to hire skilled staff.

Having personnel with technical knowledge is important since, depending on the type of business or industry, a requirement of the municipal operating license is an expert opinion from the Ecology Department. Department personnel also have to carry out inspections of workshops or companies in the event of citizen complaints. Castellanos stated that they receive several complaints a month. In Ocotlán, he said, "an inspection of a furniture maker is very common, we are a city that has around two thousand furniture workshops."[77] A good number of these furniture production sites are small workshops in houses that operate clandestinely. This sector, he indicated, is responsible for discharges of toxic substances into storm sewers that discharge into the Zula River, which borders Ocotlán until it joins the Santiago River.

Inspections of industries take place in response to citizen complaints or, if they are undertaken by initiative of the Ecology Department, facilities are notified before the inspection. Without this prior notification, Castellanos stated that it is not possible to proceed with the inspection: "Because if I want to, right now I go to a company, I say, 'I'm from the Ecology Department, I've come to do an inspection,' and they can close the door . . . but if you provide written notice, 'You know what, I'm going to go . . . ,' you have something to back you up." In any case, few inspections are carried out at the initiative of the department: "How often do we do it? Very sporadically because really, I tell you, I don't have enough staff." At the same time, when visits are made to the small workshops, the inspections "are very flexible." Castellanos shared, "I'm very honest, when I go to do an inspection, I always try to ensure that they have the bare minimum, so that we don't pollute."[78] It is difficult to demand more from microbusinesses, he asserted, which are not the most polluting either in his opinion.

To conclude this section, I would like to refer to the testimony of a former official of the El Salto municipal government who carried out inspections in coordination with personnel from the Ecology Department. This former official, on condition of anonymity, claimed to have witnessed acts of corruption and to have been fired for his insistence on penalizing irregularities when detected: "I was told, 'You're getting a bad reputation because you really go to the bottom of things.'" The former inspector narrated specific cases where he observed that polluting activities were covered up. For instance, he related that he stopped a tanker truck that was discharging waste into a stream near the El Ahogado Dam: "There was a grassy area and they were emptying a tanker truck containing three thousand liters of pollutants directly into the stream. . . . It was something oily, brownish—three thousand liters directly to the stream!" His attempt to stop this was insufficient, however: "For God's sake, I removed the plates from the truck . . .

they stopped the truck and took everything away, but it turns out that they released the truck again and then nothing, everything was fixed up."[79] In these "fix-ups," he affirmed, both bribes directly to inspectors and agreements with the mayor played a role. He stated that he was offered money directly and that other city inspectors received bribes.

* * *

At the end of this lengthy chapter, we have the anonymous testimony of a municipal inspector alleging acts of bribery, acts that meet the accepted definition of corruption. As illegal acts, there is no easily verifiable documentation or evidence to determine their prevalence. However, the bulk of the chapter has been devoted to examining the application of "official" regulations, both direct and indirect, drawing from interviews with officials from the various agencies involved at the federal, state, and municipal levels, as well as government documents and statistics. A common theme across all three levels is insufficient human resources. At the municipal level, the lack of personnel with the necessary technical qualifications is more acute. In the case of CONAGUA, which continues to centralize key functions in the control of discharges, there has been a substantial decline from 34,000 staff at its creation in 1989 (Wester et al. 2009), to 13,193 employees in 2014.[80] Beyond the issues of human resources, however, the regulatory system suffers from other weaknesses that have been charted throughout the chapter.

Key characteristics are the minimal level of regulatory enforcement and the omission in the oversight of self-reported information—information that is also branded as unreliable by water authorities. Based on information requests to CONAGUA, in addition, it is possible to conclude that there is a lack of transparency and access to information that may result from improper handling of data within the commission or from a refusal to make transparent information about the penalties applied to companies, as well as their reports emanating from the mandatory discharge sampling required of permit holders. The panorama of the RETC, which should respond to communities' right to know about chemical risks, is one of noncontinuous reports by companies and information of dubious quality. Regarding emissions to water, the weaknesses of the RETC are apparent both when comparing the volumes reported with those in Canada and the United States and when observing that the reported emissions to water are almost exclusively the substances included in the NOM-001 (heavy metals and cyanide). This implies that almost no emissions of synthetic toxic substances to water bodies are reported in Mexico.

For the voluntary certification program, CI, both its role in motivating long-term improvements in the environmental performance of participating companies and the interest of the industrial sector in participating remain in doubt. Its state-level counterpart, SEMADET's VEC program, has sparked very little interest, despite its greater flexibility. With only a cursory review, I highlighted some of the weaknesses of the regulation of industrial activity by the state government and municipalities, where there is evidence of companies evading their responsibilities to complete procedures such as the state COA, as well as an inadequate inspection capacity and limited powers to control effluent discharge.

I opened this chapter by asking, what institutional logics predominate in water and pollution management? To answer this question, we can ask, Who are the winners and losers of the current configurations? If regulations do not work to protect aquatic ecosystems or to ensure living rivers; if they do not function to safeguard the well-being of the communities that live in the vicinity of water bodies and industrial facilities, they do, nonetheless, work to normalize and regulate polluting activities. So far, I have not dwelt on the role of industry in shaping this system, which is functional for some. That is one of the objectives of chapter 4, which delves into the processes whereby environmental standards are developed and negotiated, a topic that will allow me to analyze with greater clarity the relations between government authorities and the industrial sector.

4 The Enemy at Home: Regulatory Capture and Wastewater Discharge

March 2022 saw a modified standard for wastewater discharge into surface waters approved in Mexico, after twenty-five years with only the lax NOM-001-SEMARNAT-1996 (NOM-001) in effect. This news, celebrated by environmental organizations, was not welcomed by the industrial sector. Complying with the new regulation will be "materially impossible," affirmed José Abugaber, president of the Confederation of Mexican Chambers of Industry (CONCAMIN, Confederación de Cámaras Industriales de los Estados Unidos Mexicanos), who stated that "there will be a severe economic impact. . . . We call on the authorities to open a dialogue to discuss this" (De la Rosa 2022). The new standard "will cause an increase in the prices of industrial and agricultural products, which will end up impacting the economy of families, [and lead to] a loss of competitiveness of Mexican products abroad and a rain of injunctions for being unconstitutional and unconventional," stated CONCAMIN days after the new standard was published (*Forbes* 2022). Catastrophic scenarios of bankrupt companies and escalating consumer prices aside, this regulation and the process through which it was modified constitute a window into an important facet of institutional logics and the power relations governing environmental regulation.

In chapter 3, my discussion focused almost exclusively on the actions of water and environmental authorities, with some mention of the perceptions of industry actors. These actors in industry, however, do not passively receive and accept government regulations. In this regard, I have discerned a state-centric tendency in much academic research, which focuses on "state-society" relations, leaving aside the private sector and thus exempting one of the major causes of environmental degradation from analysis. How can we understand the flows of power in environmental regulation if we do not also put the focus on the regulated parties? Curiously, this fits very well with the conception of the state presented by neoliberal ideologues, who encounter a source of danger in the excessive powers of the state. Milton Friedman, for example, writes,

> Freedom is a rare and delicate plant. Our minds tell us, and history confirms, that the great threat to freedom is the concentration of power. Government is necessary to preserve our freedom, it is an instrument through which we can exercise our freedom; yet by concentrating power in political hands, it is also a threat to freedom. (1982, 2)

"Competitive capitalism," affirms Friedman, is the antidote to this threat, where government should be at the lowest level possible, limited to enforcing law and order, ensuring adherence to private contracts, and fostering competitive markets (2). In this competitive capitalism, moreover, "economic freedom . . . also promotes political freedom because it separates economic power from political power and in this way enables the one to offset the other" (9). Beyond the professions of blind faith in the wisdom of markets, this formulation fails to consider the threats to "freedom" from the concentration of power in private hands. It also overlooks the possible "colonization" of the state by economic power (Tirado 2012, 342).

In this chapter, I explore the power relations between industry and government in the setting of environmental standards through the case of the national wastewater discharge standard (NOM-001). In the first section, I question "pluralist" visions of the state to spotlight the concentration of economic power and its influence on the state. From there the following four sections explore the institutions and actors involved in the case of the NOM-001, which I argue represents not only an example of the institutionalized corruption I seek to demonstrate but also a case of regulatory capture.

In their useful formulation, Daniel Carpenter and David Moss characterize regulatory capture as "the result or process by which regulation, in law or application, is consistently or repeatedly directed away from the public interest and toward the interests of the regulated industry, by the intent and action of the industry itself" (2014, 13). This definition highlights three central concepts. The first is the public interest, which must be defined through a "defeasible model," and which in this case may be understood as the protection of a healthy environment and the rights to health, water, and sanitation, among others. The second is intent, and here the key challenge is demonstrating that industry has actively sought to drive regulations toward its interests and away from the public interest, as opposed to simply establishing that regulations are favorable to industry. The third element is identifying the regulated industry. Early studies of capture after World War II in the United States from the fields of law, economics, and political science focused largely on independent regulatory commissions setting rules for particular industries (Stigler 1975; Novak 2014). In fact, Ernesto Dal Bó (2006) highlights that the bulk of scholarship on regulatory capture has centered on regulated monopolies, particularly utilities regulation. Where environmental regulations are concerned, a range of industries and other interests may be affected (Zinn 2002). In the case explored in this chapter, I will describe the intent and actions of industry that helped maintain the NOM-001 of 1996 in effect until 2022.

4.1 Flows of Power

Though I do not wish to suggest that they are equivalent, one way to gauge the concentration of power is by looking at accumulated global wealth on the side of "economic power" by comparing the revenue of some of the world's largest corporations with the gross domestic product (GDP) of countries, as I have done in table 4.1 with data for 2020. The table includes the GDP of Mexico and the United States, as reference points, as well as the revenue of the top ten corporations in the *Fortune* 500 Global 2020 ranking. In addition, from Honda Motor onward, it includes a series of *Fortune* 500 Global companies with plants in the industrial corridor under study, as well as several countries with GDPs similar to the revenues of these corporations. From this it follows, for example, that the GDP of Mexico, the fifteenth-largest global economy, was equivalent to roughly double Walmart's 2020 revenue. German auto parts manufacturer ZF Friedrichshafen, which has a plant in El Salto, had a higher revenue in 2020 than the GDP of Bolivia, a South American country with a population of approximately 11.7 million inhabitants. In total, the 2020 revenue of the five hundred largest corporations equaled 39 percent of global GDP ($33.3 trillion of revenue from the five hundred companies versus a global GDP of $84.7 trillion) (*Fortune*, n.d.-a; World Bank 2022).

Another way to calculate this concentration is by analyzing the wealth of the richest individuals on the planet. In its 2021 *Global Wealth Report*, financial services company Credit Suisse estimated that the richest 1 percent

Table 4.1

Selection of countries and companies with GDP or revenue and global ranking (2020)

Country or company	GDP or 2020 revenue (billion $USD)	Ranking of country or company
United States	$20,953	1
Mexico	$1,074	15
Sweden	$541	22
Walmart (US)	$524	1
Belgium	$522	23
Sinopec Group (China)	$407	2
Argentina	$389	29
State Grid (China)	$384	3
China National Petroleum (China)	$379	4
Egypt	$365	30
Royal Dutch Shell (Netherlands)	$352	5
South Africa	$335	38
Saudi Aramco (Saudi Arabia)	$329	6
Volkswagen (Germany)	$282	7
BP (UK)	$282	8
Amazon (US)	$281	9
Toyota Motor (Japan)	$275	10
Colombia	$271	40
Algeria	$145	56
Honda Motor (Japan)	$137	39
Ecuador	$99	65
Siemens (Germany)	$98	74
Nestlé (Switzerland)	$92	82
Guatemala	$78	69
IBM (US)	$77	118
PepsiCo (US)	$67	160
Costa Rica	$62	75
Continental (Germany)	$50	230
ZF Friedrichshafen (Germany)	$41	302
Bolivia	$37	92

Source: Author's elaboration based on data from *Fortune* (n.d.-a) and World Bank (2022).

of adults owned 45 percent of global wealth, while the top 10 percent held 82 percent of household assets (Credit Suisse 2021). At the other extreme, the 50 percent of adults at the bottom of the wealth pyramid possessed just 1 percent of global wealth in 2020. The trend is similar in Mexico. In 2014, Credit Suisse rated the country as an emerging market with high inequality, where the wealthiest 10 percent controlled 64.4 percent of national wealth (2014, 33). For the Mexican case it is essential to underscore the economic power of billionaires, numbering sixteen in 2014 with a combined fortune of US$142.9 billion. Between 2011 and 2014, the wealth of four billionaires, Carlos Slim, Germán Larrea, Alberto Baillères, and Ricardo Salinas Pliego, was equivalent on average to 9 percent of GDP (Esquivel Hernández 2015, 17, 19). Furthermore, these four billionaires derived part of their wealth from "sectors that were privatized, concessioned and/or regulated by the public sector" (20). Adding two others to the list—Eva Gonda de Rivera (FEMSA) and María Asunción Aramburuzabala (owner of Grupo Modelo until its 2013 sale to Anheuser-Busch Inbev)—Oxfam Mexico reported in early 2020 that the six richest people in the country had "more wealth than the poorest 50%" (Oxfam México 2020).

Another facet of this private power, its influence on politics, is often difficult to assess, due to the lack of transparency regarding lobbying activities, networks of relationships, and acts of corruption. Despite this, various observers have stressed the growing power of business elites in the previously more autonomous sphere of public policy in Mexico (Puga 2004; Alba Vega 2006; Hogenboom 2007). Thus, James Cypher and Raúl Delgado Wise (2010, 77) describe the "deep interpenetration between the state and the private sector," resulting from the transformations toward neoliberal policies during the presidency of Miguel de la Madrid (1982–1988) and decisively consolidated during the presidential term of Carlos Salinas (1988–1994). The Business Coordinating Council (CCE, Consejo Coordinador Empresarial) and other apex business organizations became embedded in the development of public policy, as evidenced in the numerous meetings held between these organizations and the president and senior officials (43).

In contrast to Friedman's implausible stance, which maintains that political and economic powers balance each other, Ralph Miliband asserts that "economic life cannot be separated from political life" (1969, 265). Miliband attempts to remedy what he identifies as a deficiency in Marxist analyses, which he maintains rarely examine "the question of the state" for real capitalist societies, while upholding the thesis that the state in capitalist societies is no more than a "coercive instrument of a ruling class" (5, 6). Written in the late 1960s, Miliband's analysis focuses on the cases of certain "advanced capitalist societies" (the United States, England, France, Federal Germany, and Japan), and he concludes that "unequal economic power, on the scale and of the kind encountered in advanced capitalist societies, inherently *produces* political inequality, on a more or less commensurate scale" (265; emphasis in original). Furthermore, this critical vision diverges from another still-dominant one that conceives power in Western societies as diffuse and fragmented. From this "pluralist" perspective, the state is the entity that accommodates and reconciles the interests of the various groups, without any bias (4). While for Mexico, the history and economic, political, and social factors are very different from the cases analyzed by Miliband, and global conditions have also changed in the period since his study, the need to analyze real capitalist states, in this case the Mexican state, remains pertinent, as does the need to understand the penetration of the interests of economic elites.

A key starting point is the recognition that capitalist states understand as among their main functions those of increasing GDP, attracting investment, and creating a business-friendly environment. As Harvard economist Michael Porter states, "National competitiveness has become one of the central preoccupations of government and industry in every nation" (1990, 76). It is to be expected, then, that entrepreneurs will have political influence in a market economy. If, for instance, a government carries out reforms that put private profit and investment at risk, "the economy may go into crisis and that will have political consequences that can be serious for the state" (Tirado 2012, 331). Even acknowledging this "structural dependency," however, Ricardo Tirado points out that the particular style of capitalist development of each country will be determined in particular by the level of influence on policy of economic actors, an effect mediated by the power relations between political and business elites (332). Tirado coincides with Carlos Alba Vega (2006) and Cypher and Delgado Wise (2010) in identifying the growing influence on policy of Mexican business elites, and in particular the CCE. Two phenomena identified by Tirado as forms of undue corporate influence are the "colonization and capture of state agencies" (342). "Colonization" refers to "making a public regulatory agency assume as its own the rules made by those who are going to be regulated by them," while "capture" applies to situations where a person loyal to business interests is charged with regulating precisely those interests.

At times during this investigation, it was possible to get a glimpse of the relations between political and economic actors that are difficult to study directly. Thus, for example, during the Mexico Business Summit, held in Guadalajara in October 2013, the minister of economy, Idelfonso Guajardo, reported proudly to the businesspeople present that when then–president Enrique Peña Nieto (2012–2018) attended the Sun Valley conference of technology and media executives in California earlier in the year, he met with

> the president of HP, with the presidents of Google and of Apple. First to my surprise, the president led the meeting with them and said, "Gentlemen, I am not going to give you the sales speech for Mexico, I already gave you that in the morning. I want to take advantage of these fifty minutes of meeting with you, so that you can tell me what we have to do as a country to become the alternative to Silicon Valley. In other words, what public policies do we need to boost the information technology sector?" . . . The four agreed that the state best positioned in the IT cluster is Jalisco.[1]

Thus, Guajardo not only shared this joyous news for Jalisco but also revealed a certain vision wherein good politicians orient their policies according to the needs of large foreign corporations.

A further facet of the relationship between government and the private sector came to my attention at a 2014 event organized by a now-defunct arm of the Ministry of Economy, ProMéxico. In a panel on the successful cooperation between government and business during the negotiations for the Pacific Alliance, a trade agreement between Mexico, Chile, Colombia, and Peru, Moisés Kalach, president of the National Chamber of the Textile Industry, spoke of the "novelty" of the Peña Nieto government in not presenting its own vision in the negotiations "but rather obtaining information from the industry from the bottom up" and developing a "seamless" relationship with the industry representatives, who established a "*cuarto de junto*" (adjoining meeting room) in the negotiations where the government representatives went to "consult" them throughout the process (see also Schneider 2002). During the same panel, Sergio Contreras, the vice president of the Mexican Business Council for Foreign Trade, Investment and Technology, stressed that for them, ProMéxico "is not a government agency but rather . . . an agency that is hand in hand, with us."[2] The council is a member of the CCE and includes among its members not only the large Mexican conglomerates (Cemex, FEMSA, Grupo México, Alfa, Bimbo, etc.) but also such transnational corporations as Walmart, Iberdrola, Chrysler, Nissan, and FedEx (COMCE 2010). This work "hand in hand" with the government, particularly the Ministry of Economy, to establish an international agreement, then, cannot be interpreted either as work on behalf of only national capitals.

There is another powerful reason to avoid state-centric analyses, or an evaluation that assumes, Friedman-style, that the state exists as an autonomous sphere of political power separate from the realm of economic power. Under this assumption, the state is often assigned the role of "balancing" the interests of economic growth and environmental protection—under the rubric of sustainable development. This is the function that Mark Whitehead and colleagues (2006), for example, assign to the state when they maintain that "the state plays a crucial role in developing political and ecological strategies which ensure that prevailing capitalist ideologies of nature as an exploitable and abundant resource are made compatible with the role of nature as both a context for social reproduction and a broader arena for cultural existence" (54). In addition to this, an exclusive focus on the state facilitates "stageist" interpretations that assign environmental problems and deficiencies in environmental regulation to the level of development. This explanation obviates the need to analyze the power relations around environmental regulation and, more specifically, the role of nonstate actors, including domestic and transnational corporations. In the next section, I delve into these relations through the case of the NOM-001.

4.2 The Process of Modifying the NOM-001 Standard

From its emission until its modification in March 2022, the NOM-001 was the only standard applicable for discharges to national waters, rivers, lakes, groundwater, and so on, and it set limits for just a score of parameters. Yolanda Pica, a researcher at the Mexican Institute of Water Technology (IMTA, Instituto Mexicano de Tecnología del Agua), explained the deficiencies of the 1996 standard: "If you analyze in detail the parameters included, it somehow evades toxic organic substances, because there is no way, no parameter to suggest the presence of that type of substance." With this "myopic" standard, she elaborated, "the bodies of water now have a load of organic substances that, since no one has ever monitored [for them], our water bodies are in the condition they are in."[3] In the case of the Santiago River, it was due to this myopia that IMTA determined that compliance with the NOM-001 would be insufficient to commence river restoration. This is a conclusion of the 2011 IMTA study, which included a draft declaration of classification of the Santiago River. The National Water Law (Article 87) empowers the National Water Commission (CONAGUA, Comisión Nacional del Agua) to issue classification declarations of water bodies as instruments to establish wastewater regulations that go beyond the limited NOM-001, as well as water quality goals and deadlines to meet them.

The draft regulatory impact statement (RIS) presented in the IMTA study concluded, in reference to the NOM-001, that it "does not regulate pollutants that are hazardous to the ecosystem and people, such as toxic organic compounds," among others, though monitoring of the Santiago River provided "evidence of the presence of these pollutants." Thus, using mathematical models, the study authors asserted that, "even with compliance with the NOM-001-SEMARNAT-1996, the water quality goals in the Santiago River are not met" (IMTA and CEA 2011, X-2).

Not being a technical expert on this issue, I sought the opinion on the Mexican standard of an official at the German Federal Environment Agency (Umweltbundesamt), Michael Suhr, who specializes in industrial effluent quality standards and the best available technique for effluent treatment. Based on an initial review of the NOM-001, Suhr observed several technical shortcomings, commenting that, "from a German perspective, it will not protect the environment." He considered the limits for the discharge of phosphorus to rivers to be "nonsense," specifying that "you have to add double the phosphorus for untreated municipal wastewater to reach 20 or 30 [mg/L]," which is the maximum limit in the standard for type A and type B classified rivers. Suhr concluded that "this has nothing to do with environmental protection." Similarly, he pointed out that the limit set for biochemical oxygen demand for type A rivers of 200 mg/L "is not so far away from [the levels in] untreated municipal wastewater," which would be in the range of 200 to 350 mg/L. This implies that "you can discharge in these rivers whatever you like more or less." Overall, Suhr concluded from this standard that "the state more or less has given up that these rivers should reach sooner or later a better quality."[4] These permissive limits explain why, in an interview, the head of environmental management at an American electronics company in El Salto commented on the NOM-001 that she "complied with it with one hand tied behind my back."[5]

In Germany, as in many other countries, there is no single standard for all effluent. Rather, wastewater is regulated by industrial sector, and the

German wastewater ordinance includes fifty-seven appendices, with the specific parameters established for domestic discharges and fifty-six industrial sectors or processes (Federal Ministry for the Environment, Nature Conservation and Nuclear Safety, Germany 2004). As the types of contaminants, and the levels of technically achievable treatment, will vary between, for example, a food and beverage company and a pharmaceutical factory or an electroplating plant, Suhr explained that "not looking at the source of pollution normally leads to requirements which are not technically based" and that "are somehow arbitrary and difficult to justify." He stated that regulating not based on the distinctions between industrial sectors but rather, as in Mexico, based on a classification that establishes categories for the use of the body of water (agricultural irrigation, public-urban use, or protection of aquatic life) "doesn't lead to a good protection level." It appears, he opined, that "the target here is not to reach really a good water quality level but rather to avoid maybe catastrophe."[6]

To round out the contrast with the regulatory system in Germany, I would highlight that Germany applies a "combined approach," with both requirements based on sectoral regulations and "quality requirements that take into account the waterbody status" (Irmer and Kirschbaum 2010, 9). This is in accordance with the EU Water Framework Directive (Directive 2000/60/EC), which stipulates that pollution prevention and regulation should contemplate the "control of pollution at source through the setting of emission limit values and of environmental quality standards" (European Union 2000). According to a report from the German Federal Environment Agency, the goal for surface waters in Germany is to achieve "good hygienic, ecological and chemical status in which aquatic communities differ only marginally from their natural state, and which are suitable for unrestricted use as bathing or fishing waters or for the abstraction of drinking water" (Irmer and Kirschbaum 2010, 9). In consequence, many industrial facilities have made progress on reducing pollutant emissions through measures such as closed-loop systems and the substitution of hazardous substances. Even so, challenges persist in attaining the goal of good ecological and hygienic status, and quality objectives are frequently not achieved for heavy metals, as well as for certain pesticides, industrial chemicals, and pharmaceuticals (Irmer and Kirschbaum 2010). In Mexico, CONAGUA's National Monitoring Network does not contemplate the monitoring of heavy metals, pesticides, industrial chemicals, or pharmaceuticals.

The Enemy at Home 179

Turning to a more local analysis of the standard, a 2011 evaluation by the Ministry of Environment and Natural Resources (SEMARNAT, Secretaría de Medio Ambiente y Recursos Naturales) concludes that the NOM-001 has had "*zero effect or impact*" (45; emphasis added). In blunt terms, the document states that this standard "is not complied with, which represents the uninhibited discharge of pollutants." From the polluters' perspective, it states, "it is more costly to comply with the NOM than to face the consequences of non-compliance (sanctions)" (45). In the assessment of the federal government, then, the failure to enforce this standard is unmistakable.

4.2.1 Understanding Standard Setting

When beginning this investigation, I was acutely aware of the technical deficiencies of the current standard, as well as the demands for its modification by environmental organizations. However, what was unclear was the actual possibility of modifying or substituting this standard; I was also unacquainted with the entities involved in that process. In my attempts to fill in these gaps, a picture began to emerge of the standard-setting process, whereby environmental technical standards are generated or modified. Shortly after commencing my research, I was able to confirm that the NOM-001 standard was in the process of being modified. At an environment, safety, and hygiene congress of the National Chemical Industry Association (ANIQ, Asociación Nacional de la Industria Química) in June 2013, Yolanda Pica of IMTA presented a preliminary draft of this modification.

To explain why the standard needed to be updated, during her presentation at the congress, Pica narrated how the NOM-001 "was developed in response to the demands of industry that said, 'It's that in Mexico there are no laboratories that perform more complex analyses.'" For this reason, there was only an "ephemeral" period during which the forty-four standards with regulations by industrial sector were in force. These standards were questioned by industry representatives who alleged a shortage of laboratories able to analyze the parameters established therein. Pica gave the example of effluents from a Mexican oil refinery that complied with all the parameters of the current regulation and that, nonetheless, were highly toxic. Those effluents complied with the NOM-001, she explained, because releasing these types of toxic substances "is not even evaluated, it's not even punished." Thus, Pica argued that it has been amply demonstrated that the "[NOM-]001—and everyone knows it—does not do much to protect the environment. Why?

Well, because we have these effluents that pass the standard and, nevertheless, they have a toxic load."[7] The preliminary draft she presented of a modified NOM-001 contemplated new parameters: acute toxicity, as well as chemical oxygen demand (COD) and color. At the congress, it was mentioned that this draft had been circulated among ANIQ members.

How was the draft standard generated? At what point in the discussion and approval process was it currently? Would this new standard enable greater environmental protection? These were the questions I wanted to answer at the time. Following the trail of this draft entailed attempting to understand two government bodies: the National Environment and Natural Resources Standards Advisory Committee (COMARNAT, Comité Consultivo Nacional de Normalización de Medio Ambiente y Recursos Naturales) and the Federal Regulatory Improvement Commission (COFEMER, Comisión Federal de Mejora Regulatoria). At the same time, I encountered secrecy surrounding the topic of the new standard, and the standard-setting process in general, much of which is not subject to transparency procedures. In addition to the interviews with officials and members of nongovernmental organizations (NGOs) cited in this chapter, the analysis is based on the review of the minutes of COMARNAT meetings from 2007 to the fall of 2020. In these little-known councils and commissions, the prevailing power relations in environmental regulation are on full display.

4.3 Regulations via Negotiation and Consensus

The first entity that is key to understanding how regulations are developed in the environmental sector is COMARNAT. The Federal Law on Metrology and Standardization (LFMN, Ley Federal de Metrología y Normalización) establishes that federal agencies are responsible for issuing Official Mexican Standards (NOMs) related to the matters within their jurisdiction (Article 38). To this end, ministries must create national advisory committees, which are "bodies for the development of official Mexican standards and the promotion of their compliance" (Article 62). In the environment sector, that committee is COMARNAT. COMARNAT is chaired by the deputy minister of environmental promotion and regulation at SEMARNAT and brings together representatives of forty-six institutions. As of January 2019, COMARNAT members included representatives of nine government

The Enemy at Home

ministries, six decentralized government agencies, three universities or research bodies, three parastatal organizations, eight NGOs, a producers' organization, and sixteen industry chambers or associations (table 4.2).[8]

Business-sector representation is greater than this would indicate, as at least three of the NGOs represent business interests. The GEMI Initiative defines itself as a "non-profit business organization" whose members include Nestlé, Procter & Gamble Mexico, Grupo Jumex, DOW, and Colgate-Palmolive. The Private Sector Center for Studies of Sustainable Development (CESPEDES, Comisión de Estudios del Sector Privado para el Desarrollo Sustentable) belongs to the CCE and is also the Mexican chapter of the World Business Council for Sustainable Development (CESPEDES 2015). The Center for Public Policy for Sustainable Development (CEDES, Centro de Políticas Públicas para el Desarrollo Sustentable) is the third NGO with political and business ties.[9] At the same time, the interests of the national oil and gas corporation PEMEX and the Federal Electricity Commission, among the largest polluters in the country, could be aligned on environmental regulatory issues with those of the private sector.

Table 4.2
Members of COMARNAT

Government
Presidency: deputy minister of environmental promotion and regulation, SEMARNAT
Ministry of the Interior
Ministry of the Navy
Ministry of Energy
Ministry of Economy
Ministry of Agriculture, Livestock, Rural Development, Fisheries and Food
Ministry of Tourism
Ministry of Communications and Transportation
Ministry of Labor and Social Security
Ministry of Health, Federal Commission for the Protection against Sanitary Risks
National Forestry Commission
National Institute of Ecology and Climate Change
National Water Commission (CONAGUA)
Federal Bureau of Environmental Protection
National Commission of Protected Natural Areas
Federal Consumer Protection Office

(continued)

Table 4.2

(Continued)

Parastatal Agencies

Federal Electricity Commission
Mexican Petroleum Institute
Petróleos Mexicanos (PEMEX)

Industry Chambers and Associations

Confederation of Mexican Chambers of Industry (CONCAMIN)
Mexican Confederation of Business Owners
National Chamber of the Transformation Industry
Nuevo León Chamber of the Transformation Industry
Mining Chamber of Mexico
Mexican Cement Chamber
National Chamber of the Iron and Steel Industry
National Chamber of the Fats, Oils, Soap and Detergent Industry
National Chamber of the Cellulose and Paper Industries (Cámara del Papel)
National Chamber of the Rubber Industry
National Chamber of the Timber Industry
National Chamber of the Perfume, Cosmetics and Personal Care Products Industry
Mexican Automotive Industry Association (AMIA)
National Chemical Industry Association (ANIQ)
National Association of Soft Drink and Carbonated Beverage Producers
Crop Protection Science and Technology

Research Centers

National Autonomous University of Mexico
National Commission for the Knowledge and Use of Biodiversity
Autonomous University of Chapingo

NGOs

Private Sector Center for Studies of Sustainable Development (CESPEDES)*
Center for Public Policy for Sustainable Development (CEDES)*
GEMI Initiative*
Mexican Environmental Law Center (CEMDA)
Mario Molina Center
World Resources Institute Mexico
Mexican Civil Council for Sustainable Forestry
Friends of Sian Ka'an

Producer Organizations

National Union of Ejidos and Forestry Communities

---

* Business-sector NGO.

The bias in the representation in COMARNAT was recognized by Norma Munguía, then general director of the primary sector and renewable natural resources at SEMARNAT, under whose supervision the modification of the NOM-001 was being developed. Munguía asserted that "COMARNAT is not balanced. In other words, if we really want COMARNAT to be representative of the different sectors potentially interested in environmental regulations, then no, currently the composition is mainly industry chambers."[10] In contrast, she affirmed, "the social sector, civil society, is underrepresented." The legal structure of these committees, as established in the LFMN, places little emphasis on the participation of civil society. Article 62 indicates that, in addition to technical personnel from government agencies, these committees will include representatives of "organizations of industrialists, service providers, merchants, producers from the agriculture, forestry or fisheries sectors; scientific or technological research centers, professional and consumer associations."[11] Thus, social representation is conceived of only in terms of "consumers." Furthermore, there are obstacles for the inclusion of more NGOs, as Munguía indicated: "the industry chambers are not very interested in bringing in more civil society," and any new organization has to be approved in a plenary session of COMARNAT.[12]

Government officials and NGO members of COMARNAT confirm that the overrepresentation of industrial interests in COMARNAT has consequences for environmental regulations. In this way, although Munguía recognized that the private-sector representatives in COMARNAT "participate actively, they are constructive, they have a lot of information, *but they can also permanently block something that goes against their interests.*"[13] Interviewed in this regard, Leticia Pineda of the Mexican Environmental Law Center (CEMDA, Centro Mexicano de Derecho Ambiental), who attended COMARNAT meetings on behalf of CEMDA, commented on some "advocacy" strategies applied by industry representatives. "It's been my experience," she related, "that sometimes someone from industry calls, and they take the COMARNAT list and start calling everyone and say, 'Hey, I want to tell you about the standard that is going to be voted on.'" She explained that on those occasions,

> they call you and say, "Hey look, I want to give you our position as the industry [sector], because in reality . . . the process was not followed properly, or they have not informed us, or SEMARNAT did not create a working group where we were all included." . . . But it is very clear . . . that industry takes great care to protect its interests, and we can say that it does take advantage of this type of committee.[14]

To understand the claims of the industry representatives referred to by Pineda, and controversies surrounding the NOM-001, I will address several procedural issues and the use of working groups to develop and modify standards.

A recurring controversy within COMARNAT is regarding who should prepare the draft standards. The LFMN empowers federal agencies to "prepare the preliminary draft of Official Mexican Standards and submit them to the national standardization advisory committees" (Article 44). This is a route whereby the government ministry prepares and presents the new NOM project or a draft modification of an existing standard, but there is also another route. As Rodrigo Ortega, then director of standardization at the Ministry of Economy, explained, "The other way is through a working group, . . . instead of the agency preparing a preliminary draft, that preliminary draft is elaborated in a working group."[15] This second route is the one preferred by the private sector, as I will illustrate in the cases of two disputed regulations that passed through COMARNAT in the period analyzed. These working groups, of course, include industry representatives.

The issue of external working groups came up during debates on a new regulation for the Pollutant Emissions and Transfers Registry (RETC, Registro de Emisiones y Transferencia de Contaminantes), the NOM-165-SEMARNAT-2013, "which establishes the list of substances subject to reporting in the pollutant emission and transfer registry" (*Official Gazette of the Federation* [DOF, *Diario Oficial de la Federación*], January 24, 2014). When SEMARNAT staff presented the draft of this standard to COMARNAT in March 2012, numerous complaints were voiced by industry representatives. The representative of ANIQ, Javier Pérez, stated for instance that "it is indispensable that a working group be formed to technically analyze this standard." In representation of the iron and steel industries, Mónica Lizbeth Barrera expressed that "it is very worrying how various regulations have been developed without forming working groups that include the participation of the affected or regulated sectors."[16] In the end, members voted to approve the creation of a working group to analyze the preliminary draft.

Several NGOs participated in that working group, including Fronteras Comunes, an environmental justice organization founded in 1991 that works with communities on issues of chemical pollution. Marisa Jacott of Fronteras Comunes described the process in the working group for the RETC standard as "very difficult" and called particular attention to the role of officials from the Department of Industry at SEMARNAT. "They

The Enemy at Home

all feel they are agents for industry within the government," she commented, recounting how they prevented the full participation of NGO representatives or disqualified their points: "They argued against us and then the industry people were very at ease because they knew SEMARNAT and the Department of Industry were going to defend them." In her judgment, certain SEMARNAT officials "defend [the industrialists] tooth and nail, instead of seeing themselves as public servants who should seek and ensure the protection of the environment, which is the function that I believe they should have."[17]

All in all, experienced observers believe that the development of the RETC standard was expeditious. This was the perspective of Maricruz Rodríguez, who promoted it as director of industrial regulation and the RETC at SEMARNAT: "There are regulations that take ten or fifteen years in this country. So having negotiated it in two years was a bargain." Rodríguez also highlighted that it was a "very participatory" process, which included people from the National Autonomous University of Mexico, the National Polytechnic Institute, and NGOs.[18] From his experience as director of standardization at the Ministry of Economy, Ortega evaluated that, on average, "the issuance of an official Mexican standard takes at least from ten months to a year," although "there are standards that have taken more than ten years." In those cases, he noted, while the aim is for technical criteria to prevail, the influence of industry resistance makes itself felt. From industry, he stated, "many times the argument is, 'You are not consulting me.' Obviously, *sometimes the sector is going to confuse consultation with you are not taking dictation from me.*"[19] This can lengthen the process of standard negotiations and provides an indication of the relationship between regulators and the regulated parties.

In this sense, Norma Munguía was critical of the way this relationship has developed in COMARNAT. She reflected that "for a long time we have been complacent. [With the idea that] 'Oh, they don't want this?' 'No.' 'Well, okay, then, this one no, then, not this one either.' But the issue isn't what they want, and if you have to cast the deciding vote, or if it has to be a decision of the majority, then so be it."[20] Munguía argued that without seeking to be "authoritarian," government agencies should acknowledge the powers they are granted by law, and in the rules governing COMARNAT, wherein, "at the end of the day, it is the obligation of the federal administration to issue standards." However, the idea that consensus should exist has become so ingrained that, when COMARNAT's operating rules were discussed in a 2015 meeting, representatives of business organizations not only questioned the "unilateralism" of draft standards being developed by the authorities in absence of multistakeholder working groups, but several petitioned for a rule to ensure that within working groups all decisions on regulations be taken by consensus.[21]

Munguía felt that it is based on a certain interpretation of "democracy" that officials believe it is necessary to "reconcile interests" and achieve consensus, but she observed that "there are things that you cannot reconcile." She contrasted the situation in US government agencies to clarify this point:

> We need to be more forceful and tougher when it comes to saying, "Well, this is the standard." In other words, the FDA [Food and Drug Administration] and the EPA [Environmental Protection Agency] are not asking the laboratories if they agree to dump their sewage into the rivers or not, they tell them no, and that's the end of it.[22]

Munguía narrated that during one COMARNAT session, when a SEMARNAT official urged voting on a regulation despite the lack of consensus, this sparked a reaction from the industrial sector: "There were threats from, 'Well, we are going to ask to speak with the minister.' 'Well, okay, what's more I'll give you the extension. Call right now, but we're voting.'" In that case, she said, this was possible because "authorities higher up were also emphatic."[23]

That has not always been the case, as Pineda related regarding the "very controversial" standard that was finally emitted in June 2013 as "NOM-163-SEMARNAT-ENER-SCFI-2013, carbon dioxide emissions from the exhaust and its equivalent in terms of fuel efficiency, applicable to new motor vehicles with a gross vehicle weight of up to 3,857 kilograms." When a draft of this standard was presented in the May 2012 session, it was opposed by the Mexican Automotive Industry Association (AMIA, Asociación Mexicana de la Industria Automotriz), even though the association's representatives had attended a series of meetings on the standard organized by SEMARNAT. The president of the AMIA, Eduardo Solís, considered it a "very significant setback," maintaining that the AMIA had not participated in preparing the preliminary draft, and arguing that "the stringency of the standard proposed by the Federal Government, above the levels achievable in our country, puts investments and important sources of employment at risk, damaging entire regions of our country."[24] Once again, the main complaint was the fact that the norm had not been developed in a working group; as

Alejandro Sosa of the GEMI Initiative stated, "it is not clear why consensus and dialogue are not given an opportunity."[25]

Industry representatives voted against this standard in a session held before the change in the federal administration. In that session, Solís declared that "the standard as it stands is absolutely unacceptable" and emphasized on behalf of AMIA that "the one we have been discussing is in fact more flexible."[26] The opposition of the automotive sector did not stop there. Months later, Toyota and other AMIA member companies (Nissan Mexicana, Ford Motor Company, General Motors, Volkswagen, and Chrysler) filed a nullity lawsuit against the standard to suspend the approval process (Rosagel 2012). Pineda—who represented CEMDA in COMARNAT during this process—commented, "What the industry also did at the time was to stop this standard with that administration and then, a few months later, the Peña administration was about to take over."[27]

In the first COMARNAT session in 2013, now under the administration of Enrique Peña Nieto, a new version of the NOM-163 was received with the evident endorsement of industry representatives. Solís of the AMIA, in addition to stating that "they are totally in favor" of the norm, lauded the "leadership" of government officials and particularly the new minister at SEMARNAT, Juan José Guerra Abud, who for many years chaired the National Association of Manufacturers of Buses, Trucks and Tractors, "for bringing to a successful conclusion this standard which is important for the country and transcendent for the automotive industry."[28]

The new version of the standard was criticized by some of the NGOs, in particular the Mexican chapter of the Institute for Transportation and Development Policy and the Center for Sustainable Transportation (CTS, Centro de Transporte Sustentable)–Embarq, which condemned the "flexibilities" it contemplates and the lack of response to their comments during the new public consultation process. The representative of CTS-Embarq, Jorge Macías, pointed out that this standard has implications for the energy efficiency of millions of new vehicles in Mexico and, therefore, for climate change, noting the environmental goal purportedly pursued by COMARNAT and that "the flexibility mechanisms as stipulated in the NOM-163-SEMARNAT-ENER-SCFI-2013, do not fulfill this obligation, but rather significantly reduce the expected environmental benefits."[29] In fact, Macías petitioned for the new standard to be modified as soon as it was issued. On the other hand, the new president of COMARNAT, Cuauhtémoc Ochoa, as deputy minister of environmental promotion and regulation, reaffirmed the administration's commitment to maintaining "open dialogue and consensus" and "working in harmony."[30]

This particular standard became a topic of public debate in the spring of 2016, during one of the worst air-quality emergencies in a decade in Mexico City. During this crisis, the media reported that vehicles that remain in Mexico are more polluting than those that are exported to Europe and the United States (see, for example, Bloomberg 2016; *El Universal* 2016). Air pollution expert José Luis Lezama stressed this point in an opinion piece: "The automotive industry manufactures vehicles with a double standard and dual morality. Those sold in the US market meet American environmental and safety standards. And those that are sold in the Mexican market do not meet these standards" (Lezama 2016). During this air-quality crisis, Rodolfo Lacy, SEMARNAT's deputy minister of planning and environmental policy, declared in the press that emission standards would be reviewed, including the NOM-163 (E. Cervantes 2016). In fact, since 2015 the standard has been slated for modification in the National Standardization Program (*DOF*, October 2, 2015).

For an official with many years of experience dealing with issues of industrial regulation at SEMARNAT, the actions of the environmental promotion and regulation area—which heads COMARNAT—are highly questionable: "In Promotion, in our ministry, we have major ineptitude. I think it is the most inept area at SEMARNAT. . . . Those responsible for establishing regulations are the most inept." The ineptitude, according to this official, is evidenced in the fact that in this area "they don't generate studies, . . . they don't know how to do their job, [and] they have sellout attitudes to industry."[31] On COMARNAT in general, this official declared, "We have the enemy at home." The controversies and perceptions outlined here form the context to understand the tardy process of changing the NOM-001, and the complexity of the interests at play in COMARNAT.

4.3.1 Stagnated Modification

In 2007, the NOM-001 was first registered in the National Standardization Program (PNN, Programa Nacional de Normalización), the annual publication specifying the new standards that will be developed, as well as the current standards that will be modified or canceled. In the PNN, the need for modification was justified by stating that the limits and parameters of the regulation needed to be changed since "they have lagged behind the protection needs of the country's water bodies" and fall short vis-à-vis international norms and agreements (*DOF*, April 24, 2015). When it was first announced in COMARNAT that the NOM-001 had been included in the PNN Supplement, objections were forthcoming. On behalf of the National Chamber of the Fats, Oils, Soap and Detergent Industry, Federico Grimaldi expressed concern that existing treatment plants were built to comply with the current standard, and thus with stricter limits "considerable investments will have to be made to be able to comply and [this change] is not the most appropriate" course of action.[32] Several industry representatives emphasized that many municipalities do not comply with the current standard and that it is not enforced through verifications or inspections. For this reason, Fernando Gutiérrez of the Nuevo León Chamber of the Transformation Industry, opined that "the standard should be taken out of the Supplement and efforts made to ensure that the current standard is complied with."[33]

To quell the concerns of industry, the representative of the Ministry of Economy, Alberto Castaños, recalled that any standard has to go through the filter of regulatory quality, "which requires overseeing that the matter does not imply higher costs for private parties."[34] The agency in charge of guaranteeing this regulatory quality was COFEMER, within the Ministry of Economy, and which I will discuss in the following section.

The tale told by the COMARNAT minutes is one of glacial progress on the NOM-001 modification. In the final session of 2007, a SEMARNAT official stated that a government working group had been formed but that a draft did not yet exist. In 2008, the standard was not mentioned in committee sessions. In the last session of 2009, SEMARNAT reported that the modification was 68 percent complete, based on an internal working group with members from SEMARNAT and CONAGUA. Two years later, the internal evaluation was ongoing.[35] The standard remained 68 percent complete in November 2012. Luis Alberto López of SEMARNAT reported then that they were working on a more consolidated document: "There is a proposal, a draft on which to some extent a consensus has been reached by some of the strongest sectors in terms of wastewater discharge, such as municipal service providers and also industrial sectors that use water as one of their process inputs." This pursuit of "consensus" from the diverse sectors was not easy, according to López, as some of the comments received "really cause serious problems as there are totally different positions between the regulated sectors on a standard that is general for all."[36]

These informal consultations with sectors came out as a contentious issue in the interviews I carried out. The draft modification presented to ANIQ by Yolanda Pica, which incorporated the new parameters of acute toxicity, COD, and color, had been received and analyzed by various members of the Association of Industrialists of El Salto (Asociación de Industriales de El Salto) in Jalisco. At the chemical company Cytec, for instance, the plant manager stated that this draft "is impossible." They had already transmitted this opinion, the manager explained: "We have put forward our respective complaint, through the Association of Industrialists of El Salto, and our determination that this cannot be complied with. The same thing in the ANIQ, we have done our part."[37] Likewise, CONCAMIN consulted its members asking them to indicate the pros, the cons, and their general observations regarding the modification of the NOM-001.[38]

These consultations are contentious given that, according to SEMARNAT officials, the preliminary draft should not have been circulated at that time. In May 2014, when I interviewed María del Carmen Porras, director of economic and legal analysis for the primary sector at SEMARNAT, who oversaw the NOM-001 process, she stated regarding the reactions to the modification from the industrial sector that "the new [NOM], in theory nobody has seen it."[39] This is particularly noteworthy because, when Porras participated in the COMARNAT session of November 2013, she reiterated the "stable" progress of the NOM-001 at 68 percent, and reported that "an informal consultation was undertaken with the sectors to receive feedback on the draft."[40] How were sectors consulted if "in theory" no one had seen the draft? This contradiction speaks of the closed nature of the regulatory process, where only the participants in COMARNAT and members of industry associations have access to information, through both formal and informal channels.

This closed-loop process has repercussions in terms of achieving improved effluent regulations. An official who participated in the internal NOM-001 working group stated in 2013, "We need help, that is, for society to do something, because . . . this matter of the 001 it's so closed. No one knows when things are being done well, and then later, really good work gets torn down." In fact, she affirmed that during the administration of Felipe Calderón (2006–2012), a draft NOM-001 had been on the verge of receiving internal approval. This did not happen, she related, because CONAGUA wanted to make further changes. This led her to question the internal process: "Since this takes place behind closed doors . . . we don't know how the

The Enemy at Home 191

matter will end. In addition, things changed so much that there are parameters that [IMTA] defended, all this evidence based on technical arguments, and now the people who saw it in SEMARNAT are gone."[41]

CONAGUA's position is conflicted, owing to its involvement in financing municipal wastewater treatment plants. Although the responsibility for urban wastewater treatment lies with municipalities (Section III of Article 115 of the Constitution), CONAGUA provides the bulk of the funding for plant construction and has maintained programs to subsidize their operation. A new wastewater standard implies many plants will require investment in upgrades in order to achieve compliance. Eric Gutiérrez of CONAGUA explained the dilemma this represents from the commission's point of view:

> Because from a plant [built to comply with] a regulation that practically requires primary [treatment], or advanced primary or some with secondary treatment, by increasing the parameters we would need to build tertiary plants or even if it meant having secondary plants in the whole country, that is going to imply an enormous cost, and one wonders, where is the money going to come from to do that?[42]

CONAGUA's ambivalent position with respect to the NOM-001 was also evident in the 2013–2018 National Water Program, where despite acknowledging that water pollution "damages ecosystems, human health and the availability of sources of water," the document maintained that "current regulations on this issue do not consider some pollutants, *they have strict thresholds that make compliance difficult given the Mexican reality* and there are official parameters that are not measured" (CONAGUA 2014b, 34; emphasis added). Hence, resistance to a more stringent regulation did not emanate solely from industry but from the government itself.

The secrecy that I asserted exists around the regulatory process encompasses even other branches of government. In November 2013, the Environment, Natural Resources and Fisheries Committee of the Senate requested that the head of SEMARNAT modify the NOM-001, "in order to update it to meet the current needs of the country as well as [to reflect] technological advances and international regulations" (Comisión de Medio Ambiente y Recursos Naturales 2018). The Ministry of the Interior responded to the Senate committee in April 2014, attaching a preliminary draft of the regulation and indicating that the version sent was discussed by SEMARNAT and CONAGUA in July 2013 (Cámara de Senadores 2014). Unlike the draft presented at the ANIQ congress in June of the same year, however, the version sent to the Senate did not include the parameter of acute toxicity.

In the preliminary draft that included toxicity, of which I obtained a version during the investigation, its inclusion is justified with the argument that "chemical analyses cannot predict or measure biological effects in the aquatic system, and toxicity tests integrate information on the effects that the total effluent discharge could cause on the receiving body, particularly on biodiversity and ecosystems." When I interviewed Porras at SEMARNAT in February 2014, she confirmed that the draft under consideration still contemplated toxicity: "That is still in the version, but as I said, the element of feedback from the regulated sectors is still missing."[43] The fact that the version submitted to the Senate did not include toxicity implied that, if it were not considered in a draft amendment sent for public consultation, there would be no public record of this change or the exclusion of this important parameter. Once again, we are facing a closed process where it is officially argued that technical criteria prevail, while the evidence indicates that what occurs involves a significant degree of political negotiation with the regulated sectors.

In November 2015, a project to modify the NOM-001 was finally presented to COMARNAT. On behalf of SEMARNAT, Porras presented the draft modification, which contemplated the parameters of COD, acute toxicity, and color, while acknowledging that "the parameters established in the current NOM not only do not prevent the pollution of bodies of water but are also lax with respect to those established in other countries such as Argentina, Venezuela, Uruguay, and Peru."[44]

Multiple expressions of dissent were recorded. Representatives from various industry associations protested that a multisector working group had not been created. On behalf of the pulp and paper industries, Pedro Silva stressed that "the standard applies to a large number of users from very diverse sectors throughout the national territory and has severe environmental, social, economic, and political implications," and he objected that "the proposed modification has not been enriched with the open and direct participation of the sectors involved." Before voting on whether the proposal would be published in the *DOF* for public consultation, Alejandro Sosa of the GEMI Initiative insisted that there was no "urgency" to updating the standard, declaring that in the past, "many difficult standards have been developed, where there were diametrically opposed positions, and in all cases consensus was reached." In the end, the vote was tied, and seventy-five days were granted for COMARNAT members to send their comments on the proposed modification.

Subsequently, CONCAMIN expressed its displeasure with the NOM-001 process in its 2015/2016 Results Report, voicing its disapproval that an external working group had not been convened for its drafting. Industry representatives promoted a particular interpretation of the LFMN and COMARNAT's operating rules whereby the authorities are obliged to always create external working groups. For example, the CONCAMIN report affirms that there was a breach of Article 22, Section III, of the operating rules, according to which one of the functions of the COMARNAT sub-committees is to "instruct the Coordinators and Executive Coordinators to integrate the working groups necessary for the development of their tasks" (SEMARNAT 2015). This, however, does not imply an obligation to generate such a working group in all cases.

To emphasize this last point, I would refer to a debate on a possible new standard for the sustainable use of nontimber forest resources in the March 2012 COMARNAT session. In response to demands from industry representatives to open an external working group, the general director of standards of the Ministry of Economy clarified that the LFMN "establishes that it is a prerogative of the ministry to prepare the draft. . . . Article 44 of the law is very clear, the draft is prepared by the ministry and they are being *too democratic*."[45] Later that year, the particularly "democratic" character of COMARNAT was touched on again, during a discussion of proposed changes to the committee's operating rules. Faced with petitions from various chambers and associations that a working group also be opened to evaluate these changes, the then deputy minister of environmental promotion and regulation, Sandra Denisse Herrera, asserted regarding COMARNAT that "this body has stood out for being very inclusive, much more inclusive than other committees in other ministries," where representatives of the same chambers also participate.[46]

The same 2015/2016 CONCAMIN report alludes to the particularly "inclusive" nature of this committee, while insisting on the creation of an external working group for the NOM-001. The report states,

> It is surprising and worrying that, this being an issue of great importance at the national level for all sectors in the country[,] . . . that [external experts] were not invited and that the well-known procedure for the elaboration or modification of

regulations has not been followed, which the Ministry of Economy through the General Directorate of Standards has utilized in each of the Committees and Subcommittees that exist and function, and *especially in COMARNAT*. (CONCAMIN 2016, 25; emphasis added)

According to Porras at SEMARNAT, when the decision is made to form an external working group, the ministry makes the invitations based on technical criteria: "Once a group is opened, we send out invitations to people that we think are closest to the topic, because as we say in this phase it is exclusively the technical part." Normally, she said, invitations are made to "representatives of the economic sectors, the chambers . . . and nongovernmental organizations, academics. It is a balanced group."[47]

In the opinion of Leticia Pineda of CEMDA, on the other hand, the process is "discretionary." An individual or organization can petition SEMARNAT to join a working group and be accredited as an expert on the specific topic, but only if there is information about the existence of the working group. As Pineda stated, "If you are an external organization, how can you find out that there is a working group? . . . What mechanism do you have to inform yourself?" In short, she asserted, "That information is very closed off. . . . Actually, there is no way that someone outside [COMARNAT] or an organization can find out about that."[48]

The technical criteria that SEMARNAT officials assert predominate, according to some participants in the process, may even leave the industrial sector at an advantage. This is because industry associations have greater access to specialized experts than even government agencies. Thus, Rodrigo Ortega, then–director of standardization at the Ministry of Economy, pointed out that "they have a bit of an advantage over us because in the end the [industry] chambers, since they bring together many companies, sometimes they have the appropriate technical staff for each of the committees . . . which the public sector lacks. We are not experts on all the matters that we regulate."[49] This also has to do, he pointed out, with access to information, where "sometimes only industry has the information," since the data from the National Institute of Statistics and Geography (Instituto Nacional de Estadística y Geografía) or other official sources are not up-to-date or lack the necessary level of detail. On the other hand, industry has access to international experts as well as people at the forefront of technology. Pineda of CEMDA also cited a dearth of information and expertise: "SEMARNAT does not have the capacity in personnel and sometimes their people are not so technically qualified either." This helps explain why the standard-setting process is "extremely inefficient," in terms of the time required to approve or modify a standard.[50]

Despite the insistence from industry, the NOM-001 continued its course without an external working group, but the process was not swift either. The seventy-five-day period to receive comments expired on January 20, 2016, and SEMARNAT received 288 comments from nine COMARNAT members. Because of the work required to adjust the draft standard to take the comments into account, almost two years went by before the amended proposal was ready. Hence, an extraordinary meeting of COMARNAT was called on December 19, 2017, to once again vote on the publication of the modified NOM-001 for public consultation. The meeting did not go smoothly, but when the vote was again tied, SEMARNAT cast the deciding vote and its publication was approved.

Finally, on January 5, 2018, the "draft modification of the Official Mexican Standard PROY-NOM-001-SEMARNAT-2017, which establishes the permissible limits of pollutants in wastewater discharges in receiving bodies owned by the nation," appeared in the *DOF*. The general public had sixty days to submit comments on the draft. In that period, SEMARNAT received 1,800 comments from eighty-three individuals and organizations. Several years would go by before further progress was made. These delays also have to do with the other filter through which technical standards and other federal regulations must pass: the cost-benefit analysis carried out by COFEMER within the Ministry of Economy. The next section addresses this issue and its implications for environmental standards.

4.4 Costs and Benefits: The Logic of COFEMER

COFEMER, rebaptized in 2018 as the National Regulatory Improvement Commission (CONAMER, Comisión Nacional de Mejora Regulatoria), performs ex ante evaluations of government regulations and procedures through the regulatory impact assessment (RIA) process. COFEMER was governed by the Federal Administrative Procedure Law (Ley Federal de Procedimiento Administrativo), which stipulated that every draft law, legislative decree, or administrative act (which includes the NOMs) prepared by a decentralized agency or ministry of the federal public administration first requires approval through the RIA process (Article 69-H). COFEMER became CONAMER with the issuance of the General Regulatory Improvement Law on May 18, 2018, but retains the functions outlined in the following discussion as regards the cost-benefit analysis of federal regulations.

As reported by Leonora Rojas-Bracho and colleagues, in the late 1990s the Organisation for Economic Co-operation and Development (OECD) recommended that member countries "adopt regulatory impact assessments (RIAs) for the systematic analysis of potential social impacts of regulations" (2013, 162). In Mexico, the creation of COFEMER was in response to OECD recommendations on regulatory reform and improvement (OECD 2004). These recommendations were made in a report published in 2000, the same year that reforms were made to the Federal Administrative Procedure Law and that COFEMER was established (OECD 2000). COFEMER's legal mandate focuses on promoting "transparency in the preparation and application of regulations and [ensuring] that these generate benefits that exceed their costs and the maximum benefit for society" (Article 69-E). However, in the environmental sector there are doubts regarding the way in which the "maximum benefit for society" is conceived of and measured.

In 2007, during the presidency of Felipe Calderón (2006–2012), a Regulatory Quality Agreement was published to set guidelines for federal agencies "on the issuance of regulations that involve compliance costs for individuals" (*DOF*, February 2, 2007). One of the requirements in order to emit regulations was that "the benefits provided by the regulation, in terms of competitiveness and the efficient functioning of markets, among others, are *higher than the costs of compliance by private parties*" (Article 3, Section V; emphasis added). In turn, this requirement became one of the criteria in the RIAs undertaken by COFEMER, as established in the Regulatory Impact Assessment Manual (*DOF*, July 26, 2010). To this end, the manual details that the federal agency must demonstrate in any RIA application, "in a clear and forceful way, preferably through monetized information, that the potential benefits of the proposed regulation are markedly higher than the cost of compliance." As is well known, there are multiple difficulties involved in attempting to monetize both the costs of the deterioration of ecosystems and the consequent impact on the health of the population, as well as the benefits of improving environmental quality and community well-being.

Eric Gutiérrez of CONAGUA had experience with RIAs, prepared in the run-up to several classification declarations for highly polluted rivers in

The Enemy at Home

the country. The challenge for authorities to demonstrate that "the benefits far outweigh the costs" has not been an easy one, in his experience: "When we want to value a species in economic terms, it is very difficult." Gutiérrez explained that outside assistance has been required in the attempt to complete the cost-benefit analysis required by COFEMER: "We don't have the expertise to demonstrate in environmental terms. . . . It is very difficult. So, we have made a lot of effort to work with environmental economists, to help us . . . and develop ad hoc the methodologies." In general, he concludes regarding COFEMER that, "from an environmental point of view, it does not help. Sincerely." This is because "they only consider the economic aspect."[51]

Norma Munguía from SEMARNAT had a similar experience. She stated that, due to the design of the RIA process, "the true environmental costs, which are the ones of interest to us as a sector, are not measured." COFEMER's procedures do not consider longer-term effects or what Munguía described as the "unpayable" costs of inadequate regulations. Munguía characterized the rationale of COFEMER in the following terms:

> "How much is it going to cost me today, tomorrow to improve my treatment plant? Oh no, it's very expensive, no, you can't." Well, yes, but in the long term the benefit is not only for you, but for the whole community living here and for the next community over, and for those upriver and those downstream, and if you [take action], and the next person does as well, and the next. . . . "No, but I can't afford to do it right now, it's very expensive, it's not possible." So, yes they are concerned basically about the now.[52]

The prioritization of protecting investment or economic growth reaches such a degree, Munguía asserted, that "there are ridiculous cases" where the generation of a handful of jobs means more to COFEMER, for example, than the protection of an ecosystem: "Ten jobs can't compete against what is going to happen to this ecosystem, 'But, there are ten jobs!'"[53]

The analysis of cost-benefit evaluation methodologies is a specialized field beyond the scope of this research. Nonetheless, I would make a few brief remarks in relation to the RIA process. First, as Gutiérrez mentioned, COFEMER establishes no clear criteria as regards the appropriate methodologies, and agencies such as CONAGUA have had to seek advice from experts. The lack of clarity in the methodologies is a fact noted by Rojas-Bracho and colleagues (2013), who reflect on their own experience with a cost-benefit analysis of a project to reduce sulfur in the gasoline and diesel supplied by PEMEX. They conclude that, "to date, guidelines produced by the two agencies that require cost-benefit analysis in Mexico [the Ministry of Finance and Public Credit and COFEMER] do not include methods for placing a monetary value on health or other intangible environmental benefits" (172). This entails the risk that, without the oversight of a central agency, "different agencies may take advantage of the absence of federal standards to manipulate results" (172). This same text notes a further deficiency of the system in Mexico: the high social discount rate.

A social discount rate is employed in the economic analysis of investment projects and "reflects the opportunity cost of capital from an intertemporal perspective for society as a whole" (European Commission 2015, 301). In simpler terms, it "reflects the social view of how future benefits and costs are to be valued against present ones" (301). A rate of zero, then, would imply giving the same value to future costs as present ones, while a positive rate indicates that present consumption is given greater value than future consumption. According to Emilio Padilla, "A higher discount rate implies a greater discrimination against future generations . . . although any positive discount rate leads the analysis to devalue and almost ignore distant impacts" (2002, 70). In Mexico, the social discount rate is high. Rojas-Bracho and colleagues point out that while the rate for cost-benefit analyses in the United States has varied between 3 percent and 7 percent, in Mexico it was 12 percent. In this regard, they affirm that "working with federal authorities to lower the discount rate would allow us to value future generations as much as we value our own" (2013, 172). A slight improvement was later made when the Ministry of Finance and Public Credit (SHCP, Secretaría de Hacienda y Crédito Público) announced in January 2014 that, as a result of a drop in interest rates and in order to promote public investment in the country, the social discount rate would decrease from 12 percent to 10 percent (SHCP 2014).

The RIA process overseen by COFEMER and now CONAMER also includes a public consultation that can represent another forum for private parties to lobby for the protection of their interests. When an RIS is published on the CONAMER website, a public consultation period is opened to submit comments on the proposed regulation. A pertinent illustration is the case of the draft of the new General Water Law presented to COFEMER in October 2014. When this proposal was later discussed in Congress in February 2015, it sparked widespread public debate, was opposed by both NGOs and academics, and was extensively reported in the media. The motivation for the

General Water Law, to replace the National Waters Law of 1992 (reformed in 2004), was the 2012 constitutional reform enshrining the human right to water and sanitation. In the wake of this reform, a broad-based coalition, Water for All, Water for Life, began to promote a citizen initiative for the General Water Law, with the participation of communities, grassroots organizations, and university researchers (Moctezuma Barragán 2020).

The interesting thing to note here is that, during the public RIA consultation process, of the twenty comments received by COFEMER, nine were from the business sector, while only two were from civil society organizations.[54] The remainder came from government agencies, irrigation users, and a private individual. Half of the comments were from COMARNAT members. Given the interest in and debate on this law from an array of actors in civil society and academia, it is my hypothesis that both the general public and many social organizations have scant knowledge or awareness of the RIA process, beyond organizations participating in COMARNAT. On the other hand, industry associations ensure the flow of information to their member companies.

On the subject of comments presented in the RIA process, Lizbeth Urbina Bravo, then director of energy, infrastructure, and environment at COFEMER, affirmed that if an RIA generates an abundance of comments, this is evidence that the government body promoting the regulation had not reached a prior consensus with the potentially affected sectors. Thus, Urbina asserted that "when they don't reach a consensus with the sector, you can tell by the number of comments that we receive."[55] She indicated that, starting the RIA process with COFEMER, "we hope that they . . . reach a consensus with the affected sector because in the end [the version of the regulation] that arrives here with us and becomes public may delay the regulatory improvement process." This refers, again, to the general nature of regulatory processes, where the idea that prevails is that regulations should be negotiated or agreed on with regulated sectors.

4.5 Consolidating the Modification of the NOM-001 Standard

Before its publication for public consultation on January 5, 2018, at the end of December 2017 the draft modification of the NOM-001 was presented to COFEMER with its respective RIS. COFEMER's response came quickly, putting the process on hold via communication with SEMARNAT the same day the proposal appeared in the *DOF*. COFEMER adduced an omission on the part of SEMARNAT, given a new legal framework known colloquially as the 2 for 1 Agreement (*DOF*, March 8, 2017). This 2017 accord, which replaced the 2007 Regulatory Quality Agreement, establishes that agencies must avoid issuing regulations with costs for private parties, unless they comply with a series of exceptions, one being the precept of benefits greater than the costs of compliance by said private parties. It is known as the 2 for 1 Agreement because the fifth article stipulates that, "for the issuance of new administrative acts of a general nature, the decentralized agencies and other agencies must expressly indicate in the corresponding draft the two regulatory obligations or the two acts that will be abrogated or repealed." In the case of the NOM-001, COFEMER informed SEMARNAT that the ministry had not complied with this article, abrogating or repealing other regulations, and requested a corrected RIS (COFEMER 2018b). In the weeks and months that followed, comments on this proposal also began to reach COFEMER, and individual companies and industry associations expressed their rejection in unequivocal terms.

Unsurprisingly, in these comments the fact that government agencies had developed the draft was characterized as making the process "unilateral"; industry associations asserted that the new parameters (toxicity, COD, and color) were not justified, and they predicted grave economic effects if the new standard were to be approved.[56] The comment from ANIQ, for example, stressed the investments in treatment technology that would be required, claiming this would lead to plant closures and would "directly affect the competitiveness of our country."[57] The lack of compliance with the current standard was also adduced as reason to avoid bringing in stricter controls, which would mean even higher levels of noncompliance.

Patricia Tovar, director of legal and economic analysis of the primary sector at SEMARNAT, who has led the NOM-001 process in the most recent period, also commented in 2020 that following the 2017 vote, relations in COMARNAT were strained:

> The pressure in COMARNAT is quite strong. . . . Every time we present a standard, COMARNAT itself has punished us. Since 2017, [when] the [NOM-001] was approved by a casting vote, all of 2018 COMARNAT punished us with all the standards that were presented to it for its vote and for publication as drafts or as definitive standards; it has been a difficult situation. The waters have started to calm, but that does not mean that COMARNAT has lowered its guard.[58]

The view here of COMARNAT as an opponent is clear. Tovar also affirmed that "there is a perception in which they practically want to limit us so that all standards must have a working group" and noted how different organizations had sent identical comments, making the NOM-001 the most commented standard in the country such that "they wanted to inundate us, to tire us and so we wouldn't be able to conclude the consultation."

Three and half years would pass before a reformulated draft would be presented to COMARNAT. This led, in June 2021, to the formation of a working group with industry, academics, and several NGOs—all COMARNAT members—to discuss four controversial parameters: temperature, color, COD, and toxicity. Following the sessions of this working group, the draft returned to the COMARNAT agenda on August 27, 2021, and in a close vote its publication in the *DOF* was approved. This vote was celebrated by SEMARNAT as progress after "25 years of paralysis" (SEMARNAT 2021c). The story did not end here, however, as the official publication of the standard could not take place without the approval from CONAMER. The same day as the vote in COMARNAT, the new version of the standard was presented to CONAMER, and almost fifty comments from industry associations and individual companies began to be registered, many discounting the process as "unilateral," despite the working group sessions held; arguing inaccuracies in the cost-benefit analysis; decrying the potential economic impact of the new regulation; and calling for the designation of an expert to review the RIA as well as the formation of a working group to review the draft and reach consensus with the regulated sectors.[59] About a dozen NGOs and academics attempted to counter these voices with comments supporting the modified standard.

The opposition to the new standard was also echoed in the media and opinion columns. Along with the familiar critiques, business representatives stressed to the media that the new standard would violate international trade agreements, particularly the United States–Mexico–Canada Agreement (Mares 2021). Given that the agreement expressly acknowledges "the sovereign right of each Party to establish its own levels of domestic environmental protection and its own environmental priorities, and to establish, adopt, or modify its environmental laws and policies accordingly," it is not clear in what sense strengthened control on water pollution would violate the agreement (Article 24.3).

Despite such last-ditch efforts to stall or block the passing of the modified NOM-001, it was issued on March 11, 2022, and is set to come into effect a year later, while allowing four years for compliance with the parameters of acute toxicity and color. This is almost fifteen years after the NOM-001 was first slated for modification and first discussed in COMARNAT. Eight years were required for SEMARNAT and the internal working group to present a draft in COMARNAT, and a further three years for that draft to be published for public consultation. The four years that passed between the draft modification of 2018 and its final publication are testament to the contentious nature of the modification, to industry opposition in institutional and non-institutional arenas, to bureaucratic inefficiency, and to legal roadblocks that favor private interests, in particular regarding the RIA process. With the new standard, the challenge of enforcement, in a context of shrinking capacity as outlined in the previous chapter, will come to the fore.

*   *   *

Rodrigo Ortega from the Ministry of Economy, specifying in an interview that he was speaking in a personal capacity, claimed that lax regulations are not used to attract investment, asserting that even though standards "function as a development lever to promote sectors," "in the end the main objective is the mitigation of the risks that you've identified." The risks to which Ortega refers are those set out in Article 40 of the LFMN, which stipulates that NOMs are meant to address the characteristics of products or processes that may constitute "a risk to the safety of people or to human, animal and plant health, the general and work environment, or to the preservation of natural resources" (Article 40, Section I). For Ortega, when these NOMs are developed within the various government ministries, "always, always, always, what we want is to avoid risk," and supporting any particular industrial sector is secondary.[60]

Can the public interest be prioritized in a system of environmental regulation based on a logic of consensus and negotiation with the regulated sectors? The evidence presented here, in particular the interviews with critical officials and members of NGOs who have participated in these processes, paints a picture where the interests of private parties tend to predominate. In the case of COFEMER/CONAMER, in addition, the legal guidelines for its operation privilege private interests. We can speak of regulatory capture in the process of environmental standard setting, then, where the private sector has been empowered and this prevents or delays the approval of regulations that protect the health of the population and ecosystems. In the case of COMARNAT, a process of regulatory capture can be verified due both to the preponderance of the participation of industrial associations and to the action of industry actors within and outside institutional spaces to impede or delay the approval of a new wastewater discharge standard. In chapter 5, I turn again to actors in industry, to chart the difference between the discourse and reality of the environmental performance of companies in the industrial corridor in Jalisco.

5 Corporate Sustainability: Myths and Realities

Much of this research has to do with distinguishing appearances from realities, as well as identifying areas where there is so little reliable information that fiction cannot be discerned from fact. There are two areas where this exercise is necessary: the environmental regulation enacted by state actors and the environmental performance of industries, both national and transnational. In both cases, according to the prevailing discourses, we are already at the height of a green and sustainable era, with robust environmental laws and regulations. According to the most recent Organisation for Economic Co-operation and Development evaluation of environmental performance in Mexico, for example, "Mexico has significantly strengthened its national environmental policies and demonstrated impressive international leadership in areas such as climate change and water management" (2013, 61). Here, my general argument is that this strengthening represents, to a large extent, a simulation that responds to the need to demonstrate global parity in the levels of regulation, without the intention of full or strict enforcement. Regarding industry, it is possible to reveal another area of simulation by analyzing its discourses and corporate social responsibility (CSR) and sustainability reports and contrasting them with some indications of the actual performance of factories in the Santiago River Basin.

While exploring these ideas, we encounter a series of brilliant mirages that this case allows us to examine in greater detail. Furthermore, these closer analyses allow us to question one of the most persistent hegemonic logics relevant to pollution in the South: that the answers, solutions, and best practices will come from the North, from free trade and from transnational corporations bearing leading technology and know-how. This is the "common sense" that appears in the discourse from both the governmental and private sectors regarding the problem of the Santiago River, as well as in some optimistic studies on the topic of industrial pollution (for example, Cole 2004). In this way, Elizabeth Economy, in her book *The River Runs Black*, which investigates environmental degradation in China, particularly the severe river pollution prevalent there, contends that as China becomes more integrated into the global economy, "there is also the potential for environmental objectives to be advanced by environmental activities or requirements embodied in the various trade regimes to which China accedes" (2004, 201). For promoters of the policies of neoliberalization, foreign direct investment (FDI) entails environmental benefits. Thus, a World Bank publication on green growth claims that "the best way to facilitate access to green technologies is through openness to international trade, foreign direct investment, . . . and other forms of global connectedness" (2012, 78). In this narrative, transnational corporations, the sources of FDI, are portrayed not only as clean and responsible actors but also as necessary sources of the technological advances that will curb environmental deterioration.

Kevin Gallagher and Lyuba Zarsky (2007, 29) identify four assumptions that support the hypothesis of the environmental boons of FDI: (1) Global competition has pushed transnational corporations (TNCs) toward technological changes that reduce pollution and the intensity of resource use. (2) TNCs transfer cleaner technologies to their facilities in "developing countries." (3) Due to the need to comply with stricter standards and consumer preferences in their home countries (in the Global North), TNCs have invested in the development of cleaner and safer technologies and products. (4) TNCs operate under company-level environmental standards, regardless of the production site, and these reflect the highest levels of control required by their home country. These assumptions differ greatly from the reality. First, they assume the behavior of TNCs in the Global North is environmentally innocuous, which is certainly not always the case. An example of this was the scandal unleashed in September 2015 by the deceptive practices of German car maker Volkswagen. The company was called to account for equipping 11 million vehicles, mainly with diesel engines, with software that activated during emissions tests to report lower levels of polluting emissions and thus feign legal compliance (Jolly 2019). Second, when we contrast these assumptions with the reality of a case like that of the Santiago, we see how they become "myths" that do not rely on facts

Corporate Sustainability

but, nonetheless, have an ideological weight in shoring up flexible regulations and self-regulation.

In the conflict over the Santiago River, only in rare instances have social demands, research, and government power turned to scrutinize the activities of the private sector. "They make you believe that . . . we must support economic development and if you act against that . . . they make you believe that you're crazy or, how dare you go against the empire of money?" reflects Graciela González, an activist from Leap of Life (Un Salto de Vida), the organization that in 2012 denounced the industrial sector together with Greenpeace Mexico. Thus, both in citizen claims and in many investigations, the focus is either on denouncing or studying the state. Why is the industrial sector studied and called to account so infrequently? Graciela has pointed out one of the key reasons, stemming from its association with development, progress, and employment.

There are also practical reasons, in the sense that often companies act with a high level of opacity and secrecy. Speeches about open doors abound, but when assailed by direct request, those doors often remain firmly closed. The lack of data on industrial discharges is not an exclusive phenomenon of the Santiago River, but rather a situation that prevails at the national level. Researchers from the Tecnológico de Monterrey assert in an evaluation that "official information on water and industry in Mexico is confusing, is not up-to-date, is imprecise and unsystematic, is poorly accessible and is used very little by the government apparatus itself" (López and Flores 2010, 179). They highlight the failures on the part of both the government and industry to comply with roles and responsibilities, as well as the institutional inability to monitor the wastewater management systems of the industrial facilities in the country (198).

A sector for which there is such limited reliable information available and, moreover, for which it is difficult to generate accurate information is not immediately attractive as the subject of academic research. Furthermore, for a researcher or a community organization, generating critical investigations or public complaints about specific companies in the absence of strong evidence raises such risks as defamation lawsuits. In the epilogue to the second edition of their excellent book *Deceit and Denial: The Deadly Politics of Industrial Pollution*, historians Gerald Markowitz and David Rosner (2013) relate how several of the researchers who reviewed their manuscript were summoned by corporate attorneys to testify about the book's peer-review process, after one of the authors acted as an expert witness in a trial about worker exposure to toxins in the vinyl chloride industry (used in the manufacture of PVC). In response to this, the authors created a website where they published much of the empirical basis for their research (308).

Conscious of the obstacle of a dearth of reliable data on the environmental performance of industries in Mexico, I proposed to test the limits of the available and accessible information, and to interrogate the lack of information as part of a system that masks polluting activities. This concern is not limited to water and effluents, but more generally relates to the environmental impacts of industry in Mexico. Rhys Jenkins and Alfonso Mercado García, for example, perceive that, "[given] the importance of the relationship between industrial development and environmental sustainability in Mexico, the scarcity of information and studies in this regard is surprising" (2008, 20). Miguel Ángel López and Blanca Nelly Flores point out that, on water consumption as well as wastewater generation, treatment, and reuse, "the real situation . . . is not known with exactitude due to the precarious availability of information and the inability of the institutions of the three levels of government to monitor and supervise industry" (2010, 179). Acknowledging this challenge, then, what questions can be answered with some level of certainty about industrial activity and its environmental impacts?

To determine this, I identified several spheres of information, each of which is addressed in this chapter. First, there is information about the companies located in the industrial corridor, whether they are of domestic or foreign capital, as well as their sector, location, and size, determined by the number of factory employees. In chapter 1, I presented data on the composition and distribution of industrial activities in my study area. This provides an idea of the magnitude of the challenge for the future restoration of the Santiago River. Of this universe of companies, my research has delved deeper into only a fraction, where I conducted interviews or obtained government information on their activities and polluting emissions. The selection of this fraction was not random, nor is the fraction representative of all the activity in the area. My sample is biased, but this is due to methodological and tactical decisions that I will now explain (see also the appendix).

In methodological terms, I sought to focus on companies for which there was some analysis of their effluents in existing official studies. Along with this, I took into account the polluting potential of these discharges, according to the industrial sector. Both factors led me to choose larger-than-average companies and a higher proportion of companies in the chemical sector. To explain the tactical decisions, some of my previous considerations have to be taken into account. I knew beforehand that it would be difficult to meet with factory personnel and that excessively incisive questions about their discharges (volumes, substances, and concentrations) would not be welcome. This was not simply a suspicion or commonsense deduction. In 2003, I interviewed engineers from the environment, health and safety (EHS) areas of three factories in the industrial corridor (Ciba, Celanese, and Nestlé). From that experience, I took the lesson that if I asked specific questions about the pollution emanating from factories, I risked not being able to obtain the interviews or gleaning little information from them. But what approach with companies would allow me to engage in a dialogue about their environmental impacts?

Recent decades have witnessed a surge in the adoption of environmental sustainability or management policies and programs by the private sector, with the concomitant publication of annual reports or statements on environmental and social policies. As Dara O'Rourke (2004b) notes, however, the trend has not been homogeneous; rather, larger companies tend to generate these voluntary reports, and they are more common in certain industries and regions. Overall, O'Rourke observes that "large, branded manufacturing firms are currently the most likely to voluntarily report on CSR issues" (vii). This is because they are the most sensitive regarding their reputation and negative news about their practices. For this research, this trend toward reports and programs, even given their uneven adoption, represented a possible strategy to engage in a dialogue with factory representatives. By framing my interest in the language of corporate sustainability and environmental management, however, I again inclined my sample of companies to the largest and, to a certain extent, to those of foreign capital.

In general terms, this strategy was successful, in that it allowed me to enter into a dialogue on environmental management with representatives of a series of companies without, of course, discussing in detail their emissions or quantitative indicators, information that is considered confidential. The language and level of detail were in line with what is customary in corporate sustainability reports or standards such as the Global Reporting Initiative (GRI). In addition to the tactical aspect of this decision, from an anthropological perspective it permitted me to understand the vision of the companies vis-à-vis their environmental management and performance, as well as their assessment of environmental authorities. The limitations and scope of this strategy will become clear throughout the chapter. Although I chose this option as the best one to be able to interview the EHS managers of the companies that had this type of program, it was not an infallible strategy. Various companies, including some of the largest in the corridor, declined my interview requests.

Most of the largest companies in the area are also members of the Association of Industrialists of El Salto (AISAC, Asociación de Industriales de El Salto). AISAC was founded in 1982 with the objective, according to manager Silvia Vega, of addressing specific problems of the industrial area of El Salto, which was then well outside the metropolitan area, as well as "working hand in hand with federal, state, and municipal governments on industrial issues." AISAC brings together around seventy companies from the area that they define as the Industrial Corridor of El Salto. Vega affirmed that member companies have an "open-door" policy. This policy is in response, Vega said, to negative opinions from community members: "A lot of times people speak from lack of knowledge and say, well it's a company and it's polluting. . . . So, . . . how are you going to convince someone of the opposite? With information." For this reason, Vega stated that "the policy of the companies is to say, if the community has doubts, the door is open."[1] In this research, I found that this is not always the case.

After requesting interviews to discuss their sustainability or environmental management strategies, I received negative responses from factory staff at Honda, cardboard producer Empaques Modernos de Guadalajara, and the synthetic fiber producer Zoltek, part of the Japanese Toray Group, all AISAC members. In several other cases there was simply no response, even after I reiterated requests over periods of up to one year. Such was the case at the local Huntsman and AlEn plants (companies where I was able to interview representatives at their corporate headquarters), also AISAC members. The doors may not be as open as claimed, or at least the policy has not been embraced by all the companies in the association. Interview requests were denied or did not receive a response, in addition, from non-AISAC companies such as Celanese (refusal by the headquarters in the United States and no response from the factory in Poncitlán) and Siemens (no response). Nonetheless, it was possible to carry out interviews at sixteen companies and, in ten cases, tours of their facilities: AlEn (headquarters only), Corporación de Occidente, Cytec, DSM, Huntsman (headquarters only), Infineum, Mexichem, Nestlé, Omnilife, Oxiteno, Quimikao (Kao Group), Urrea (Grivatec), and ZF, as well as three other US companies under the condition of confidentiality, two from the electronics industry and one from the food sector.

The sources of information that I turned to in addition to interviews included the information that each company makes public on its website, government records obtained via information requests, and, finally, water quality studies that included analyses of industrial effluents. All this allowed me to draw on diverse spheres of information and enrich the analysis. Thus, in the first section, I review the information from a series of sustainability reports and policies of a selection of companies to determine to what extent they contribute to transparency regarding their activities, the environmental improvements they claim to have achieved, and whether these reports are useful in gauging the local activities and emissions of these corporations. This is the discursive and promotional level of the companies.

In the second section of the chapter, I contrast this discursive level with the existing information on discharges and environmental management practices of four companies. This is done to explain the role of what I consider a myth surrounding the environmental performance of transnational corporations that, at least in the cases for which we have empirical evidence, is far from being verified in reality. Here the intention is to question the prevailing discourse on industry and environmental regulation, which assumes that large companies, particularly transnationals, are self-regulating and responsible, while small and clandestine companies are the sources of environmental deterioration.

At the heart of this investigation are the relations between government and the private sector. In this sense, it was interesting in the interviews I undertook with factory representatives to discuss their perspectives on the actions, level of knowledge, and effectiveness of government authorities, as well as their vision of the correct role of environmental regulations. In the third section, I consider these viewpoints to analyze them in terms of the configuration of power relations. From there, the chapter closes by reflecting on the limits of access to information on industrial activities and whether there indeed exists a "right to know" in the interest of protecting the health and well-being of communities and ecosystems.

5.1 Between Sustainability and Greenwashing

As mentioned, the recent trend of most large companies, both transnational and Mexican, is to adopt environmental management policies, obtain related certifications, and, in many cases, generate annual sustainability reports. Based on specified criteria, in what follows I examine to what extent these policies and documents present evidence of improved environmental performance, particularly in the case of wastewater, while questioning the reliability of the information presented. The term "greenwashing" was coined to refer to "disinformation disseminated by an organization so as to present an environmentally responsible public image" (Maxwell 2005). According to Jacob Vos, greenwashing does not normally imply that companies provide false information, but rather, "the deception often lies in the emphasis corporations place on their ecological projects, rather than in the existence of the projects themselves" (2009, 674). This is a good starting point to analyze what some of the companies of the corridor publish in their sustainability reports.

To undertake this analysis, I selected a series of recent reports for the years 2009 to 2019 from nine companies with factories in the area under study. For each company, I examined from three to six reports, focusing on the information provided on their environmental performance. Only one of these nine companies, Urrea (Grivatec), does not generate annual reports but rather has a sustainability section on its website, which was the basis for this review (Urrea 2016). I included in the selection both Mexican and foreign companies, as well as companies from several different sectors. The companies contemplated were Nestlé (Switzerland, food and beverages); Huntsman (United States, chemical); Celanese (United States, chemical); Quimikao (Japan, chemical); Flextronics (United States, electronics); AlEn (Mexico, chemical); Urrea (Mexico, metal industries); Mexichem (Mexico, chemical); and Oxiteno (Brazil, chemical). Various other companies where I did interviews do not generate this type of annual report; several only publish their environmental or sustainability policy, and one, Omnilife Manufacturing (Mexico, pharmaceutical), does not address the issue on its website.

The growth of this type of corporate report began in the late 1980s and early 1990s, with an emphasis first on environmental metrics, and later incorporating social or occupational health and safety issues (Milne

Corporate Sustainability

and Gray 2013). Initially, the reports did not usually refer to sustainability or sustainable development, but now many have been "repackaged" as sustainability reports (Aras and Crowther 2009, 279). Aside from noting that most of these reports do not define sustainability or sustainable development—notoriously slippery concepts—Markus Milne and Rob Gray (2013) highlight that reporting alone is often interpreted as being "sustainable": "Many organizations seem to confuse narrow and incomplete, partial reporting with claims to be *reporting on being sustainable*, actually *being sustainable*, or more commonly, with claims to be *moving towards sustainability*" (24; emphasis in original). The predominant logic of these documents, and therefore the interpretation of corporate sustainability, is to report according to the "triple bottom line" (TBL), or the results of the organization in economic, environmental, and social terms. The critique of these authors is that "the concept of the TBL is very unlikely to be a sufficient condition for sustainability, and indeed may lead to greater levels of *un*-sustainability" (14). In light of these precautions, let us explore the content of the reports from the selected companies.

First, the assumption of the TBL framework is evident in most cases, whether it is referred to as the "triple bottom line model" (Mexichem 2010); or an analogous concept such as "people, planet, profit," as in Huntsman's reports, which also refer to "ecology, economy and equity" (2012, 19); or, in the terms of the Kao Group (owners of Quimikao), conservation, community, and culture (Kao 2015). These reports are awash with commitments, codes of ethics, principles, programs, self-adulations, sketches of ecological products, philanthropic activities, energy- or water-saving projects, and, in some cases, goals and quantitative indicators. In terms of sustainability "metrics," despite the fact that most companies make some reference to their compliance with the guidelines of the GRI, the variables reported tend to vary significantly, which impedes comparisons. This fact was also remarked on by O'Rourke (2004b, 27), who observes that CSR reports employ "widely varying indicators, some of which are vague, unclear, irrelevant to major impacts, misleading, or worse."

In general terms, it is not an exaggeration to assert that these reports portray a win-win wonderland of innovation, efficiency, and continuous improvement where companies are now also contributing to the achievement of the UN Sustainable Development Goals. As Milne and Gray remark, in the discourse surrounding these reports, from the GRI or the

Carbon Disclosure Project, "the message of sustainability is unquestioned: an industry of endeavour is successfully constructing—and rewarding—sustainable performances and achievements of sustainability by many of the world's largest corporations in a hyper-reality which is entirely divorced from any planetary or human realities" (2013, 19). Furthermore, there are very clear absences in the alternate reality that is presented in the reports.

One of the most conspicuous absences from the perspective of this research is the lack of data on the environmental impacts of corporations at the factory level. Almost exclusively, companies present global data on their water and energy consumption or greenhouse gas emissions, waste, or wastewater generation without distinguishing between regions, much less individual factories. An exception to this rule is the 2010 report of the Kao Group, which included a table with a breakdown of the emissions for its Quimikao factory in El Salto, as well as for its plants in Japan and other countries (Kao 2010). However, the corporation did not continue the practice of presenting disaggregated information in subsequent reports (Kao 2013, 2015, 2019). This is particularly striking given that many companies stress that local communities are among the stakeholders considered the main audience for their reports. For communities, however, global consumption and emissions data say little about the impacts of a local factory.

Focusing on water use and discharge, the panorama is of inconsistent or even nonexistent data. As summarized in table 5.1, of the reports from nine companies, *four do not provide any quantitative data on their wastewater discharge*, one reports a reduction in the volume it discharges, and the other four provide some global data regarding their effluent quality. On this topic, Huntsman reports the total tons of chemical oxygen demand (COD) that it discharges from its more than seventy manufacturing and research and development sites in thirty countries, as well as a trend line of pollution intensity in terms of production. For 2017, Huntsman reported a slight reduction in the tons of COD it emits versus previous years, indicating that the "reductions are due in part to tighter permit limits and additional government controls over discharges" (Huntsman 2017, 38). So these reductions did not derive from internal decisions but rather were due to regulatory pressure. Furthermore, global data for a single parameter, in this case COD, do not represent evidence that the company does not discharge toxins or affect specific water bodies where it operates.

Table 5.1
Summary of water and discharge data from selected corporate reports

Company	Topic	Data provided
AlEn (2018)	Water	• % reduction in consumption per ton of production compared with 2017
	Effluent discharge	• % reduction in volume of discharge compared with 2017
Celanese (2017)	Water	• No quantitative data
	Effluent discharge	• No quantitative data
Flextronics (2018)	Water	• Reduction in volume of extracted water compared with the previous year
	Effluent discharge	• No quantitative data
Huntsman (2017)	Water	• Total volume (*water in*) • Intensity in cubic meters (m^3) per ton of production
	Effluent discharge	• Discharge volume (*water out*) • Tons of COD discharged • Trend in COD intensity versus production
Mexichem (Orbia 2018)	Water	• Water consumption in operations by source (surface and underground water, m^3/year) • Water recycled and reused (m^3/year) • Intensity of extracted water by ton sold
	Effluent discharge	• Total discharge volume (m^3/year) • Tons discharged for several parameters: COD, total suspended solid, biochemical oxygen demand, and total organic carbon
Nestlé (2018)	Water	• Total water extracted (m^3/year) • Total water extracted (m^3) per ton of product • % reduction in water extracted per ton of product compared with 2010
	Effluent discharge	• Discharge volume (m^3/year) • Total effluent discharged (m^3) per ton of product • Average quality of effluent discharged (mg COD/L)
Oxiteno (2018)	Water	• Total water extracted (m^3/year) per type of source and country • Total water consumption (m^3) per ton of product
	Effluent discharge	• No quantitative data

(continued)

Table 5.1
(Continued)

Company	Topic	Data provided
Quimikao (Kao 2019)	Water	• Total volume used per year (indicating proportion in Japan and three regions of the world where the company has operations) • Rate of annual decrease per unit of sales (compared with base year 2005)
	Effluent discharge	• Total COD load discharged in tons (indicating proportion in Japan and three regions of the world where the company has operations)
Urrea	Water	• No quantitative data
	Effluent discharge	• No quantitative data

Source: Author's elaboration.

Unsurprisingly, the company that provides the most data is Nestlé. Nestlé is a global brand with direct sales to the consumer and is also under scrutiny as the target of campaigns against water privatization—given its role in the bottled water industry. In 2021, Nestlé was the seventy-ninth company on the *Fortune* Global 500 list, with more than US$93 billion in revenue and 273,000 employees globally (*Fortune*, n.d.-c). Among other controversies, Nestlé faced a lawsuit in California, where it was alleged that it was extracting water for bottling from a national forest with an expired permit, this in the midst of a historic drought in the state (Morris 2016).

Nestlé is known for framing its CSR strategy in terms of what it calls "shared value" (Porter and Kramer 2011; Porter et al. 2012). Nestlé applies its shared value strategy to "drive growth and competitive success in Nutrition, Health and Wellness, while addressing societal issues that impact our business, including water, rural development and sustainability" (Nestlé 2015, 11). This often involves working with suppliers, as is the case for its plant in Ocotlán. The plant manager related how they have worked with their milk suppliers:

> I can have a business relationship with a milk supplier where the traditional approach is, pay me more because everything is very expensive. And so, Nestlé does not fall into that vicious circle of saying, I pay you more and then you

Corporate Sustainability

charge me more. So, what does Nestlé do? Nestlé tells you, "Why don't we study your cost structure together?" We detect areas of opportunity, I share best practices, I help you where I can support you, for example, with supplies of cheaper inputs. . . . I help you by getting you cheaper credits, I help you to be more productive so that your cost is lower and in that way we both win.[2]

This is an example of shared value's win-win approach, which Michael Porter and Mark Kramer describe as "a more sophisticated form of capitalism, one imbued with a social purpose" that "should arise not out of charity but out of a deeper understanding of competition and economic value creation" (2011, 77).

In its 2018 shared value report, Nestlé provides data on the total volume of its wastewater discharge, the volume per ton of product, and effluent quality measured in terms of the average COD concentration discharged from all its plants and warehouses. The average COD concentration has varied in recent years, with the 2018 value of 41 milligrams per liter (mg/L) being considerably lower than the 83.8 mg/L reported in 2017 (Nestlé 2018). Despite the multiple commitments that I will summarize later, Nestlé does not undertake to achieve a specific average reduction or concentration (Nestlé 2012, 2015, 2018). I will return to this issue of effluent quality, and the data presented, when I go into detail on the Nestlé factory in Ocotlán in the next section.

In general, more quantitative data are reported for water consumption than for discharge. Only Celanese and Urrea neglect to specify even the total volume of water that they extract or use in their operations. Even so, the data also reveal the absence of clear criteria to generate this information. While AlEn indicates only the percentage reduction in its water consumption, Flextronics' reporting is circumscribed to its total withdrawal. The other companies provide some indicator of the "intensity" of water use, but there are also various ways to characterize that intensity. Thus, Nestlé (2018) reports intensity in terms of cubic meters per ton of production, Mexichem (Orbia 2018) in terms of cubic meters per ton sold, and the Kao Group (Kao 2019) as the rate of water use per unit of sales (compared with its 2005 base year). These different criteria (production and sales) prevent comparison. The measure that would come closest to gauging the efficiency of production in environmental terms would be water use per ton of production, since an indicator such as sales is influenced by economic factors unrelated to the production process.

218   Chapter 5

Turning again to effluents, it is worthwhile to examine not only the quantitative data reported but also the companies' commitments regarding their discharges. The base level found in many reports is a commitment to legal compliance. For instance, while Celanese does not provide quantitative data on water or discharges in its reports, it states among its guiding principles that "we will comply with all applicable laws and regulations in each country in which we do business" (2015, 24). In vague terms, Flextronics asserts that wastewater "generated from operations, industrial processes and sanitation facilities are characterized, monitored, controlled and treated as required prior to discharge or disposal" (2015, 56). One would suppose that "as required" refers to legal stipulations, but the phrase is ambiguous. In a previous report, Flextronics made reference to the construction of wastewater treatment plants in Guadalajara and the Chinese city of Zhuhai and stated, "We are not only focusing on meeting these laws, but striving to achieve the highest environmental standards" (2011, 51). Another indeterminate commitment.

AlEn, a Monterrey-based manufacturer of cleaning products, has transitioned from imprecise to hyperbolic statements. In its 2014 report, it stated that its effluents "comply with the maximum permissible limits established by law" and that "AlEn does not affect any water resource due to discharges or runoff waters," since its discharges "are made into municipal sewers" (2014, 45). While I cannot address whether the first assertion is accurate, the second is false, at least in the case of its plant in El Salto. In accordance with the discharge permit issued by the National Water Commission (CONAGUA, Comisión Nacional del Agua) in 2004, the receiving body for the discharge from its industrial process is an unnamed stream (Permit 08JAL127506/12FMGR04). If AlEn's discharge were into a municipal sewer, it would in fact not require a permit from CONAGUA. More recently, in its 2018 report, AlEn maintains that "at the end of the water use cycle, we have treatment plants at all our operations that allow us to return the water in the same or better conditions than we received it" (35). Not only does it not degrade water, then, it even improves its quality.

The smallest company in this sample, valve and faucet producer Urrea, echoes AlEn's words and makes false statements. The company affirmed on its website that "caring for the environment is incorporated into our practices with the acquisition of the new water treatment plant, which allows zero discharges to the drainage network, returning the water in the same or

Corporate Sustainability

better conditions than when it was taken from mother earth" (Urrea 2016). How would Urrea substantiate that the treated effluents from its nickel and chrome electroplating tanks and so on have a quality equal to or better than that of the water it extracted "from mother earth"? In another unverifiable statement, Urrea maintained that its plant "complies with the highest international standards" (Urrea 2016). What standards? From which countries? It may be good marketing, but these are not clear or testable statements.

Of these Urrea claims, what is false is the assertion regarding achieving "zero discharge," as I mentioned in chapter 3. This became evident during my visit to the facilities in El Salto, where the person in charge of environmental management explained that, although the treatment plant in the electroplating area ensures compliance with the NOM-001-SEMARNAT-1996 standard (NOM-001), they are unable to use all the treated water in irrigation of their property (what they consider to be zero discharge) because it kills the grass. Therefore, a part of this discharge is released into the El Ahogado Canal.[3] The Mexican CSR magazine *Ganar-Ganar* (Win-win) published that at the Urrea plant in El Salto, "all the water consumed is recycled [and] the company is committed to taking care of the flora living there, giving life to its landscape" (Ortega 2010, 52). The water from that particular treatment plant, at least, is not what would give "life" to the landscape.

Two of the nine companies allude to reaching levels of wastewater treatment beyond what is stipulated by law. While Huntsman attributes the drop in the COD load it emits globally to stricter regulations, it also professes that "we are complying with—and in many cases exceeding—increasingly strict water quality standards" (2017, 38). This is a vague statement that does not commit the company to specific actions beyond compliance. The company that purports to hold itself to a higher bar is Nestlé. Nonetheless, its commitment is ambiguous. Nestlé affirms that in 2012, "we strengthened our Nestlé Environmental Requirements (NER) for water quality and effluent discharge to ensure we go beyond compliance with the legal requirements of the markets in which we operate" (2015, 153). It indicates that its starting point is regulatory compliance and that since 2017 it has employed a digital monitoring tool that ensures that "all our plants meet the exacting standards of our Nestlé Environmental Requirements for water quality" (2018, 41).

Nonetheless, neither the report nor its website indicates what the "Nestlé Environmental Requirements" actually are, so there would be no way to verify that, for example, its factory in Ocotlán adheres to them. Despite the repeated mention of the Nestlé Environmental Requirements, these are not in fact defined and, when an activist from the Transnational Institute contacted Nestlé in July 2020 regarding its requirements for wastewater discharge, the response from Nestlé Consumer Care was that "Nestlé's effluent discharge requirements are always to comply with the requirements of the country or locality where we operate." In Ocotlán, as we will see, Nestlé has not fulfilled this commitment, violating Mexican regulations in repeated monitoring. In general, then, most companies limit their public commitments regarding effluent discharge to mere legal compliance (which is also not optional), and the few that commit to something beyond that make only equivocal claims.

Although I will not go into the goals and indicators that each company provides for other environmental parameters, I would note that a number of these companies set goals and highlight their progress on indicators such as energy consumption, greenhouse gas generation (obviously linked to energy consumption), and sometimes waste. To put this in context, I would return to the question of how the notion of "sustainability" is envisioned in these reports. While the title of Celanese's interim 2011 report was *Sustainability Is Good Business*, Milne and Gray (2013, 16) pose two key questions to decipher these reports: "First, is it even fair to suggest that businesses should sacrifice profit within capitalism? and, second . . . is there any credence whatsoever in businesses' own claims that they are able to do so?"

The general picture that emerges from this sample of reports is of progress in certain areas directly linked to economic savings (such as reductions in energy consumption) and setbacks in other areas that are justified by acquisitions of new plants or increases in production, or which pass without comment. In AlEn's reports, for example, great detail is provided on its recycling program, from which it recovers material to produce bottles for its products at its two recycling plants. Without underestimating the value of this recycling, what is relevant here is to note that it is also good business for the company: "At AlEn we have shown that by taking advantage of the waste from PET and HDPE bottles, not only is the environment protected, but also there is an economic benefit that makes these projects profitable initiatives" (2012, 11). Likewise, Mexichem emphasizes that, taking into account "the growing cost structure of energy and water, we continually work in search of improving eco-efficiency in the use of these resources" (2010, 43). In these cases, clearly, there seems to be a confluence between

Corporate Sustainability

being "sustainable" and doing good business, so no further changes or sacrifices are required.

In several cases, simply reporting on certain environmental metrics is presented as constituting a sustainability strategy or evidence of improving environmental performance. An interesting case, in this sense, is that of Celanese, which publishes data on four environmental variables for its operations in eighteen countries: the intensity of its generation of greenhouse gases, intensity of air emissions (volatile organic compounds), intensity of waste generation, and intensity of energy consumption—all measured in terms of production. Its 2011 interim report set out goals for these indicators, with percentage reductions to be achieved by 2015, and asserted that they were "among the most aggressive [goals] in the chemical industry" (3). However, in 2013 it retreated from these goals, declaring that, instead, it was going to seek "continuous, cumulative progress through local, site-level improvement projects, moving our focus away from overly aggressive longer-term goals that may not account for variables such as an expanding footprint associated with company growth strategies" (2013, 12). Although Celanese is also one of the companies that affirms that "ecological and economic benefits often align" (2015, 16), when this is not the case, there is no doubt what the priorities are.

Huntsman (2010) set a modest goal in 2010 of reducing its energy consumption by 2 percent each year for a period of ten years. However, total energy consumption underwent ups and downs in subsequent reports, and no progressive reductions in energy intensity have been achieved (Huntsman 2014, 2017). Its 2014 report attributes an increase in energy consumption to the "record" levels of profitability and production, nonetheless asserting that Huntsman "continued to stay competitive by improving the energy efficiency of our operations" (2014, 31). The annual goal is no longer mentioned. Similarly, when Mexichem reported in 2015 that both the total and intensity of its electricity consumption increased (as well as the intensity of greenhouse gas emissions and waste generation), this was simply explained by an acquisition, as well as a "ramp-up of operations, and an increase in productive activity" (2015, 95). This is far from a previous statement claiming to have an "eco-efficiency approach, that is, doing more with less and going for more" (2010, 39). It seems that even data indicative of decreases in efficiency and increases in total materials consumption can be smoothly rebranded as evidence of a company's productivity and profitability.

Of course, there are also companies that report achieving quantitative goals in terms of resource efficiency. The Kao Group set 2020 goals for the reduction of CO_2 generation in the life cycle of its products, as well as for water consumed during use of its cleaning and personal hygiene products, and made progress toward those goals (Kao 2015, 2019). Nestlé (2015) highlights a series of goals and achievements in its eco-efficiency, compared with its 2005 base year: a 56 percent reduction in water discharge per ton of product, a 41.2 percent reduction in water extraction per ton of product, and a 42.7 percent drop in direct greenhouse gas emissions per ton of product, among others. Based on these "achievements" Nestlé avers, "We've continued to decouple environmental impacts from growth" (182). In some cases, however, greater efficiency does not translate into a decrease in consumption. Thus, Nestlé indicates that its energy use has risen 6.6 percent since 2005, although it stresses that in the same period its production volume increased 50.2 percent. In other cases, it presents data that I consider a misrepresentation of their performance. On the subject of the "optimization" of its packaging, Nestlé boasts that "the cumulative amount of packaging we have avoided since 1991 is more than 771,830 tonnes and CHF [Swiss francs] 1356 million in packaging costs" (186). Against what scenario does it make the comparison to determine these figures? Compared with using the worst possible packaging? In addition, this presents Nestlé as a responsible company by reducing, for example, the weight of its PET bottles for its bottled waters, instead of identifying it as one of the major contributors to the problem of waste generated globally due to water consumed in disposable bottles.

Two final comments on how these reports tend to embellish the environmental virtues of companies. First, many companies emphasize the ecological characteristics of specific products. One of the clearest cases is from Huntsman, which repeatedly makes reference in its reports to a particular dye, Avitera, a product of its Textile Effects division, to which its factory in Jalisco belongs. According to the vice president of this division, "If the entire world's reactive dyed cotton was processed with AVITERA® SE . . . more than 820 billion liters of water per year could be saved—the equivalent of 1.3 liters of fresh water per person per day in the major Asian textile-processing countries, such as India, Bangladesh and China" (Huntsman 2014, 19). Not only does it magnify the possible impacts of this product—with the "savings" achievable in the most populous countries in the world—but it has emphasized this particular dye in almost all the

Corporate Sustainability

company's sustainability reports. What is not specified in these reports is that the Textile Effects division alone has more than two thousand products (according to its website) and that this division represented only 11 percent of the company's revenue in 2019 (Huntsman 2019). Highlighting a single product not only says little about the characteristics of all the products of the company's four divisions but also provides scant information on the environmental impacts of the company's manufacturing activities. This tactic of overemphasizing an "ecological" product is one of the features of greenwashing identified by Vos (2009), since here a single product is taken to highlight the "green" character of a company's total operations.

The last observation I would like to make on these reports is the way in which a number of companies maintain that "sustainability" is nothing new, characterizing it as part of their legacies transmitted from their founders. The Kao Group, for instance, maintains that since its first soap came onto the market in 1890, "Kao has consistently operated in line with its CSR perspective, and in 2004, it incorporated the founding spirit into the corporate philosophy, the Kao Way" (Kao 2010, 11). Nestlé, for its part, appeals to the story of its founder, Henri Nestlé, who started the company with an infant formula, motivated by his desire to "help save the life of a neighbour's child and, more broadly, to help alleviate infant mortality" (2015, 9). The company claims that, in this story, "one can see the beginnings of our conviction that for a company to be successful over the long term and create value for shareholders, it must create value for society" (9). So what it now calls "creating shared value" apparently dates back to 1866. When we see these examples, we can also take it as an indication of how "sustainability" and CSR more broadly are interpreted as business as usual, remaining firmly within prevailing business logic.

From the point of view of a skeptic, it would be easy to dismiss these reports as mere advertising materials. They clearly function to a large extent to that end, and with a growing group of consumers concerned with buying responsible and environmentally friendly products, generating a reputation as a "sustainable" company may mean accessing other markets and consumers. However, that is not the only purpose or result of these reports. From the point of view of local communities, they contribute very little toward being able to determine the risks, emissions, or even production processes of a local factory. But for companies, the claim to or reputation for good environmental performance can have regulatory repercussions.

Vos sustains that "companies and organizations can rest on their good reputations to some extent, and may get more leniency from regulating authorities" (2009, 685). In a similar vein, Laufer notes, "Corporations can rely on their reputations for compliance and social responsibility with lesser scrutiny. The emblem of certification to certain standards and the reputational advantage of membership or participation in socially responsible organizations distances the firm from any alleged deviance" (2003, 257). This is a point I will explore in the next section.

The panorama of these reports is of an extremely partial selection of data, spotlighting instances where there is a "win-win" in economic and environmental terms, as well as specific products or projects that do not necessarily represent the total operations or impacts of the companies. This is also consistent with the outlook that emerged in the interviews with company representatives when they were asked about the integration of sustainability or environmental management in their organizations. In the vast majority of cases, the answers alluded to the fact that they were already typical company practices, such as seeking legal compliance or savings in materials and consumption of energy and inputs. Thus, adopting a sustainability strategy simply involved integrating scattered practices under a single, more ordered system, together with the recording and monitoring of quantitative metrics. Although AlEn, for example, does not have a formal sustainability strategy, according to the representative interviewed at its corporate headquarters, for AlEn sustainability is something as old as the company itself:

> The company has been in the Mexican market for more than sixty years, so it has always sought to incorporate this type of process. Everything that has happened with sustainability was not a conscious issue, it was not an issue of let's take care of the environment, it was a business issue, of how we make this move faster, how we can reduce costs, this type of thing, so it has always been there.[4]

So, together with the references to the strong ethical or altruistic values of company founders, it is argued that with sustainability there is nothing new under the sun. What this means crucially for this analysis is that there is no change in logic either, and the main drivers of any change will be—in addition to reputation—regulatory compliance and input efficiencies that also result in financial savings.

Two other testimonies support this critique, highlighting how the fundamental logic of companies does not change. Huntsman's sustainability coordinator for global operations touched on this point when discussing the

Corporate Sustainability

challenges of adopting a sustainability vision. The coordinator explained that, as a company listed on the New York Stock Exchange, Huntsman is also "guilty" of working from a short-term perspective, due to pressure from its investors:

> We're not so much looking out broadly, more long term into the future. There are some exceptions, but for the most part, the general community in Wall Street is still of the mindset that they're looking at specific metrics in a very short time frame. So, they're having a hard time getting their arms around what's the value of sustainability.[5]

Beyond external pressures, the director of EHS issues of the National Chemical Industry Association (ANIQ, Asociación Nacional de la Industria Química) highlighted the internal logics of companies that prevent progress. Describing a process of trying to generate sustainability indicators for the chemical industry in Mexico, he stated that while companies have reported efficiency improvements in terms of waste generation, this has not been the case for energy or water. His explanation was that "we assume that at the end of the day, because what we want is to sell more, we want to produce more, and well, at the end of the day that requires or demands more use of resources."[6] This is the logic of "eco-efficiency" that William McDonough and Michael Braungart declare only presents an "illusion of change." Beyond appearances, they argue that "relying on eco-efficiency to save the environment will in fact achieve the opposite—it will let industry finish off everything quietly, persistently, and completely" (1998). Win-win seems to translate, in practice, into the company always winning and the environment winning when it suits them.

5.2 A Myth of the Multinational

A key factor that, at least at the discursive level, contributes to a minimization of industry responsibility for the pollution of the Santiago River and, at the same time, weakens the arguments for stricter standards is something that may be considered a myth, in the sense that it is a widely held belief expressed and repeated by different actors that does not stand up in the face of existing evidence. According to this myth, because large transnational corporations have international certifications as well as environmental management systems or internal guidelines, they comply with environmental standards that are stricter than required by Mexican environmental regulations: their ethics and internal commitments are a higher bar than official standards, and Mexican legal requirements are secondary given their internal codes. This argument supports a system based on self-regulation and the independence of corporations that, apparently, don't require the stick of inspections or standards because their international and corporate commitments are more than sufficient.

To illustrate this myth, I will cite two people who work in different spheres but who express the same idea. Silvia Vega, who for decades has been the manager of the Association of Industrialists of El Salto (AISAC, Asociación de Industriales de El Salto), states regarding the work on environmental issues of the member companies that "many of them are large corporations, [and] they have to comply with the standards or policies laid out by their own companies and many times they go beyond what is called for in Mexican regulations."[7] In the municipality of Ocotlán, the director of ecology, Víctor Castellanos, expressed a similar idea. In the context of explaining a fine applied to the Nestlé factory in his municipality, he maintained an optimistic vision of the performance of this company and of the Celanese factory, located across the river in the municipality of Poncitlán. "Nestlé and Celanese are companies with high levels of health and safety, I mean, they are with OSHA [US Occupational Safety and Health Administration], they work with international environmental protection standards," he said, while explaining the Nestlé fine related to records for its wastewater treatment plant. Even given evidence to the contrary, therefore, the belief in the responsible action of this type of company is maintained.

Is there some truth to this myth, or are virtues attributed to these companies that cannot be confirmed in practice? In order to attempt to answer this question, I will review available data for four companies that discharge into the river or the El Ahogado Canal, with reference to both their compliance with the NOM-001 and their reaction to changes in Mexican regulations. The companies are the global food giant Nestlé; two American chemical companies, Huntsman and Celanese; and the Japanese chemical corporation Quimikao (Kao Group). Briefly, I will review evidence from five main sources: the 2011 study of the Santiago River undertaken by the Mexican Institute of Water Technology (IMTA, Instituto Mexicano de Tecnología del Agua), which included analysis of a number of industrial discharges in the river basin; two earlier studies contracted out by the Jalisco State Water Commission (CEA, Comisión Estatal del Agua) to the consulting company

Corporate Sustainability

AyMA Ingeniería y Consultoría (AyMA Ingeniería y Consultoría 2003; CEAS and AyMA Ingeniería y Consultoría 2006), with analysis of the effluent of these companies; records of CONAGUA inspection visits; and data provided by the companies to the Ministry of Environment and Natural Resources (SEMARNAT, Secretaría de Medio Ambiente y Recursos Naturales) in reports submitted to obtain their annual operating certificates (COAs, *cédulas de operación anual*). There are few studies analyzing industrial effluent discharged into the Santiago; however, the wastewaters of the selected companies were included in at least two of the three studies just cited.

The Nestlé factory in Ocotlán produces baby formula for twenty-one Latin American countries and was the company's first factory in Mexico, established in 1935. Unlike the other companies I will analyze, Nestlé, the world's largest food and beverage corporation, is not a likely source of toxic emissions at this site. Still, the studies of the Santiago River that have included analysis of Nestlé's effluent have consistently demonstrated noncompliance with the NOM-001. The two AyMA studies were undertaken in the context of plans to build the Arcediano Dam on the Santiago. In the 2003 study, samples of Nestlé's effluent were taken on three occasions, revealing a level of biochemical oxygen demand (BOD) almost twelve times what is permitted for type B rivers, with an average of 898 mg/L versus a maximum monthly average of 75 mg/L. Here, it should be recalled that the NOM-001 contemplates three classifications for the country's rivers, types A, B, and C, where type A, for use in agricultural irrigation, has the least stringent limits; type B, for public-urban use, is somewhat more restrictive; and type C, for protection of aquatic life, sets the strictest limits for the same parameters. In 2003, the Santiago in Ocotlán was classified as type B, although the river classification from Ocotlán and until the Arcediano site (to the north of the Guadalajara Metropolitan Area) was changed to type C on January 1, 2009.[8]

Nestlé's effluent also failed to comply on other parameters, with almost double the limit for fats and oils (29.2 mg/L versus 15 mg/L in the standard) and for total nitrogen (76.3 mg/L versus 40 mg/L), as well as an excess of total suspended solids (TSS) (AyMA Ingeniería y Consultoría 2003, 4-39). A further parameter that is worth noting, despite its absence from the NOM-001, is COD, an indicator of the presence of organic and inorganic substances in a sample susceptible to oxidization by a strong oxidizing agent, which includes substances not biologically degradable. In 2003, average COD in Nestlé's wastewater was 1,263 mg/L. COD is not regulated in the 1996 standard;

however, when it was included in the Federal Duties Law (LFD, Ley Federal de Derechos; Article 278-B), at the end of 2007, taxes were applicable for concentrations of this parameter above 200 mg/L for type B water bodies. The limits set in the LFD differ from those indicated in the NOM-001, as they are for tax purposes, with levels above the limits set being the basis for calculation of duties, ostensibly as part of the "polluter pays" principle.

Noncompliance continued in 2006, when a sample of Nestlé's effluent was again analyzed, with BOD levels almost five times the limit for the daily average (738 mg/L versus 150 mg/L), more than 50 percent above the limit for fats and oils at 39.5 mg/L, and slightly above the limit for TSS. COD was also high, at a level of 1,152 mg/L (CEAS and AyMA Ingeniería y Consultoría 2006, 4-3). In the more recent IMTA study, the researchers used as the reference the limits for type C rivers, as the river reclassification had taken place. In their results for Nestlé, noncompliance continued for the same parameters in three monitoring campaigns undertaken in 2009 and 2010. For BOD, with a maximum daily average of 60 mg/L, Nestlé discharged at *almost twenty times* this concentration (1,175 mg/L); for nitrogen, it was five times the limit (131 mg/L versus 25 mg/L); *more than nineteen times* the limit for phosphorus (193 mg/L versus 10 mg/L); and in one sample, the factory released a concentration of COD *thirty-eight times the applicable limit* in the LFD at that time for type C rivers (3,841 mg/L versus 100 mg/L) (IMTA and CEA 2011, 5-67, 5-69, 5-102). Here it is worth making the comparison also with what Nestlé (2010, 41) reported as the average COD concentration in its effluents globally: 78 mg/L in 2010. Thus, the effluent sample from its Ocotlán factory exceeded that average almost fifty times.

More recently, in 2018, CONAGUA undertook inspections at the Nestlé factory on the banks of the river in Ocotlán, as well as its second infant formula factory, inaugurated in 2016 in the same municipality. Laboratory analyses found that the effluents from both factories exceeded the limits established in their discharge permits (in one case for fecal coliforms and in the other for total nitrogen, total phosphorus, and fecal coliforms), and each factory was fined MX$132,540 as a result.[9] Noncompliance continues to be the constant.

Returning to the myth outlined, Nestlé should not only comply with Mexican standards but also meet stricter limits set in its internal standards, as it proclaims in its "shared value" reports. In effect, according to the manager of the Ocotlán factory, Nestlé has its own environmental emissions

Corporate Sustainability   229

standards. However, this does not imply that they go beyond the regulations in the countries where it operates. He explained the situation in this way: "Mexico has emission standards, so Nestlé asks us, 'Respect the emission standards of that country.' . . . If there were no standard, for example for wastewater discharge, Nestlé has a standard for water discharge, but Mexico has one, so we respect the Mexican standard."[10] In light of the analyses just cited, this respect for Mexican regulations is clearly in doubt. Further, Nestlé does not set out to exceed national legal requirements for its wastewater. Here is an apparent contradiction with what the company reports on its new, globally applicable environmental requirements. When the government of Jalisco made public a list of twenty-nine companies that violated the discharge standard in their emissions to the Santiago River in early 2020, the list included both of Nestlé's factories in Ocotlán (de la Peña 2020). Thus, there is evidence of compliance neither with unknown internal requirements nor with Mexican regulations.

Continuing downstream, the next of the four companies is Celanese and its factory that commenced operations in 1947 and announced its closure in October 2019. Celanese, headquartered in Irving, Texas, is among the five hundred largest companies in the United States, with more than 7,600 employees and 2020 revenues of US$5.6 billion.[11] Its plant in Poncitlán was dedicated for decades to the manufacture of cellulose acetate and acetic anhydride. Cellulose acetate is the material used, for example, in cigarette filters. With respect to its voluminous discharge into the Santiago,[12] there are data that suggest noncompliance with the Mexican standard. In the 2006 AyMA study, of note is the concentration of TSS of 1,342 mg/L, almost *eleven times the average daily limit* for type B rivers (CEAS and AyMA Ingeniería y Consultoría 2006, 4-4). That same year, as a result of the inspection of its discharge on November 23, 2006, CONAGUA fined Celanese MX$243,298.[13]

In the IMTA study, Celanese released high levels of phosphorus in the three samples analyzed, at about five times the official limit in each sample (IMTA and CEA 2011, 5-29, 5-67, 5-103). In the first sample, compared with the limits for a type C classification, its effluent was *twenty-six times above the limit for TSS* (1,058 mg/L versus 60 mg/L), *seventeen times the limit for BOD* (855 mg/L versus 60 mg/L), and almost *twenty-one times the limit for COD* in the LFD, with a concentration of 2,088 mg/L (2011, 5-29–5-31). Further, one sample failed to comply with permissible pH (5–10 units), with an acidic pH of 2.3 (5-189). With respect to parameters not contemplated in either the LFD or the NOM-001, the IMTA study found a concentration of phenols of 0.19 mg/L, a class of substances the authors affirm "affect organisms due to their toxicity," and at a level they consider "very high" (5-199). In the analysis of volatile and semivolatile organic compounds, referred to previously in this text, forty-eight different substances were detected in Celanese's wastewater, including high levels of chloroform (212).

The inspection record from 2010 provides a further piece of interesting evidence in order to interrogate the myth that transnational corporations go above and beyond national environmental regulations.[14] Among the appendices is a 2010 letter from the legal representative of Celanese in Mexico to the director of the Lerma-Santiago-Pacific (LSP) Basin Agency, Raúl Antonio Iglesias Benítez, requesting changes to the specific discharge conditions in its wastewater permit. The letter explains the nature of its process, indicating that due to the characteristics of its discharge and available technologies, "treatment of the phosphorus and Chemical Oxygen Demand present in the wastewaters of the Complex is difficult." For this reason, they request that the permitted level of phosphorus be raised to a monthly average of 59 mg/L, almost three times the official limit of 20 mg/L (set both in its own discharge permit and in the NOM-001 for type C rivers). The concession they request for COD is to be able to discharge an average concentration of 240 mg/L, 2.4 times the limit in the LFD. On arguing in favor of these allowances, they indicate that their discharge is not a source of "heavy metals, cyanide or toxic substances," contrary to the results of the IMTA study (IMTA and CEA 2011). The request received an initial negative response, though the story did not end there.

Celanese expressed its disagreement with the initial refusal from CONAGUA and filed an appeal for review, arguing that the authority "omitted to expressly address the issue of obtaining a maximum limit for the average monthly concentrations for phosphorus of 59 mg/L and chemical oxygen demand of 240 mg/L."[15] In response, the then-director of the commission, David Korenfeld, accepted the arguments and revoked the resolution on the discharge permit, concluding that the authority also left the company in a situation of "uncertainty," since it "failed to provide sufficient and duly justified reasons that would allow the applicant to know the reasons why they classified the receiving body as 'Type C' and also modified their particular discharge conditions."[16] It remained pending, therefore, for the LSP Basin Agency to issue a new response to Celanese's request.

Corporate Sustainability

In May 2015, investigators from the Attorney General's Office (Procuraduría General de la República) "raided" the Celanese factory in Poncitlán for alleged "violations of Mexican environmental legislation for contaminating the Santiago River and the neighboring lands with mercury and methyl-ethyl-ketone" (Del Toro Carazo Abogados and Ramos and Hermosillo Abogados 2015). This was related to a lawsuit (writ of amparo) initiated by the owner of the neighboring property, Javier Salcedo Sahagún, who asserted culpability on the part of the director of the LSP Basin Agency and CONAGUA for omissions such as failing to cancel Celanese's discharge permit (No. 08JAL133533/12FMOC09), failing to verify compliance with permit requirements, and not issuing sanctions. Salcedo was looking to build a high-density residential subdivision, to be called La Ribera Residencia (Riverside Residence), on a property bordering the Celanese factory.

In evidence of the allegations, the amparo cited an expert opinion on environmental crimes of April 2015, prepared by Lucía Rueda Quintana of the Attorney General's Office Criminal Investigation Agency (preliminary investigation A.P. 1235/UEIDAPLE/DA/33/2014).[17] The report detailed the collection and analysis of water and soil samples, and concluded there were violations of the NOM-001, with Celanese exceeding levels for mercury in its discharge. Likewise, it cited the discharge into the soil of methyl ethyl ketone "that [according to] NOM-052-SEMARNAT-2005 is considered a hazardous waste."[18] Finally, the report underscored that an unauthorized discharge was detected during a visit to the plant in October 2014.

In March 2016, the Water Quality Office of the LSP Basin Agency once again denied the company's request for changes to its permit, and it presented the average concentration of phosphorus in the Santiago River for samples taken between 2012 and 2015. Those averages for the stations on the river from upstream of Celanese until the Salto de Juanacatlán waterfall were in a range between 0.74 mg/L and 2.87 mg/L, thus greatly exceeding the value of 0.05 mg/L established in the LFD (Article 224, Section V), in the Water Quality Guidelines for the protection of aquatic life. As the intention is "to cleanup and reduce the concentrations of all the pollutants that currently affect the quality" of the Santiago River, they concluded that an adjustment to the company's permit was not recommended.[19] However, other documents raise doubts as to whether Celanese in fact made the necessary modifications to achieve compliance with the standard for phosphorus.

In this regard, the key document is a technical assessment of the treatment capacity of the system at the Celanese plant dated November 2009, prepared by the American engineering and consulting firm CH2M Hill.[20] The experts at CH2M Hill concluded that Celanese's wastewater treatment plants could not comply with the NOM-001 for type C rivers, specifically for the parameters of phosphorus, TSS, and COD (the last in relation to the level of 100 mg/L set out in the LFD). They recommended adjustments to the system to incorporate a chemical precipitation process and tertiary ultrafiltration technology with membranes, but even so they indicated that the aforementioned "alternative limits" would be needed for phosphorus and COD. Nonetheless, when CONAGUA carried out another inspection of the Celanese plant on October 14, 2015, the inspection record indicated that the company had a treatment system consisting of "sedimentation, homogenization, separation of fats, aeration with activated sludge, clarification and chlorination" (Record PNI-2015-LSP-112). This is the same system it had in 2009, as described by CH2M Hill. If the inspection report is accurate, then, chemical precipitation and ultrafiltration were not incorporated, which implies that it was not complying with the limits for phosphorus, and possibly for TSS, just to mention the two parameters controlled by the NOM-001. More generally, Celanese's request to CONAGUA makes evident that not only did the company not go beyond the Mexican standard, it even sought official consent for its noncompliance.

Downriver from Celanese, in the community of Atotonilquillo, we find the Huntsman factory, acquired from Ciba Specialty Chemicals in 2006. The Ciba factory was established on this site in 1965 and over the course of its history produced a range of substances from pesticides and epoxy resins to pharmaceutical products (STPS 2006). On taking over the factory, Huntsman informed the basin agency at CONAGUA of its plans to expand its production lines as well as continue with those of Ciba in the "production of dyes for such industries as the carpet, automotive, and home and apparel textile [industries]" (Inspection Record VI-PNI-VIII-07-205). This expansion was motivated by "several advantages" of the Atotonilquillo plant, as well as the closing of a Huntsman factory in the United States; it was also going to require the use of large volumes of water, as its production "is highly intensive in the use of said resource." When the factory's fiftieth anniversary was celebrated in 2015, it was pronounced the premier manufacturing facility in the Americas for Huntsman's Textile Effects division, producing over 150 dyes and chemicals (Huntsman 2015).

Corporate Sustainability

The 2006 AyMA study analyzed samples of Huntsman's effluent, taken just months after the factory acquisition in July 2006. In the results, noncompliance was found with almost three times the daily limit for nitrogen (172 mg/L versus 60 mg/L), a high level of COD at 1,066 mg/L, and an electrical conductivity, indicative of the presence of dissolved solids, of 26,100 µmhos/cm, classified in the study as "excessively high" (CEAS and AyMA Ingeniería y Consultoría 2006, 4-4). This was also the only study that included toxicity analysis, finding a level of acute toxicity classified as significant for this discharge, at thirty-three units (4-22).[21] In the 2011 study, the IMTA analysis found noncompliance in concentrations of nitrogen, with up to four times the allowed limit; COD values of up to 528 mg/L; and once again high levels of electrical conductivity at 17,230 µmhos/cm (IMTA and CEA 2011, 5-103, 5-105, 5-449). In terms of volatile and semivolatile organic compounds, between nineteen and twenty-three different substances were detected in each of the three monitoring campaigns. Given an ongoing campaign focused on the apparel sector, in 2012 Greenpeace Mexico had two samples of Huntsman's effluent analyzed. It identified the presence in one sample of thirty-one different substances and in the other of fifty-two synthetic organic compounds. Among these, it highlighted the presence of diverse compounds considered "extremely toxic substances, including for aquatic organisms," with reference to dimethyl benzenamine, diethyl benzenamine, and 1-methylethyl benzenamine, among other toxins detected (Greenpeace Mexico 2012a).

Additional evidence of the fictitious nature of the myth being analyzed is found in the appendices to another CONAGUA inspection at Huntsman, from October 20, 2011 (Record PNI-2011-LSP-623).[22] What is notable here is Huntsman's response to the change in the classification of the Santiago to type C. Together with a letter of February 2010 addressed to the basin authority is a Huntsman presentation explaining the proposed modifications to its wastewater treatment plant. "In the production of our dyes," states the presentation from 2009, "we face the problem of the generation of liquid wastes with a low potential for treatment by conventional methods." What it proposes are adjustments to lower nitrogen and COD levels in its effluent in order to comply with the new limits. While this is not evidence of any noncompliance, it is an indication that this multinational headquartered in Salt Lake City, Utah, responds to changes in Mexican regulations, and not solely to its own standards, which are assumed to exceed national requirements. This is consistent with the comments of

234   Chapter 5

the global sustainability coordinator at Huntsman, whom I interviewed in early 2014.

For the coordinator, the decision to surpass the environmental standards of any of the thirty countries where Huntsman has manufacturing facilities is linked to its pillars of sustainability: people, planet, and profit (Huntsman 2014). This means, as he explained, that there must be more than an environmental reason to set itself a stricter limit: "Generally, my rule of thumb with them," he said, "is that if it impacts only one of these things [people, planet, and profit], the likelihood is it's not a true corporate sustainability project. It needs to impact more than one."[23] Taking the example of regulation of air emissions in Mexico, the coordinator commented that, "for us to go above and beyond that, there needs to be another reason for us to do that, beyond just saying, 'Hey, we met the environmental obligations here.'" That "above and beyond" means bringing added value to the company in terms, he indicated, of either improvements for the community given some specific complaint or, of course, higher profit. Corporate sustainability is not an environmental agenda, and for Huntsman there is no preexisting internal obligation to exceed the requirements of the environmental regulations in the countries where it operates.

For the last company to be examined, Quimikao, located in the heart of the industrial area in El Salto, there is an interesting source of evidence of noncompliance: its own reports presented to SEMARNAT for its COA. Quimikao, part of the Japanese Kao Group, produces surfactants from fatty acids, mainly for fabric softeners and other personal care products, as well as additives for asphalt. Constantly, in nine reports presented by Quimikao between 2002 and 2012, the company reported high levels of nitrogen *up to twenty-four times the legal limit*, in the case of the concentration reported in 2006 of 984 mg/L, compared with a limit for the monthly average of 40 mg/L with the lax type A classification. Noncompliance is also a constant in more recent years, with the obligation to achieve a maximum monthly average of 15 mg/L with the type C classification: Quimikao reported 388 mg/L in 2009, 344 mg/L in 2010, 120 mg/L in 2011, and 333 mg/L in 2012.[24]

Analyses of its effluent have also detected noncompliance. The 2006 AyMA study found 369 mg/L of nitrogen, a level of BOD_5 almost three times the limit for type A (538 mg/L), and a COD of 1,172 mg/L (CEAS and AyMA Ingeniería y Consultoría 2006, 4-3). This effluent was also found to have a significant level of acute toxicity, at twenty-one units according to

Corporate Sustainability

the test with the organism *Vibrio fischeri* (4-22). Levels of contaminants in industrial wastewater may vary significantly during the course of a day or from one day to the next. In this way, one of the samples analyzed as part of the 2011 IMTA study found even higher levels of pollutants. With the type C classification now applicable, *BOD limits were exceeded sixty-two times, with 3,745 mg/L versus a limit of 60 mg/L, while the concentration of fats and oils was forty-six times the limit* (1,159 mg/L versus 25 mg/L); nitrogen was high once again at 366 mg/L; and the *COD was at a level sixty-five times above the limit in the LFD*, at 6,486 mg/L (5-100). In the same sample, fifty-six distinct volatile and semivolatile organic compounds were detected.

In this rather long and detailed discussion of effluent analyses, limits, and river classifications, I have sought to demonstrate basically two things. First, there is a pattern of noncompliance with the NOM-001 on behalf of these four companies and, although there is no continuous monitoring of these discharges, there is evidence of this noncompliance over time. Second, based on evidence from interviews with company representatives and official documents, I have shown that these companies do not comply with internal standards that are stricter than Mexican regulations for industrial effluent and revealed how they respond to changes in Mexican standards. Thus, at least in the case of these factories that belong to important global corporations and for which there are greater external data on their effluent quality, the myth of the foreign corporation adhering to self-imposed environmental rules that surpass the quality levels called for by law cannot be sustained.

5.3 Government through the Eyes of Industry

In previous chapters, I have examined the actions of government authorities to regulate industry, drawing from government documents and statistics, as well as interviews with public officials. Likewise, I have analyzed the NOM-001 and the regulatory capture that hampered its modification. Now I will turn to explore how both authorities and environmental regulations are viewed from the perspective of industry, specifically the outlook of EHS personnel at various factories in the corridor. Although, as would be expected, a number express their conformity with the (low) level of enforcement and the (lack of) stringency of environmental standards, the perspectives are not one-dimensional and provide insight into regulatory practices as experienced by the regulated parties, as well as the relationship between government authorities and the private sector. Finally, several interviewees also shared their opinions on the problems of the Santiago River, which, in general, they believe are not their concern.

As regards government authorities, while many of the EHS managers whom I interviewed affirm that there are capable and knowledgeable personnel among government officials, they acknowledge that levels of enforcement and sanctions are low. This is the opinion even of those who feel that regulations are adequate, such as the EHS manager at Urrea, who asserted that "standards as such are very good, industrial compliance as such is very bad." In his opinion, "if they had the possibility of more inspectors . . . and if there were not so much corruption, people would comply more."[25] Several referred to the lack of inspectors at the Federal Bureau of Environmental Protection (Procuraduría Federal de Protección al Ambiente) and, repeatedly, at CONAGUA, a reality that I laid out in detail in chapter 3. The head of sustainable development at AlEn observed, moreover, that CONAGUA often fails to follow through on sanctions. After declaring that the fines for water and discharge violations are "very expensive," she tempered this affirmation by clarifying that "many times the authority does not have the human resources, that is, the people to present the cases and apply the sanctions." When fines are announced, she stated, the cases are "very dramatic, very popular with the media," but later, "little by little they are forgotten, it is no longer on television . . . and in the end there is no sanction."[26] Up to this point, these perspectives are consistent with the data presented previously.

At an American electronics company in the corridor, an EHS engineer related his experience complying with environmental regulations: "As long as you present the documents on time, they do not question further, which is sometimes necessary, isn't it? That questioning." In this way, he stated, "with the government, it is during the first months [of the year] that you have to provide documentation and the rest of the year . . . they don't ask you for anything." There is also no oversight, he said: "Very rarely do we receive an [inspection] visit, very rarely." Unsurprisingly, he concludes that "they have a long way to go to become agencies such as we see in other countries."[27]

The head of EHS at a different electronics plant also underscored the carelessness of the authorities. She related that, "at the municipal level,

Corporate Sustainability

since they have all the documents from past years—because they have files for each company—they just look at the file and say, 'Ah, okay, ask them for the same things.'" From her point of view, at the end of the day, this is not a problem: "If you don't ask me, if you don't require anything from me, all the better for me." We have already touched on the shortcomings of municipal oversight, but this interviewee also questioned the seriousness of the work at the federal level. In this case, she recounted an experience with the SEMARNAT delegation in Jalisco. As her company has several industrial plants, each registered with a different company name and with its respective environmental registration number with SEMARNAT, she presented numerous COAs reporting the annual emissions of the various industrial installations. After several years of doing this, she narrated, "The girl from SEMARNAT asked me, 'Why is it that you present so many duplicates of your COAs?' 'No, I am not providing duplicates, I am presenting COAs for each industrial warehouse.' . . . I said to her, 'So what has been happening for the past ten years that I presented my COAs?' She said to me, 'Well, they were all filed as duplicates,' and . . . I was very surprised, considering that they are the authorities." So the information for the complete operations of the company had not been taken into account. Given this, she asserted, "I believe that it is information that is irrelevant to them. I'm not so sure they really analyze it."[28] The evidence supports her conclusion.

An oft-mentioned problem in interviews were the delays of the environmental authorities, at all levels, in dealing with permit requests, renewals, and other procedures. Although this was the case for distinct agencies, CONAGUA clearly stands out due to its inefficiency. The head of EHS at the small Infineum plant in El Salto, producing additives for lubricants, explained that it took CONAGUA six years to issue the concession title for its well. Repeatedly facing such government nonresponsiveness, she said that one strategy has been to take group action: "We have to take steps together as AISAC to ensure things move forward."[29] Another of the interviewees, from the Dutch company DSM, at its vitamin premix plant, reported that the inability to register its water permit under the company's current name even prevented it from being certified in the Clean Industry program. He described CONAGUA as "very inefficient," detailing that DSM had spent twelve or thirteen years trying to change the registration.[30] Silvia Vega from AISAC agreed that "you have to take legal action" if you want to conclude a process with the commission, stating that "CONAGUA is where you see the most bureaucracy, and the least commitment, and the least willingness" to get things done.[31]

Perhaps surprisingly, several EHS managers interviewed voiced strong criticisms of the laxity of regulations. The head of EHS at Oxiteno, a Brazilian company that produces surfactants and fatty acids from ethylene oxide at its Tlaquepaque factory, discussed the gaps in legislation on environmental emissions, particularly for greenhouse gases and wastewater. In these cases, he said, "the rules now are very benign." Regarding the NOM-001, he highlighted the fact that it does not contemplate COD: "If you have COD, you know whether or not you are polluting, and it is not considered in the standard."[32] Similarly, the EHS manager at the car suspension factory of the German corporation ZF maintained that the standards are "lax" and stated with regard to the NOM-001 that "They should change it, now. A more accurate view of our reality, how many more companies have been established, and also, within companies, the variety of pollutants that we release into the environment. I think that yes, it should be more stringent."[33] However, not everyone welcomed a stricter standard.

This issue was directly touched on by one of the interviewees, who commented on the concern that the approval of stricter controls could lead to the flight of companies from the country. He recounted an informal chat with colleagues who work in the EHS departments at other factories, where the topic of a new effluent standard came up and one person expressed, "Imagine, my headquarters said, speaking of the wastewater standard . . . that they were going to think about moving somewhere else. . . . No, man, just imagine I'm going to be out of a job." This was not the main concern of the interviewee, who responded, "My friend, I'd prefer that they actually regulate and to be left without a job. Don't be offended, but you are not an environmentalist as you say, you aren't. You're just another worker."[34] What surfaces here is the role of standards either in attracting companies seeking more "flexible" regulatory systems or in scaring away industries if overly rigorous. In this sense, several of the interviewees spoke about the ideal and real role played by environmental norms.

Repeatedly, the interviewees—accurately—linked Mexican environmental regulations with the country's signing of the North American Free Trade Agreement (NAFTA). Many said that the standards are "copy-pasted" from US environmental standards, which, as we have seen, is not true, at least in the case of effluent discharge. The origin of standards in regulatory systems

Corporate Sustainability

from other latitudes has its problems, but also its usefulness, according to some. The head of EHS at an American food company with a factory in El Salto, who asserted that "the Mexican regulations were a copy of European and American regulations," said that when they were modified for the Mexican context, "things didn't fit together well in the changes made and . . . there are some that are very lax, there are others that don't fit, they are not appropriate for the national context, but at the end of the day we now have regulations, which before we did not have."[35]

Mexichem's corporate EHS manager explained the importance of having these environmental standards. "The fact that Mexico has regulations that are equivalent to another country, for the products we produce in Mexico, allows us to compete in those countries. In other words, I have regulations and we avoid accusations of unfair trade or dumping," he said. From his point of view, regulations play a balancing role, in the style of ideas of sustainable development: "There must be a balance. The standard must protect the public good, but it is also the function of the government to promote the development of industry, so that citizens have income and we have a better economy." In this sense, he believed that companies should keep track and "participate or find out how the legislation is moving to indicate when a public policy is generating more harm than the benefit it can provide."[36] That is accomplished, he said, through industry associations and chambers.

In the case of ANIQ, for example, the head of the association's EHS committee explained how this committee was established between 1995 and 1996, in response to the development of many new environmental laws and regulations after the signing of NAFTA. In his words, this led this industrial sector to seek to

> build a common front against all the legislation that was being generated. Honestly, we just wanted to defend ourselves and say what we wanted and what we didn't. Anyhow, it was a lot of that, *the defense of our interests at all costs* . . . not to have such broad and specific legislation. At that time, it was so vast that we found our interests jeopardized. Our productivity and our competitiveness looked like they were very threatened.[37]

The relationship with authorities has evolved since then, and he is now pleased with the participation of industrialists in the generation of new environmental regulations. "The channels are open," said the ANIQ representative, even if the desired results are not always achieved: "Maybe at the end of the day the laws or regulations approved aren't exactly as ANIQ would have liked or wished. But I think that in the end we do have the possibility to speak."[38] That opportunity to speak, negotiate, and reach consensus is what I discussed in chapter 4.

On the topic of developing and modifying environmental standards, the environmental manager at Infineum perceived that the industrial sector is more informed of the regulatory processes than even many government officials. Evidence of this was her experience as a member of an advisory council at the SEMARNAT delegation in Jalisco, where she found that "we were the ones who knew about the regulations because the information had not reached their delegation; communication is lacking within the government."[39] Despite the channels of participation enjoyed by the industrial sector, there are also those who express concern that the positions of the private sector are not taken into account. Thus, according to the manager of the Cytec plant in Atequiza, for whom current standards are "at a competitive level," although "they are less stringent than in other latitudes," the concern was the lack of certainty for industries as regards regulatory issues. "We cannot live," he declared, "thinking that new laws will appear overnight; laws that we have not seen, that we have not commented on and that have no applicability." He maintained that "we need to have a government that has its feet on the ground," lamenting the existence of a "very important disconnection" between government and industry, where in the government "they feel that they possess the absolute truth."[40] This is striking, particularly given the influence exerted by industry in regulatory processes.

From a more international perspective, Huntsman's coordinator of environmental sustainability for global operations shared his vision on the approval of new environmental regulations by national governments. He gave the example of the greenhouse gas emission rights trading scheme in the European Union and stated:

> That's something countries have to take into account, . . . if you're going to force that kind of . . . further and further tightening, further and further scrutiny, and if you cannot justify it very efficiently in saying this is the added value it brings by having this take place, added value to community, added value to the region, to the abilities of that region to support itself sustainably, etc., then it's going to be really hard for companies to continue to justify the fact that they have a presence there.[41]

In this sense, he explained that, while there has been "displacement of locations because of labor costs, there certainly has also been displacement of things because of regulatory burden." Here we return to the power of companies to exercise "locational blackmail" (Acselrad 2014, 379).

If many interviewees acknowledge that regulations are weak but believe modifying them could put "competitiveness" at risk, what is the option to guarantee environmental protection? According to some company representatives, the alternative is to rely on the ethics and responsibility of the companies themselves. Rather than complain about the authorities or focus on the laxity of regulations, said an engineer from an American food factory, attention should be centered on the actions of the individual company. This is directly linked to the "myth of the multinational." At his company, he stated, "we always go by the highest standard," whether it be the US or the local one, and maintained that, rather than questioning the norms, "the truth is that it depends a lot on the responsibility of each company." Where there are gaps in the legislation, he affirmed, "if there is no law, well there is no law, but then I am going to act such that I do not pollute." This is the option in the face of the trend that "as Mexicans we always tend to complain about the government."[42] The constructive can-do attitude sounds commendable, but can a system be based on the presumption of such goodwill? It would no doubt be naïve to think that the motivation of each company is sufficient to guarantee environmental protection.

The last two topics that I will deal with are the dwindling underground water sources in the corridor—the main source supplying industry and communities—and the perspectives from industry on the conflict surrounding the Santiago River. The territory covered by the El Ahogado Subbasin corresponds approximately to the territory of the Toluquilla aquifer, according to the characterization of CONAGUA. This aquifer is overexploited, with extraction reported to exceed recharge at a rate of 73.1 million cubic meters per year (*Official Gazette of the Federation* [*Diario Oficial de la Federación*], January 4, 2018). The manager at AISAC described as "worrying" the situation in this area, where "industries with high water consumption can no longer be authorized."[43] The scarcity of water for industrial expansion is inextricably linked to the rapid urban expansion in this area. This urban expansion, in addition, has brought other problems for some factories, particularly high-risk ones.

In the case of the Mexichem plant, where they produce chlorine gas, in addition to caustic soda and hydrogen gas, the EHS manager explained that, together with AISAC and its neighbors at Quimikao, they have worked to establish an "intermediate buffer zone . . . to avoid putting in housing units that we could affect."[44] Vega claimed that real estate developers are "very voracious," which is why the association has opposed projects such as the Tierra Mojada, which sought to build twenty thousand homes on land of the El Ahogado Dam. On that occasion, AISAC opposed the municipalities of El Salto and Tlajomulco, asking, according to Vega, "How is it possible that on these contaminated lands they intend to install housing . . . ? It's not fair, it's not fair to deceive the people."[45] At the Cytec chemical plant in Atequiza, they reported a similar issue of housing developments creeping closer to their installations. The plant manager indicated that the authorities "do not quite understand what we are talking about." In his view, "they are protecting other interests, not the interests of the industrialists."[46] City councils have tended to give preference to permits requested by real estate developers, instead of protecting the population and establishing the necessary safeguard zones around high-risk industries.

On the conflict around the Santiago River, at several of the companies where I raised the question of whether the river pollution problem affected them, representatives' responses coincided in that they claimed there was no direct impact for them as long as they complied with regulations. In the case of Cytec, they were called to appear as part of a criminal investigation involving several companies after the death of Miguel Ángel López. Given this, the manager stated, "I can proudly mention that we did not contribute in any way to what happened, nor did any of the companies in El Salto." At Quimikao, the EHS engineer interviewed maintained that, "based on the results, we know that we are not, well one can't say exactly nonpolluting, [but] we are within parameters, we are complying with parameters and what we do know, for example, is that there are some heavy metals but they already come from upstream, there are some small companies, they are the ones that pollute much more." He lamented that the large companies are under the greatest scrutiny, noting that the interest has been from the media, not the authorities, and the media can contribute to people thinking, "It's that company, it's the big ones. So yes, it does affect you a little."[47]

This sense of the injustice of blaming large companies for the situation of the river was a recurring theme. It was expressed, for example, by the environmental manager at Corporación de Occidente, an association between the local cooperative Tradoc (Trabajadores Democráticos de Occidente) and American tire company Cooper Tires (42 percent Tradoc and 58 percent

Cooper Tires, at the time of the interview). Tradoc is known for its strike of more than three years against the German corporation Continental Tire. The strike started in early 2002 and did not end until the factory was recovered by workers in 2005. The interviewee, Federico Martínez Barba, was a member of the union leadership during the strike and recounted how, with the support of European organizations, the union's general secretary, Jesús Torres, was able to speak at a Continental shareholders' meeting in Hanover, Germany. In a case study of the solidarity economy in Latin America, José Guillermo Díaz Muñoz highlights the experience of these workers at the former Euzkadi factory, established in 1971 and purchased by Continental in 1998. The factory is now run by members of the Tradoc cooperative and is emblematic in Mexico and internationally, both for "their triumph over a large transnational like Continental" and for the "reopening and reinstallation and its subsequent appropriation to become co-owners" (2011, 72).

As part of the administration of Corporación de Occidente, Martínez stated that the cooperative has been sensitive to the problems of the Santiago River, treating its effluent and also providing some support to local activist Raúl Muñoz, of the Citizen Committee for Environmental Defense. For Martínez, however, it is an error to single out industries as the source of the problem: "What I believe now that I am on this side and I tell you with all honesty, I believe that the majority of companies, in my opinion, they do comply.... At least the companies that are in AISAC, I believe that they do comply." The problem lies, in his opinion, in another area: "I believe that a factor that affects the contamination of the Santiago River is the lack of control of municipal sewage." On the other hand, Martínez pointed to a phenomenon that has also been denounced by local activists, affirming that "there are many companies [that] irresponsibly are delegating part of their polluting activities to family workshops."[48] Documenting the outsourcing of polluting activities remains for other studies in this area. In general terms, however, we can see that the cooperative is aligned with the position of AISAC on this issue: industry is not to blame.

The sense of injustice in singling out industry was expressed even more clearly by the Cytec manager: "We have problems that do not necessarily have to do with the industry, but with the municipalities themselves, and one wishes they were treated the same way they treat transnational industries." Evidence of discrepancies in the treatment of companies and municipalities is found in the river itself, he said:

> We have, for example, particular discharge conditions that the government authorizes us for our wastewater discharge and, sadly, these are much stricter than quality of the water in the river into which we discharge. . . . So, the river is much more polluted—much, much more polluted than what they are demanding of us.[49]

In the same vein, Silvia Vega of AISAC reported hearing the complaint from companies, "Hey, I'm discharging, . . . but I look beside me, and I have no idea what's in this other discharge, right? And why are [the regulations] applied to me, when the municipality does not even treat its waters?" This is part of a more generalized feeling of inconsistency or lack of parity in the application of the standards; Vega stated in this regard that "the rules must be the same for everyone, because otherwise it discourages those who are doing things well."[50]

At this point I would note, first, that the "demanding" particular discharge conditions to which the Cytec manager alludes are, in fact, the laxest category in the NOM-001 for type A rivers. Second, I would pose a question, especially in the case of transnational corporations: In what sense is it unfair if they are not treated the same as the municipalities? On the one hand, their effluents come from a diversity of sectors and processes and, for simple technical reasons, require control through differentiated parameters. On the other hand, if a transnational company decides to establish itself in a country where, in addition to cheap labor, there are deficiencies in public infrastructure, including municipal wastewater treatment plants, how do these deficiencies become an argument to excuse them from even minimal environmental compliance? If they wanted to be located where local governments meet all their obligations, presumably they could have maintained operations in developed countries with adequate infrastructure and strong environmental controls. Finally, it is clear how the pollution of the river itself becomes a pretext for not requiring that companies adequately treat effluent. Here we see, then, how a *sewer of progress* is perpetuated.

* * *

In this chapter, I have examined the practices and discourses of companies in the Ocotlán–El Salto Industrial Corridor. For a series of companies, I questioned the information they publish in reports and online platforms, in terms of both the data on their use and discharge of water and their commitments in this regard. I analyzed their corporate reports from the

Corporate Sustainability

lens of critiques of greenwashing and eco-efficiency, or the TBL, to tease out the rationale behind these corporate promotional materials. Here, the picture that emerged is of partial or nonexistent information about local facilities and industrial effluent, together with (at best) ambiguous commitments. Although the reputation enjoyed by large companies—particularly transnational corporations—is that of adherence to "the highest international standards," in the reports reviewed, in most cases there are no real commitments to go beyond legal compliance in the different countries where they operate. Where a broader commitment is expressed—as in the case of Nestlé—the environmental standards to which the company is committed are never specified.

From there, I questioned this myth of the multinational from a different angle, to contrast the idea of the compliance of transnationals with exacting international standards with evidence for four companies with factories in the corridor, where studies found repeated noncompliance with the discharge standard. Documents I received through information requests as appendixes to inspection reports also illustrated how several companies either asked for concessions to have the consent of the authority to comply with more "flexible" parameters, as in the case of Celanese, or made changes to their treatment system in response to the reclassification of the Santiago River, as in the case of Huntsman. We are a long way, therefore, from businesses complying of their own volition with the environmental standards of Switzerland, Japan, or the United States.

Finally, I explored the perceptions of EHS managers in the corridor regarding environmental regulations and local water problems. Here, even these regulated parties stressed the laxity of the regulatory system. These testimonies also present a vision of regulations as a requirement for international trade—to avoid accusations of dumping—regardless of their stringency or level of enforcement. One of the underlying logics from these actors in industry is that tightening regulations could motivate the flight of companies. At the same time, in their view, the blame for the deteriorated state of the Santiago River lies elsewhere—with municipalities and small or clandestine companies—while the largest factories are unfairly accused. It is unfair, they maintain, that they are monitored or required to comply with stricter parameters than the municipalities, or to meet quality requirements exceeding the current state of water in the river itself. In short, they sketch the image of a sector under the weight of rigorous oversight and plagued by unfounded accusations. The answer to current environmental woes, some propose, would be for the conscientious companies to voluntarily self-regulate based on their own environmental ethics. This is contrasted with the evidence of both scarce inspections and permissive standards.

A critical and objective analysis of the situation should also draw attention to the lack of transparency regarding the environmental performance of companies. Indeed, communities do not have the "right to know" about the types of risks to which they are exposed by industrial activities. The possible implications of this situation are described in detail by Lilia Albert and Marisa Jacott (2015) in their book on chemical emergencies in Mexico. Therein, they narrate five cases of industrial accidents, from the fire at the Anaversa agrochemical factory in Córdoba, Veracruz, in 1991 to the 2014 spill of forty thousand cubic meters of copper sulfate from a tailings pond into the Sonora River at Grupo México's Buenavista del Cobre mine. When analyzing the common causes of these accidents, Albert and Jacott underscore that, despite registering complaints before the accidents, in the vast majority of cases the nearby communities "had not been informed of the processes that were carried out at the nearby factories, nor did they know the type or level of toxicity of the substances that were used or generated in those processes" (2015, 239). Even the emergency response and fire authorities lacked the necessary information—in addition to the resources—to deal with these industrial accidents. The exposure to toxic substances in the El Salto area has been chronic, and not due to major accidents or spills, but the lack of access to basic information is equally worrisome. The local population must have information on the types of risks to which inhabitants are exposed.

6 Conclusions: The Road Ahead

"We all approve of development," Graciela González of Leap of Life (Un Salto de Vida) told a group of university students in May 2022, "because that's what we've been taught, that we have to develop, be productive, be competitive. It's the theme that permeates all knowledge currently." This was her introduction to a presentation titled "Industrial Paradises = Environmental Hells," a formula, she stated, "that has converted us into sacrifice zones."[1] In summing up this story of the Santiago River, the notion of development and its link to industrialization is a fitting starting point. Ideas of development, progress, and modernization permeate many conventional worldviews and serve as a logic that rationalizes pollution. In this discursive game, I argue that there exists a double standard of modernization, whereby the state assumes both the responsibility of being the bearer of environmental modernization—whether garbed in the vocabulary of sustainable development, integrated water resource management, or inclusive green growth—and the blame for not achieving the desired "balance," with the (often tacit) explanation that at its current stage of development, the country needs to prioritize development or progress.

At the same time, private actors are not silent in these debates, particularly when, as in the case of the Santiago River, they are called to account for what local actors call "environmental devastation." Generally, these companies, particularly large transnationals, present themselves as exemplars of efficiency and environmental awareness and, in the event of failures attributed to the private sector, often turn the finger of blame on the state. If they have done wrong, it is the Mexican state that should punish and control the companies. When the state does not fulfill this function, nobody is surprised.

"Terribly predictable" was the epithet I heard from a European water researcher after listening to a description of the situation of the Santiago River. Certainly, the story of a river polluted by industry in a country in the South and of a government unable or unwilling to act to protect it is far from unique or—from a certain hegemonic logic—surprising. The teleological idea prevails, in practice if not in public statements, that Mexico cannot afford a more restrictive level of regulation on environmental issues due to its level of development. This idea is crystallized in the so-called environmental Kuznets curve, a model that postulates an inverted-U relationship between development and environmental pollution, which first increases until a certain level of development or per capita income is reached, after which it decreases. The model takes its name from the economist Simon Kuznets, who hypothesized that as countries grew economically, income inequality first increased and then decreased (Kuznets 1955). Translated to the arena of pollution, it can be interpreted at the policy level in so-called developing countries in the imperative: "Grow first, then clean up" (Dasgupta et al. 2002, 147).

This modernizing and optimistic outlook is confronted, in practice, with the challenge that one "often cannot (as yet) detect pollution leveling or declines in developing countries" (Perz 2007, 419, 422). In fact, the hypothesis has already been questioned by one of the principal promoters of this concept: the World Bank (see IBRD 1992; Hettige et al. 1997). After affirming that there is no evidence to support Kuznets's hypothesis regarding income inequality, the World Bank report on "inclusive green growth" acknowledges that "overall environmental performance does not first get worse and then improve with income—no Kuznets curve here either" (2012, 5; see also Damania et al. 2019). Although there may be improvements in certain areas, such as local air quality, the World Bank asserts, this is not the case when it comes to the accumulation of toxic chemicals and pesticides in water and soil, nor for global pollutants such as greenhouse gases.

This recognition also comes from the authors of the *Global Competitiveness Report 2014–2015*, a publication of the World Economic Forum. In this ranking of 144 countries around twelve "pillars of competitiveness," the authors present an analysis of what they term "sustainable competitiveness" (Schwab 2014, xiii). Here, progress is slow, with growing concerns regarding pollution and biodiversity loss, and they conclude that "the world is not moving toward a more sustainable path and concrete results

Conclusions

are yet to be achieved" (54). To carry out the ranking, the authors classify countries according to their "stage of development," divided between the countries dependent on natural resources and unskilled labor (factor driven), those that have advanced in their productivity (efficiency driven), and those in the target stage, when the economy is innovation driven. Mexico, in this modern hierarchy, seems to be on the threshold of optimal "competitiveness" (modernity, civilization), placed in the transition stage between efficiency and innovation.

In evolutionary narratives and competitiveness rankings, nations are represented as coherent and relatively autonomous units that only have to follow certain political and regulatory prescriptions to advance on the path of efficiency and toward innovation. What is conspicuous by its absence in this representation of the world is any analysis of historical or global power relations. Highlighting the weight of history in shaping these relationships, Héctor Alimonda maintains that "the catastrophic trauma of conquest and integration in a subordinate, colonial position in the international system . . . is the origin marking of Latin America" (2011, 21). Despite the mirage of a "global-centric" world, Alimonda points to this "hidden underside of modernity," describing an enduring coloniality that maintains inequalities and turns Latin American nature into "a subordinate space, which can be exploited, razed, [and] reconfigured, according to the needs of the current accumulation regimes" (25, 23). This reflects the criticisms of the narratives of progressive development based on dependency theory, which affirm that "one part of the world is poor *because* the other is rich" (Biel 2007, 116; emphasis in original). In this sense, it resonates with Alf Hornborg's critique of the "zero-sum" model of development, which acknowledges that the "economic and technological expansion" of core capitalist nations occurs at the expense of peripheral areas (2009, 245). If there were no economies to provide raw materials, cheap labor, and spaces for toxic waste, could the *innovative* economies be sustained?

Eric Wolf points out that there is a tendency among social scientists to conceive of nations or societies or cultures as "internally homogeneous and externally distinctive and bounded objects," and from there to represent the world as a "global pool hall in which the entities spin off each other like so many hard and round billiard balls" (2010, 6). In this vision, social relations are usually understood as between individuals and removed from their political, economic, and ideological context, which facilitates a conception "of the nation-state as a structure of social ties informed by moral consensus rather than as a nexus of economic, political, and ideological relationships connected to other nexuses" (9). Such an understanding of the state facilitates, for example, the conception of environmental problems as derived from a supposed Mexican "culture" or Mexican "values" that undervalue the environment or promote corruption, instead of encouraging an analysis of power relations in and around the Mexican state and between this state and other "nexuses" in the global economy.

Without addressing the environment, Michael Porter presents a clear vision of the link between a certain idea of national cultures and economic performance: "Differences in national values, culture, economic structures, institutions, and histories all contribute to competitive success" (1990, 73). Porter presumes that nations will host competitive industries if their "home-environment is the most forward-looking, dynamic, and challenging" (73). This is part of the ideology of capitalism, also expressed in the idea of the "American dream," with the notion that there exists a meritocracy where hard work and its corollaries—talent, efficiency, and so on—may lead individuals or nations to higher levels of wealth and well-being. Immanuel Wallerstein criticizes the notion of nations as coincident with "societies"— problematizing the concept of society as "one half of an antithetic tandem in which the other is the state" (2000, 137). Perceiving the world through the lens of the nation-state facilitates a belief that certain countries have overcome this or that environmental problem, in this case industrial water pollution. But if we consider the world-system, then capitalist production has not overcome the problem; the critical sites of its manifestation have simply changed. The country-by-country approach does not allow this to be seen as a phenomenon of production for the global market, while allowing global corporations to take advantage of existing double standards so as to continue on with low-cost polluting production practices.

The environmental impacts of industry in the Global South are increasingly important given the shifting geographies of capitalism and the global division of labor. "The financial command and control functions of the global economy may still be concentrated in New York, Tokyo, and London," observes Neil Smith, but "the new global cities of Asia and Latin America and now increasingly Africa are very much the workshops of global capital" (2008, 263). Since 2010, China has been the top global manufacturer in terms of manufacturing value added (MVA), and in 2019, it accounted

Conclusions

for 27.4 percent of global MVA, more than the United States (16.8 percent) and Japan (7.5 percent) combined (World Bank, 2022). Overall, the share of MVA of "industrialized economies" in Europe, North America, and Asia has dropped from 60.3 percent in 2010 to 50.5 percent in 2020 as part of a "gradual shift of manufacturing production, in relative terms, away from industrialized countries to developing economies" (UNIDO 2021, 16). Mexico was the eleventh global producer in 2019, generating 1.6 percent of global MVA. That year, manufacturing accounted for 17.3 percent of GDP and employed 6.5 million people (INEGI 2019, 2021b).

In this sense, the "predictable" case of the Santiago River is a conflict that makes clear some of the most elemental contradictions of our time and to which conventional approaches are not responding: the tension between the degradation of our environment and continued economic growth. What we find, therefore, although not surprising, is important, since these are the mechanisms that sustain appropriation.

6.1 The Contradictions in "Reviving" the Santiago River

In August 2019, as part of the Revive the Santiago River strategy, the Jalisco Ministry of Economic Development (Secretaría de Desarrollo Económico) signed an agreement with the main industry associations in the state. The voluntary pact "committed" the chambers and associations to "guarantee the compliance of their members with municipal, state and federal environmental regulations, related to the generation of emissions into the atmosphere, waste, use of water resources, and wastewater discharge."[2] Why was it deemed necessary to *voluntarily* express the intention of complying with the law? The representative of the Council of Industrial Chambers of Jalisco (Consejo de Cámaras Industriales de Jalisco) explained that "complying with the standards is a matter of willingness [because] our system of government does not have the capacity to ensure that we all comply. It is a conviction that we must have" (Mora 2019). Faced with official incapacity, should we celebrate their amenability to complying with the country's lax regulations?

Lamentably, there is not much more to report on the Jalisco government's actions vis-à-vis industry even within the framework of its grand "strategy." At the beginning of 2020, the media reverberated for several weeks with news of the health impact study that the authorities of the State

Water Commission (CEA, Comisión Estatal del Agua) Jalisco had kept under wraps. The study, completed in 2011 by researchers from the Autonomous University of San Luis Potosí, revealed serious damage to the cognitive abilities of boys and girls in El Salto, Juanacatlán, and two other riverside communities, where the children also "presented high levels of exposure to lead, arsenic, cadmium, mercury, benzene and [persistent organic pollutants]" (UASLP and CEA 2011, 268). The lead researcher, Gabriela Domínguez, told the media, "Finding so many metals in such a percentage of children is very worrying, because we do not see the effect of each of them in isolation, but rather a combined effect where synergies occur, and damage is aggravated" (Olvera 2020). Domínguez was prevented from sharing the study before 2020, due to the confidentiality clause signed with the CEA.

As part of an effort by the Alfaro government to demonstrate that it was taking action, on February 5, 2020, the governor made an open invitation to what he called a "macro-excursion" to visit municipal wastewater treatment plants that were being constructed or rehabilitated as part of the Santiago River strategy. During this excursion, Alfaro released a list of twenty-nine companies where effluent samples had exceeded the limits of the NOM-001-SEMARNAT-1996 standard (NOM-001). The list included large transnationals, several of which I analyzed in greater detail in chapter 5: Nestlé, Honda, Hershey's, Mexichem, Cytec, Quimikao, Zoltek, José Cuervo, and Tequila Patrón (de la Peña 2020). The noncompliance is ongoing.

In many ways, the tale told in this book has not been a hopeful one. It has not been encouraging in terms of what has been achieved thus far in efforts to clean up the Upper Santiago River, from its source in Ocotlán and up to the El Ahogado Subbasin. Neither have the failings of the environmental regulatory system provided for an encouraging narrative. Looking at the companies, likewise, there is little to spur hopes of imminent improvements in treatment levels or of a willingness to assume responsibility as a sector for the future restoration of the river.

"The devastation," says Graciela González, "is more and more profound." In April 2021, the vehicle of two Leap of Life activists was set on fire outside their home, leading them to seek safety out of the country for several months. Living in a violent and polluted environment in El Salto, Graciela states, "we are shot at, imprisoned, malnourished, contaminated, and besides that with the threat of things getting worse." So, when asked about the alternatives and the struggle of Leap of Life, she alludes to the diversity

Conclusions

of creative actions they have taken, from their tree nursery to workshops in schools to collective art projects: "We embroider, we tackle the issue, and we fight, we scratch, we bite, we denounce in the media, file complaints, lawsuits, direct fights with those in front of us . . . hugs and kisses for the families of those who have left us."[3]

Despite the fact that this is not a story with a happy ending, then, community actors continue to seek allies and take an array of actions seeking to shift the balance of power toward river restoration. At the same time, I believe that clarifying aspects of the current panorama can contribute to understanding the real challenges involved in the cleanup of this river, and environmental protection in a globalized world more broadly. The intention of this work and, I dare say, that of the organizations that struggle to protect the health of riverside communities, is to challenge the status quo whereby the river functions as a sewer, and to reimagine it as a space for life, recreation, and sustenance.

Restoration of a healthy river is an impossibility from the perspective of the bureaucratic pragmatism that has prevailed to date; neither is it accordant with the double standards applied by transnational corporations or with the plans for continuing industrial development in this region. In short, the defense of this river directly challenges the prevailing logic of industrialization and economic growth and, as such, cannot be assimilated within the current strategies for inserting this region into the national and global economy. This is not a result of a lack of adequate technologies to treat wastewater or a lack of funds to invest in the necessary works; that is, it is not principally a problem of a technological or financial nature. The problem derives from economic and political decisions that devalue both the environment, in this case the life of the river, and the lives of the workers and poor or relatively poor people who live in the periurban and rural communities bordering the river. The persistence of this problem cannot be understood without acknowledging this devaluation of certain human lives.

This book has focused on how human lives are devalued in everyday practices involving permits, classifications, duties, inspections, certifications, and the various ways in which industrial effluents are (not) regulated and monitored in a system that masks polluting activities. To the extent possible, I have also touched on the role of the private sector in keeping Mexican environmental regulations as lenient as possible. Lax regulations allow for transnationals to maintain affirmations of environmental compliance at

254   Chapter 6

a global level while enjoying the flexibility of multiple regulatory regimes: they can advocate not to tighten regulations in Mexico, while complying with the most demanding limits in Germany, the United States, or any other country in the North. The two main concepts that I have used to understand the persistence of industrial pollution in the Santiago River are institutionalized corruption and the myth of the multinational. Next, I highlight what I have sought to argue and demonstrate with these notions.

6.2 Institutionalized Corruption

Before recapitulating what I define as institutionalized corruption, I would reiterate what it is not. In addition to trying to achieve conceptual clarity, I emphasize this because I do not wish to label the wide range of government officials in the water and environment sectors, many of whom carry out their work with intelligence, honesty, and commitment, as corrupt. Nor do I wish to apply this general qualifier to those working at factories in the industrial corridor. If not for numerous critical government employees concerned about the degradation of water bodies in the country, I would not have understood many of the weaknesses of the current regulatory system: through their incisive observations, I began to understand how regulation is applied and how environmental standards are generated and modified.

As I specified in the introduction, the term "institutionalized corruption" does not refer to illicit acts that generate undue enrichment for individual public officials. Rather, the concept seeks to highlight the logic that underlies the configuration of the system of environmental regulation in Mexico characterized by lax and poorly enforced standards, dependent on self-monitoring and self-regulation, and wherein the private sector has been empowered in the formulation and modification of environmental regulations such that there exists a form of regulatory capture. It designates a system that normalizes and obscures polluting activities, and environmental degradation in general, and is a fundamental part of what has unfortunately granted *resilience* to the phenomenon of industrial pollution of the Santiago River. Throughout this book, I have sought to present evidence of, as well as to explain theoretically, the existence of this institutionalized corruption.

The weakness of the inspection regime is evident. If at the national level the National Water Commission (CONAGUA, Comisión Nacional del Agua) is capable of inspecting all users holding a concession title or permit *once*

Conclusions

every sixty-eight years, then it is clear that the level of inspection is derisory. Moreover, although CONAGUA is not obliged to notify those inspected in advance, discharge inspections are carried out on consecutive dates and this translates into de facto notification, allowing users to quickly identify when an inspection might occur. In addition, there are testimonies that illegal notifications of users continue. This is linked to the low levels of penalties derived from the inspections carried out.

Self-monitoring is another key point for discharge regulations, since the main source of information on effluent quality is the users themselves, who are obliged to report the results of wastewater sampling to CONAGUA on a quarterly, bimonthly, or annual basis. Various officials from CONAGUA and the Mexican Institute of Water Technology (Instituto Mexicano de Tecnología del Agua) stated that they do not consider this self-reported information to be reliable, also affirming that it is not systematically reviewed within CONAGUA. The pattern, unsurprisingly, is to always report within the legal parameters, and here the role of the laboratories was also highlighted in perhaps masking the polluting activity of private parties. For around thirty companies in the industrial corridor, in response to a request for information, CONAGUA denied having this self-reported information for the period from 2000 to 2013. This implies a generalized noncompliance by the companies or, more likely, the reluctance of the commission to make this information public.[4]

In another case of self-reported information, the Pollutant Emissions and Transfers Registry (RETC, Registro de Emisiones y Transferencia de Contaminantes) should in theory provide information on toxic substances released by industry into Mexican waters. However, the panorama is of a low level of reporting and of approximate information that is not subject to sufficient governmental scrutiny. In addition, for discharges to water, companies in the country almost exclusively report amounts of heavy metals and cyanide—parameters contemplated in the NOM-001—while an extremely low number of establishments report the discharge of other RETC substances, even following the expansion of mandatory reportable substances to two hundred (NOM-165-SEMARNAT-2013). The comparison of the amount of pollutants reported as discharged into the waters of the three North American Free Trade Agreement (now the United States–Mexico–Canada Agreement) countries, even taking into account the differences between the Mexican RETC, the National Pollutant Release Inventory in Canada, and the US Toxic Release Inventory, makes clear that the system in Mexico is not working. I would recall here that establishments in Mexico reported only 0.4 percent of total emissions to water in the three countries in 2015 and 1.6 percent in 2016.[5]

Grasping how the industrial sector has been empowered in the system of environmental regulation in Mexico becomes clearer when we look at how technical standards are formulated and modified within the National Environment and Natural Resources Standards Advisory Committee (Comité Consultivo Nacional de Normalización de Medio Ambiente y Recursos Naturales). With a culture of consensus and often the de facto veto power of industry, the situation can be aptly described as regulatory capture or "colonization of the state" (Tirado 2012; Carpenter and Moss 2014). On examining the protracted process of achieving a modification to the Mexican effluent discharge standard, the NOM-001, I related how the process stagnated from 2007 to the end of 2017. Even when a proposal to modify this obsolete standard was finally published in the *Official Gazette of the Federation* (*Diario Oficial de la Federación*) at the beginning of 2018, it was not until March 2022 that it was finally issued, amid a flurry of statements from industry rejecting the addition of new parameters to better control the release of toxic pollutants to Mexican waters.

The importance of the regulatory capture argument also has to do with how power is distributed in society and where the analytical emphasis is placed. From studies of movements for environmental justice, David Pellow critiques the "state-centric" approach of many social movements and theoretical analyses, arguing that given the growing power of corporations, including in policy-making, a focus on the political-economic process is required that "decenters" the state. This is in recognition of the fact that the private sector is often "the most powerful player in these [social] conflicts, frequently usurping state policy-making authority and sovereignty" (2001, 52; see also Pellow 2006). With the expansion of neoliberal policies and the implementation of free trade agreements, the power of corporations over national governments has increased.

To understand institutionalized corruption in more theoretical terms, I turned to discussions of the neoliberalization of nature and the critique of market environmentalism as an "environmental fix," which empowers the private sector in environmental regulation, and which is part of a response to the "endemic problem of sustained economic growth" (Castree 2008, 146).

Conclusions

The assumptions of free-market environmentalism bolster arguments in favor of reducing the regulatory capacity of the state, particularly traditional command-and-control regulations, while expanding initiatives centered on taxes, self-regulation, and self-monitoring. Even these schemes, however, are implemented in Mexico with low payment levels—in the case of duties for wastewater discharge—and without the oversight required to be functional. Taken to the context of developing countries, moreover, arguments of the lack of political will and scarce government resources are employed to justify a reliance on business self-monitoring and the generation of standards through dialogue, negotiation, and consensus with regulated sectors. In affirming the necessity and validity of this type of arrangement, there is an essential foundation: the myth of the multinational.

The logic that I call institutionalized corruption plays important roles, since it supports a regulatory structure that formally meets the needs of the state and of the corporations operating in Mexico, in order to deflect accusations of environmental dumping and maintain a facade of global parity in the levels of environmental regulation. In the case of effluent discharge, even without taking into account the paucity of inspections, and the lack of personnel for both inspection and review of self-reported emissions data, current regulations clearly demonstrate the unwillingness to protect bodies of water and human health. Taking into account the other elements that hinder enforcement, it is clear that environmental regulations are not designed for those purposes.

The concept of institutionalized corruption attempts to explain why, in the words of the head of the legal department in Jalisco at the Federal Bureau of Environmental Protection (Procuraduría Federal de Protección al Ambiente) that I cited in the introduction, there is no damage to the aquatic ecosystem of the Santiago River since the pollution that exists occurs within the system of permits and classifications overseen by CONAGUA.[6] That is a purpose fulfilled by the regulatory system. In this sense, institutionalized corruption works by shielding polluting activities with the automatic response that there exists "compliance" or, at least, there is no evidence to the contrary. Conflicts such as that of the Santiago River expose the logic of institutionalized corruption because they assert that ecosystems and human lives are worth protecting: they exist, they have value, they are not cannon fodder to support an industrial development strategy that offers up not only cheap labor but the rivers and the health of populations in the Global South.

6.3 The Myth of the Multinational

The figure of the large corporation, particularly the transnational, bringing to the South its environmentally innocuous technology and environmental management and control systems devised in countries of the North with the strictest regulations—friend of the government and international ideal—is the justification of a system based on self-monitoring, self-regulation, and standard setting by consensus. Thus, it is a system that does not work, in an important part, because it is based on a fallacy.

The myth of the multinational affirms that multi- or transnational corporations comply with international environmental standards, beyond what is required by Mexican legislation, and that they are a minor source of environmental deterioration. In chapter 5, I questioned this myth in light of evidence for some large companies in the Ocotlán–El Salto Industrial Corridor. From an analysis of the sustainability reports of nine companies, I found that they do not make clear commitments to exceed compliance with the environmental legislation of each country—even when there is ambiguous mention of complying with the highest international standards. Where there was sufficient empirical evidence, I also questioned this myth based on data that show the ongoing noncompliance of four transnational companies even with Mexican discharge regulations.

The importance of the myth does not lie, however, in the empirical basis of the good environmental performance of these companies. Rather, it lies in its functionality to justify the empowerment of private actors in the system of environmental regulation. It is useful, furthermore, to divert the attention of both authorities and the general population from large corporations, by assigning the responsibility for polluting activities only to small companies and municipalities. The figure of the conscientious and efficient large corporation is contrasted with the small business incapable of controlling emissions and corrupt or inept municipalities that do not treat their waters. I highlight this not because there is not a grain of truth regarding the practices of many smaller companies or municipalities but because the contrast should be questioned.

We can recall the recommendation of Milton Friedman regarding the social responsibility of business, which consists of using "its resources and engag[ing] in activities designed to increase its profits," with the only limitation of staying within the "rules of the game" (1982, 133). What if

Conclusions

the rules of the game are subject to manipulation by the same businesses? Well, this will simply facilitate fulfilling its main function. A system of environmental regulation cannot, I believe, be based on a naïve reading of corporations—transnational or Mexican—nor on an innocent vision of the state that assigns it a function of balancing interests instead of empirically observing that, in most cases, in socio-environmental conflicts and in the generation and application of environmental regulations, the state defends private interests.

6.4 From Sewer of Progress to River of Life

After this analysis, an obligatory question is, what implications does it have for the struggle to clean up the Santiago River or similar socio-environmental conflicts? What recommendations can I make, either in terms of necessary changes in environmental regulations or for activists in El Salto and Juanacatlán and their allies? Here I see an important dilemma that must be addressed before presenting some ideas. Due to the critical analysis of government practices and the observations on the structural nature of environmental degradation linked to the country's strategy of insertion in the global economy, a blunt response could dismiss any attempt to pressure the state to improve or strengthen regulations as naïve or ineffective, or even as an attempt to patch up the system in such a way as to prolong capitalist devastation. I understand these criticisms, but do not share them in their entirety.

Toxic pollution is daily damaging health and degrading ecosystems. These impacts must be controlled or eliminated, and damages must be compensated. A more radical approach that would focus solely on the autonomous actions that emanate from local communities and without engaging with state actors, in my opinion, fails to grant serious consideration to the context of a severely degraded environment in this area, where many people live in conditions of extreme economic and social marginalization while also suffering physically due to environmental pollution. This limits people's ability to sustain themselves autonomously, because certain lands and waters are not suitable to provide sustenance; hence emphasizing only local initiatives implies ignoring the real material conditions in which several hundred thousand people live.

In his intriguing book, Joel Bakan argues that the corporation is a "pathological institution" and even "psychopathic," given the legal mandate that forces corporations to pursue their own interests "relentlessly and without exception . . . regardless of the often harmful consequences it might cause to others" (2005, intro.). Based on this vision, which is supported by evidence and analysis, Bakan is critical of the strategies of activists who propose to refrain from any interaction with the state, due to its inability to control corporate power. Without discounting the existence of regulatory capture, he advocates strong regulatory controls and surveillance systems that oblige corporations by legal means, maintaining that "there is little democracy in a system that relies on market forces and nongovernmental organizations to promote socially responsible behavior from corporations" (chap. 6). He shares the observation of many, which is confirmed here, that state power has been deployed in favor of private interests, with the ideological justifications of neoliberalism.

In the case of the Santiago River, I believe that the strategies that directly target both the industrial sector and, if possible with the evidence gathered, specific companies contributing to environmental deterioration and quality of life are important. Demonstrating the responsibility of specific companies entails its own challenges, but there is a history with the work of Greenpeace Mexico, and intelligent strategies will surely come from the creativity and concern of those affected and their allies. At the same time, I consider it essential to put pressure on the government sector in various ways.

With the modified version of the NOM-001 approved and set to come into effect in 2023, this represents a step forward in protecting Mexican waters. In the future, further progress will still be needed to shift toward technical standards that take into account the origin of the discharge and that differentiate between industrial sectors. All this will be in vain, however, if there are no real changes in enforcement and in the regulatory framework more broadly to decrease reliance on self-monitoring and change the practices surrounding standard setting to shift the balance of powers and alter the mentality that standards should be devised via consensus with the regulated sectors. Strengthening the water quality monitoring system of surface and groundwater will also be key.

How much of this is actually possible if institutionalized corruption exists? Obviously, the previous recommendations can be characterized as "reformist" and are not suggestions that I make from a naïve reading of the state or the industrial sector. However, I believe they are justified for two

Conclusions

reasons. First, because immediate action is essential to protect the health of people and ecosystems. Second, I believe they are changes that cannot be assimilated within the logic of institutionalized corruption, since their purpose is to protect the commons and, therefore, they have the potential to contribute to more fundamental changes.

For many, the Santiago River as a living river does not exist: not only does it not exist in practice but it also does not exist in the imagination or as a possibility for the future. Various organizations, both local and their national and international allies, contribute to another vision not only of this river but of the value of human lives. They strongly contradict and reject a system where some human lives are worth more than others and where the double standards of the global economy must be naturalized or attributed to a question of "cultural" differences. The road will be long and uncertain, and it will also bring together divergent political positions, but in the end, the road to a living Santiago River is a road of hope.

Appendix: Methodological Strategy

Undertaking this research represented an opportunity to dedicate myself for several years to understanding the problems of the Santiago River and, with a large dose of humility, attempting to provide activists and other interested parties with pertinent analysis and data to strengthen the demands for river cleanup and restoration. What approaches, questions, and research strategy would help me do that? I had previously prepared a report for the Mexican Institute for Community Development (Instituto Mexicano para el Desarrollo Comunitario), a nongovernmental organization (NGO), in an initial attempt to bring together the available information on the industrial corridor and the polluting potential of its discharges. That process reinforced for me both the relevance of the issue and the challenges involved in making industrial pollution the subject of my research. However, my project when I commenced this research as part of my PhD studies had a substantially different approach from the research I eventually undertook. Initially, I proposed to study the socio-environmental conflict that has been unleashed by the contamination of the Santiago River in El Salto and Juanacatlán, Jalisco, by asking how this conflict had developed in its political, economic, technological, and social dimensions. Without underestimating what such a study could yield, this question left me with lingering concerns.

Was I going to analyze the strategies, achievements, and limitations of local activists and grassroots organizations in El Salto and Juanacatlán? Certainly, much valuable research adopts a focus on the actors of socio-environmental conflicts, and I had previously collaborated in a collective piece with this analytical focus (McCulligh et al. 2012). On that occasion, although in the end we decided not to delve into the subject in our text, we faced the challenge of how to address the differences and conflicts between the various grassroots organizations. Beyond that challenge, when thinking about the best way to take advantage of a period of in-depth research, I did not want the final product to be a series of conclusions focused on the work or perceptions of activists or the local population of El Salto and Juanacatlán. If in my work for an NGO I had collaborated with others to demand the cleanup of the river, now, in my academic research, was I going to analyze precisely the type of work that I had done? On several occasions, I also heard members of Leap of Life (Un Salto de Vida) express their refusal to become the "objects" of academic inquiry. Added to this valid concern was my own perception that a focus on the social movement or social conflict as such would not lead me to contribute elements to understand the causes of ongoing river pollution, which in my view might strengthen the demands for its eventual restoration as a place of life.

I began to read about institutional ethnography when I was making decisions about how to focus my research. It struck me then that the narrations of Canadian sociologist Dorothy Smith (2005) on what led her to propose this way of approaching research reflected the dilemma I was struggling with at the time. Smith describes her experience with feminist students seeking to study the women's movement through the lens of social movements:

> Imposing the social movement frame reconstructed as an object that of which we were part. We became conceptual outsiders. It seemed not possible to take up a topic sociologically without transforming people and people's doings into objects. It wasn't a matter of intention. Once the sociological frame was committed, inquiry and discovery *from within* the women's movement was precluded. (28; emphasis in original)

This account mirrored my own concerns and bolstered my decision to focus my research on one of the important causes of river deterioration: the industrial sector and its regulators in government. At the same time, broader concerns also informed my research strategy.

I am referring to the methodological concerns, arising especially from poststructuralism, feminism, and the elaborations of complex thought, that problematize the relationship between the researcher and the subjects of research, as well as the manner of conceiving scientific knowledge more broadly. In this sense, Patti Lather describes how, particularly in the social sciences, science is distinguished from nonscience based on "a method that is supposedly a trans-historical, culture-free, disinterested, replicable,

Appendix

testable and empirical substantiation of theory" (1992, 88). This claim to "universal" and "objective" methods and knowledge obviates the relationship between the researcher and the researched. In this way, Edgar Morin explains, "Western science was founded on the positivist elimination of the subject based on the idea that objects, existing independently of the subject, could be observed and explained as such" (1990, 65). In this research, I was concerned not only with recognizing my relationship as researcher with my research subjects but also with seeking a reflexive practice as a way of trying to "study the shifting, multiple subject positionings of the researcher in order to take responsibility for the knowledge being produced" (Chaudhry 2000, 109).

The alternative to universal objectivity, then, is not relativism, described by Donna Haraway as "a way of being nowhere while claiming to be everywhere equally" (1988, 584). Haraway advocates for knowledge that is "partial, locatable and critical," and for the practice of an objectivity that "privileges contestation, deconstruction, passionate construction, [and] webbed connections" (585). In my research, and given my previous experience working on these issues in an NGO with certain "naturalized" conceptions of the problem under study and the actors involved, it was important for me to recognize and explicitly discuss my experience and critical views on the role of government and industry in perpetuating environmental degradation in this region.

Acknowledging these concerns, however, did not imply that I adopted a radical poststructuralist or constructivist position, which denies a reality beyond discourse or subjective perceptions and constructions. Nor does it mean that I abandoned my interest in analyzing the strategies of local and national organizations. I would locate my approach along the lines of what Samantha Jones qualifies as "moderate" or "contextual" constructivism, which starts from accepting "epistemological relativism (i.e. that we can never know reality exactly as it is), while rejecting ontological relativism (i.e. that our accounts of the world are not constrained by nature)" (2002, 248). My intent is not to argue, in the words of Arturo Escobar, that "there is no real nature out there," but to highlight how discourses manifest certain articulations between knowledge and power (1996, 46). My interest is in the link highlighted by Michel Foucault between relations of power and discourse: "There can be no possible exercise of power without a certain economy of discourses of truth which operates through and on the basis of this association" (1980, 93). The discursive construction of an environmental problem has "effects of power" that have material implications (94).

Critiques of postmodernism and poststructuralism have called attention to the lack of any criteria to decipher between different representations of that "real nature." Beyond the rejection of the Archimedean viewpoint of the universal subject, Dorothy Smith reflects that much postmodernist and poststructuralist work also rejects "the notion that there can be an overriding truth to which alternative views, theories, and versions of the world must be subordinated" (1996, 174). Since there is no reality or truth external to the text or discourse to which to appeal, Smith asserts that "discourse as a field of study is an endless resource without destination or conclusion" (177). In a similar sense, from the field of political ecology (PE), Piers Blaikie questions the usefulness of a poststructuralist PE given that the political and ethical goal of much work in the field has been environmental justice, and he calls to "resist the lures of post-structuralism" (2012, 233). Blaikie's concern is to be able to communicate with actors outside the academy and to achieve the political goals of PE. He calls for a "critical realist" PE that acknowledges the "unequal power" generated by and generative of language and discourse but that also acknowledges an external reality and makes use of empirical research and evidence (234).

While the analysis in this book centers on empirical evidence, both the results of my own research and those taken from other sources, primarily data generated by the government apparatus itself, I also touch on ways in which discourse constitutes a key part of the practices that lead to the persistence of problems such as the industrial pollution of the Santiago River. Despite clearly situating his approach in the style of materialist (realist) PE, in the materialist-constructivist distinction, Joan Martínez-Alier (2002) stresses that both styles are connected. Thus, the interest in discourse from a constructivist PE is linked to the materialist perspective in that "struggles over resources, even when they have tangible material origins, have always been struggles over meanings" (Guha and Martínez-Alier cited in Martínez-Alier 2002, 256). In the end, Martínez-Alier suggests that the "two styles of Political Ecology must thus be combined" (256). I undertook this research with the intention of combining the materialist and constructivist approaches to PE.

This leaves unanswered, perhaps, the question of how to address the challenge of discerning different versions or discourses of reality. For example, in the case of the Santiago River, even when all actors are confronted

Appendix 267

by the same evidence of water-quality testing or the same reality of pollution that can be smelled and perceived directly, their discourses and interpretations diverge significantly. For many local residents and activists, what they perceive is a matter of life and death, of injustice and grievance, while for others, including many in government, it is a minor issue that is already under control. Boaventura de Sousa Santos describes his criterion, affirming that "knowledge-as-intervention-in-reality is the measure of realism, not knowledge-as-a-representation-of-reality," while also acknowledging the "incompleteness" of any knowledge (2009, 115, 187). When Blaikie asks, "Can some political ecology be useful?" his response is a resounding "YES" (2012, 238). The commitment to be useful in the face of a problem that I believe is urgent—with my criterion of usefulness strongly formed by my own experience on the subject—is my yardstick for distinguishing between different approaches to and representations of reality.

A.1 Institutional Ethnography

It was in the work of Escobar (1995) that I first read about institutional ethnography, in his insightful critique of development understood as an inevitable route to modernization, industrialization, and urbanization, *Encountering Development: The Making and Unmaking of the Third World*. Escobar applies institutional ethnography to policies and programs to combat hunger in Colombia in the period from 1975 to 1990 as an analytical tool to reveal the practices of institutions that often remain hidden because they are seen as "rational" (1995, 105). By analyzing documentary practices, and the processes through which institutions develop plans and label populations, Escobar makes explicit the role of institutions in structuring the conditions under which people live and conceive of their lives. This is part of a process to "train ourselves to see culturally what we have been taught to overlook, namely, the participation of institutional practices in the making of the world" (113). It seemed to me at that time that a strategy based in institutional ethnography would permit me to scrutinize how federal, state, and municipal authorities conceive, communicate, and implement water policies and regulations, as well as how industrial water pollution is normalized in the country and in the case of the Santiago River.

Thus, as set out in the introduction, I turned to strategies of institutional ethnography to study the administrative, legal, economic, and discursive practices of private and governmental actors. Given the predominant role of texts in organizing local practices "extralocally," institutional ethnography stresses methods including analysis of texts and mapping, in addition to interviews and participant observation (Devault 2006, 295). While semistructured interviews were a key part of the research I undertook, I also carefully sifted through government documents, many obtained through public information requests, to supplement the information gleaned from interviews, assess and understand bureaucratic practices, and call into question narratives of environmental compliance based on contrasting evidence.

A.2 Brief Sketch of Research Undertaken

After two decades of citizen demands for the cleanup of the Santiago River, the guiding question of my research was, why does this river continue to be polluted by discharges of industrial origin? From there, I sought clues to answer that question within government practices and the practices and discourses of the companies established in the area. Before undertaking this research, I was uncertain whether I would be able to obtain the interviews I deemed necessary to be able to try to answer this question. In particular, my limited experience speaking with industry representatives left me with the certainty that I needed a clear strategy for how to present my research interest.

With industry actors, the answer I landed on was to approach them through the language and focus now adopted by many companies: sustainability strategies and environmental management programs. Given the boom in sustainability and environmental policies, programs, and reports, I saw an opening to dialogue with personnel from the factories in the industrial corridor based on their own discourse, reports, and commitments. This way of approaching my research made sense to me, moreover, because I had collaborated as a consultant in several sustainability assessments for agrifood companies and I felt I understood the methods, certifications, and jargon associated with corporate sustainability strategies. Although I evaluate the results positively, this approach also imposed certain limitations on the research. I designed the interviews to be consistent with a focus on corporate sustainability and to avoid defensive postures that could result from making the interviewee feel questioned or accused. My experience

Appendix

confirmed the importance of this strategy, since even presenting my research in this way, in several cases I perceived an environment of extreme caution and even suspicion in the face of my interest in a company's environmental management strategies.

This focus also limited the research in directing it toward larger companies that have more established environmental policies or sustainability strategies. At the same time, this way of framing my interest did not guarantee obtaining the interviews I sought. In fact, obtaining interviews with factory representatives and tours of the factories was both tedious and time consuming, requiring some luck as well as persistence in calls, emails, and letters and, when required, the signing of confidentiality agreements. The arrangements for these interviews generally took from one to eight months, sometimes even more. As I detailed in chapter 5, receiving negative responses was also part of the process. In the end, I was able to interview representatives of sixteen companies: in thirteen companies it was with the person in charge of environment, health and safety at the local factory or the director of the local plant; in two cases I only interviewed staff from the companies' headquarters (via telephone); and in one case I interviewed staff both at their headquarters and at the local factory. In ten companies it was possible to take a tour of their facilities, some being more complete tours than others.

A.3   Actor-Oriented Political Ecology

My research methodology combined an actor-centered analysis, institutional ethnography, and elements of PE. I proposed combining these strategies because they allowed me to analyze the practices that favor industrial pollution and the private sector and governmental actors involved in these processes, without losing sight of the country's strategy of insertion in the global economy; and, in addition, to undertake work with the organizations of the socio-environmental movement around the Santiago River, to exchange pertinent information and learn about the analysis and proposals of the groups in relation to industrial pollution.

Based in PE, Raymond Bryant and Sinead Bailey (1997, 25) affirm that by putting the actor at the center, importance is given to the political in PE, and they understand the interaction between actors as the essence of politics. Bryant and Bailey point out that, in general, PE research seeks to "explain the topography of a politicized environment" (187). Central to their idea of a politicized environment is their conception of power, which they understand as encompassing both material and nonmaterial considerations and the fluidity of power itself, where, for example, in the realm of ideas and legitimacy, weaker actors can significantly challenge powerful actors such as the state and corporations. In tracing complex power relations, they emphasize that "the ability of an actor to control or resist other actors is never permanent or fixed but always in flux" (44). Thus, while the state and corporations have often contributed to environmental deterioration, in an "alliance" that rests on "a combination of a quest for profits by [transnational corporations] and a desire for development by Third World leaders" (109), their interests also diverge in many cases, and it is essential to probe this complexity.

A deficiency of much research located in the field of PE, according to Jeff Bury (2008, 309), has been the tendency to "essentialize actors such as the state, NGOs, or local community organizations and treat them as monolithic entities." In his study of a US mining company and the effects of its operations on community access to resources near Cajamarca in Peru, Bury particularly emphasizes the importance of treating corporations as complex actors. In the ethnographies of the transnational companies that he studies, Bury combines archival research (financial statements, annual reports, and external investigations) with interviews with corporation employees; he describes as "delicate" the process of gaining access to these employees, something that, as mentioned, I also faced in this investigation (310). For Bury, an actor-centered approach also allows us to glimpse the complexity of the relationships that link particular sites with broader scales of analysis. He conceives the challenge of this perspective as being able to "navigate between the overdetermining essentialism of structuralism and the complexity of atomized localism" (309).

To close this section, I would like to turn to a "methodological precaution" that Foucault suggests for the study of power. Foucault calls for not trying to understand power in its legitimate and regular formulations but to apprehend it "at its extremities," in its more local "capillary" manifestations, where it breaks the rules and employs even violent mechanisms (1980, 96). In other words, he recommends observing power where it is "less legal in character" (97). I highlight this because in my research I was fundamentally interested in the illegal or unethical exercise of power,

Appendix 271

both by government actors and by the companies in question. On the government side, my intention was to demonstrate the nonenforcement of environmental laws as well as the preparation of inadequate regulations to control pollution: practices that, as I have pointed out, are part of institutionalized corruption.

In the case of companies, likewise, the aim was to go beyond the "official version" of their environmental performance, manifested in their sustainability reports or in their affiliation with programs such as the Clean Industry program of the Federal Bureau of Environmental Protection (PROFEPA, Procuraduría Federal de Protección al Ambiente) or ISO 14000–type certifications. "Who certifies the certifiers?" asks Martínez-Alier, asserting that to separate "greenwashing" from true environmental responsibility, the state or international organizations are required to "sanction" environmental audits (2002, 197). In the Mexican case, the reliability of the authorities in that role remains in doubt. The government endorsement perhaps reflects the "governmentalization" highlighted by Foucault, without actually representing a transfer of power. Foucault notes that in contemporary societies, power relations are increasingly centralized under the auspices of state institutions, although he maintains that this "is not because they are derived [from the state]; it is rather because power relations have come more and more under state control" (1982, 793). Here, the distinction made by Barry Barnes between authority and power is also relevant. According to Barnes (1986, 182), authority should be understood as "power minus discretion"; in contrast, a power "directs a routine, and directs it with discretion." In relation to transnational companies and the state, then, my hypothesis was that although government actors have the authority to monitor, sanction, and endorse, it is the corporations that have the power, in this case to dump pollutants into the Santiago River with impunity.

A.4 Research Techniques

The main research techniques that I used to characterize the practices of companies and business associations were the following:

1. I analyzed documents, including
   a. financial and sustainability reports, web page content, and advertising materials of each company;

b. environmental certifications;

c. the public information available on the activities of the selected companies as well as the Association of Industrialists of El Salto (AISAC, Asociación de Industriales de El Salto) and the National Association of the Chemical Industry (ANIQ, Asociación Nacional de la Industria Química); and

d. a compiled database of the companies in my study area with information the National Statistical Directory of Economic Units (Directorio Estadístico Nacional de Unidades Económicas).

2. I conducted structured interviews with representatives of AISAC and ANIQ and with the environment, health and safety representatives of sixteen companies.

3. I engaged in participant observation of meetings and events convened by ANIQ and several business and economic promotion forums. In particular, I attended events related to issues of sustainability and corporate responsibility.

The main techniques I used to analyze the practices of the water, environment, and economic promotion authorities were the following:

1. I analyzed documents, including

a. engaging in a systematic review of the information available on the Santiago River and, in particular, the Ocotlán–El Salto Industrial Corridor, in government reports, public statements, documentary videos, and media coverage;

b. generating information on industrial pollution monitoring and enforcement practices through a targeted strategy of public information requests to the main government institutions involved; and

c. analyzing laws, regulations, and standards, as well as documents that outline policies and programs, related to water management, industrial pollution control, and environmental audits.

2. I conducted semistructured interviews with water, environment, and economic promotion officials.

3. I engaged in participant observation of the Academic Water Council of the Jalisco State Water Commission (CEA, Comisión Estatal del Agua).

Due to its importance in my study, I will make some additional comments on access to government public information and its limits. As mentioned

Appendix

in the introduction, I made around two hundred information requests as part of this investigation, most of them to federal authorities (the Ministry of Environment and Natural Resources [Secretaría de Medio Ambiente y Recursos Naturales], the National Water Commission [CONAGUA, Comisión Nacional del Agua], and PROFEPA), and a smaller number to agencies at the state level (the CEA, the Ministry of Environment and Territorial Development [Secretaría de Medio Ambiente y Desarrollo Territorial], and the Jalisco Ministry of Health [Secretaría de Salud Jalisco]). Experience confirms this route as an important way to access relevant information on the formulation and application of environmental regulations. In fact, chapters 3–5 examine in-depth information obtained through requests for information, in addition to interviews. I consider it essential to highlight access to government information as key to transparency, particularly given the recent trend of providing less access through the websites of federal agencies.

In the process of requesting public government information, I encountered recurring problems that are worth pointing out. The main problem is that the information provided is often incomplete or even contradictory. In chapter 3, I detailed various examples of contradictory and incomplete information provided by CONAGUA. Formulating the requests requires precision, to prevent them from being discarded or the information from being classified as nonexistent due to the use of inaccurate terminology. In many cases, although I requested the information in electronic format, the agencies responded that it could only be made available on paper. Because of this, I paid for more than twelve thousand sheets of information in the course of the investigation. This could clearly be a limitation in access to information. At the same time, I found that requests are perceived by government agencies as an excess and unimportant workload, as I was met with annoyance and complaints at times due to the amount of information requested.

All in all, the system renders mixed results wherein, despite applicants' presenting well-formulated requests, the willingness of agencies and perhaps even individual officials to provide complete and reliable information to them plays an important role. Appeals do not always provide adequate outcomes either, in addition to requiring a significant investment of time, as well as greater technical knowledge to present appropriate legal justifications.

*   *   *

In this research, then, I took up elements of institutional ethnography, PE, and an actor-centered approach to understand the power relations around the formulation and application of regulations governing industrial discharges to water bodies in Mexico. This allowed me to understand practices in government agencies and the private sector without losing sight of structural factors related to the way in which manufacturing in Mexico is inserted into the flows of goods and capital in a globalized world. At the same time, I attempted to take seriously the "power effects" of discourse, which create meaning and limit serious discussion of the environmental and health effects of industrial pollution. Finally, I think it is important to underline that, in the interest of reflexivity and making both my interest and my experiences on the subject transparent, at different points in this text, I reflect on my own experiences, a fact that I hope also contributes to a more complex and interesting narrative for the reader.

Notes

Introduction

1. At present, this dam only functions to divert water to the Aurora irrigation canal located above the waterfall, supplying water to Irrigation District 013.

2. Interview, August 2003.

3. ¡Qué poca madre tuvimos!

4. Interview, August 2003.

5. This coincides with the year cited by Durán and Torres (2009), who indicate that fishermen reported fish floating in the Santiago River in 1973.

6. Interview, July 29, 2014.

7. Interview, October 16, 2013.

8. Interview, August 2003.

9. On March 1, 2013, the Ministry of Environment for Sustainable Development changed its name to the Ministry of Environment and Territorial Development (SEMA-DET, Secretaría de Medio Ambiente y Desarrollo Territorial).

10. Taken from the undated document *Historial: Reuniones del Problema de olores de Juanacatlán*, provided by the Jalisco State Human Rights Commission (Comisión Estatal de Derechos Humanos Jalisco) to Instituto VIDA and IMDEC with regard to complaint no. 986/07/III.

11. Unless otherwise noted, all translations of texts originally in Spanish are my own.

12. Since 1997, Mexico has been divided into thirteen hydrological-administrative regions, which are groupings of several river basins.

13. According to information from CONAGUA's Public Water Rights Registry (Registro Público de Derechos de Agua), in Jalisco there are only 17 permits (representing

less than 0.1 percent of total volume) for industrial use of surface water versus 636 for groundwater extraction (CONAGUA 2022b).

14. Interview, December 9, 2013; emphasis added.

15. Interview, December 9, 2013.

16. Harvey's concept of accumulation by dispossession is criticized by Robert Brenner (2006, 102) for seeking to encompass an overly broad range of processes. Brenner posits that its distinctive characteristic is the focus on the subjection to capitalist logics of pre- and noncapitalist economies and nationalized sectors of capitalist economies (98). What is "counterproductive," Brenner suggests, is the inclusion of processes "that are quite normal aspects or by-products of the already well-established sway of capital," such as the exacerbation of the exploitation of the workforce or the protection of a state of its own capitalists (100).

Chapter 1

1. Site visit, March 5, 2022.

2. Wester et al. define the hydrocracy as the bearer of the "hydraulic mission," understood as the "the strong conviction that every drop of water flowing to the ocean is a waste and that the state should develop hydraulic infrastructure to capture as much water as possible for human uses" (2009, 396).

3. Held in Mexico City, September 13, 2013.

4. The United Nations (2014) defines water stress as arising in a region where the water supply is less than 1,700 m^3 per person per year; water scarcity is defined as arising in an area with less than 1,000 m^3 per person, and absolute scarcity exists where less than 500 m^3 of water is available per person.

5. BOD measures the amount of oxygen required or consumed by the microbiological decomposition of organic matter in water, typically measured in milligrams per liter of oxygen consumed in five days at a constant temperature of 20°C in the dark (Worsfold et al. 2005).

6. COD is understood as the amount of organic and inorganic matter in a body of water that can be oxidized by a strong oxidant (Worsfold et al. 2005).

7. TSS is defined as the settleable solids, solids, and suspended or colloidal organic matter that is retained in a filter element (SE 2015).

8. The source of basic information for this analysis is the National Statistical Directory of Economic Units (DENUE, Directorio Estadístico Nacional de Unidades Económicas) maintained by INEGI, supplemented in specific instances with data from the Mexican Business Information System (Sistema de Información Empresarial Mexicano) of the Ministry of Economy. The version of the DENUE consulted was

Notes

updated based on the Economic Census of 2014 with verification work undertaken by INEGI in the second half of 2015 (INEGI 2016).

9. Economic units of the manufacturing industries classification (31–33). To more clearly identify industrial manufacturing activities, I excluded from the database companies with 11 to 30 employees and dedicated to traditional baking and tortilla preparation, which are activities typical of any community.

10. Based on information available on the internet, I categorized the companies as Mexican or, with foreign capital, by their host country. Where the company had no website or other information available online, I assumed they were Mexican companies.

11. Field notes, CONAGUA offices in Ocotlán, August 14, 2014.

12. According to information from the Agency for Toxic Substances and Disease Registry (2022) of the United States and the EPA (2002).

Chapter 2

1. Interview, August 27, 2020.

2. Interview, August 27, 2020.

3. Interview, August 27, 2020.

4. Interview, August 27, 2020.

5. Interview, December 18, 2009.

6. Letter of July 10, 2002, in author's possession.

7. The regional offices of CONAGUA changed their name to basin agencies, in this case the Lerma-Santiago-Pacific Basin Agency, in 2007.

8. Iglesias oversaw the CONAGUA Regional Office from 2002 until November 2012, when he was fired for having granted hydraulic works to a company in which he had family interests. He was subsequently disqualified from public service for a period of ten years (Velazco 2013).

9. Letter No. BOO.00.R12.07.3/123, December 17, 2002.

10. Letter No. BOO.00.R09.07.3/111, November 25, 2003.

11. Oficio DG/DI/3259/2003, December 15, 2003.

12. Letter of March 3, 2003.

13. Third Investigative Unit, investigation report 23/03/III, September 29, 2003.

14. Interview, February 18, 2008.

15. The CEAS was established in May 2001, and in 2006 its name was changed to the State Water Commission of Jalisco (CEA, Comisión Estatal del Agua).

16. Zona de emergencia ambiental y de acción extraordinaria en materia de salud.

17. These responses were gleaned from a series of letters, including a letter from SEMADES (1317/2008) dated April 25, 2008, from then-minister Martha Ruth del Toro Gaytán, and a letter from the CONAGUA Basin Agency (folio B00.00.R12.07.3/24) dated May 6, 2008.

18. This change was included in the sixth transitory article of the LFD, November 13, 2008.

19. Interview, June 6, 2014.

20. Decree 19985 of May 12, 2003, reformed via decree 20564 of July 9, 2004.

21. INFOMEX Jalisco folio 07913120.

22. Polígono de Fragilidad Ambiental de la zona de la cuenca El Ahogado.

23. Interview, February 25, 2013.

24. Interview, October 16, 2013.

25. Field notes, CONAGUA offices in Ocotlán, August 14, 2014.

Chapter 3

1. Part of a speech given on May 21, 2014; emphasis added.

2. Part of a speech given on May 21, 2014.

3. The Internal Regulations of SEMARNAT were modified on November 26, 2012 (*Diario Oficial de la Federación*, Article 45, Section I).

4. Interview, March 27, 2014.

5. Azuela was head of PROFEPA from December 1994 to 2000 and is now a researcher at the Institute of Social Research at the National Autonomous University of Mexico.

6. Interview, March 28, 2014.

7. Request for government public information folio 1610100175314. All documentation received in response to the information requests cited are in the possession of the author.

8. Personal communication, June 2021.

9. Interview, May 7, 2015.

10. Interview, May 7, 2015.

Notes 279

11. Interview, October 10, 2013.

12. Information from a CONAGUA administrative resolution of May 23, 2013, referring to inspection visit PNI-2012-LSP-256.

13. Request for government public information folio 1610100215514.

14. Interview, February 25, 2013.

15. Information obtained through information request to the Federal Institute for Access to Information and Data Protection (IFAI, Instituto Federal de Acceso a la Información y Protección de Datos) folio 1610100154214.

16. Information obtained through information request to the IFAI folio 1610100211013, inspection report PNI-2012-LSP-285.

17. Notes from site visit, May 10, 2014.

18. Information obtained through information request to the IFAI folio 1610100154419.

19. Interview, October 10, 2013.

20. Interview, July 4, 2014.

21. Interview, June 6, 2014.

22. Interview, June 6, 2014.

23. Interview, May 7, 2015.

24. Interview, May 7, 2015.

25. Interview, May 7, 2015.

26. Interview, May 13, 2014.

27. Information obtained through information request to the IFAI folio 1610100154214.

28. Interview, October 3, 2013.

29. Interview, October 3, 2013.

30. Interview, November 28, 2013.

31. Interview, October 10, 2013.

32. Interview, February 11, 2014.

33. Interview, June 6, 2014.

34. Interview, September 11, 2013.

35. Interview, September 26, 2013.

36. Interview, October 10, 2013.

37. Interview, February 25, 2013.

38. Interview, September 11, 2013.

39. Interview, October 10, 2013.

40. Interview, September 26, 2013.

41. Interview, September 26, 2013.

42. Information obtained through information request to the IFAI folio 1610100072914.

43. The Law of Transparency and Access to Public Government Information of June 11, 2002, stipulated in Article 14 that reserved information will include "commercial, industrial secrets, fiscal, banking, fiduciary or other considered as such by a legal provision." The General Law of Transparency and Access to Public Information (Article 116), issued on May 4, 2015, and the Federal Law of Transparency and Access to Public Information of May 9, 2016, maintained similar provisions (Article 113, Section II).

44. Information obtained through information request to the IFAI folio 1610100160214.

45. The fourteen substances that are not mandatory for reporting in Mexico and that are among the twenty most important pollutants discharged into water in the region are nitric acid and nitrate compounds, total ammonia, total phosphorus, manganese and compounds, methanol, sodium nitrite, ethylene glycol, zinc and compounds, barium and compounds, chlorine, copper and compounds, vanadium and compounds, formic acid, and total reduced sulfur (CEC 2014, 32).

46. Interview, August 6, 2014.

47. Interview, May 22, 2014.

48. Interview, August 6, 2014.

49. Interview, February 12, 2014.

50. Interview, August 6, 2014.

51. Comments during the public meeting of the North American PRTR Initiative convened by the CEC on February 26, 2020, in Montreal, Canada.

52. Interview, April 24, 2014.

53. Interview, September 27, 2013.

54. Interview, September 27, 2013.

55. Environmental Diploma 2013 of the National Chemical Industry Association, Module VII. Assessment of environmental aspects, Mexico City, November 7–8, 2013.

56. Interview, March 27, 2014.

57. Interview, September 27, 2013.

Notes 281

58. Interview, December 9, 2013.

59. Interview, March 27, 2014.

60. Interview, August 6, 2014.

61. Interview, May 15, 2014.

62. Interview, June 13, 2014.

63. Interview, September 4, 2014.

64. Interview, December 11, 2013.

65. Interview, May 5, 2014.

66. Interview, December 3, 2013.

67. Interview, November 28, 2013.

68. Interview, February 13, 2014.

69. Interview, October 15, 2021.

70. Interview, August 6, 2014.

71. http://siga.jalisco.gob.mx/cumplimientov/, accessed July 2016.

72. Interview, August 6, 2014.

73. Information obtained through information request submitted via INFOMEX Jalisco folio 01425014.

74. Document PC/CPCP/384/2014, October 29, 2014, resolution of the appeal for review 453/2014 of the ITEI Jalisco.

75. SEMADET document, November 12, 2014, Transparency Unit, SEMADET/UT/No. 0894/2014.

76. Interview, August 14, 2014.

77. Interview, August 14, 2014.

78. Interview, August 14, 2014.

79. Interview, July 22, 2014.

80. Information obtained through information request to the IFAI folio 1610100101314.

Chapter 4

1. Part of a speech given during the Eleventh Mexico Business Summit (México Cumbre de Negocios), October 20, 2013.

2. Speeches delivered at the event ProMéxico Global, Mexico City, March 25, 2014.

3. Interview, September 11, 2013.

4. Interview, September 30, 2015.

5. Interview, September 4, 2014. "La cumplo con la mano en la cintura."

6. Interview, September 30, 2015.

7. Speech made during the Environment, Health and Safety Congress of ANIQ, June 14, 2013.

8. Public access to government information request folio 0001600009119.

9. The CEDES director in 2003 was Gabriel Quadri de la Torre. Quadri was also director of CESPEDES from 1998 to 2003 and in 2012 was a candidate for the presidency for the New Alliance Party.

10. Interview, May 19, 2014.

11. The same general definition of members of these committees is maintained in the Quality Infrastructure Law (Article 26) that replaced the LFMN in January 2020.

12. Interview, May 19, 2014.

13. Interview, May 19, 2014; emphasis added.

14. Interview, May 19, 2014.

15. Interview, March 27, 2014.

16. Minutes of March 29, 2012. The minutes cited in this chapter were obtained through information requests to the IFAI folios 0001600082414, 0001600082614, 0001600049215, 0001600009019, and 0001600085221.

17. Interview, August 6, 2014.

18. Interview, February 12, 2014.

19. Interview, March 27, 2014; emphasis added.

20. Interview, May 19, 2014.

21. Minutes of June 24, 2015.

22. Interview, May 19, 2014.

23. Interview, May 19, 2014.

24. Minutes of May 9, 2012.

25. Minutes of May 9, 2012.

26. Minutes of July 4, 2012.

Notes

27. Interview, May 19, 2014.

28. Minutes of February 8, 2013.

29. Minutes of May 31, 2013.

30. Minutes of February 8, 2013.

31. Personal communication, interview conducted under condition of anonymity.

32. Minutes of June 29, 2007.

33. Minutes of June 29, 2007.

34. Minutes of June 29, 2007.

35. Minutes of November 29, 2011.

36. Minutes of November 23, 2012.

37. Interview, October 3, 2013.

38. Agenda of the CONCAMIN Water and Environment Commission, January 22, 2013.

39. Interview, May 19, 2014.

40. Minutes of November 15, 2013.

41. Interview, September 11, 2013.

42. Interview, June 6, 2014.

43. Interview, February 12, 2014.

44. Minutes of November 6, 2015.

45. Minutes of March 29, 2012; emphasis added.

46. Minutes of June 27, 2012.

47. Interview, February 12, 2014.

48. Interview, February 12, 2014.

49. Interview, March 27, 2014.

50. Interview, May 19, 2014.

51. Interview, September 26, 2013.

52. Interview, May 19, 2014.

53. Interview, May 19, 2014.

54. One of the comments came from CEMDA, the other from an organization called Legal, Political and Social Studies (Estudios Jurídicos, Políticos y Sociales).

55. Interview, October 9, 2013.

56. All comments registered with COFEMER/CONAMER on the modification of the NOM-001 can be consulted on the institutional website (CONAMER, n.d.).

57. Comment from ANIQ registered in the COFEMER system on January 7, 2018 (COFEMER 2018a).

58. Comments made during the event "Reflections and Actions towards the Publication of NOM-001-SEMARNAT-2017," October 5, 2020 (virtual event).

59. The comment from CONCAMIN was replicated by other associations and reflects the tenor of industry comments. CONCAMIN comment registered in the CONAMER system on August 31, 2021 (CONAMER 2021).

60. Interview, March 27, 2014.

Chapter 5

1. Interview, December 13, 2013.

2. Interview, June 13, 2014.

3. Notes from site visit, March 4, 2014.

4. Interview, October 24, 2013.

5. Interview, January 16, 2014.

6. Interview, November 12, 2014.

7. Interview, December 13, 2013.

8. This change was made to transitory Article 6 of the Federal Duties Law published in the *Official Gazette of the Federation* (*Diario Oficial de la Federación*) on November 13, 2008.

9. Inspection reports accessed through governmental public information request folios 1610100157220 and 1610100157320, related to inspections PNI-2018-LSP-149 and PNI-2018-LSP-168. Other inspection acts cited come from the request folios 1610100211113, 1610100211213, 1610100211413, 1610100211013, and 1610100014915. These requests can be consulted through the website www.infomex.org.mx.

10. Interview, June 13, 2014.

11. Celanese was ranked at number 477 in the *Fortune* 500 (*Fortune*, n.d.-b).

12. In 2010, Celanese requested an increase to the volume of discharge to allow 3,156,753 cubic meters per year (Permit 08JAL133533/12FMOC12).

13. Information provided by CONAGUA in response to access to information request folio 1610100157614.

Notes

14. Information provided by CONAGUA in response to access to information request folio 1610100211213.

15. File 14-1055, Official Letter No. B00.-292, October 2, 2014.

16. File 14-1055, Official Letter No. B00.-292, October 2, 2014. Information provided by CONAGUA in response to access to information request folio 1610100052816.

17. The amparo was obtained as part of information provided by CONAGUA in response to access to information request folio 1610100052816.

18. Report prepared by Lucía Rueda Quintana, April 1, 2015, folios 25759, and 13676, A.P. 1235/UEIDAPLE/DA/33/2103.

19. Memorandum No. No. B00.812.3-16. Information provided by CONAGUA in response to access to information request folio 1610100052816.

20. Information provided by CONAGUA in response to access to information request folio 1610100294416. Among the documents provided by CONAGUA is a Spanish translation of the memorandum from CH2M Hill.

21. A toxicity test is a procedure to determine the toxicity of a chemical, effluent, or water sample using living organisms. It measures the level of effect on the test organism exposed to a specific chemical, effluent, or water sample.

22. Information provided by CONAGUA in response to access to information request folio 1610100211313.

23. Interview, January 16, 2014.

24. Information provided by CONAGUA in response to access to information request folio 0001600323313.

25. Interview, December 3, 2013.

26. Interview, October 24, 2013.

27. Interview, May 5, 2014.

28. Interview, September 4, 2014.

29. Interview, November 28, 2013.

30. Interview, January 30, 2014.

31. Interview, December 13, 2013.

32. Interview, November 1, 2013.

33. Interview, December 11, 2013.

34. Interview, December 11, 2013.

35. Interview, May 15, 2014.

36. Interview, March 21, 2014.

37. Interview, November 12, 2014; emphasis added.

38. Interview, November 12, 2014.

39. Interview, November 28, 2013.

40. Interview, October 3, 2013.

41. Interview, January 16, 2016.

42. Interview, May 15, 2014.

43. Interview, December 13, 2013.

44. Interview, July 22, 2014.

45. Interview, December 13, 2013.

46. Interview, October 3, 2013.

47. Interview, November 28, 2013.

48. Interview, April 29, 2014.

49. Interview, October 3, 2013.

50. Interview, December 13, 2013.

Chapter 6

1. Presentation at the Tonalá University Center of the University of Guadalajara, May 18, 2022.

2. Received in response to a request for information in Jalisco folio 06390319.

3. Interview, August 28, 2020.

4. Request for access to information folio 1610100072914.

5. With information from the Commission for Environmental Cooperation database (CEC, n.d.).

6. Interview, December 9, 2013.

References

Aboites, Luis. 2009. *La decadencia del agua de la nación: Estudio sobre desigualdad social y cambio político en México, segunda mitad del siglo XX*. Mexico City: El Colegio de México.

Aboites, Luis, Enrique Cifuentes, Blanca Jiménez Cisneros, and María Luisa Torregrosa. 2008. *Agenda del agua*. Mexico City: Academia Mexicana de Ciencias–Red del Agua.

Aboites, Luis, Diana Birrichaga Gardida, and Jorge Alfredo Garay Trejo. 2010. El manejo de las aguas mexicanas en el siglo XX. In *El agua en México: Cauces y encauces*, edited by Blanca Jiménez Cisneros, María Luisa Torregrosa, and Luis Aboites, 21–49. Mexico City: Academia Mexicana de Ciencias.

Acselrad, Henri. 2014. El movimiento de justicia ambiental y la crítica al desarrollo: La desigualdad ambiental como categoría constitutiva de la acumulación por despojo en América Latina. In *Territorios en disputa: Despojo capitalista, luchas en defensa de los bienes comunes naturales y alternativas emancipatorias para América Latina*, edited by Claudia Composto and Mina Lorena Navarro, 376–396. Mexico City: Bajo Tierra Ediciones.

Agencia Subversiones. 2017. Tour del horror: De la dictadura de la normalidad a la cotidiana resistencia. *Subversiones: Agencia Autónoma de Comunicación*, March 23. https://subversiones.org/archivos/30367#:~:text=El%20Tour%20del%20Horror%20es,en%20complicidad%20con%20el%20Estado.

Agency for Toxic Substances and Disease Registry. 2022. Homepage. Last updated August 16. http://www.atsdr.cdc.gov/.

Aguilar Ibarra, Alonso, Marisa Mazari, and Blanca Jiménez Cisneros. 2010a. El marco jurídico e institucional para la gestión de la calidad del agua en México. In *Calidad del agua: Un enfoque multidisciplinario*, edited by Alonso Aguilar Ibarra, 281–303. Mexico City: UNAM.

Aguilar Ibarra, Alonso, Rosario Pérez Espejo, and Sara Ávila Forcada. 2010b. Soluciones de la teoría económica para la contaminación del agua. In *Calidad del agua: Un enfoque multidisciplinario*, edited by Alonso Aguilar Ibarra, 221–243. Mexico City: UNAM.

Alba Vega, Carlos. 2006. Los empresarios y la democracia en México. *Foro Internacional* 46 (1) (January–March): 122–149.

Albert, Lilia, and Marisa Jacott. 2015. *México tóxico: Emergencias químicas*. Mexico City: Siglo XXI Editores.

AlEn. 2012. *AlEn Informe de Sustentabilidad 2012*. Monterrey, Mexico: Industrias AlEn.

AlEn. 2014. *Multiplicando acciones: Informe de Sustentabilidad 2014*. Monterrey, Mexico: Industrias AlEn.

AlEn. 2018. *Informe de Sustentabilidad 2018*. Monterrey, Mexico: Industrias AlEn.

Alimonda, Héctor. 2011. La colonialidad de la naturaleza: Una aproximación a la ecología política latinoamericana. In *La naturaleza colonizada: Ecología política y minería en América Latina*, edited by Héctor Alimonda, 21–58. Buenos Aires: CLACSO.

Alonso Torres, José, Mariana Jaime, and Margarita Valle. 2009. Prefieren dinero a río limpio. *Mural*, March 21.

Anderson, Terry, and Donald Leal. 2001. *Free Market Environmentalism*. Rev. ed. New York: Palgrave.

Aras, Güler, and David Crowther. 2009. Corporate Sustainability Reporting: A Study in Disingenuity? *Journal of Business Ethics* 87 (1): 279–288. https://doi.org/10.1007/s10551-008-9806-0.

Arellano-Aguilar, Omar, Laura Ortega Elorza, and Pablo Gesundheit. 2012. *Estudio de la contaminación en la cuenca del río Santiago y la salud pública en la región*. Mexico City: Greenpeace México and Unión de Científicos Comprometidos con la Sociedad.

Arias, Patricia, ed. 1985. *Guadalajara, la gran ciudad de la pequeña industria*. Zamora, Mexico: Colegio de Michoacán.

Arrojo, Pedro. 2009. El reto ético de la crisis global del agua. *Relaciones Internacionales* 12 (October): 33–53.

Atilano, Alejandra, and Sergio Hernández. 2007. Niegan realizar estudio. *Mural*, October 26.

Auyero, Javier, and Débora Alejandra Swistun. 2009. *Flammable: Environmental Suffering in an Argentine Shantytown*. New York: Oxford University Press.

AyMA Ingeniería y Consultoría. 2003. *Estudio de monitoreo y modelación de la calidad del agua de los ríos Santiago y Verde del estado de Jalisco*. Guadalajara, Mexico: Comisión Estatal de Agua y Saneamiento de Jalisco.

Ayuntamiento de Juanacatlán. 1997. Escudo de Juanacatlán (Xonacatlan). Boletín Cultural No. 1. https://congresoweb.congresojal.gob.mx/bibliotecavirtual/Kardex/kardex.cfm#:~:text=ganader%C3%ADa-,her%C3%A1ldica,-Himno%20del%20Estado.

Bakan, Joel. 2005. *The Corporation: The Pathological Pursuit of Profit and Power*. London: Constable and Robinson. Kobo edition.

References

Bakker, Karen. 2009. Neoliberal Nature, Ecological Fixes, and the Pitfalls of Comparative Research. *Environment and Planning A* 41 (8): 1781–1787. https://doi.org/10.1068/a4277.

Bakker, Karen. 2010. The Limits of "Neoliberal Natures": Debating Green Neoliberalism. *Progress in Human Geography* 34 (6): 715–735. https://doi.org/10.1177/030913 2510376849.

Bakker, Karen. 2014. The Business of Water: Market Environmentalism in the Water Sector. *Annual Review of Environment and Resources* 39 (2014): 469–494. https://doi .org/10.1146/annurev-environ-070312-132730.

Banerjee, Subhabrata Bobby. 2003. Who Sustains Whose Development? Sustainable Development and the Reinvention of Nature. *Organization Studies* 24 (1): 143–180. https://doi.org/10.1177/0170840603024001341.

Barba, Carlos, and Fernando Pozos. 2001. El mercado de trabajo de los trabajadores no manuales de la industria electrónica de la zona metropolitana de Guadalajara: Un estudio de caso. *Espiral, Estudios sobre Estado y Sociedad* 8 (22): 197–221.

Barlow, Maude. 2007. *Blue Covenant: The Global Water Crisis and the Coming Battle for the Right to Water.* Toronto: McClelland and Stewart.

Barnes, Barry. 1986. On Authority and Its Relationship to Power. In *Power, Action and Belief*, edited by John Law, 180–195. London: Routledge.

Behre, Christopher. 2003. Mexican Environmental Law: Enforcement and Public Participation since the Signing of NAFTA's Environmental Cooperation Agreement. *Journal of Transnational Law and Policy* 12 (2): 327–343.

Bernache, Gerardo. 2012. El riesgo para los habitantes de El Salto. In *Riesgos socioambientales en México*, edited by Mauricio Sánchez, Elena Lazos, and Roberto Melville, 193–216. Mexico City: CIESAS.

Biel, Robert. 2007. *El nuevo imperialismo: Crisis y contradicciones en las relaciones Norte-Sur.* Mexico City: Siglo XXI Editores.

Bizberg, Ilán. 2015. Tipos de capitalismo en América Latina. In *Variedades de capitalismo en América Latina: Los casos de México, Brasil, Argentina y Chile*, edited by Ilán Bizberg, 41–94. Mexico City: El Colegio de México.

Blackman, Allen, Bidisha Lahiri, William Pizer, Marisol Rivera Planter, and Carlos Muñoz Piña. 2010. Voluntary Environmental Regulation in Developing Countries: Mexico's Clean Industry Program. *Journal of Environmental Economics and Management* 60 (3): 182–192. https://doi.org/10.1016/j.jeem.2010.05.006.

Blackman, Allen, and Nicholas Sisto. 2005. *Muddling Through while Environmental Regulatory Capacity Evolves: What Role for Voluntary Agreements?* Washington, DC: Resources for the Future. http://www.rff.org/files/sharepoint/WorkImages/Download/RFF-DP-05 -16.pdf.

Blaikie, Piers. 2012. Should Some Political Ecology Be Useful? The Inaugural Lecture for the Cultural and Political Ecology Specialty Group, Annual Meeting of the Association of American Geographers, April 2010. *Geoforum* 43 (2) (March): 231–239. https://doi.org/10.1016/j.geoforum.2011.08.010.

Bloomberg. 2016. Éste es el pequeño y sucio secreto de la contaminación en la CDMX. *El Financiero*, April 4. http://www.elfinanciero.com.mx/bloomberg/este-es-el -pequeno-y-sucio-secreto-de-la-contaminacion-en-la-cdmx.html.

Bollo Manent, Manuel, Rodolfo Montaño Salazar, and José Ramón Hernández Santana, eds. 2017. *Situación ambiental de la Cuenca del Río Santiago–Guadalajara*. Morelia, Mexico: CIGA-UNAM, SEMARNAT, and SEMADET.

Brenner, Neil, Jamie Peck, and Nik Theodore. 2010. Variegated Neoliberalization: Geographies, Modalities, Pathways. *Global Networks* 10 (2): 182–222. https://doi.org /10.1111/j.1471-0374.2009.00277.x.

Brenner, Robert. 2006. What Is, and What Is Not, Imperialism? *Historical Materialism* 14 (4): 79–105. https://doi.org/10.1163/156920606778982464.

Bryant, Raymond. 1997. Beyond the Impasse: The Power of Political Ecology in Third World Environmental Research. *Natural Resources and Environment* 29 (1) (March): 5–19.

Bryant, Raymond, and Sinead Bailey. 1997. *Third World Political Ecology*. London: Routledge.

Bullard, Robert. 1993. The Threat of Environmental Racism. *Natural Resources and Environment* 7 (3) (Winter): 23–26, 55–56.

Bury, Jeff. 2008. Transnational Corporations and Livelihood Transformations in the Peruvian Andes: An Actor-Oriented Political Ecology. *Human Organization* 67 (3) (Fall): 307–321.

Bussell, Jennifer. 2015. Typologies of Corruption: A Pragmatic Approach. In *Greed, Corruption, and the Modern State: Essays in Political Economy*, edited by Susan Rose-Ackerman and Paul Lagunes, 21–45. Northampton, MA: Edward Elgar.

Cabrales, Luis Felipe. 2010. El de atrás paga: El modelo metropolitano de Guadalajara. In *La reinvención de la metrópoli: Algunas propuestas*, edited by Octavio Urquídez, 75–96. Guadalajara, Mexico: Colegio de Jalisco.

Cámara de Senadores. 2014. Oficio No. DGPL-2P2A.-4520. Mexico City: Senado de la República. https://www.senado.gob.mx/comisiones/medio_ambiente/docs/puntos /FOLIO%20401.pdf.

Cárdenas, Enrique. 2000. The Process of Accelerated Industrialization in Mexico, 1929–1982. In *An Economic History of Twentieth-Century Latin America*, edited by Enrique Cárdenas, José Antonio Ocampo, and Rosemary Thorp, 176–204. New York: Palgrave.

References

Carpenter, Daniel, and David Moss. 2014. Introduction to *Preventing Regulatory Capture: Special Interest Influence and How to Limit It,* edited by Daniel Carpenter and David Moss, 1–22. New York: Cambridge University Press.

Carruthers, David, ed. 2008. *Environmental Justice in Latin America: Problems, Promise, and Practice.* Cambridge, MA: MIT Press.

Castree, Noel. 2008. Neoliberalising Nature: The Logics of Deregulation and Reregulation. *Environment and Planning A* 40 (1): 131–152. https://doi.org/10.1068/a3999.

Castree, Noel. 2009. Researching Neoliberal Environmental Governance: A Reply to Karen Bakker. *Environment and Planning A* 41 (8): 1788–1794. https://doi.org/10.1068/a42204.

Castree, Noel. 2010a. Neoliberalism and the Biophysical Environment 1: What "Neoliberalism" Is, and What Difference Nature Makes to It. *Geography Compass* 4 (12) (December): 1725–1733. https://doi.org/10.1111/j.1749-8198.2010.00405.x.

Castree, Noel. 2010b. Neoliberalism and the Biophysical Environment 2: Theorising the Neoliberalisation of Nature. *Geography Compass* 4 (12) (December): 1734–1746. https://doi.org/10.1111/j.1749-8198.2010.00407.x.

Castree, Noel. 2011. Neoliberalism and the Biophysical Environment 3: Putting Theory into Practice. *Geography Compass* 5 (1) (January): 35–49. https://doi.org/10.1111/j.1749-8198.2010.00406.x.

CEA (Comisión Estatal del Agua Jalisco). 2008. *Oficio DUEAS-204/2008.* Guadalajara, Mexico: CEA.

CEA (Comisión Estatal del Agua Jalisco). 2009. *Resultados del monitoreo Río Santiago, Río Zula y Arroyo El Ahogado en mayo de 2009.* Guadalajara, Mexico: CEA.

CEA (Comisión Estatal del Agua Jalisco). 2012. *Rectificación Arroyo El Ahogado.* Guadalajara, Mexico: CEA. http://www.ceajalisco.gob.mx/notas/documentos/rectificacion_ahogado.pdf.

CEAS (Comisión Estatal de Agua y Saneamiento, Jalisco) and AyMA Ingeniería y Consultoría. 2006. *Identificación y Caracterización de Fuentes de Contaminación de las Cuencas Directa del Río Santiago entre los Municipios de Ocotlán y Tonalá, y Directa del Río Zula.* Guadalajara, Mexico: CEAS.

CEAS (Comisión Estatal de Agua y Saneamiento, Jalisco) and AyMA Ingeniería y Consultoría. 2007. *Estudio de actualización de clasificación del río Verde y la parte Alta del río Santiago, Jalisco.* Guadalajara, Mexico: CEAS.

CEAS (Comisión Estatal de Agua y Saneamiento, Jalisco) and Gobierno del Estado de Jalisco. 2005. *Estudio y diagnóstico en la Cuenca Baja "El Ahogado" y monitoreo de la Laguna Cajititlán.* Guadalajara, Mexico: CEAS.

CEAS (Comisión Estatal de Agua y Saneamiento, Jalisco) and Universidad de Guadalajara–CUCEI (Centro Universitario de Ciencias Exactas e Ingenierías). 2004. *Estudio para la caracterización de los lodos de los ríos Verde y Santiago*. Guadalajara, Mexico: CEAS.

CEC (Commission for Environmental Cooperation). 2012. *Expediente de hechos relativo a la petición SEM-03-003 (Lago de Chapala II)*. Montreal: CEC. http://www.cec .org/files/documents/publications/11004-north-american-environmental-law-and -policy-volume-29-es.pdf.

CEC (Commission for Environmental Cooperation). 2014. *Taking Stock 14: Exploring Changes in PRTR Reporting, 2005–2010*. Montreal: CEC. http://www.cec.org/files /documents/publications/11581-taking-stock-vol-14-en.pdf.

CEC (Commission for Environmental Cooperation). n.d. Taking Stock. Accessed March 30, 2022. http://takingstock.cec.org/.

CEDHJ (Comisión Estatal de Derechos Humanos Jalisco). 2008. *Informe especial sobre la contaminación del río Santiago a su paso por los municipios de El Salto y Juanacatlán*. Guadalajara, Mexico: CEDHJ. http://cedhj.org.mx/recomendaciones/inf.%20especi ales/2008/rio_santiago.pdf.

CEDHJ (Comisión Estatal de Derechos Humanos Jalisco). 2009. *Recomendación 1/2009*. Guadalajara, Mexico: CEDHJ. http://cedhj.org.mx/recomendaciones/emitidas/2009 /rec0901.pdf.

CEDHJ (Comisión Estatal de Derechos Humanos Jalisco). 2022. *Recomendación 5/2022*. Guadalajara, Mexico: CEDHJ. http://cedhj.org.mx/recomendaciones/emitidas/2022 /Reco%205-2022%20VP.pdf.

Celanese. 2011. *Sustainability Is Good Business: 2011 Interim Report*. Irving, TX: Celanese.

Celanese. 2013. *Empower: 2013 Stewardship Report*. Irving, TX: Celanese.

Celanese. 2015. *In Our Hands: 2015 Celanese Stewardship Report*. Irving, TX: Celanese.

Celanese. 2017. *Celanese 2017 Stewardship Report*. Irving, TX: Celanese.

CEREAL (Centro de Reflexión y Acción Laboral). 2015. *El precio de la flexibilidad: Experiencias de trabajadores en la industria electrónica en México*. Guadalajara, Mexico: CEREAL and GoodElectronics. https://goodelectronics.org/wp-content/uploads/sites /3/2015/03/filesnamePaying20the20price20for20flexibility20-20workers2720experi ences20in20the20electronics20industry20in20Mexico_Spanish.pdf.

Cervantes, Evlyn. 2016. Buscan con ley mejorar el aire. *El Norte*, April 24. http:// www.elnorte.com/aplicaciones/articulo/default.aspx?id=826577&sc=319.

Cervantes, Rosario, and Jorge Villaseñor. 2014. Perfil exportador de Jalisco: Valor agregado nacional y local contenido en sus exportaciones manufactureras. *Carta económica regional* 26 (113) (January–June): 166–200.

References

CESPEDES (Comisión de Estudios del Sector Privado para el Desarrollo Sustentable). 2015. *¿Quiénes somos?* https://cespedes.org.mx/2015/03/19/quienes-somos/.

Chaudhry, Lubna Nazir. 2000. Researching "My People" Researching Myself: Fragments of a Reflexive Tale. In *Working the Ruins: Feminist Poststructural Theory and Methods in Education*, edited by Elizabeth St. Pierre and Wanda Pillow, 96–113. New York: Routledge.

CIATEJ (Centro de Investigación y Asistencia en Tecnología y Diseño del Estado de Jalisco). 2012. *Diagnóstico Integral del Polígono de Fragilidad Ambiental (POFA) y su entorno 2012*. Guadalajara, Mexico: CIATEJ.

Citlalli de Dios, Vania. 2009. Solicitan otro año para tratar el agua. *Mural*, January 20.

CNDH (Comisión Nacional de los Derechos Humanos). 2010. *Recomendación No. 12/2010, sobre la omisión de cumplimiento de las normas de medio ambiente en agravio de V1*. Mexico City: CNDH.

CNN Expansión. 2016. *Las 500 empresas más importantes de México*. Mexico City: CNNMéxico.

COCURS (Consejo de Cuenca del río Santiago). 2021. *Programa Hídrico Regional 2021–2024, VIII Región Hidrológico-Administrativa Lerma Santiago Pacífico, Unidad de Planeación Río Santiago, versión preliminar*. Mexico City: CONAGUA.

COFEMER (Comisión Federal de Mejora Regulatoria). 2018a. JRL-NFG-LCF-B000180058. Mexico City: COFEMER. https://cofemersimir.gob.mx/expediente/21218/recibido/58940/B000180058.

COFEMER (Comisión Federal de Mejora Regulatoria). 2018b. Of. No. COFEME/18/0036. Mexico City: COFEMER. https://cofemersimir.gob.mx/expediente/21218/emitido/47550/COFEME_18_0036.

Cole, Matthew. 2004. Trade, the Pollution Haven Hypothesis and the Environmental Kuznets Curve: Examining the Linkages. *Ecological Economics* 48 (1) (January): 71–81. https://doi.org/10.1016/j.ecolecon.2003.09.007.

COMCE (Consejo Empresarial Mexicano de Comercio Exterior Inversión y Tecnología). 2010. Consejo Empresarial Mexicano de Comercio Exterior Inversión y Tecnología. http://www.protlcuem.gob.mx/swb/work/models/Protlcuem/Resource/39/1/images/SContreras.pdf.

Comisión de Medio Ambiente y Recursos Naturales. 2018. *Puntos de acuerdo turnados en la LXII Legislatura*. Mexico City: Senado de la República. https://www.senado.gob.mx/comisiones/medio_ambiente/puntos.php.

Composto, Claudia, and Mina Lorena Navarro. 2014. Claves de lectura para comprender el despojo y las luchas por los bienes comunes naturales en América Latina. In *Territorios en disputa: Despojo capitalista, luchas en defensa de los bienes comunes naturales y alternativas emancipatorias para América Latina*, edited by Claudia Composto and Mina Lorena Navarro, 33–75. Mexico City: Bajo Tierra Ediciones.

CONAGUA (Comisión Nacional del Agua). 2003. *Estadísticas del agua en México 2003*. Mexico City: CONAGUA.

CONAGUA (Comisión Nacional del Agua). 2011a. *Agenda del Agua 2030*. Mexico City: SEMARNAT.

CONAGUA (Comisión Nacional del Agua). 2011b. *Estadísticas del agua en México, edición 2011*. Mexico City: SEMARNAT.

CONAGUA (Comisión Nacional del Agua). 2014a. *Estadísticas del agua en México, edición 2014*. Mexico City: SEMARNAT.

CONAGUA (Comisión Nacional del Agua). 2014b. *Programa Nacional Hídrico 2013–2018*. Mexico City: SEMARNAT.

CONAGUA (Comisión Nacional del Agua). 2015. *Preservación y recuperación de acuíferos en México*. Mexico City: CONAGUA.

CONAGUA (Comisión Nacional del Agua). 2017. *Estadísticas del agua en México, edición 2017*. Mexico City: SEMARNAT.

CONAGUA (Comisión Nacional del Agua). 2018. *Estadísticas del agua en México, edición 2018*. Mexico City: SEMARNAT.

CONAGUA (Comisión Nacional del Agua). 2020. *Programa Nacional Hídrico, 2020–2024*. Mexico City: CONAGUA.

CONAGUA (Comisión Nacional del Agua). 2022a. *Sistema Nacional de Información del Agua*. http://sina.conagua.gob.mx/sina/.

CONAGUA (Comisión Nacional del Agua). 2022b. *Títulos y volúmenes de aguas nacionales y bienes inherentes por uso de agua clasificados a nivel nacional, Avance de inscripciones en el Registro Público de Derechos de Agua (Repda)*. https://www.gob.mx/conagua/acciones-y-programas/informacion-estadistica-62159.

CONAGUA (Comisión Nacional del Agua). 2022c. *Versión Pública de visitas de Inspección*. https://www.gob.mx/conagua/documentos/derechos-y-obligaciones-de-los-usuarios-ante-una-visita-de-inspeccion.

CONAMER (Comisión Nacional de Mejora Regulatoria). 2021. JCRL-LCF-AMMDC-AMB-B00212418. Mexico City: CONAMER. https://cofemersimir.gob.mx/expediente/21218/recibido/66224/B000212418.

CONAMER (Comisión Nacional de Mejora Regulatoria). n.d. No. Expediente: 04/0097/201217. https://cofemersimir.gob.mx/expedientes/21218.

CONCAMIN (Confederación de Cámaras Industriales de los Estados Unidos Mexicanos). 2016. *Informe de resultados periodo 2015/2016*. Mexico City: CONCAMIN.

References

Conde, Marta. 2014. Activism Mobilising Science. *Ecological Economics* 105 (September): 67–77. https://doi.org/10.1016/j.ecolecon.2014.05.012.

Corcoran, Emily, Christian Nellemann, Elaine Baker, Robert Bos, David Osborn, and Heidi Savelli, eds. 2010. *Sick Water? The Central Role of Wastewater Management in Sustainable Development: A Rapid Response Assessment.* Arendal, Norway: United Nations Environment Programme, UN-HABITAT, and GRID-Arendal.

Credit Suisse. 2014. *Global Wealth Report 2014.* Zurich, Switzerland: Credit Suisse. https://www.credit-suisse.com/about-us/en/reports-research/global-wealth-report .html.

Credit Suisse. 2021. *Global Wealth Report 2021.* Zurich, Switzerland: Credit Suisse. https://www.credit-suisse.com/about-us/en/reports-research/global-wealth-report .html.

Cypher, James. 2013. Neodevelopmentalism vs. Neoliberalism: Differential Evolutionary Institutional Structures and Policy Response in Brazil and Mexico. *Journal of Economic Issues* 47 (2) (June): 391–399. https://doi.org/10.2753/JEI0021-3624470212.

Cypher, James, and Raúl Delgado Wise. 2010. *Mexico's Economic Dilemma: The Developmental Failure of Neoliberalism.* New York: Rowman and Littlefield.

Dabat Latrubesse, Alejandro. 2004. Globalización, economía del conocimiento y nueva industria electrónica de exportación en México. *Revista Latinoamericana de Economía* 35 (137): 11–40. https://doi.org/10.22201/iiec.20078951e.2004.137.7532.

Dal Bó, Ernesto. 2006. Regulatory Capture: A Review. *Oxford Review of Economic Policy* 22 (2) (Summer): 203–225. https://doi.org/10.1093/oxrep/grj013.

Damania, Richard, Sébastien Desbureaux, Aude-Sophie Rodella, Jason Russ, and Esha Zaveri. 2019. *Quality Unknown: The Invisible Water Crisis.* Washington, DC: World Bank.

Dasgupta, Susmita, Benoit Laplante, Hua Wang, and David Wheeler. 2002. Confronting the Environmental Kuznets Curve. *Journal of Economic Perspectives* 16 (1) (Winter): 147–168. https://doi.org/10.1257/0895330027157.

de la Garza Toledo, Enrique. 2004. Manufacturing Neoliberalism: Industrial Relations, Trade Union Corporatism and Politics. In *Mexico in Transition: Neoliberal Globalism, the State and Civil Society,* edited by Gerardo Otero, 104–120. New York: Zed Books.

de la Peña, Andrés. 2020. Ventilan a 29 empresas que contaminan el río Santiago. *Partidero,* February 5. https://partidero.com/ventilan-a-29-empresas-que-contaminan -el-rio-santiago/.

De la Rosa, Eduardo. 2022. La NOM de aguas residuales provocará quiebras y encarecerá canasta básica: IP. *Milenio,* April 19. https://www.milenio.com/negocios/nom -aguas-residuales-provocara-quiebras-encarecera-canasta.

del Castillo, Agustín. 2008. Industrias de El Salto están al límite de la norma, pero en gran volumen. *Público*, February 28.

del Castillo, Agustín. 2016. Metales pesados, los asesinos silenciosos en el río Santiago. *Milenio*, September 12.

Delgado, Gian Carlo. 2012. Metabolismo social y minería. *Ecología Política* 43: 16–20.

Del Toro Carazo Abogados and Ramos and Hermosillo Abogados. 2015. Grupo Celanese Indagada por la PGR por Responsabilidad Penal Por Violaciones al Medio Ambiente. *PR Newswire*, May 8. https://www.prnewswire.com/news-releases/grupo-celanese-indagada -por-la-pgr-por-responsabilidad-penal-por-violaciones-al-medio-ambiente-informado -por-del-toro-carazo-abogados-y-ramos--hermosillo-abogados-503084851.html.

Demaria, Federico, François Schneider, Filka Skeulova, and Joan Martínez-Alier. 2013. What Is Degrowth? From an Activist Slogan to a Social Movement. *Environmental Values* 22 (2) (April): 191–215. https://doi.org/10.3197/096327113X13581561725194.

de Paula Sandoval, Francisco. 1981. *Obras sucesos y fantasías en el Lago Chapala*. Guadalajara, Mexico: Unidad Editorial, Gobierno de Jalisco.

Devault, Marjorie. 2006. Introduction: What Is Institutional Ethnography? *Social Problems* 53 (3) (August): 294–298. https://doi.org/10.1525/sp.2006.53.3.294.

Díaz Muñoz, José Guillermo. 2011. Las economías solidarias latinoamericanas como construcción de alternativas de resistencia y liberación desde abajo: Un estudio comparado de casos micro y macro de México, Argentina, Brasil y Bolivia (1989–2009). PhD dissertation, ITESO.

Dickens, Charles. 1905. *Hard Times*. New York: Charles Scribner's Sons.

Durán, Juan Manuel, Raquel Partida, and Alicia Torres. 1999. Cuencas hidrológicas y ejes industriales: El caso de la Cuenca Lerma-Chapala-Santiago. *Relaciones 80* 20 (Fall): 99–129.

Durán, Juan Manuel, and Alicia Torres. 2009. La sustentabilidad de la cuenca del río Santiago y su relación con la metropolización de Guadalajara. *Cultura, Tecnología y Patrimonio* 4 (7) (January–June): 5–31.

Durand, Jorge. 1985. Siglo y medio en el camino de la industrialización. In *Guadalajara, la gran ciudad de la pequeña industria*, edited by Patricia Arias, 159–189. Zamora, Mexico: Colegio de Michoacán.

Durand, Jorge. 1986. *Los obreros de Río Grande*. Zamora, Mexico: El Colegio de Michoacán.

Dussel Peters, Enrique, and Samuel Ortiz. 2015. *Monitor de la manufactura mexicana, año 10, número 11, febrero de 2015*. Mexico City: Universidad Nacional Autónoma de México.

Economist. 1992. Let Them Eat Pollution. *Economist*, February 8, 66.

References

Economy, Elizabeth. 2004. *The River Runs Black: The Environmental Challenge to China's Future*. Ithaca, NY: Cornell University Press.

Ehrlich, Paul R. 1968. *The Population Bomb*. London: Ballantine.

El Universal. 2016. Problema de contaminación por tipo de vehículos: Blumberg. *El Universal*, May 10. https://www.eluniversal.com.mx/articulo/nacion/sociedad/2016/05/10/problema-de-contaminacion-por-tipo-de-vehiculos-blumberg.

Enciso, Angélica, and Raúl Torres. 2008. Represión, respuesta gubernamental a los que defienden el medio ambiente. *La Jornada Jalisco*, May 30.

EPA (Environmental Protection Agency). 1991. *Mexican Environmental Laws, Regulations and Standards: Preliminary Report on EPA Findings*. Washington, DC: Office of Enforcement, EPA. https://nepis.epa.gov/Exe/ZyPURL.cgi?Dockey=90010O00.txt.

EPA (Environmental Protection Agency). 2002. *Toxicological Review of Phenol*. EPA/635/R-02/006. https://iris.epa.gov/static/pdfs/0088tr.pdf.

EPA (Environmental Protection Agency). 2022. Industrial Effluent Guidelines. https://www.epa.gov/eg/industrial-effluent-guidelines.

Escobar, Arturo. 1995. *Encountering Development: The Making and Unmaking of the Third World*. Princeton, NJ: Princeton University Press. Kobo edition.

Escobar, Arturo. 1996. Constructing Nature: Elements for a Poststructural Political Ecology. In *Liberation Ecologies: Environment, Development, Social Movements*, edited by Richard Peet and Michael Watts, 46–68. New York: Routledge.

Escobar, Arturo. 2005. El "postdesarrollo" como concepto y práctica social. In *Políticas de economía, ambiente y sociedad en tiempos de globalización*, edited by Daniel Mato, 17–32. Caracas, Venezuela: Facultad de Ciencias Económicas y Sociales, Universidad Central de Venezuela.

Esquivel Hernández, Gerardo. 2015. *Desigualdad extrema en México: Concentración del poder político y económico*. Mexico City: Oxfam México.

Estrada, Jesús. 2008. Sancionar al que contamine aguas, piden los industriales. *Público*, February 20.

Etzioni, Amitai. 2009. The Capture Theory of Regulations—Revisited. *Society* 46 (4): 319–323. https://doi.org/10.1007/s12115-009-9228-3.

European Commission. 2015. *Guide to Cost-Benefit Analysis of Investment Projects: Economic Appraisal Tool for Cohesion Policy 2014–2020*. Brussels: European Union. http://ec.europa.eu/regional_policy/sources/docgener/studies/pdf/cba_guide.pdf.

European Union. 2000. Directive 2000/60/EC. *Official Journal of the European Communities*, L. 327. https://eur-lex.europa.eu/resource.html?uri=cellar:5c835afb-2ec6-4577-bdf8-756d3d694eeb.0004.02/DOC_1&format=PDF.

Fagin, Dan. 2014. *Toms River: A Story of Science and Salvation*. New York: Bantam Books. Kobo edition.

Federal Ministry for the Environment, Nature Conservation and Nuclear Safety, Germany. 2004. *Promulgation of the New Version of the Ordinance on Requirements for the Discharge of Waste Water into Waters*. https://www.bmuv.de/fileadmin/bmu-import /files/pdfs/allgemein/application/pdf/wastewater_ordinance.pdf.

Ferrer, Mauricio. 2005. Confiables, los estudios de la UdeG, sobre Arcediano. *La gaceta*, November 28.

Ferrer, Mauricio. 2008. Miguel Ángel murió porque ingirió agua muy contaminada, expresó. *La Jornada Jalisco*, February 23.

Ferrer, Mauricio. 2012. Calderón se compromete a sanear el Santiago; cambiará de la noche a la mañana: Iglesias. *La Jornada Jalisco*, March 18.

Flextronics. 2011. *Flextronics Corporate Social and Environmental Responsibility Program Sustainability Report 2010/2011*. Singapore: Flextronics International.

Flextronics. 2015. *Flex 2015 Global Citizenship Report*. Singapore: Flextronics International.

Flextronics. 2018. *Sustainable Living: 2018 Sustainability Executive Report*. Singapore: Flextronics International.

Forbes. 2019. Billionaires 2019: Menos multimillonarios y menos riqueza a nivel global. *Forbes*, March 5. https://www.forbes.com.mx/billionaires-2019-menos-multimillonarios -y-menos-riqueza-a-nivel-global/.

Forbes. 2022. Concamin advierte afectación de 2.2 billones de pesos por nueva NOM de aguas residuales. *Forbes*, March 14. https://www.forbes.com.mx/concamin -advierte-afectacion-de-2-2-billones-de-pesos-por-nueva-nom-de-aguas-residuales/.

Fortune. n.d.-a. Global 500. *Fortune*. Accessed April 15, 2022. https://fortune.com /global500/2020/search/.

Fortune. n.d.-b. Global 500: Celanese. *Fortune*. Accessed April 15, 2022. https://for tune.com/company/celanese/fortune500/.

Fortune. n.d.-c. Global 500: Nestlé. *Fortune*. Accessed March 30, 2022. https://fortune .com/company/nestle/global500/.

Foster, John Bellamy. 2002. Capitalism and Ecology: The Nature of the Contradiction. *Monthly Review* 54 (4) (September): 6–16.

Foucault, Michel. 1980. Two Lectures. In *Power/Knowledge: Selected Interviews & Other Writings, 1972–1977*, edited by Colin Gordon, 78–108. New York: Pantheon Books.

Foucault, Michel. 1982. The Subject and Power. *Critical Inquiry* 8 (4) (Summer): 777–795.

References 299

Friedman, Milton. 1982. *Capitalism and Freedom*. Chicago: University of Chicago Press.

Gallagher, Kevin, and Lyuba Zarsky. 2007. *Enclave Economy: Foreign Investment and Sustainable Development in Mexico's Silicon Valley*. Cambridge, MA: MIT Press.

Gallardo, Juan. 2005. Estudio Ambiental del Ácido Sulfhídrico como contaminante del aire en las comunidades de Juanacatlán y El Salto, Jalisco, 2004–2005. Master's thesis, Universidad de Guadalajara.

Gandy, Matthew. 1999. Rethinking the Ecological Leviathan: Environmental Regulation in an Age of Risk. *Global Environmental Change* 9 (1) (April): 59–69. https://doi .org/10.1016/S0959-3780(98)00023-5.

Gobierno del Estado de Jalisco. 1974. *Jalisco: Estrategia de Desarrollo, Plan Industrial, Posibilidades de inversión*. Guadalajara, Mexico: Gobierno del Estado.

Gobierno del Estado de Jalisco. 2017. *Evaluación al Programa Cumplimiento Ambiental Voluntario: Evaluación de Consistencia y Resultados 2016*. Guadalajara, Mexico: Secretaría de Planeación, Administración y Finanzas.

Gobierno del Estado de Jalisco. 2022. Presupuesto de egresos. Guadalajara, Mexico: Secretaría de Administración. https://transparenciafiscal.jalisco.gob.mx/transparencia -fiscal/programatico_presupuestal/presupuesto-de-egresos.

Gómez-Meda, B. C., G. M. Zúñiga-González, L. V. Sánchez-Orozco, A. L. Zamora-Perez, J. P. Rojas-Ramírez, A. D. Rocha-Muñoz, A. A. Sobrevilla-Navarro, M. A. Arellano-Avelar, A. A. Guerrero-de León, J. S. Armendáriz-Borunda, and M. G. Sánchez-Parada. 2017. Buccal Micronucleus Cytome Assay of Populations under Chronic Heavy Metal and Other Metal Exposure along the Santiago River, Mexico. *Environmental Monitoring and Assessment* 189 (10): article 522. https://doi.org/10.1007 /s10661-017-6237-3.

González Corona, Elías. 1989. *El Salto, industria y urbanización de Guadalajara*. Cuadernos de Difusión Científica 15. Guadalajara, Mexico: Universidad de Guadalajara.

Greenberg, James, Thomas Weaver, Anne Browning-Aiken, and William Alexander. 2012. The Neoliberal Transformation of Mexico. In *Neoliberalism and Commodity Production in Mexico*, edited by Thomas Weaver, James Greenberg, William Alexander, and Anne Browning-Aiken, 1–31. Boulder: University Press of Colorado.

Greene, Joshua, and Solène Morvant-Roux. 2020. Social Reproduction, Ecological Dispossession and Dependency: Life beside the Río Santiago in Mexico. *Development and Change* 51 (6): 1481–1510. https://doi.org/10.1111/dech.12617.

Greenpeace Mexico. 2012a. *Metales pesados y contaminantes orgánicos en descargas de aguas residuales de la empresa Huntsman, en Atotonilquillo*. Mexico City: Greenpeace México.

Greenpeace Mexico. 2012b. *Ríos tóxicos en México: Hoja informativa*. Mexico City: Greenpeace México.

Greenpeace Mexico. 2016. *Alto a la catástrofe ecológica del río Santiago: Reporte técnico*. Mexico City: Greenpeace México.

Gudynas, Eduardo. 2013. Debates on Development and Its Alternatives in Latin America: A Brief Heterodox Guide. In *Beyond Development: Alternative Visions from Latin America*, edited by Miriam Lang and Dunia Mokrani, 15–39. Quito, Ecuador: Fundación Rosa Luxemburg.

Guillén, Héctor. 2013. México: De la sustitución de importaciones al nuevo modelo económico. *Comercio Exterior* 63 (4) (July and August): 34–60.

Haber, Stephen. 1993. La industrialización de México: Historiografía y análisis. *Historia mexicana* 42 (3): 649–688.

Haraway, Donna. 1988. Situated Knowledges: The Science Question in Feminism and the Privilege of Partial Perspective. *Feminist Studies* 14 (3) (Autumn): 575–599.

Hardin, Garrett. (1968) 2009. The Tragedy of the Commons. *Journal of Natural Resources Policy Research* 1 (3): 243–253. https://doi.org/10.1080/19390450903037302.

Harvey, David. 1996. *Justice, Nature and the Geography of Difference*. Malden, MA: Blackwell.

Harvey, David. 2003. *The New Imperialism*. New York: Oxford University Press.

Harvey, David. 2005. *A Brief History of Neoliberalism*. New York: Oxford University Press.

Hayek, Friedrich A. 1944. *The Road to Serfdom*. Chicago: University of Chicago Press.

Hettige, Hemamala, Muthukumara Mani, and David Wheeler. 1997. *Industrial Pollution in Economic Development: Kuznets Revisited*. Washington, DC: World Bank.

Heynen, Nik, James McCarthy, Scott Prudham, and Paul Robbins. 2007. Introduction: False Promises. In *Neoliberal Environments: False Promises and Unnatural Consequences*, edited by Nik Heynen, James McCarthy, Scott Prudham, and Paul Robbins, 1–21. New York: Routledge.

Hogenboom, Barbara. 2007. The Changing Politics of Lobbying: Private Sector Organizations in Mexico. *Journal of Public Affairs* 14 (3): 296–309. https://doi.org/10.1002/pa.1456.

Hornborg, Alf. 2009. Zero-Sum World: Challenges in Conceptualizing Environmental Load Displacement and Ecologically Unequal Exchange in the World-System. *International Journal of Comparative Sociology* 50 (3–4): 237–262. https://doi.org/10.1177/0020715209105141.

References 301

Huntsman. 2010. *We See a Better World: 2010 Sustainability Report*. Woodlands, TX: Huntsman. https://d1io3yog0oux5.cloudfront.net/_88bef8faca9b14bb737538f4792 a719e/huntsman/db/861/10264/pdf/SustainabilityReport2010.pdf.

Huntsman. 2012. *Conversations about Sustainability: 2012 Sustainability Report*. Woodlands, TX: Huntsman. https://d1io3yog0oux5.cloudfront.net/_88bef8faca9b14bb73 7538f4792a719e/huntsman/db/861/10262/pdf/SustainabilityReport2012.pdf.

Huntsman. 2014. *Water Dependent, Water Responsible: Focused on a Precious Resource, 2014 Sustainability Report*. Woodlands, TX: Huntsman. https://d1io3yog0oux5.cloud front.net/_88bef8faca9b14bb737538f4792a719e/huntsman/db/861/10260/pdf /SustainabilityReport2014.pdf.

Huntsman. 2015. Huntsman Textile Effects Commemorates 50th Anniversary of Its Mexico Manufacturing Facility. October 13. https://www.huntsman.com/about /textile-effects/news/detail/12679/huntsman-textile-effects-commemorates-50th -anniversary-of.

Huntsman. 2017. *Bringing Chemistry to Life, Growth and Sustainability in Asia Pacific: 2017 Sustainability Report*. Woodlands, TX: Huntsman. https://d1io3yog0oux5.cloud front.net/_88bef8faca9b14bb737538f4792a719e/huntsman/db/861/10257/pdf /SustainabilityReport2017.pdf.

Huntsman. 2019. *Huntsman 2019 Annual Report*. Woodlands, TX: Huntsman. https:// d1io3yog0oux5.cloudfront.net/_88bef8faca9b14bb737538f4792a719e/huntsman /db/735/7886/annual_report/Huntsman+2019+Annual+Report++Web+Posting+Book marked+PDF.pdf.

IACHR (Inter-American Commission on Human Rights). 2020. *Resolution 7/20, Precautionary Measure No. 708-19*. https://www.oas.org/en/iachr/decisions/pdf/2020/7-20 MC708-19-ME.pdf.

IBRD (International Bank for Reconstruction and Development). 1992. *World Development Report 1992: Development and the Environment*. Oxford: Oxford University Press.

IFAI (Instituto Federal de Acceso a la Información y Protección de Datos). 2012. *Resolución de recurso de revisión por solicitud folio 1611100006011*. Mexico City: IFAI.

IIEG (Instituto de Información Estadística y Geográfica). 2016. *Industria eléctrica, ficha sectorial, septiembre 2016*. Guadalajara, Mexico: IIEG.

IIEG (Instituto de Información Estadística y Geográfica). 2019. *Producto Interno Bruto por entidad federativa y sector de actividad, 2003–2018, IIEG*. Guadalajara, Mexico: IIEG.

ILO (International Labour Organization). 2018. *Global Wage Report 2018/19: What Lies behind Gender Pay Gaps*. Geneva: ILO. https://www.ilo.org/wcmsp5/groups/pub lic/---dgreports/---dcomm/---publ/documents/publication/wcms_650553.pdf.

IMTA (Instituto Mexicano de Tecnología del Agua). 2006. *La importancia de incluir análisis de toxicidad en descargas industriales y municipales que afectan a los cuerpos receptores.* Jiutepec, Mexico: IMTA.

IMTA (Instituto Mexicano de Tecnología del Agua) and CEA (Comisión Estatal del Agua) Jalisco. 2011. *Actualización del estudio de calidad del agua del Río Santiago (desde su nacimiento en el Lago de Chapala, hasta la Presa Santa Rosa).* Jiutepec, Mexico: IMTA.

INEGI (Instituto Nacional de Estadística Geografía e Informática). 1984. *X Censo General de Población y Vivienda, 1980, Estado de Jalisco.* Aguascalientes, Mexico: INEGI.

INEGI (Instituto Nacional de Estadística Geografía e Informática). 1991. *Jalisco Resultados Definitivos, Datos por Localidad, XI Censo General de Población y Vivienda, 1990.* Aguascalientes, Mexico: INEGI.

INEGI (Instituto Nacional de Estadística Geografía e Informática). 2016. *Directorio Estadístico Nacional de Unidades Económicas.* Aguascalientes, Mexico: INEGI. https:// www.inegi.org.mx/app/mapa/denue/.

INEGI (Instituto Nacional de Estadística Geografía e Informática). 2017. *Anuario estadístico y geográfico de Jalisco 2017.* Aguascalientes, Mexico: INEGI. http://internet .contenidos.inegi.org.mx/contenidos/Productos/prod_serv/contenidos/espanol /bvinegi/productos/nueva_estruc/anuarios_2017/702825092085.pdf.

INEGI (Instituto Nacional de Estadística Geografía e Informática). 2019. *Censos Económicos 2019.* Aguascalientes, Mexico: INEGI. https://www.inegi.org.mx/programas /ce/2019/.

INEGI (Instituto Nacional de Estadística Geografía e Informática). 2020a. *Censo de Población y Vivienda 2020.* Aguascalientes, Mexico: INEGI. https://www.inegi.org.mx /programas/ccpv/2020/.

INEGI (Instituto Nacional de Estadística Geografía e Informática). 2020b. *Censos económicos 2019: Micro, pequeña, mediana y gran empresa: Estratificación de los establecimientos.* Aguascalientes, Mexico: INEGI. https://www.inegi.org.mx/contenidos /productos/prod_serv/contenidos/espanol/bvinegi/productos/nueva_estruc /702825198657.pdf.

INEGI (Instituto Nacional de Estadística Geografía e Informática). 2021a. *Balanza Comercial de Mercancías de México.* Aguascalientes, Mexico: INEGI. https://www.inegi .org.mx/programas/comext/#Tabulados.

INEGI (Instituto Nacional de Estadística Geografía e Informática). 2021b. *PIB y cuentas nacionales.* Aguascalientes, Mexico: INEGI. https://www.inegi.org.mx/temas/pib /#Tabulados.

Informador. 1973. Alto porcentaje de contaminación en las aguas del Lerma-Santiago. *Informador,* January 24.

References

Informador. 1974. Nivel de contaminación que presenta el río Santiago. *Informador,* April 1.

Informador. 2007. Pobladores exigen declaratoria de emergencia en Juanacatlán y El Salto. *Informador,* April 26.

Informador. 2010. Anuncia Semades protección de la cuenca de El Ahogado. *Informador,* February 16. http://www.informador.com.mx/jalisco/2010/179066/6/anuncia-semades -proteccion-de-la-cuenca-de-el-ahogado.htm.

Informador. 2012. La CEA prepara denuncias penales por daño ambiental. *Informador,* December 6. http://www.informador.com.mx/jalisco/2012/422540/6/la-cea-prepara -denuncias-penales-por-dano-ambiental.htm.

Informador. 2019. Pactan cierre de basurero Los Laureles. *Informador,* September 18. https://www.informador.mx/Pactan-cierre-de-basurero-Los-Laureles-l201909180001 .html.

Irmer, Ulrich, and B. Kirschbaum. 2010. *Water Resource Management in Germany. Part 1: Fundamentals.* Dessau-Roßlau, Germany: Umweltbundesamt.

Jenkins, Rhys, and Alfonso Mercado García. 2008. Ambiente e industria en México. In *Ambiente e industria en México: Tendencias, regulación y comportamiento ambiental,* edited by Rhys Jenkins and Alfonso Mercado García, 15–33. Mexico City: El Colegio de México.

Jiménez, Blanca. 2001. *La contaminación ambiental en México: Causas, efectos y tecnología apropiada.* Mexico City: Limusa, Colegio de Ingenierios Ambientales de México, and FEMISCA.

Jiménez, Blanca. 2007. Información y calidad del agua en México. *Trayectorias* 9 (24): 45–56.

Jolly, Jasper. 2019. Volkswagen Emissions Scandal: Mass Lawsuit Opens in Germany. *Guardian,* September 30. https://www.theguardian.com/business/2019/sep/30/volks wagen-emissions-scandal-mass-lawsuit-opens-in-germany.

Jones, Samantha. 2002. Social Constructionism and the Environment: Through the Quagmire. *Global Environmental Change* 12 (4) (December): 247–251. https://doi.org /10.1016/S0959-3780(02)00062-6.

Kallis, Giorgos. 2011. In Defense of Degrowth. *Ecological Economics* 70 (5) (March): 873–880. https://doi.org/10.1016/j.ecolecon.2010.12.007.

Kao. 2010. *Kao CSR/Sustainability Report 2010.* Tokyo: Kao. https://www.kao.com /content/dam/sites/kao/www-kao-com/global/en/sustainability/pdf/csr_sustainabil ity_2010_all.pdf.

Kao. 2013. *Kao Sustainability Report 2013.* Tokyo: Kao. https://www.kao.com/content /dam/sites/kao/www-kao-com/global/en/sustainability/pdf/sustainability2013_e_all.pdf.

Kao. 2015. *Kao Sustainability Report 2015: Highlights*. Tokyo: Kao. https://www.kao.com/content/dam/sites/kao/www-kao-com/global/en/sustainability/pdf/sustainability2015_e_all.pdf.

Kao. 2019. *Kao Sustainability Data Book 2019*. Tokyo: Kao. https://www.kao.com/content/dam/sites/kao/www-kao-com/global/en/sustainability/pdf/sustainability2019-e-all.pdf.

Krausmann, Fridolin, Christian Lauk, Willi Haas, and Dominik Wiedenhofer. 2018. From Resource Extraction to Outflows of Wastes and Emissions: The Socioeconomic Metabolism of the Global Economy, 1900–2015. *Global Environmental Change* 52: 131–140. https://doi.org/10.1016/j.gloenvcha.2018.07.003.

Kuznets, Simon. 1955. Economic Growth and Income Inequality. *American Economic Review* 45 (1) (March): 1–28.

Kwan Yuk, Pan. 2016. Want Cheap Labour? Head to Mexico, Not China. *Financial Times*, January 14. https://www.ft.com/content/bddc8121-a7a0-3788-a74c-cd2b49cd3230.

Lara, Guadalupe, and Cindy McCulligh. 2014. *Yo vi a mi pueblo llorar: Historias de la lucha contra la presa de Arcediano*. Guadalajara, Mexico: Instituto Mexicano para el Desarrollo Comunitario.

Lather, Patti. 1992. Critical Frames in Educational Research: Feminist and Poststructural Perspectives. *Theory into Practice* 31 (2): 87–99. https://doi.org/10.1080/00405849209543529.

Latouche, Serge. 2008. *La apuesta por el decrecimiento: ¿Cómo salir del imaginario dominante?* Barcelona: Icaria & Antrazyt.

Laufer, William. 2003. Social Accountability and Corporate Greenwashing. *Journal of Business Ethics* 43 (3) (March): 253–261. https://doi.org/10.1023/A:1022962719299.

Legislatura XLVIII. 1972. *Diario de los debates de la Cámara de Diputados del Congreso de los Estados Unidos Mexicanos, 17 octubre 1972*. http://cronica.diputados.gob.mx/DDebates/48/3er/Ord/19721017.html.

Lezama, Cecilia. 2004. *Percepción del riesgo y comportamiento ambiental en la industria*. Guadalajara, Mexico: El Colegio de Jalisco.

Lezama, José Luis. 2016. Simulación y mitos en el combate a la contaminación. *Aristegui Noticias*, May 10. http://aristeguinoticias.com/1005/mexico/simulacion-y-mitos-en-el-combate-a-la-contaminacion-jose-luis-lezama/.

Liverman, Diana, and Silvina Vilas. 2006. Neoliberalism and the Environment in Latin America. *Annual Review of Environment and Resources* 31:327–363. https://doi.org/10.1146/annurev.energy.29.102403.140729.

References

305

Lomelí, Daniela. 2015. Entre nostalgía y contaminación. *La Cascada*, May 8. https://www.cascadanoticias.com/noticias/educacion-y-cultura/educacion/entre-nostalgia-y-contaminacion.

López, Miguel Ángel, and Blanca Nelly Flores. 2010. Industria. In *El agua en México: Cauces y encauces*, edited by Blanca Jiménez, María Luisa Torregrosa, and Luis Aboites, 179–202. Mexico City: Academia Mexicana de Ciencias.

Lora-Wainwright, Anna. 2021. *Resigned Activism: Living with Pollution in Rural China*. Rev. ed. Cambridge, MA: MIT Press.

Mahayni, Basil. 2013. Producing Crisis: Hegemonic Debates, Mediations and Representations of Water Scarcity. In *Contemporary Water Governance in the Global South: Scarcity, Marketization and Participation*, edited by Leila Harris, Jacqueline Goldin, and Christopher Sneddon, 35–44. New York: Routledge.

MAPDER (Movimiento Mexicano de Afectados por las Presas y en Defensa de los Ríos). 2005. *Declaración de Arcediano*. Arcediano, Mexico. https://archive.internationalrivers.org/sites/default/files/attached-files/mapder_segundo.pdf.

Mares, Marco. 2021. NOM-001: Tsunami de aguas residuales. *El Economista*, August 30. https://www.eleconomista.com.mx/opinion/NOM-001-tsunami-de-aguas-residuales-20210830-0146.html.

Markowitz, Gerald, and David Rosner. 2013. *Deceit and Denial: The Deadly Politics of Industrial Pollution*. Berkeley: University of California Press.

Martín, Rubén. 2008. Un grupo ciudadano ha contabilizado 477 casos en la zona desde junio a la fecha. *Público*, February 8.

Martínez, C. M. A., and G. A. Gavilán. 2015. *Elementos para la creación del Registro Nacional de Sustancias Químicas*. Mexico City: Instituto Nacional de Ecología y Cambio Climático.

Martínez-Alier, Joan. 2002. *The Environmentalism of the Poor: A Study of Ecological Conflicts and Valuation*. Northampton, MA: Edward Elgar.

Martínez-Alier, Joan. 2008. Conflictos ecológicos y justicia Ambiental. *Papeles de relaciones ecosociales y cambio global* 103 (2008): 11–27.

Martínez-Alier, Joan, and Jordi Roca Jusmet. 2000. *Economía ecológica y política ambiental*. Mexico City: Fondo de Cultura Económica.

Martínez-Alier, Joan, Leah Temper, and Federico Demaria. 2014. Social Metabolism and Environmental Conflicts in India. *Indi@logs* 1 (1): 51–83.

Maxwell, Kerry. 2005. Buzzword: Greenwash also Green-wash. *Macmillan Dictionary*, January 10. https://www.macmillandictionary.com/buzzword/entries/greenwash.html.

McCarthy, James. 2004. Privatizing Conditions of Production: Trade Agreements as Neoliberal Environmental Governance. *Geoforum* 35 (3) (May): 327–341. https://doi.org/10.1016/j.geoforum.2003.07.002.

McCarthy, James, and Scott Prudham. 2004. Neoliberal Nature and the Nature of Neoliberalism. *Geoforum* 35 (3) (May): 275–283. https://doi.org/10.1016/j.geoforum.2003.07.003.

McCulligh, Cindy. 2011. Un mal con muchas máscaras: Las diversas caras de la privatización. In *Las turbias aguas de la privatización en México*, edited by Carmen Díaz and Claudia Campero, 9–16. Mexico City: Coalición de Organizaciones Mexicanas por el Derecho al Agua.

McCulligh, Cindy. 2022. Wastewater and Wishful Thinking: Treatment Plants to "Revive" the Santiago River in Mexico. *Environment and Planning E: Nature and Space*, September 18. https://doi.org/10.1177/25148486221125230.

McCulligh, Cindy, Luis Arellano-García, and Diego Casas-Beltrán. 2020. Unsafe Waters: The Hydrosocial Cycle of Drinking Water in Western Mexico. *Local Environment* 25 (8): 576–596. https://doi.org/10.1080/13549839.2020.1805598.

McCulligh, Cindy, Juan Carlos Páez, and Gerardo Moya. 2007. *Mártires del Río Santiago: Informe sobre violaciones al derecho a la salud y a un medio ambiente sano en Juanacatlán y El Salto, Jalisco, México*. Guadalajara, Mexico: Instituto Mexicano para el Desarrollo Comunitario.

McCulligh, Cindy, and Xavier Romo, dirs. 2003. *Creando desiertos: Historias del Lago de Chapala y el Alto Santiago*. Guadalajara, Mexico: Instituto Mexicano para el Desarrollo Comunitario. 30 mins. VHS.

McCulligh, Cindy, Darcy Tetreault, and Paulina Martínez. 2012. Conflicto y contaminación: El movimiento socio-ecológico en torno al Río Santiago. In *Gobernanza y Gestión del Agua en el Occidente de México: La metrópoli de Guadalajara*, edited by Heliodoro Ochoa and Hans-Joachim Bürkner, 129–172. Tlaquepaque, Mexico: ITESO.

McDonough, William, and Michael Braungart. 1998. The NEXT Industrial Revolution. *Atlantic*, October. http://www.theatlantic.com/magazine/archive/1998/10/the-next-industrial-revolution/304695/.

Meadows, Donnella, Dennis Meadows, Jørgen Randers, and William Behrens. 1972. *The Limits to Growth*. New York: Universe Books.

Medina-Ross, Verónica. 2005. Los negocios y el ambiente: Una relación cambiante. In *Sustentabilidad ambiental en la industria: Conceptos, tendencias internacionales y experiencias mexicanas*, edited by Alfonso Mercado García and Ismael Aguilar Barajas, 63–106. Mexico City: El Colegio de México.

Medina-Ross, Verónica. 2008. La gestión ambiental voluntaria en el sector químico en México. In *Ambiente e industria en México: Tendencias, regulación y comportamiento*

References

ambiental, edited by Rhys Jenkins and Alfonso Mercado García, 197–246. Mexico City: El Colegio de México.

Mehta, Lyla. 2007. Whose Scarcity? Whose Property? The Case of Water in Western India. *Land Use Policy* 24 (4) (October): 654–663. https://doi.org/10.1016/j.landusepol.2006.05.009.

Meléndez, Violeta. 2016. Solapa Conagua contaminación del río Santiago. *El Diario NTR: Periodismo crítico*, November 28. http://www.ntrguadalajara.com/post.php?id_nota=57732.

Menell, Peter. 1992. Institutional Fantasylands: From Scientific Management to Free Market Environmentalism. *Harvard Journal of Law and Public Policy* 15 (2): 489–510. https://doi.org/10.2139/ssrn.2222384.

Mercado García, Alfonso, and María Lourdes Blanco. 2005. ¿Exigencia gubernamental y responsabilidad corporativa? Un estudio sobre las normas ecológicas aplicables a la industria mexicana. In *Sustentabilidad ambiental en la industria: Conceptos, tendencias internacionales y experiencias mexicanas*, edited by Alfonso Mercado García and Ismael Aguilar Barajas, 217–246. Mexico City: El Colegio de México.

Mexichem. 2010. *Sustainable Development Report 2010*. Mexico City: Mexichem. https://www.orbia.com/4a0df8/siteassets/6.-sustainability/sustainability-reports/2010/desarrollosustentable2010_ing.pdf.

Mexichem. 2015. *Integrated Report 2015 Mexichem*. Mexico City: Mexichem. https://www.orbia.com/4a0e3b/siteassets/6.-sustainability/sustainability-reports/2015/mexichem_2015-final.pdf.

Michaels, David, and Celeste Monforton. 2005. Manufacturing Uncertainty: Contested Science and the Protection of the Public's Health and Environment. *American Journal of Public Health* 95 (S1) (July): S39–S48. https://doi.org/10.2105/AJPH.2004.043059.

Miliband, Ralph. 1969. *The State in Capitalist Society*. London: Weidenfeld and Nicolson.

Milne, Markus, and Rob Gray. 2013. W(h)ither Ecology? The Triple Bottom Line, the Global Reporting Initiative, and Corporate Sustainability Reporting. *Journal of Business Ethics* 118: 13–29. https://doi.org/10.1007/s10551-012-1543-8.

Mitsui. 2014. *Newsletter to Shareholders: 2014 Winter*. https://www.mitsui.com/jp/en/ir/library/shareholder/__icsFiles/afieldfile/2015/07/16/en_kabu14wi.pdf.

Moctezuma Barragán, Pedro. 2020. La iniciativa ciudadana de Ley General de Aguas: Hacia un cambio de paradigma. *Argumentos* 33 (93): 109–130. https://doi.org/10.24275/uamxoc-dcsh/argumentos/202093-05.

Mol, Arthur, Gert Spaargaren, and David Sonnenfeld. 2013. Ecological Modernization Theory: Taking Stock, Moving Forward. In *Routledge International Handbook of*

Social and Environmental Change, edited by Stewart Lockie, David Sonnenfeld, and Dana Fisher, 15–30. New York: Routledge.

Molle, François, Peter Mollinga, and Philippus Wester. 2009. Hydraulic Bureaucracies and the Hydraulic Mission: Flows of Water, Flows of Power. *Water Alternatives* 2 (3): 328–349.

Mora, Yunuen. 2019. Firman pacto "voluntario" para saneamiento del Río Santiago. *Informador*, August 7. https://www.informador.mx/jalisco/Firman-pacto-voluntario -para-saneamiento-del-Rio-Santiago-20190807-0115.html.

Moreno-Brid, Juan Carlos. 2013. Industrial Policy: A Missing Link in Mexico's Quest for Export-Led Growth. *Latin American Policy* 4 (2): 216–237. https://doi.org/10.1111/lamp .12015.

Moreno-Brid, Juan Carlos, and Jaime Ros. 2009. *Development and Growth in the Mexican Economy: A Historical Perspective*. New York: Oxford University Press.

Moreno Vázquez, José Luis, Boris Marañón, and Dania López. 2010. Los acuíferos sobreexplotados: Origen, crisis y gestión social. In *El agua en México: Cauces y encauces*, edited by Blanca Jiménez Cisneros, María Luisa Torregrosa, and Luis Aboites, 79–115. Mexico City: Academia Mexicana de Ciencias and CONAGUA.

Morin, Edgar. 1990. *Introducción al pensamiento complejo*. Paris: Ediciones ESF.

Morris, Regan. 2016. Nestle: Bottling Water in Drought-Hit California. BBC News, May 3. http://www.bbc.com/news/business-36161580.

Mumme, Stephen. 1992. Maintenance and Environmental Reform in Mexico: Salinas's Preemptive Strategy. *Latin American Perspectives* 19 (1) (Winter): 123–143.

Navarro, Mina Lorena. 2015. *Luchas por lo común: Antagonismo social contra el despojo capitalista de los bienes naturales en México*. Mexico City: Bajo Tierra.

Nestlé. 2010. *Nestlé Creating Shared Value Update 2010*. Vevey, Switzerland: Nestlé. https://www.nestle.com/sites/default/files/asset-library/documents/library/documents /corporate_social_responsibility/nestle_creating_shared_value_update_2010.pdf.

Nestlé. 2012. *Nestlé in Society: Creating Shared Value and Meeting Our Commitments 2012*. Vevey, Switzerland: Nestlé. https://www.nestle.com/sites/default/files/asset -library/documents/library/documents/corporate_social_responsibility/nestle-csv-full -report-2012-en.pdf.

Nestlé. 2015. *Nestlé in Society: Creating Shared Value and Meeting Our Commitments 2015*. Vevey, Switzerland: Nestlé. https://www.nestle.com/sites/default/files/asset-libra ry/documents/library/documents/corporate_social_responsibility/nestle-csv-full -report-2015-en.pdf.

Nestlé. 2018. *Creating Shared Value and Meeting Our Commitments 2018*. Vevey, Switzerland: Nestlé. https://www.nestle.com/sites/default/files/2020-10/nestle-creating -shared-value-summary-report-2018-en.pdf.

References

Novak, William J. 2014. A Revisionist History of Regulatory Capture. In *Preventing Regulatory Capture: Special Interest Influence and How to Limit It*, edited by Daniel Carpenter and David Moss, 25–48. New York: Cambridge University Press.

Nuño, Analy S. 2008. No se sancionará a empresas que no cumplan: Conagua. *La Jornada Jalisco*, November 13.

Occupational Knowledge International and Fronteras Comunes. 2011. *Exportando riesgos: Envíos de baterías de plomo usadas desde Estados Unidos hacia México aprovechan la debilidad de las normas de protección ambiental y de salud de los trabajadores*. San Francisco: Occupational Knowledge International. http://www.okinternational.org/docs/ExportingHazards_Spanish.pdf.

O'Connor, David, and David Turnham. 1992. *Managing the Environment in Developing Countries*. Policy Brief No. 2. OECD Development Center. https://doi.org/10.1787/480585052668.

O'Connor, James. 1994. Is Sustainable Capitalism Possible? In *Is Capitalism Sustainable? Political Economy and the Politics of Ecology*, edited by Martin O'Connor, 152–175. New York: Guilford.

OECD (Organisation for Economic Co-operation and Development). 1992. *The Polluter-Pays Principle: OECD Analyses and Recommendations*. Paris: OECD. http://www.oecd.org/officialdocuments/publicdisplaydocumentpdf/?cote=OCDE/GD(92)81&docLanguage=En.

OECD (Organisation for Economic Co-operation and Development). 1998. *OECD Environmental Performance Reviews: Mexico 1998*. Paris: OECD.

OECD (Organisation for Economic Co-operation and Development). 2000. *OECD Reviews of Regulatory Reform: Regulatory Reform in Mexico 1999*. Paris: OECD.

OECD (Organisation for Economic Co-operation and Development). 2003. *OECD Environmental Performance Reviews: Mexico 2003*. Paris: OECD.

OECD (Organisation for Economic Co-operation and Development). 2004. *OECD Reviews of Regulatory Reform: Mexico Progress in Implementing Regulatory Reform*. Paris: OECD.

OECD (Organisation for Economic Co-operation and Development). 2013. *OECD Environmental Performance Reviews: Mexico 2013*. Paris: OECD.

OHCHR (Office of the United Nations High Commissioner for Human Rights). 2016. *Declaración del Grupo de trabajo de Naciones Unidas sobre empresas y derechos humanos al final de su visita a México*. Mexico City: OHCHR. https://hchr.org.mx/relatorias_grupos/declaracion-del-grupo-de-trabajo-de-naciones-unidas-sobre-empresas-y-derechos-humanos-al-final-de-su-visita-a-mexico-ciudad-de-mexico-7-de-septiembre-de-2016/.

Olsen, Douglas, and Gustavo Saltiel. 2007. Water Resources—Averting a Water Crisis in Mexico. In *Mexico 2006–2012: Creating the Foundations for Equitable Growth*,

219–318. Washington, DC: World Bank. http://documents.worldbank.org/curated/en/44650146877456646/pdf/P0948670English0Public.pdf.

Olvera, Dulce. 2020. Funcionarios en Jalisco sabían el daño que el río Santiago le hizo a los niños. ONGs: Deben ir a prisión. *Sin embargo*, February 2. https://www.sinembargo.mx/02-02-2020/3720289.

Orbia. 2018. *Sustainability Report 2018*. Mexico City: Orbia. https://www.orbia.com/sustainability/sustainability-reports/.

Ordóñez, Sergio. 2006. Crisis y restructuración de la industria electrónica mundial y reconversión en México. *Comercio Exterior* 56 (7): 550–564.

O'Rourke, Dara. 2004a. *Community-Driven Regulation: Balancing Development and the Environment in Vietnam*. Cambridge, MA: MIT Press.

O'Rourke, Dara. 2004b. *Opportunities and Obstacles for Corporate Social Responsibility Reporting in Developing Countries*. Washington, DC: World Bank Group.

Ortega, J. 2010. Agua, protagonista principal en la vida de una empresa. *Ganar-Ganar*, November/December.

Ostrom, Elinor. 1990. *Governing the Commons: The Evolution of Institutions for Collective Action*. New York: Cambridge University Press.

Oxfam México. 2020. *Tiempo para el cuidado: El trabajo de cuidados y la crisis global de desigualdad*. Mexico City: Oxfam México. https://oxfammexico.org/tiempo-para-el-cuidado-el-trabajo-de-cuidados-y-la-crisis-global-de-desigualdad/.

Oxiteno. 2018. *Sustainability Report 2018*. https://cdn.oxiteno.com/links/Relatorio+de+Sustentabilidade+2018+ENG.pdf.

Padilla, Emilio. 2002. Intergenerational Equity and Sustainability. *Ecological Economics* 41 (1) (April): 69–83. https://doi.org/10.1016/S0921-8009(02)00026-5.

Palacios, Juan José. 1992. Guadalajara: ¿Valle del Silicio mexicano? La industria electrónica en un área que se abre a la exportación. *Revista EURE* 18 (55): 47–59.

Palaniappan, Meena, Peter Gleick, Lucy Allen, Michael Cohen, Juliet Christian-Smith, and Courtney Smith. 2010. *Clearing the Waters: A Focus on Water Quality Solutions*. Nairobi, Kenya: United Nations Environment Programme.

Palomero, R. 2007. Impresiona contaminación del río Santiago a TLA. *Público*, October 8.

Parra, Francisco Javier. 2006. Signos, síntomas y concentraciones de tiosulfatos urinarios, asociados a exposición al ácido sulfhídrico, como principal contaminante atmosférico, en niños escolares de la localidad de Juanacatlán y El Salto Jalisco. Master's thesis, Universidad Autónoma de México.

References   311

Patronato de Conservación y Fomento del Lago de Chapala. 1997. *El río Lerma Santiago.* Guadalajara, Mexico: Editorial Ágata.

Paz, María Fernanda. 2012. Deterioro y resistencias: Conflictos socioambientales en México. In *Conflictos socioambientales y alternativas de la sociedad civil,* edited by Darcy Tetreault, Heliodoro Ochoa, and Eduardo Hernández, 27–48. Tlaquepaque, Mexico: ITESO.

Paz, María Fernanda. 2014. Conflictos socioambientales en México: ¿Qué está en disputa? In *Conflictos, conflictividades y movilizaciones socioambientales en México: Problemas comunes, lecturas diversas,* edited by María Fernanda Paz and Nicholas Risdell, 13–58. Mexico City: Miguel Ángel Porrúa.

Peck, Jamie. 2010. *Constructions of Neoliberal Reason.* New York: Oxford University Press.

Pellow, David. 2001. Environmental Justice and the Political Process: Movements, Corporations, and the State. *Sociological Quarterly* 42 (1): 47–67. https://doi.org/10.1111/j.1533-8525.2001.tb02374.x.

Pellow, David. 2006. Transnational Alliances and Global Politics: New Geographies of Urban Environmental Justice Struggles. In *In the Nature of Cities: Urban Political Ecology and the Politics of Urban Metabolism,* edited by Nik Heynen, Maria Kaika, and Erik Swyngedouw, 216–233. New York: Routledge.

Peregrina, Angélica. 1994. *Chapala: Visto por viajeros.* Guadalajara, Mexico: El Colegio de Jalisco.

Pérez, Matilde. 2007. Habitantes de Jalisco claman ayuda al TLA; el río Santiago, "fuente de muerte." *La Jornada Jalisco,* October 11.

Perz, Stephen. 2007. Reformulating Modernization-Based Environmental Social Theories: Challenges on the Road to an Interdisciplinary Environmental Science. *Society and Natural Resources* 20 (5): 415–430. https://doi.org/10.1080/08941920701211777.

Polanyi, Karl. (1944) 2001. *The Great Transformation: The Political and Economic Origins of Our Time.* Boston: Beacon Press.

Porter, Michael. 1990. The Competitive Advantage of Nations. *Harvard Business Review* (March–April): 73–91.

Porter, Michael, Greg Hills, Marc Pfitzer, Sonja Patscheke, and Elizabeth Hawkins. 2012. *Measuring Shared Value: How to Unlock Value by Linking Social and Business Results.* San Francisco: FSG. http://www.fsg.org/publications/measuring-shared-value.

Porter, Michael, and Mark Kramer. 2011. Creating Shared Value: How to Reinvent Capitalism—and Unleash a Wave of Innovation and Growth. *Harvard Business Review* (January–February): 62–77.

PPT (Permanent Peoples' Tribunal). 2013. *Dictamen de la audiencia temática "Devastación ambiental y derechos de los pueblos."* Mexico City: PPT. https://www.tppmexico

.org/dictamen-de-la-audiencia-tematica-devastacion-ambiental-y-derechos-de-los-pueblos/.

PROFEPA (Procuraduría Federal de Protección al Ambiente). 2014. *Busca PROFEPA estímulos fiscales para empresas que se certifiquen en materia ambiental*. Mexico City: PROFEPA. http://www.Profepa.gob.mx/innovaportal/v/6228/1/mx/busca_Profepa_estimulos_fiscales_para_empresas_que_se_certifiquen_en_materia_ambiental.html.

PROFEPA (Procuraduría Federal de Protección al Ambiente). 2016. *Informe de Actividades 2015*. Mexico City: PROFEPA.

PROFEPA (Procuraduría Federal de Protección al Ambiente). 2017. *Informe de Actividades 2016*. Mexico City: PROFEPA.

PROFEPA (Procuraduría Federal de Protección al Ambiente). 2018. *Informe de Actividades 2017*. Mexico City: PROFEPA.

PROFEPA (Procuraduría Federal de Protección al Ambiente). 2019. *Informe de Actividades 2018*. Mexico City: PROFEPA.

PROFEPA (Procuraduría Federal de Protección al Ambiente). 2020. *Informe de Actividades 2019*. Mexico City: PROFEPA.

PROFEPA (Procuraduría Federal de Protección al Ambiente). 2021a. *Informe de Actividades 2020*. Mexico City: PROFEPA.

PROFEPA (Procuraduría Federal de Protección al Ambiente). 2021b. *Resultados Obtenidos PNAA*. Mexico City: PROFEPA. https://www.gob.mx/profepa/acciones-y-programas/resultados-obtenidos?idiom=es.

PROFEPA (Procuraduría Federal de Protección al Ambiente). 2022a. *Empresas con Certificado Vigente en el estado de Jalisco*. Mexico City: PROFEPA. http://sirev.profepa.gob.mx:9080/EmpresasCertificadasSIIP/EmpresasCertificadas/EmpresasCertificadas.html?estado=14.

PROFEPA (Procuraduría Federal de Protección al Ambiente). 2022b. *Padrón de Auditores Ambientales*. Mexico City: PROFEPA. http://www.profepa.gob.mx/innovaportal/v/3981/1/mx/padron_de_auditores_ambientales.html.

Prüss-Üstün, Annette, and Carlos Corvalán. 2006. *Preventing Disease through Healthy Environments: Towards an Estimate of the Environmental Burden of Disease*. Geneva: World Health Organization. https://apps.who.int/iris/handle/10665/43457.

Prüss-Üstün, Annette, J. Wolf, Carlos Corvalán, R. V. Bos, and María Purificación Neira. 2016. *Preventing Disease through Healthy Environments: A Global Assessment of the Burden of Disease from Environmental Risks*. Geneva: World Health Organization. https://www.who.int/publications/i/item/9789241565196.

Puga, Cristina. 2004. *Los empresarios organizados y el Tratado de libre comercio de América del Norte*. Mexico City: UNAM and Miguel Ángel Porrúa.

References

Restrepo, Eduardo. 2007. Antropología y colonialidad. In *El giro decolonial: Reflexiones para una diversidad epistémica más allá del capitalismo global*, edited by Santiago Castro-Gómez and Ramón Grosfoguel, 289–304. Bogotá, Colombia: Siglo del Hombre Editores.

Ribeiro, Gustavo Lins. 2007. Poder, redes e ideología en el campo del desarrollo. *Tabula Rasa* 6 (January–June): 173–193.

Ribeiro, Silvia. 2005. Las caras de la privatización del agua. *La Jornada*, April 30.

Ríos, Julio. 2015. Semadet sigue con pendientes en la cuenca del Río Santiago. *La Jornada Jalisco*, February 17.

Robinson, John. 2004. Squaring the Circle? Some Thoughts on the Idea of Sustainable Development. *Ecological Economics* 48 (4) (April): 369–384. https://doi.org/10.1016/j.ecolecon.2003.10.017.

Robles, Vanesa. 2008. Arsénico, en la sangre del niño que cayó al río. *Público*, February 13.

Rojas-Bracho, Leonora, Verónica Garibay-Bravo, Gretchen Stevens, and Georgina Echániz-Pellicer. 2013. Environmental Fuel Quality Improvements in Mexico: A Case Study of the Role of Cost-Benefit Analysis in the Decision-Making Process. In *The Globalization of Cost-Benefit Analysis in Environmental Policy*, edited by Michael Livermore and Richard Revesz, 161–177. New York: Oxford University Press.

Romero, Dubraska. 2008. Descarta CCIJ arsénico en Río Santiago. *Mural*, February 20.

Rosagel, S. 2012. AMIA confirma suspensión de NOM-163. *Manufactura*, October 12.

Rostow, Walt Whitman. 1960. *The Stages of Economic Growth: A Non-Communist Manifesto*. Cambridge: Cambridge University Press.

Saavedra Ponce, Viridiana. 2010. No está en riesgo la salud de la población que vive alrededor del río Santiago: Petersen Farah. *La Jornada Jalisco*, February 11.

Salas-Mercado, Manuel. 2001. *Una mirada al pasado: El Salto, Jal.* Guadalajara: Universidad de Guadalajara.

Sanmina. n.d. Guadalajara. Accessed March 15, 2020. http://www.sanmina.com/locations/guadalajara/index.php.

Santos, Boaventura de Sousa. 2009. *Una epistemología del sur: La reinvención del conocimiento y la emancipación social*. Mexico City: Siglo XXI Editores.

Schlosberg, David. 2007. *Defining Environmental Justice: Theories, Movements, and Nature*. Oxford: Oxford University Press.

Schneider, Ben Ross. 2002. Why Is Mexican Business So Organized? *Latin American Research Review* 37 (1): 77–118.

Schwab, Klaus, ed. 2014. *The Global Competitiveness Report 2014–2015: Full Data Edition*. Geneva: World Economic Forum. http://www3.weforum.org/docs/WEF_Global CompetitivenessReport_2014-15.pdf.

Schwarzenbach, René, Thomas Egli, Thomas Hofstetter, Urs von Gunten, and Bernhard Wehrli. 2010. Global Water Pollution and Human Health. *Annual Review of Environment and Resources* 35 (November): 109–136. https://doi.org/10.1146/annurev-environ-100809-125342.

SE (Secretaría de Economía). 1950. *Séptimo Censo General de Población, Estado de Jalisco*. Mexico City: Secretaría de Economía. https://www.inegi.org.mx/app/biblioteca/ficha .html?upc=702825412579.

SE (Secretaría de Economía). 2015. NMX-AA-034-SCFI-2015, Análisis de agua—medición de sólidos y sales disueltas en aguas naturales, residuales y residuales tratadas—método de prueba. https://www.gob.mx/cms/uploads/attachment/file /166146/nmx-aa-034-scfi-2015.pdf.

SE (Secretaría de Economía). 2016. Balanza comercial de México año previo de entrada en vigor de los TLCs vs. 2016. Estadísticas de comercio exterior de México. https://www .gob.mx/cms/uploads/attachment/file/110340/TOTAL_2016_enero-abril.pdf.

SEMADES (Secretaría de Medio Ambiente para el Desarrollo Sustentable). 2012. *V Reunión Ordinaria del Órgano Técnico Mixto*. Guadalajara, Jalisco: SEMADES. https:// semadet.jalisco.gob.mx/sites/semadet.jalisco.gob.mx/files/05_minuta_otm_0.pdf.

SEMADES (Secretaría de Medio Ambiente para el Desarrollo Sustentable). 2013. Parque Ecológico en El Salto–Juanacatlán. YouTube video, 10:43. Posted February 8. https://www.youtube.com/watch?v=oS0-tGYhzdg.

SEMARNAT (Secretaría de Medio Ambiente y Recursos Naturales). 2011. *Evaluación de Instrumentos Normativos del Sector Ambiental*. Mexico City: SEMARNAT. http:// biblioteca.Semarnat.gob.mx/janium/Documentos/Ciga/Libros2011/CD001056 .pdf.

SEMARNAT (Secretaría de Medio Ambiente y Recursos Naturales). 2013. *Presentación RETC 2013*. http://apps1.Semarnat.gob.mx/retc/retc/PresentacionRETC2013.pdf.

SEMARNAT (Secretaría de Medio Ambiente y Recursos Naturales). 2014. *El agua que mueve a México: XXV aniversario de la Comisión Nacional del Agua*. Mexico City: SEMARNAT.

SEMARNAT (Secretaría de Medio Ambiente y Recursos Naturales). 2015. *Reglas de Operación del Comité Consultivo Nacional de Normalización de Medio Ambiente y Recursos Naturales*. Mexico City: SEMARNAT. https://www.semarnat.gob.mx/sites/default /files/documentos/leyesynormas/comites/reglas_de_operacion_comarnat_2015.pdf.

SEMARNAT (Secretaría de Medio Ambiente y Recursos Naturales). 2021a. *Presupuesto asignado a la SEMARNAT por unidad administrativa*. Mexico City: SEMARNAT.

References 315

http://dgeiawf.semarnat.gob.mx:8080/ibi_apps/WFServlet?IBIF_ex=D4_GASTOS01_03
&IBIC_user=dgeia_mce&IBIC_pass=dgeia_mce&NOMBREANIO=*.

SEMARNAT (Secretaría de Medio Ambiente y Recursos Naturales). 2021b. *Procuración de Justicia Ambiental*. Mexico City: SEMARNAT. http://dgeiawf.semarnat.gob
.mx:8080/approot/dgeia_mce/html/03_institucional/profepa.html.

SEMARNAT (Secretaría de Medio Ambiente y Recursos Naturales). 2021c. *Semarnat
actualiza NOM 001 sobre descargas de aguas residuales, tras 25 años de parálisis*. Mexico
City: SEMARNAT. https://www.gob.mx/semarnat/prensa/semarnat-actualiza-nom
-001-sobre-descargas-de-aguas-residuales-tras-25-anos-de-paralisis?idiom=es.

SEMARNAT (Secretaría de Medio Ambiente y Recursos Naturales), Delegación Jalisco.
2008. *Asunto: Respuesta a pliego de peticiones de las comunidades de El Salto, Juanacatlán y
Puente Grande, Oficio Número SPGARN.014.02.01 01.393/08*. Mexico City: SEMARNAT.

SGG (Secretaría General de Gobierno). 2009. *Oficio No. SAJ/242/2009*. Guadalajara,
Mexico: SGG.

SHCP (Secretaría de Hacienda y Crédito Público). 2014. *Oficio Circular No.
400.1.410.14009*. Mexico City: SHCP. https://www.gob.mx/cms/uploads/attachment
/file/23409/oficio_tasa_social_de_descuento.pdf.

Shiva, Vandana. 2003. *Las guerras del agua: Privatización, contaminación y lucro*. Mexico City: Siglo XXI Editores.

Short, Jodi, and Michael Toffel. 2008. Coerced Confessions: Self-Policing in the
Shadow of the Regulator. *Journal of Law, Economics and Organization* 24 (1) (May):
45–71. https://doi.org/10.1093/jleo/ewm039.

Simonian, Lane. 1999. *La defensa de la tierra del jaguar: Una historia de la conservación
en México*. Mexico City: Instituto Nacional de Ecología/SEMARNAP.

Smith, Dorothy. 1996. Telling the Truth after Postmodernism. *Symbolic Interaction*
19 (3) (Fall): 171–202. https://doi.org/10.1525/si.1996.19.3.171.

Smith, Dorothy. 2005. *Institutional Ethnography: A Sociology for People*. New York:
Altamira Press.

Smith, Neil. 2008. *Uneven Development: Nature, Capital, and the Production of Space*.
3rd ed. Athens: University of Georgia Press.

SSJ (Secretaría de Salud Jalisco). 2010. *Percepción de la morbilidad y mortalidad entre los
habitantes de El Salto y Juanacatlán comparativamente con la de Tonalá, Jalisco*. Guadalajara, Mexico: SSJ.

Stigler, George. 1975. *The Citizen and the State: Essays on Regulation*. Chicago: University of Chicago Press.

STPS (Secretaría de Trabajo y Previsión Social). 2006. *Casos de éxito 2006*. Vol. 3,
Sistemas de Administración de la Seguridad y Salud en el Trabajo. Mexico City: STPS.

http://www.stps.gob.mx/bp/secciones/dgsst/publicaciones/casos_exit/libro%20casos%20de%20exito%203.pdf.

Swyngedouw, Erik. 2005. Dispossessing H_2O: The Contested Terrain of Water Privatization. *Capitalism, Nature, Socialism* 16 (1): 81–98. https://doi.org/10.1080/1045575052000335384.

Taber, Nancy. 2010. Institutional Ethnography, Autoethnography, and Narrative: An Argument for Incorporating Multiple Methodologies. *Qualitative Research* 10 (1): 5–25. https://doi.org/10.1177/1468794109348680.

Tetreault, Darcy, Cindy McCulligh, and Rodrigo Flores. 2010. La exigibilidad de los derechos ambientales en México: El caso del Río Santiago. In *Perspectivas del universalismo en México*, edited by Enrique Valencia, 121–132. Mexico City: Fundación Konrad Adenauer, Universidad de Guadalajara, and ITESO.

Tetreault, Darcy, Cindy McCulligh, and Carlos Lucio, eds. 2018. *Social Environmental Conflicts in Mexico: Resistance to Dispossession and Alternatives from Below*. New York: Palgrave Macmillan.

Tetreault, Darcy, Heliodoro Ochoa, and Eduardo Hernández. 2012. Introduction to *Conflictos socioambientales y alternativas de la sociedad civil*, edited by Darcy Tetreault, Heliodoro Ochoa, and Eduardo Hernández, 13–26. Tlaquepaque, Mexico: ITESO.

Tirado, Ricardo. 2012. El nuevo espacio político de los empresarios. In *Gobernabilidad y gobernanza en los albores del siglo XXI y reflexiones sobre el México contemporáneo*, edited by Bertha Lerner, Ricardo Uvalle, and Roberto Moreno, 321–355. Mexico City: UNAM.

TLA (Tribunal Latinoamericano del Agua). 2006. *Veredicto del Caso: Afectación de la Cuenca Lerma-Chapala-Santiago-Pacífico*. San José, Costa Rica: TLA.

TLA (Tribunal Latinoamericano del Agua). 2007. *Veredicto del Caso: Deterioro y contaminación del Río Santiago: Municipios de El Salto y Juanacatlán, Estado de Jalisco, República Mexicana*. San José, Costa Rica: TLA.

Toledo, Víctor, David Garrido, and Narciso Barrera-Bassols. 2014. Conflictos socio-ambientales, resistencias ciudadanas y violencia neoliberal en México. *ecologíaPolítica* 46: 115–124.

Toledo, Victor, David Garrido, and Narciso Barrera-Bassols. 2015. The Struggle for Life: Socio-environmental Conflicts in Mexico. *Latin American Perspectives* 42 (5): 133–147. https://doi.org/10.1177/0094582X15588104.

Torregrosa, María Luisa, Luisa Paré, Karina Kloster, and Jordi Vera. 2010. Administración del agua. In *El agua en México: Cauces y encauces*, edited by Blanca Elena Jiménez, María Luisa Torregrosa, and Luis Aboites, 595–624. Mexico City: Academia Mexicana de Ciencias.

Torres, Raúl. 2008. "No hay materia" para intervenir en el caso de contaminación del río Santiago: CNDH. *La Jornada Jalisco*, November 26.

References

317

Tortajada, Cecilia. 2002. Abastecimiento de agua y manejo de descargas residuales en México: Un análisis de las políticas ambientales. In *Agua, cultura y sociedad en México*, edited by Patricia Ávila García, 233–244. Zamora, Mexico: El Colegio de Michoacán.

Transparency International. n.d. Political Corruption. Accessed March 30, 2022. https://www.transparency.org/en/corruptionary/political-corruption.

Transparency International Kenya. n.d. FAQs about Corruption. Accessed April 15, 2022. https://tikenya.org/faqs-about-corruption/.

Truman, Harry S. 1949. Inaugural Address of Harry S. Truman. Avalon Project. https://avalon.law.yale.edu/20th_century/truman.asp.

Tylor, Edward Burnett. 1920. *Primitive Culture: Researches into the Development of Mythology, Philosophy, Religion, Language, Art, and Custom*. Vol. 1. London: John Murray.

UASLP (Universidad Autónoma de San Luis Potosí) and CEA (Comisión Estatal del Agua Jalisco). 2011. *Propuesta metodológica para la implantación de una batería de indicadores de salud que favorezcan el establecimiento de programas de diagnóstico, intervención y vigilancia epidemiológica en las poblaciones ubicadas en la zona de influencia del proyecto de la Presa Arcediano en el estado de Jalisco*. Guadalajara, Mexico: CEA Jalisco.

Ugalde, Vicente. 2014. La coacción en la regulación ambiental en México: Una aproximación sociológica. In *El derecho ambiental en acción: Problemas de implementación, aplicación y cumplimiento*, edited by Vicente Ugalde, 83–119. Mexico City: El Colegio de México.

UNESCO (United Nations Educational, Scientific and Cultural Organization). 2003. *1st UN World Water Development Report: Water for People, Water for Life*. Paris: UNESCO and Berghahn Books.

UNESCO (United Nations Educational, Scientific and Cultural Organization). 2012. *The United Nations World Water Development Report 4: Managing Water under Uncertainty and Risk*. Paris: UNESCO.

UNIDO (United Nations Industrial Development Organization). 2021. *Statistical Indicators of Inclusive and Sustainable Industrialization: Biennial Progress Report*. Vienna: UNIDO. https://www.unido.org/sites/default/files/files/2021-09/SDG_report_2021_final.pdf.

United Nations. 1992. *Report of the United Nations Conference on Environment and Development*. Geneva: United Nations General Assembly. https://www.un.org/en/development/desa/population/migration/generalassembly/docs/globalcompact/A_CONF.151_26_Vol.I_Declaration.pdf.

United Nations. 2009. *2009 UNISDR Terminology on Disaster Risk Reduction*. Geneva: United Nations International Strategy for Disaster Risk Reduction. https://www.preventionweb.net/files/7817_UNISDRTerminologyEnglish.pdf.

United Nations. 2014. Water Scarcity. http://www.un.org/waterforlifedecade/scarcity.shtml.

UN-Water. 2013. *Mexico UN-Water Country Brief*. http://www.unwater.org/publications/un-water-country-briefs-mexico/.

Urciaga, José, Miguel Ángel Hernández, and David Carruthers. 2008. La política ambiental mexicana: Una panorámica. In *Del saqueo a la conservación: Historia ambiental contemporánea de Baja California Sur, 1940–2003*, edited by Micheline Cariño and Mario Monteforte, 67–97. Mexico City: SEMARNAT.

Urrea. 2016. *Sustentabilidad*. https://urrea.mx/es/sustentabilidad.

US Renal Data System. 2021. International Comparisons. In *2021 USRDS Annual Data Report: Epidemiology of Kidney Disease in the United States*, chap. 11. Bethesda, MD: National Institutes of Health, National Institute of Diabetes and Digestive and Kidney Diseases. https://adr.usrds.org/2021/end-stage-renal-disease/11-international-comparisons.

Vargas, Mónica, ed. 2021. *Transnational Corporations and Free Trade in Mexico: Caravan on the Social and Environmental Impacts*. Amsterdam: Transnational Institute. https://www.stopcorporateimpunity.org/wp-content/uploads/2021/10/Report_Caravan_ToxiTourMexico_ENG.pdf.

Velasco, Jorge. 2016. Empresarios de El Salto dicen que la contaminación del agua de riego vertida a la cuenca es más grave que las descargas de las industrias. *Milenio Jalisco*, September 15.

Velazco, Alejandro. 2012. Incumplen ley federal el 20% de las empresas que realizan descargas en el Santiago: Conagua. *La Jornada Jalisco*, March 27.

Velazco, Alejandro. 2013. En Conagua red de cómplices beneficiaron familia de Iglesias Benítez. *Verde Bandera: Periodismo ambiental*, March 22.

Villareal, René. 1976. *El desequilibrio externo en la industrialización en México (1929–1975): Un enfoque estructuralista*. Mexico City: Fondo de Cultura Económica.

Von Bertrab, Alejandro, and Javier Matus Pacheco. 2010. Aspectos sociales sobre la calidad del agua y los ecosistemas acuáticos: Un análisisde conflictos y controversias en torno al agua. In *Calidad del agua: Un enfoque multidisciplinario*, edited by Alonso Aguilar Ibarra, 247–279. Mexico City: UNAM.

Vos, Jacob. 2009. Actions Speak Louder Than Words: Greenwashing in Corporate America. *Notre Dame Journal of Law, Ethics and Public Policy* 23 (2): 673–697.

Walby, Kevin. 2007. On the Social Relations of Research: A Critical Assessment of Institutional Ethnography. *Qualitative Inquiry* 13 (7): 1008–1030. https://doi.org/10.1177/1077800407305809.

Wallerstein, Immanuel. 2000. *The Essential Wallerstein*. New York: New Press.

WCED (World Commission on Environment and Development). 1987. *Report of the World Commission on Environment and Development: Our Common Future*. New

References

York: United Nations. https://sustainabledevelopment.un.org/content/documents/5987our-common-future.pdf.

Wester, Philippus, Edwin Rap, and Sergio Vargas-Velázquez. 2009. The Hydraulic Mission and the Mexican Hydrocracy: Regulating and Reforming the Flows of Water and Power. *Water Alternatives* 2 (3): 395–415.

White, Leslie. 1949. *The Science of Culture: A Study of Man and Civilization.* New York: Grove Press.

Whitehead, Mark, Martin Jones, and Rhys Jones. 2006. Spatializing the Ecological Leviathan: Territorial Strategies and the Production of Regional Natures. *Geografiska Annaler: Series B, Human Geography* 88 (1): 49–65. https://doi.org/10.1111/j.0435-3684.2006.00205.x.

Wolf, Eric. 2010. *Europe and the People without History.* Los Angeles: University of California Press.

Wolf, Sidney. 1996. Fear and Loathing about the Public Right to Know: The Surprising Success of the Emergency Planning and Community Right-to-Know Act. *Journal of Land Use and Environmental Law* 1 (2): 217–319.

World Bank. 2012. *Inclusive Green Growth: The Pathway to Sustainable Development.* Washington, DC: World Bank.

World Bank. 2022. World Development Indicators. Accessed April 15, 2022. http://databank.worldbank.org/data/reports.aspx?source=world-development-indicators.

Worsfold, Paul, Alan Townshend, and Colin Poole, eds. 2005. *Encyclopedia of Analytical Science.* 2nd ed. Amsterdam: Elsevier.

Zibechi, Raúl. 2007. *Autonomías y emancipaciones: América Latina en movimiento.* Lima: Universidad Nacional Mayor de San Marcos and Fondo Editorial de la Facultad de Ciencias Sociales.

Zinn, Matthew. 2002. Policing Environmental Regulatory Enforcement: Cooperation, Capture, and Citizen Suits. *Stanford Environmental Law Journal* 21 (1): 81–174.

Index

Note: Page numbers in *italics* indicate figures and tables.

Abugaber, José, 169
Access to information, 33–34, 166,
 207–211, 271–273
 on annual operating certificates,
 163–164, 227
 in corporate sustainability reports,
 209, 211, 212–225, 244–245
 from EHS personnel, 209–211, 225,
 235–246
 on environmental performance
 vs. myth of the multinational,
 226–227
 on laboratory analyses, 132
 methodologies and, 208–211
 and myth of the multinational,
 225–235
 "open-door policy" *vs*. actual
 corporate responses, 210–211
 "right to know" and, 149, 166, 211,
 246
 on tax-related self-reporting,
 146–147
Accumulation by dispossession, 26–30,
 276n16
Actor-oriented political ecology, 269–270,
 273–274
AGyDSA, 99
Alatorre, Rocío, 6–7, 91–92

Alen del Norte (AlEn)
 access to information from, 210–211
 CI certification of, 160
 compliance claims of, 218
 corporate sustainability reports of,
 212, *215*, 217–221, 224
 effluent/discharges of, *215*, 218
 perspective of EHS official from, 236
 reports to RETC, *154*
 water consumption by, 217
Alfaro Ramírez, Enrique, 14, 102, 115,
 130, 162, 252
Álvarez, José de Jesús, 101
Amezcua, Jesús, 141
Ampugnani, Gustavo, 110–111
Anderson, Terry, 21, 25–26, 62
Annual operating certificates (COAs),
 150, 163–164, 167, 227, 237
Apoyo Técnico Industrial, 137
Arcediano Dam, 7, 63, 87–90, 96,
 103–105, 112, 227
Arcediano Declaration, 89–90
Arellano, Joel, 104–105
Armendáriz, Juan, 113–114
Arrojo, Pedro, 66
Association of Industrialists of El Salto
 (AISAC), 6, 95, 108, 114, 190, 210,
 241–244

Automatic sensors, 136
Autonomous University of Guadalajara, 12
Autonomous University of San Luis Potosí, 7–8, 252
AyMA Ingeniería Consultoría, 98–99, 104, 226–227, 229, 233
Azuela de la Cueva, Antonio, 126, 278n5

Basso, Lelio, 112
Bermejillo, José María, 38
Biochemical oxygen demand (BOD), 67–69, 97, 228, 235, 276n5
Bogantes, Javier, 90
Border Industrialization Program, 42
Bourguett, Víctor Javier, 119–120, 122
Bravo, Lizbeth Urbina, 199
Bribery, 30–32
Brundtland Report, 21–22
Business Coordinating Council (CCE), 43, 45, 173–176, 181

Caldéron, Felipe, 190, 196
Canada, self-reporting in, 149–151, 151, 166–167, 255–256
Cancer, 6–7, 113–114
Capitalism
  and accumulation by dispossession, 26–30, 276n16
  competitive, and role of state, 170
  economic and political power under, 171–176
  first contradiction of, 22
  and free-market environmentalism, 17, 19–20, 24–30, 58, 62, 256–257
  international subcontracting, 49
  second contradiction of, 22, 26
  transnational dependent, 40
Carabias, Julia, 126
Carbon dioxide emissions, standards for, 186–188
Carbon Disclosure Project, 213–214
Cárdenas, Lázaro, 41

Cárdenas Jiménez, Alberto, 70
Castañeda Nañez, Héctor, 108, 131–132, 135, 145
Castaños, Alberto, 189
Castellanos, Victor, 164–165, 226
Castree, Noel, 28–30
Celanese
  corporate sustainability reports of, 212, 215, 217–218, 220, 221
  discharge permits for, 141, 142, 230–232, 284n12
  effluents/discharges of, 78, 97, 99, 215, 229–232
  inspection records on, 230
  interviews/interview refusal, 209, 210
  myth of the multinational and, 226, 229–232, 245
  noncompliance of, 99, 229–232
  operations in industrial corridor, 10
  "raid" on and amparo against, 231
  reports to RETC, 154
  technical assessment of treatment system, 232
  water consumption by, 217
Center for Public Policy and Sustainable Development (CEDES), 181
Center for Sustainable Transportation (CTS-Embarq), 187
CH2M Hill, 232
Chemical oxygen demand (COD), 67–69, 98, 276n6
  in Celanese effluent, 229–230, 232
  duties charged for, 56
  in Huntsman effluent, 214, 219, 233
  in Nestlé effluent, 217, 227–228
  in Quimikao effluent, 234–235
  in standard modification, 180, 190, 192, 200–202
Children, health risks for, 7–8, 81–83, 89, 115–116, 251–252
China, as competitor for Mexico, 70–71
Ciba/Ciba Geigy, 3, 11, 97, 99, 209, 232

Index

Citizen Committee for Environmental Defense (CCDA), 90, 99, 100, 243
Citizen complaints, early, 83, 86–88
Citizen's Environmental Defense, 86
Clean Industry (CI) program, 57, 156–161, 167, 271
Coloniality, 122–123
Colonization, of regulatory agencies, 174–175, 256
Color parameter, in NOM-001 modification, 180, 190, 192, 200–202
Command and control measures, 55–56, 123–124
Commercial-environmental model, 124–125
Commission for Environmental Cooperation of North America (CEC), 87, 112, 150
Comprehensive Sanitation Program, 101
Comprehensive Strategy for the Recovery of the Santiago River, 14, 115
Confederation of Mexican Chambers of Industry (CONCAMIN), 169, 190, 193–194
Constructivism, 265–266
Consultative approach, 60
Continental Automotive Guadalajara, 160
Contreras, Sergio, 175
Corporacíon de Occidente, *154*, 211, 242–243
Corporate revenues, *vs.* country GDPs, 171, *172*
Corporate social responsibility (CSR), 62, 205, 224, 258–259
Corporate sustainability
access to information on, 207–211
failure of, 18
greenwashing *vs.*, 18, 212
link to legacy/reputation, 223–225
myth of the multinational and, 17, 62, 206–207, 211, 225–235, 258–259

myths *vs.* reality of, 205–207
neoliberalization and, 206
transnational corporations and, 206–207
Corporate sustainability reports, 209, 211, 212–225, 244–245, 258
compliance claims in, 218–220
effluent/wastewater information in, 214–220, *215–216*
growth of, 212–213
key questions for deciphering, 220
lack of factory-level data in, 214
Nestlé, 212, 216–217, 219–220
reporting *vs.* actual sustainability, 213, 220–225, 244–245
Corruption
definition of, 30
in inspection process, 131–132
institutionalized, 15–16, 17, 30–32, 124, 254–258, 260–261
municipal-level, 165–166
typologies of, 30
Cortés, Maite, 155–156
Cost-benefit analysis, of regulations, 195–199
Council of Industrial Chambers of Jalisco, 95–96, 251
Countercultural perspective, 20–21
Crown Envases, 98, *153*, *154*
Crysel, 11, 97
Cueto, Luz María, 94
Cultural evolution, 120–121
Cyanamid. *See* Cytec/Cytec-Solvay
Cypher, James, 13, 40, 43, 48, 173, 174
Cytec/Cytec-Solvay
discharge permit for, 141
effluents/discharges of, 252
information obtained from, 211
operations in industrial corridor, 3, 10–11
perspectives on regulation, 137–138, 190, 240, 242–244
reports to RETC, *153*, *154*

Index

Dams and hydroelectric power, 9, 27–28, 38, 63–64, 87–90
Degrowth, 16
Delgado Wise, Raúl, 40, 43, 48, 173, 174
Dependency theory, 249
Development
  vs. environmental degradation, 16–24, 247–251
  evolutionary theories and, 119–123
  Kuznets curve and, 248
  Mexican industrialization strategies and, 40–49
  myths *vs.* reality of corporate sustainability and, 205–207
  national culture and, 249–250
  neoliberalism and, 42–49
  sustainable, 16–18, 21–24
  Villareal's definition of, 43
  zero-sum model of, 249
Díaz, Porfirio, 40
Dickens, Charles, 19–20
"Dictatorship of normalcy," 82
Direct (command and control) regulation, 55–56, 123–124
Discharge permits, 139–143
  Celanese, 141, 142, 230–232, 284n12
  number issued, *127*, 127–128
  period after river reclassification (2009–), 141–142
  period of least possible regulation (2000–2008), 140–141
  period of tailoring (1994–1998), 140
  self-reporting by holders of, 144–146
"Disposal mediums," 25–26
Dispossession, accumulation by, 26–30, 276n16
Distribuidora Chocomex, 133
Domínguez, Gabriela, 7–8, 252
DSM, 142, *154*, 211, 237

Echeverría, Luis, 11, 42
Eco-efficiency, 220–222, 225, 244–245
Ecological modernization (EM), 23–24

"Ecological park," 107
Effem Mexico, 160
Efficiency/inefficiency
  of CONAGUA, 237–238
  of regulations, 55–56
Effluent/discharge, 12, 14, 75–79. *See also specific corporations, pollutants, and regulations*
  corporate claims of compliance to regulations of, 218–220
  corporate sustainability reports on, 214–220, *215–216*, 244–245
  early studies of Santiago River, 96–99
  failure to test or treat, 134–135
  myth of the multinational *vs.* actual, 225–235
  NOM-001-SEMARNAT-1996 and, 53–54
  noncompliance with regulations, 14, 78–79, 98–99, 227–235
  payments for *vs.* actual protection, 15–16
  permits for, *127*, 127–128, 139–143
  simplification of standards for, 53–54, 61–62
  technical standards for, 52, 53
  water data on, 68–69
El Ahogado Canal, death of boy who fell in, 4–5, 93–96, 99, 117, 134, 242
Eloy Ruiz, Jaime, 86
El Salto. *See also* Ocotlán–El Salto Industrial Corridor; Santiago River
  manufacturing in, 70–75, *73*
El Salto Industrial Park, 12, 134–135
Emergency Planning and Community Right-to-Know Act (US), 149
Emerson Power Transmissions, 141
Empaques Modernos de Guadalajara (EMG), 98, 130, 132, 141, *154*, 160, 210
Enciso, Enrique, 92, 111

Index

325

Enciso, Sofía, 4, 37–39, 111

Envases Universales, 98, *154*

Environment, health and safety (EHS) personnel, 209–211, 225, 235–246

Environment, National Resources and Fisheries Committee, 191

Environmental degradation
development *vs.*, 16–24, 247–251
displacement from Global North to Global South, 18, 23–24, 66, 122
evolutionary theories and, 119–123, 249
neoliberal logics and, 26–30
normalization of, 15–16, 17

"Environmentalism of the poor," 20, 85, 88

Environmental Law Institute (IDEA), 87–92

Epidemiology, 92–93

Escobar, Arturo, 22, 121–122, 265

Eurocentrism, 23, 120

European Union (EU) Water Framework Directive, 178

Euzkadi, 12, 243

Evolutionary theories, 119–123, 249

Federal Administrative Procedure Law, 195, 196

Federal Bureau of Environmental Protection (PROFEPA), 30, 52–53, 54, 57
budget of, 159
Clean Industry program, 57, 156–161, 271
complaints to and responses of, 83, 86, 92, 100–102
dismissal of Greenpeace report, 115
inspection role of, 125–128, 158–159

Federal Commission for Protection Against Sanitary Risks (COFEPRIS), 6–7, 91, 100

Federal Duties Law (LFD), 56, 98, 103–105, 227–228, 284n8

Federal Electricity Commission, 2, 28, 181

Federal Environmental Protection Law, 52

Federal Institute for Access to Information and Data Protection (IFAI), 110–111

Federal Law on Metrology and Standardization (LFMN), 180, 183, 184, 193, 202

Federal Law to Prevent and Control Environmental Pollution, 51

Federal Regulatory Improvement Commission (COFEMER), 180, 189, 195–200, 202

Fernández, Luz Marcela, 163

Flextronics, 49, *154*, 160, 212, *215*, 217–218

Foam, toxic, 2, 81–83, 109, *109*

Foreign direct investment (FDI), 18, 39, 43, 70–71, 79–80, 206
environmental boons of, hypothesis of, 206–207
neoliberalization and, 206

Forest resources, new standard for, 193–195

Foster, John Bellamy, 22–23

Foucault, Michel, 265–266, 270–271

Fox, Vincente, 94

Free-market environmentalism, 17, 19–20, 24–30, 58, 62, 256–257

Friedman, Milton, 44, 62, 170, 173, 258–259

Fronteras Comunes, 152–153, 155, 159, 184–185

Gaitán, Aciel, 63

Gandy, Matthew, 50–51, 54

GEMI Initiative, 181, 186–187, 192

General Agreement on Tariffs and Trade, 44

General Law of Ecological Balance and Environmental Protection, 52, 157

General Regulatory Improvement Law,
195–196
General Water Law, 198–199
Germany, environmental regulation in,
177–178
Global Reporting Initiative (GRI), 209,
213–214
Gonda de Rivera, Eva, 173
González, Apolinar, 137
González, Graciela, 37, 111, 207, 247
González Corona, Elías, 13
Gray, Rob, 213–214, 220
Green economy, 16–17, 21
Green growth, 16–17, 21, 69, 205–207,
248
Greenpeace Mexico, *109*, 109–115, 207,
233, 260
Greenwashing, 18, 212, 244–245, 271
Grimaldi, Federico, 189
Grivatec, 142, *154. See also* Urrea
Grupo Gondi, 130
Guadalajara Industrial Park, 98
Guajardo, Idelfonso, 175
Guerra Abud, Juan José, 187
Guerrero Villalobos, Guillermo, 126
Güitrón, Raúl, 114
Gutiérrez, Alfonso, 92, 94
Gutiérrez, Eric, 103–105, 136, 143,
145–146, 191, 196–197
Gutiérrez, Fernando, 189
Gutiérrez Treviño, Javier, 95–96

Harassment of activists, 111, 252–253
Hardin, Garrett, 21, 24
Harvey, David, 20–21, 24, 27, 45,
276n16
Hayek, Friedrich, 44
Health and illness
assessments of, 6–8, 251–252
cause-and-effect relationship with
pollution, 92–93, 116
death of boy who fell in canal, 4–5,
93–96, 99, 117, 134, 242

deaths of dam workers, 2
findings on nuclear abnormalities,
113–114
Greenpeace Mexico evaluation of,
111–115
register of illnesses, 99
risks for children, 7–8, 81–83, 89,
115–116, 251–252
Herrera, Sandra Denisse, 193
Herrera Camacho, Óscar, 129–130
Hershey's, 37, 98, *154*, 252
Hilasal Mexicana, 132–133
"Hollowing out," of state
responsibilities, 29
Honda, 37, 95, *154*, 160, 171, *172*, 210,
252
Huntsman
corporate sustainability reports
of, 212, 213, 214, *215*, 219,
221–225
effluents/discharges of, 78, 99, 214,
215, 219, 232–234
interviews with officials of, 210–211,
233–234
myth of the multinational and, 226,
232–234, 245
noncompliance of, 99, 233–234
perspective of EHS official from,
240–241
pillars of sustainability, 234
reports to RETC, *154*
"Hydraulic mission," 27, 276n2
Hydraulic Resources Committee, 6–7
Hydrocacy, 126, 276n2
Hydroelectric power, 9, 27–28, 38,
63–64
Hydroelectric System of the Santiago
River, 28

IBM, 12, 37, *154*, *172*
Iglesias Benítez, Raúl Antonio, 86–87,
95, 110, 133–134, 230, 277n8
IMI-Electronics, 135

Index

Import substitution industrialization (ISI), 11–13, 27, 41–43
Indirect regulation, 55–57
Industrial Corridor (Ocotlán–El Salto). *See* Ocotlán–El Salto Industrial Corridor
Industrial Corridor of Jalisco, 11
Industrial Development Commission of the National Congress, 11
Industrialization strategies, 40–49, 79–80
"Industrial Paradises = Environmental Hells," 247
Industrial Zone of Western Mexico, 10
Industrias Gosa, 98
Industry/industry actors. *See also specific corporations*
  colonization of state agencies by, 174–175, 256
  COMARNAT bias toward, 181–188
  COMARNAT members from, 180–181, *182*
  complaints about CONAGUA inefficiency, 237–238
  costs to *vs.* benefits of regulation, 195–199
  flows of power, 169–176
  myth of the multinational and, 17, 62, 206–207, 211, 225–235
  negotiation and consensus with, 180–195, 202
  objections to new standard, 169, 189, 190, 200–202
  pact for compliance, 251
  "pathological" and "psychopathic" corporations, 259–260
  perspective on Clean Industry program, 160–161
  perspective on government and regulation, 235–246
  perspective on inspections, 137–139, 236
  regulatory capture by, 60, 170–176, 202–203, 256

  sense of injustice over blame for pollution, 242–246
  technical advantage of, 194–195
Infineum, *154*, 211, 237, 240
Information, access to. *See* Access to information
Inspections, 123–139
  Clean Industry program and amnesty from, 156, 158–159
  corruption in process, 131–132
  demands to strengthen, 129–130
  discharge permits and, 139, 142
  industry perception of, 137–139, 236
  institutional corruption and, 254–255
  jurisdiction over and responsibility for, 125–127
  municipal-level regulations and, 164–166
  number of, 127, 128–130, *129*
  prior notification and knowledge about, 135–137
  records *vs.* myth of the multinational, 227, 228, 230, 233
  results of (penalties from), 127, 130–139
  state-level regulations and, 162–164
Inspectors, number of, 127, 128
Institute for Transportation and Development Policy, 187
Institute of Integrated Values and Environmental Development (Instituto VIDA), 2, 5–7, 86, 88–92, 100, 108
Institutional ethnography, 32–34, 263, 267–268, 273–274
Institutionalized corruption, 15–16, 17, 30–32, 124, 254–258, 260–261
Institutional Revolutionary Party, 108, 135, 162
Inter-American Commission on Human Rights (IACHR), 116
Interinstitutional processes, 5–7, 101–102
International Monetary Fund, 13, 43

International Organization for Standardization, 57
International subcontracting capitalism, 49
International Water Association, 119

Jacott, Marisa, 152–153, 155, 159, 184–185, 246
Jalisco. *See also* Ocotlán–El Salto Industrial Corridor; Santiago River
    kidney disease in, 81–83
    manufacturing in, 70–75, *72*, *73*
    water quality data for, 67–69
Jalisco Center for Research and Assistance in Technology and Design, 89
Jalisco Ecologist Collective, 155–156
Jalisco Institute of Transparency and Public Information (ITEI), 164
Jalisco Ministry of Economic Development, 251
Jalisco Ministry of Health (SSJ), 88–89, 91, 100–102, 107–108
Jalisco State Human Rights Commission (CEDHJ), 88–89, 100, 105–108, 131
Jalisco State Water Commission (CEA), 5–6, 78–79, 100–105, 130, 226–227, 278n15
Jenkins, Rhys, 55–56, 125, 208
Joint Technical Committee (JTC), 107, 108
Jornada Jalisco, La, 103
José Cuervo, 252

Kalach, Moisés, 175
Kao Group, corporate sustainability reports of, 213, 214, *216*, 217, 222, 223. *See also* Quimikao
Kidney disease, 4, 10, 81–83, 99, 111, 113–114
Korenfeld, David, 230
Kuznets curve, 248

Labor, costs and exploitation in Mexico, 39–40, 46
Laboratories, conflicts of interest, 137, 145–146
Lacy, Rodolfo, 188
Lake Chapala, 9, 114
Latin American Water Tribunal (TLA), 90–92
Law of Transparency and Access to Government Information, 280n43
Leal, Donald, 21, 25–26, 62
Leap of Life, 37–39
    access to water study data, 110–111
    activist's reflection on river, 4
    case before Permanent Peoples' Tribunal, 112–113
    founding of, 90
    harassment/violence against, 111, 252–253
    human rights complaint from, 91
    objectives, actions, and strategies of, 82, 86, 100, 102–103, 108
    Tour of Terror, 37–39, 82, 107
    work with Greenpeace Mexico, 109–115, 207
Lerma-Santiago-Pacific (LSP) Basin Agency, 95, 110, 128–130, 133–134, 137, 141, 147, 230–232, 277n7
Lerma-Santiago River, 8–9, 114
"Locational blackmail," 20, 240–241
López, Luis Alberto, 189
López Obrador, Andrés Manuel, 128–129
López Rocha, Miguel Ángel, 4–5, 93–96, 99, 117, 134, 242
Los Laureles landfill, 92, 98–102
Louisiana, pollution and health in, 93
Luege Tamargo, José Luis, 6, 104, 110

Macías, Ezequiel, 1, 3, 4
Macías, Jorge, 187
Macrorecommendation, 91, 105–108
Madrid, Miguel de la, 42–43, 173

Index

"Manufacturing uncertainty," 84, 97, 107–108, 116
Maquiladoras, 47–48
Maquiladoras de Oleaginosas, *154*
"Maquila mentality," 39–40
Markowitz, Gerald, 93, 207–208
Martínez-Alier, Joan, 20, 56, 85, 88, 266
Martínez Barba, Federico, 243
Martínez Negrete, Dolores, 38
Martínez Negrete, Francisco, 38
Martyrs of the Blanco River school, 81–82
Martyrs of the Santiago River (Instituto Vida and IMDEC), 90–91
Marx, Karl, 22, 27
Medina Ascencio, Francisco, 11
Megamarch, 100
Mercado García, Alfonso, 55–56, 125, 208
Methodology, 263–274. *See also specific approaches*
Mexican Automotive Industry Association (AMIA), 186–187
Mexican Environmental Law Center (CEMDA), 183–184
Mexican Institute for Community Development (IMDEC), 5, 7, 90–92, 108, 110–111, 263
Mexican Institute of Water Technology (IMTA)
  draft on NOM-001 modification, 179–180
  draft on river reclassification, 104
  on General Water Law, 119
  on standards and standard changes, 143
  study of Santiago River, 54, 78–79, 110–111, 131, 176–177, 226–230
"Mexicanization" laws, 42
Mexican Movement of Dam-Affected People and in Defense of Rivers (MAPDER), 89–90

Mexichem
  access to information from, 211
  corporate sustainability reports of, 211, 212, 217, 220–221
  discharge permits for, 142
  effluents/discharges of, 98, *215*, 252
  noncompliance of, 98, 252
  operations in industrial corridor, 12
  perspective of EHS manager from, 239, 241–242
  reports to RETC, *154*
Mexico. *See also specific topics*
  dual and disjointed manufacturing sector of, 48–49
  environmental performance, OECD evaluation of, 205
  environmental regulations in, 49–62, 80, 123–127 (*see also* Regulations, environmental, in Mexico)
  GDP *vs.* corporate revenues, 171, *172*
  industrialization strategies of, 11–13, 27, 40–49, 70, 79–80
  labor costs/exploitation in, 39–40, 46
  manufacturing states of, 71, *72*
  water quality data in, 67–69
Mexico Business Summit, 175
Miliband, Ralph, 173–174
Milne, Markus, 213–214, 220
"Minimal state," 29–30
Ministry of Environment and Natural Resources (SEMARNAT)
  complaints to and responses of, 100–103
  evaluation of NOM-001, 179
  industry perspective on, 237, 240
  pollutant registry and, 150–156
  responsibilities of, 54, 125
  standard modification under, 176–203
Ministry of Environment and Territorial Development (SEMADET), 7, 106, 130, 162–163

Ministry of Environment for Sustainable Development (SEMADES), 5, 100–102, 107, 275n9
Ministry of Finance and Public Credit (SHCP), 103–104, 198
Ministry of Health and Assistance, 51
Ministry of Hydraulic Resources (SRH), 51–52
Ministry of Industry and Commerce, 51–52
Ministry of Rural Development, 5
Ministry of the Environment, Natural Resources and Fisheries, 54
Ministry of the Interior, 106–107
Ministry of Urban Development and Ecology, 52
Modernization, double standard of, 247
Montoya, Armando, 157
Morales, José Domingo, 158, 159
Multinational, myth of the. *See* Myth of the multinational
"Multiple dispossession," 26–27
Munguía, Norma, 181, 185–186, 197
Municipal-level regulations, 164–166
Municipal wastewater, 6, 10, 67–68
Muñoz Delgadillo, Raúl, 4, 99, 243
Myth of the multinational, 17, 62, 206–207, 211, 225–235, 245, 254, 258–259
and Celanese, 226, 229–232, 245
and Huntsman, 226, 232–234, 245
and industry perspective on government and regulation, 241
and Nestlé, 226, 227–229
and Quimikao, 226, 234–235

National Action Party, 70, 135
National Assembly of Environmentally Affected People (ANAA), 7, 102–103, 112–113
National Association of Manufacturers of Buses, Trucks and Tractors, 187
National Autonomous University of Mexico, 79, 185
National Chamber of the Fats, Oils, Soap and Detergent Industry, 189
National Chemical Industry Association (ANIQ), 157–158, 179, 184, 190–191, 200, 225, 239–240
National Commission for the Knowledge and Use of Biodiversity, 52–53, 54
National culture, and development, 249–250
National Environmental Auditing Program, 156
National Environment and Natural Resources Standards Advisory Committee (COMARNAT), 180–195
business interests and bias on, 181–188
"democratic" character of, 186, 193–195
institutionalized corruption and, 256
members of, 180–181, *181–182*
as opponent to regulation, 200–201
progress/delays on standard modification, 188–195
regulatory capture of, 202–203, 256
working groups and draft standards of, 184–188
National Human Rights Commission (CNDH), 91, 96, 134
National Hydraulic Program, 129
National Institute of Ecology, 52–53, 54
National Institute of Statistics and Geology (INEGI), *72*, 73, *73*, 194
National Monitoring Network, 67, 86, 178
National Pollutant Release Inventory (Canada), 149–151, *151*, 255–256
National Polytechnic Institute, 185

Index

National Regulatory Improvement Commission (CONAMER), 195–199, 202
National Standardization Program (PNN), 188–189
National Statistical Directory of Economic Units (DENUE), 276n8
National Water Commission (CONAGUA), 6–7, 51–54
  complaints to and responses of, 86–88, 100–102
  declining resources of, 166
  defense of industries, 95
  discharge permits issued by, *127*, 127–128, 139–143, 230–232
  industry perspective on, 235–246
  inefficiency of, 237–238
  inspections by, 123–124, 125–139, 236 (*see also* Inspections)
  inspectors of, number of, 127, 128
  monitoring network of, 67, 86, 178
  position on standard modification, 190–191
  reclassification of Santiago River, 103–105
  self-reports to, 57–58, 124, 143–156, 166, 255–256
  on water crisis/conflicts, 64–65, 84–85
  water quality data of, 67–69, 86–87
National Water Program (NWP), 68–69, 84–85, 191
National Waters Law (LAN), 53, 104, 119, 125, 139–140, 177, 198–199
Navarro, José Ernesto, 155
Navarro, Mina Lorena, 26
Neoevolutionist perspective, 120–121
Neoliberalism, 20, 24–30, 42–49, 70, 79–80
  economic results of, 46–49, *47*
  and environmental degradation, 26–30

and environmental fixes, 28–30, 256–257
and environmental regulations, 50–51, 54–55, 62
and foreign direct investment, 206
and institutionalized corruption, 31
Mexico as bastion of, 13
and power relations, 170, 173
Neoliberalization, 13, 44–45
Neoliberalization of nature, 28–30, 58, 256
Neo-Malthusian perspective, 21
Nestlé
  access to information from, 211
  compliance claims of, 219–220
  corporate revenues of, *172*
  corporate sustainability reports of, 212, *215*, 216–217, 219–220, 222, 223
  effluents/discharges of, 78, 97, 99, *215*, 217, 219–220, 227–229
  inspection records on, 228
  interviews with officials from, 209, 211
  myth of the multinational and, 226, 227–229
  noncompliance of, 99, 227–229, 252
  operations in industrial corridor, 10
  reports to RETC, *154*
  shared value strategy of, 216–217, 223, 228–229
Nestlé Environmental Requirements (NER), 219–220
NOM-001-SEMARNAT-1996, 53–54, 61
  analysis by German expert, 177–178
  analysis by SEMARNAT, 179
  deficiencies of, 176–179
  noncompliance with, 78–79, 98–99, 227–235
  reclassification of Santiago River under, 103–105, 141–142
  regulatory capture and, 171, 202–203, 256

NOM-001-SEMARNAT-1996
modification, 176–203, 260
business interest and bias in
COMARNAT and, 180–184
CONAGUA position on, 190–191
consolidation of, 199–202
cost-benefit analysis of, 195–199
final draft and issuance of, 201–202
IMTA preliminary draft of, 179–180
industry objections to, 169, 189, 190,
200–202
institutionalized corruption and,
256
need for, 188–189
negotiations and consensus on,
180–195, 202
new parameters in, 180, 190, 191–192,
200–202
official publication of, 192, 195,
199–201
regulatory impact statement on, 177,
195–199
secrecy and closed-door process of,
190–191
stagnation/delays in, 188–195
technical advantage of industry and,
194–195
2 for 1 Agreement and, 200
understanding process of, 179–180
working groups and drafts of,
184–188
NOM-002-SEMARNAT-1996, 53, 126
NOM-003-SEMARNAT-1997, 53
NOM-163-SEMARNAT-ENER-SCFI-2013,
186–188
Nongovernmental organizations
(NGOs). *See also specific*
organizations
representation on COMARNAT,
180–183, *182*
North American Agreement on
Environmental Cooperation,
87–88

North American Free Trade Agreement
(NAFTA), 46–50
and environmental agreement, 87
and environmental degradation,
112
and greenwashing, 18
and Mexican environmental
regulations, 49–50, 55, 137–138,
149, 238–239
and Mexican manufacturing/exports,
46, 48
and neoliberalization, 40
and self-reporting in member
countries, 149–151, *151*, 166–167,
255–256
"Nuclear abnormalities," 113–114
Nuevo León Chapter of the
Transformation Industry, 189

Occidental, El, 88–89
Occupational Knowledge International,
155
Ochoa, Cuauhtémoc, 187–188
O'Connor, James, 22–23, 28
Ocotlán–El Salto Industrial Corridor,
70–75, 80
access to information on, 33–34,
207–211
corporate sustainability reports on,
211, 212–225, 244–245
discharge permits for, 139–143
early studies of effluents from,
96–99
environmental impact of, 3–4, 12–14,
37–39, 75–79
growth of, 3, 10–14, 38, 70
map of installations, *76–77*
myth of the multinational and,
225–235, 258–259
number of factories in, 14, 73–75, *74*
origin of capital (Mexican *vs.* foreign),
74, *74*, *76–77*, 277n10
reports to RETC (2010–2020), *154*

sectors represented in, 14, 72–75, *74*, 208

water supply for, 11–12, 63–67, 241–242

Odor, 1–3, 6, 82–83, 89

Office of Civil Protection, 101–102

Official Gazette of the Federation (*DOF*), 184, 192, 195, 199–201, 256

Olaéz, Edgar, 162

Omnilife Manufacturing, *154*, 211, 212

Organisation for Economic Co-Operation and Development (OECD), 16, 58, 60–62, 147, 196, 205

Ortega, Rodrigo, 184, 194, 202

Ostrom, Elinor, 24

Oxiteno, 141, *154*, 160, 211, 212, *215*, 238

Padilla Gutiérrez, Héctor, 6–7

Parra, Francisco, 2

Particular discharge conditions (PDCs), 139–143

Paz, María Fernanda, 64, 84–85

PEMEX, 181, 197

Peña Nieto, Enrique, 105, 175, 187

Pennwalt del Pacífico. *See* Mexichem

PepsiCo (Santorini), 99, *172*

Pérez, Javier, 184

Pérez Peláez, Fernando Guzmán, 106

Permanent Peoples' Tribúnal (PPT), 112–113

Permits. *See* Discharge permits

Petersen Farah, Alfonso, 108

Pica, Yolanda, 143, 145, 146, 176–177, 179–180, 190

Pineda, Leticia, 183–184, 186, 187, 194–195

Plásticos Rex, 142, *154*

Polanyi, Karl, 19–20, 23, 28

Political ecology, 17, 33–34, 266–267, 269–270, 273–274

Pollutant Emissions and Transfers Registry (RETC), 149–156, 166

developing new regulation for, 184–185

emissions reported, 143–155, *153*, *154*

institutionalized corruption and, 255–256

lack of annual reporting, 153

mandatory/nonmandatory pollutants in, 151, 280n45

vs. self-reporting in US and Canada, 149–151, *151*, 166–167, 255–256

Pollutant Release and Transfer Registry (PRTR), 152

"Polluter pays" principle, 56–57, 61, 98, 147, 228

Population growth, 13–14, 64–65

Porfiriato, 28, 40–41

Porras, María del Carmen, 190, 192

Postdevelopment, 17

Postmodernism, 266

Poststructuralism, 264–266

Power flows/relations, 169–176

economic power and, 171–176, *172*

investigation of, 211

methodological approach to, 265–266, 270–274

neoliberalism and, 170, 173

and regulatory capture, 60, 170–176

and standard modification, 180–195

Preciado, Juan Gil, 10

Precitubo, *154*

Private Sector Center for Studies of Sustainable Development (CESPEDES), 181

Privatization, 45–49, 53, 54–55, 58

ProMéxico, 175–176

Public consultation, on new regulations, 198–199

Public interest, regulatory capture *vs.*, 170–171

Public Water Rights Registry (REPDA), *127*, 127–128, 275n13

334 Index

Quadri de la Torre, Gabriel, 282n9
Quezada, Juan Rafael Elvira, 123
Quimikao
    access to information from, 211
    CI certification of, 160, 161
    corporate sustainability reports of,
        212, 213, 214, *216*, 217, 222, 223
    effluents/discharges of, 4, 78, 98, 99,
        216, 234–235, 252
    laboratory testing and, 137
    myth of the multinational and, 226,
        234–235
    noncompliance of, 98, 99, 234–235,
        252
    perception of EHS personnel at,
        241–242
    perception of inspections at, 138–139
    reports to RETC, *154*
    water consumption by, 217

Ragasa Industrias, 130–131
Ramírez Acuña, Francisco, 88
Ramírez Anguiano, Victor Manuel,
    108
Region of Environmental Fragility
    (REF), 101, 107–108
Regulation for the Protection and
    Control of Water Pollution, 51–52
Regulations, environmental
    command and control (direct),
        55–56, 123–124
    commercial-environmental model of,
        124–125
    in developing countries, 58–62
    free-market environmentalism and,
        28–30, 58, 62, 256–257
    "hollowing out" of state
        responsibilities and, 29
    hypothetical function of, 125
    indirect, 55–57
    lax, competitive advantage of, 16,
        17–18, 202, 238–240
    "minimal state" and, 29–30

neoliberalism and, 50–51, 54–55, 62
noncompliance with, 14, 78–79,
    98–99, 227–235
self-monitoring and, 57–61, 124,
    143–156
state role in, restructured and
    diminished, 55, 112–113
voluntary, 55, 56–57, 61, 156–163,
    167
Regulations, environmental, in Mexico,
    49–62, 80
agencies/ministries responsible for,
    51, 54
corporate claims of compliance with,
    218–220
cost-benefit analysis of, 195–199
enforcement of (inspections),
    123–139
evolution of, 50–58
flows of power/power relations and,
    169–176
vs. German standards, 177–178
industry perspective on, 235–246
logics of system, 59–62, 123–127,
    254–258
modification of, 176–203
municipal-level, 164–166
OECD review of, 60–62
pact for industrial compliance with,
    251
reclassification of Santiago River,
    103–105, 141–142
simplification of, 53–54, 61–62
state-level, 162–164
2 for 1 Agreement and, 200
US EPA report on, 49–50
via negotiation and consensus,
    180–195, 202
Regulatory capture, 60, 170–176, 256
    definition of, 170
    industry intent and, 170–171
    and NOM-001 modification, 202–203,
        256

Index

Regulatory Impact Assessment Manual, 196

Regulatory impact statement (RIS), 177, 195–199

Regulatory Quality Agreement, 196, 200

Relativism, 265

Reséndiz, Rubén, 95

Resilience, 8, 28

Revive the Santiago River, 115, 162, 251–254

Rhine River, 12

"Right to know," 149, 166, 211, 246

Rivas Souza, Mario, 96

Rivera, Luis Miguel, 129, 139

Rocha, María del Carmen, 94

Rodríguez, José Antonio, 129, 136–137

Rodríguez, Maricruz, 152, 155, 185

Rogers, Thomas L., 8–9

Romo, Xavier, 2

Rosner, David, 93, 207–208

Rostow, W. W., 121

Rueda Quintana, Lucía, 231

Ruíz, Magdalena, 106

Ruling relations, 32–33

Sacrifice zones, 15–16

Salcedo Sahagún, Javier, 231

Saldaña, Rodrigo, 2, 6, 82–83, 87, 92

Salinas de Gortari, Carlos, 13, 45, 173

Salzgitter Mannesmann, 135

Sandoval, Aristóteles, 108, 162

Sanmina-SCI Systems, 49, 153–155, *154*

Santiago River, 8–10. *See also specific agencies, industries, and regulations*

AyMA study of, 98–99, 104, 226–227, 229, 233

contribution to national GDP, 9–10

in "critical state," 79

damming of and power from, 9, 27–28, 38

drone flights over, 5

early citizen complaints about, 83, 86–88

early reports on pollution, 12

early study of industrial effluents into, 96–99

flow/hydraulic management of, 75, 114

former glory of, 1, 3–4, 8–9

Greenpeace Mexico campaign for, *109*, 109–115

IMTA study of, 54, 78–79, 110–111, 131, 176–177, 226–230

industrial corridor and, 3–4, 10–14, 70–75, 80

as industrial water source, 12

industry perspective on, 242–244

macrorecommendation for, 91, 105–108

media coverage of, 88–89

odor of, 1–3, 6, 82–83, 89

"predictable" case of, 248, 251

reclassification of, 103–105, 141–142

as Region of Environmental Fragility, 101, 107–108

resilience of pollution, 8, 28

as sewer of progress, 8, 15–16

state of emergency for, 106–107

struggle to clean up, 251–254, 259–264

toxic foam from, 2, 81–83

urban (population) growth along, 13–14

water analyses of, 5–6, 12, 78–79, 96–99

Santorini (PepsiCo), 99, *172*

Scarcity, water, 63–67

Science *vs.* nonscience, 264–265

Self-monitoring/self-reporting, 57–61, 124, 143–156

analysis of reports (2000–2013), 146–149

fiction *vs.* faithful measure, 143–149, 166, 255–256

institutionalized corruption and, 255–256

Self-monitoring/self-reporting (cont.)
laboratories involved in, 145–146
Mexico *vs.* US and Canada, 149–151,
151, 166–167, 255–256
pollutant registry (RETC) and,
149–156, 255–256
tax/duty-related, 144, 146–149,
148
Sewage (municipal wastewater), 6, 10,
67–68
Sewer of progress, 8, 15–16
Shared development, 42
Shared value strategy, of Nestlé, 216–217,
223, 228–229
Siemens, *172*, 210
"Silicon Valley of Mexico," 39, 70–71
Silva, Francisco Javier, 15–16, 159
Silva, Pedro, 192
SIRALAB (System for the Reception of
Laboratory Analyses), 146
Slim, Carlos, 45, 173
Smith, Dorothy, 32–33, 264, 266
Social discount rate, 198
Social environmental conflicts, 20–21,
63–64, 83–86. *See also specific*
conflicts and conflict participants
CONAGUA evaluation of, 64–65,
84–85
"environmentalism of the poor" and,
20, 85, 88
Paz's analysis of, 64, 84–85
role of state in, 84–86
structural nature of, 85
Social responsibility, corporate, 62, 205,
224, 258–259
Socio-environmental movement, 7–8,
40. *See also specific organizations and*
actions
access to water study data, 110–111
alliances of, 86, 102–103
creative strategies of, 86
early citizen complaints and, 83,
86–88

government response to, 7–8, 83–86,
99–102
Greenpeace Mexico and, *109*,
109–115
harassment/violence against activists,
111, 252–253
health of children as impetus for,
81–83, 89
media coverage for, 88–89
origins and history of, 81–96
protest actions of, 99–103
Tour of Terror, 37–39, 82, 107
Solís, Eduardo, 186–187
Sosa, Alejandro, 186–187, 192
Standard modification. *See* NOM-001-
SEMARNAT-1996 modification
State Bureau of Environmental
Protection (PROEPA), 5, 102, 131,
159, 162
State-centric approach, criticism of,
169–170, 176, 256
State-level regulation, 162–164
State of emergency, 106–107
State Water and Sanitation Commission
(CEAS), 96–99, 278n15
Suhr, Michael, 177–178
Summers, Lawrence, 122
Sustainable competitiveness, 248–249
Sustainable development, 16–18, 21–24.
See also Corporate sustainability

Taking Stock Online, 150
Taxes, self-reporting and, 144, 146–149,
148
Tecnológico de Monterrey, 207
Temperature parameter, in NOM-001
modification, 201
Tequila companies/production, 70, 75,
97, 98–99, 129, 252
Tequila Patrón, 252
Toms River, New Jersey, 93
Total suspended solids (TSS), 56, 67–69,
79, 228, 229, 232, 276n7

Index

Tour of Terror, 37–39, 82, 107
Tovar, Patricia, 200–201
Toxicity parameter, in NOM-001
    modification, 180, 190, 191–192,
    200–202
Toxicity test, 54, 192, 285n21
Toxic Release Inventory (US), 149–151,
    151, 255–256
Toxic Rivers campaign (Greenpeace
    Mexico), *109*, 109–115
Toxi-Tour, 7, 115
Tragedy of the commons, 21, 24–25
Transnational dependent capitalism, 40
Transnational Institute, 7, 220
Transnationals, arrival in industrial
    corridor, 12. *See also* Myth of the
    multinational
Transparency International, 30, 32
Triple bottom line (TBL), 213, 244–245
Truman Doctrine, 121
2 for 1 Agreement, 200
Tylor, Edward B., 120

Union Carbide disaster, 149
United Nations, 16
United Nations Department of Social
    and Economic Affairs, 121–122
United Nations Educational, Scientific
    and Cultural Organization
    (UNESCO), 65, 66
United Nations Environment
    Programme (UNEP), 57, 66–67
United Nations Office for Disaster Risk
    Reduction, 8
United Nations Working Group on
    Business and Human Rights, 113
United States (US)
    GDP *vs.* corporate revenues, 171, *172*
    self-reporting in, 144, 149–151, *151*,
    166–167, 255–256
United States–Mexico–Canada
    Agreement, 201, 255–256
University of Guadalajara, 97, 113–114

UN Sustainable Development Goals,
    213
UN-Water, 67
Urrea
    CI certification of, 161
    compliance claims/false statements
    of, 218–219
    corporate sustainability information
    from, 212, *216*, 217, 218–219
    discharge permits for, 140–142
    effluents/discharges of, 98, *216*,
    218–219
    interviews with officials from, 211
    perspective of EHS manager from,
    236
    reports to RETC, *153*
    water consumption by, 217
US Department of the Treasury, 13
US Environmental Protection Agency
    (EPA), 49–50
Utilitarian perspective, 20–22

Vega, Silvia, 210, 226, 242, 244
Vibrio fischeri, 99
Vimifos, 135
Violence, against activists, 252–253
Volkswagen, deceptive practices of, 206
Voluntary Environmental Compliance
    (VEC), 162–163, 167
Voluntary regulations, 55, 56–57, 61,
    156–163, 167

Wastewater treatment plants (WWTPs)
    effluent not treated by, 134–135
    industrial facilities lacking
    investigation of, 89
    as projected solution, 98, 99–101,
    105, 110, 116
    tender process/funding for, 105
Water, Energy and Climate Conference,
    119
Water consumption, corporate reports
    of, 217

Water crises, 63–67
Waterfall of Juanacatlán, 1, 3–4, 9, 13
Water permits, *127*, 127–128
Water regulations. *See* Regulations, environmental
Water stress, 65, 276n4
Water supply, 11–12, 63–67, 241–242
Water wars, 63
White, Leslie, 120–121
Working groups, for draft standards, 184–188
World Bank, 13, 16, 26, 43, 66, 69, 147–149, 206, 248
World Business Council for Sustainable Development, 181
World Commission on Environment and Development, 21
World Economic Forum, 248–249
World Health Organization (WHO), 92–93
World Trade Organization (WTO), 70
World Water Forum, 90

Yin, Hernández, Xóchitl, 115

Zedillo, Ernesto, 54
Zero-sum model, of development, 249
ZF
    access to information from, 211
    corporate revenues of, 171, *172*
    discharge permit for, 141
    effluents/discharges of, 98, 99
    lapse in CI certification, 160–161
    perspectives on regulation, 238
    reports to RETC, *153*, *154*
Zoltek
    discharge permits for, 141
    emission reports of, 153–155
    interviews refused by, 210
    noncompliance of, 252
    reports to RETC, *153*, *154*

Urban and Industrial Environments

Series editor: Robert Gottlieb, Henry R. Luce Professor of Urban and Environmental Policy, Occidental College

Maureen Smith, *The U.S. Paper Industry and Sustainable Production: An Argument for Restructuring*

Keith Pezzoli, *Human Settlements and Planning for Ecological Sustainability: The Case of Mexico City*

Sarah Hammond Creighton, *Greening the Ivory Tower: Improving the Environmental Track Record of Universities, Colleges, and Other Institutions*

Jan Mazurek, *Making Microchips: Policy, Globalization, and Economic Restructuring in the Semiconductor Industry*

William A. Shutkin, *The Land That Could Be: Environmentalism and Democracy in the Twenty-First Century*

Richard Hofrichter, ed., *Reclaiming the Environmental Debate: The Politics of Health in a Toxic Culture*

Robert Gottlieb, *Environmentalism Unbound: Exploring New Pathways for Change*

Kenneth Geiser, *Materials Matter: Toward a Sustainable Materials Policy*

Thomas D. Beamish, *Silent Spill: The Organization of an Industrial Crisis*

Matthew Gandy, *Concrete and Clay: Reworking Nature in New York City*

David Naguib Pellow, *Garbage Wars: The Struggle for Environmental Justice in Chicago*

Julian Agyeman, Robert D. Bullard, and Bob Evans, eds., *Just Sustainabilities: Development in an Unequal World*

Barbara L. Allen, *Uneasy Alchemy: Citizens and Experts in Louisiana's Chemical Corridor Disputes*

Dara O'Rourke, *Community-Driven Regulation: Balancing Development and the Environment in Vietnam*

Brian K. Obach, *Labor and the Environmental Movement: The Quest for Common Ground*

Peggy F. Barlett and Geoffrey W. Chase, eds., *Sustainability on Campus: Stories and Strategies for Change*

Steve Lerner, *Diamond: A Struggle for Environmental Justice in Louisiana's Chemical Corridor*

Jason Corburn, *Street Science: Community Knowledge and Environmental Health Justice*

Peggy F. Barlett, ed., *Urban Place: Reconnecting with the Natural World*

David Naguib Pellow and Robert J. Brulle, eds., *Power, Justice, and the Environment: A Critical Appraisal of the Environmental Justice Movement*

Eran Ben-Joseph, *The Code of the City: Standards and the Hidden Language of Place Making*

Nancy J. Myers and Carolyn Raffensperger, eds., *Precautionary Tools for Reshaping Environmental Policy*

Kelly Sims Gallagher, *China Shifts Gears: Automakers, Oil, Pollution, and Development*

Kerry H. Whiteside, *Precautionary Politics: Principle and Practice in Confronting Environmental Risk*

Ronald Sandler and Phaedra C. Pezzullo, eds., *Environmental Justice and Environmentalism: The Social Justice Challenge to the Environmental Movement*

Julie Sze, *Noxious New York: The Racial Politics of Urban Health and Environmental Justice*

Robert D. Bullard, ed., *Growing Smarter: Achieving Livable Communities, Environmental Justice, and Regional Equity*

Ann Rappaport and Sarah Hammond Creighton, *Degrees That Matter: Climate Change and the University*

Michael Egan, *Barry Commoner and the Science of Survival: The Remaking of American Environmentalism*

David J. Hess, *Alternative Pathways in Science and Industry: Activism, Innovation, and the Environment in an Era of Globalization*

Peter F. Cannavò, *The Working Landscape: Founding, Preservation, and the Politics of Place*

Paul Stanton Kibel, ed., *Rivertown: Rethinking Urban Rivers*

Kevin P. Gallagher and Lyuba Zarsky, *The Enclave Economy: Foreign Investment and Sustainable Development in Mexico's Silicon Valley*

David N. Pellow, *Resisting Global Toxics: Transnational Movements for Environmental Justice*

Robert Gottlieb, *Reinventing Los Angeles: Nature and Community in the Global City*

David V. Carruthers, ed., *Environmental Justice in Latin America: Problems, Promise, and Practice*

Tom Angotti, *New York for Sale: Community Planning Confronts Global Real Estate*

Paloma Pavel, ed., *Breakthrough Communities: Sustainability and Justice in the Next American Metropolis*

Anastasia Loukaitou-Sideris and Renia Ehrenfeucht, *Sidewalks: Conflict and Negotiation over Public Space*

David J. Hess, *Localist Movements in a Global Economy: Sustainability, Justice, and Urban Development in the United States*

Julian Agyeman and Yelena Ogneva-Himmelberger, eds., *Environmental Justice and Sustainability in the Former Soviet Union*

Jason Corburn, *Toward the Healthy City: People, Places, and the Politics of Urban Planning*

JoAnn Carmin and Julian Agyeman, eds., *Environmental Inequalities Beyond Borders: Local Perspectives on Global Injustices*

Louise Mozingo, *Pastoral Capitalism: A History of Suburban Corporate Landscapes*

Gwen Ottinger and Benjamin Cohen, eds., *Technoscience and Environmental Justice: Expert Cultures in a Grassroots Movement*

Samantha MacBride, *Recycling Reconsidered: The Present Failure and Future Promise of Environmental Action in the United States*

Andrew Karvonen, *Politics of Urban Runoff: Nature, Technology, and the Sustainable City*

Daniel Schneider, *Hybrid Nature: Sewage Treatment and the Contradictions of the Industrial Ecosystem*

Catherine Tumber, *Small, Gritty, and Green: The Promise of America's Smaller Industrial Cities in a Low-Carbon World*

Sam Bass Warner and Andrew H. Whittemore, *American Urban Form: A Representative History*

John Pucher and Ralph Buehler, eds., *City Cycling*

Stephanie Foote and Elizabeth Mazzolini, eds., *Histories of the Dustheap: Waste, Material Cultures, Social Justice*

David J. Hess, *Good Green Jobs in a Global Economy: Making and Keeping New Industries in the United States*

Joseph F. C. DiMento and Clifford Ellis, *Changing Lanes: Visions and Histories of Urban Freeways*

Joanna Robinson, *Contested Water: The Struggle Against Water Privatization in the United States and Canada*

William B. Meyer, *The Environmental Advantages of Cities: Countering Commonsense Antiurbanism*

Rebecca L. Henn and Andrew J. Hoffman, eds., *Constructing Green: The Social Structures of Sustainability*

Peggy F. Barlett and Geoffrey W. Chase, eds., *Sustainability in Higher Education: Stories and Strategies for Transformation*

Isabelle Anguelovski, *Neighborhood as Refuge: Community Reconstruction, Place Remaking, and Environmental Justice in the City*

Kelly Sims Gallagher, *The Globalization of Clean Energy Technology: Lessons from China*

Vinit Mukhija and Anastasia Loukaitou-Sideris, eds., *The Informal American City: Beyond Taco Trucks and Day Labor*

Roxanne Warren, *Rail and the City: Shrinking Our Carbon Footprint While Reimagining Urban Space*

Marianne E. Krasny and Keith G. Tidball, *Civic Ecology: Adaptation and Transformation from the Ground Up*

Erik Swyngedouw, *Liquid Power: Contested Hydro-Modernities in Twentieth-Century Spain*

Ken Geiser, *Chemicals without Harm: Policies for a Sustainable World*

Duncan McLaren and Julian Agyeman, *Sharing Cities: A Case for Truly Smart and Sustainable Cities*

Jessica Smartt Gullion, *Fracking the Neighborhood: Reluctant Activists and Natural Gas Drilling*

Nicholas A. Phelps, *Sequel to Suburbia: Glimpses of America's Post-Suburban Future*

Shannon Elizabeth Bell, *Fighting King Coal: The Challenges to Micromobilization in Central Appalachia*

Theresa Enright, *The Making of Grand Paris: Metropolitan Urbanism in the Twenty-First Century*

Robert Gottlieb and Simon Ng, *Global Cities: Urban Environments in Los Angeles, Hong Kong, and China*

Anna Lora-Wainwright, *Resigned Activism: Living with Pollution in Rural China*

Scott L. Cummings, *Blue and Green: The Drive for Justice at America's Port*

David Bissell, *Transit Life: Cities, Commuting, and the Politics of Everyday Mobilities*

Javiera Barandiarán, *From Empire to Umpire: Science and Environmental Conflict in Neoliberal Chile*

Benjamin Pauli, *Flint Fights Back: Environmental Justice and Democracy in the Flint Water Crisis*

Karen Chapple and Anastasia Loukaitou-Sideris, *Transit-Oriented Displacement or Community Dividends? Understanding the Effects of Smarter Growth on Communities*

Henrik Ernstson and Sverker Sörlin, eds., *Grounding Urban Natures: Histories and Futures of Urban Ecologies*

Katrina Smith Korfmacher, *Bridging the Silos: Collaborating for Environment, Health, and Justice in Urban Communities*

Jill Lindsey Harrison, *From the Inside Out: The Fight for Environmental Justice within Government Agencies*

Anastasia Loukaitou-Sideris, Dana Cuff, Todd Presner, Maite Zubiaurre, and Jonathan Jae-an Crisman, *Urban Humanities: New Practices for Reimagining the City*

Govind Gopakumar, *Installing Automobility: Emerging Politics of Mobility and Streets in Indian Cities*

Amelia Thorpe, *Everyday Ownership: PARK(ing) Day and the Practice of Property*

Tridib Banerjee, *In the Images of Development: City Design in the Global South*

Ralph Buehler and John Pucher, eds., *Cycling for Sustainable Cities*

Casey J. Dawkins, *Just Housing: The Moral Foundations of American Housing Policy*

Kian Goh, *Form and Flow: The Spatial Politics of Urban Resilience and Climate Justice*

Kian Goh, Anastasia Loukaitou-Sideris, and Vinit Mukhija, eds., *Just Urban Design: The Struggle for a Public City*

Sheila R. Foster and Christian Iaione, *Co-Cities: Innovative Transitions toward Just and Self-Sustaining Communities*

Vinit Mukhija, *Remaking the American Dream: The Informal and Formal Transformation of Single-Family Housing Cities*

Cindy McCullig, *Sewer of Progress: Corporations, Institutionalized Corruption, and the Struggle for the Santiago River*